EDUCATIONAL PSYCHOLOGY

Kelvin Seifert

The University of Manitoba

HOUGHTON MIFFLIN COMPANY

BOSTON   Dallas   Geneva, Illinois
Lawrenceville, New Jersey   Palo Alto

To Barbie,
our children,
and our parents

Part and chapter opener art by Dorothea Sierra.

Illustrations by Vytas Sakalas

Printed in the U.S.A.

Library of Congress Catalog Card Number:
LC 82-83201

ISBN: 0-395-32790-3

Contents

Preface

When I began teaching, I was impressed with both the difficulty and the ease of the job. The ease because my students were often interesting, fun, and stimulating; and because caring for their educational needs seemed possible, responsible, and important. But the difficulty, too, because I never seemed to understand my students fully, no matter what their age or personality; and because I never had time, while actually teaching, to deliberate about most of my decisions. These problems made me wish for guidelines or theories to rely on while I was teaching, to give me confidence that I was doing what my students really needed. Through the years, other teachers, from various grade levels and settings, have expressed similar concerns to me.

This book is one response to these concerns. It introduces psychology as it relates to teaching and emphasizes its practical applications. These often—perhaps even usually—do not consist of simple formulas or "recipes for teaching." They consist instead of guidelines or general strategies of response which can orient teachers to the problems they and their students face. These problems and strategies, which cut across age groups and teaching institutions, have in common a psychological quality: they involve individual behavior, thinking, and motivation. This fact has dictated many features of the text, beyond the fundamental need for a book that is readable, practical, comprehensive, and concise.

Audience

Educational Psychology is intended for all teachers, whatever their instructional setting or the ages of their students. The text assumes that, although most individuals studying educational psychology do so expecting to teach in public schools, a significant minority have other teaching experiences or expectations—in nursing, for example, or in business, military training, or recreational work. The text's coverage and examples try to take these nonschool settings into account while paying special attention to the most common application of educational psychology, public school teaching.

Coverage

Educational Psychology focuses on four topics essential to effective teaching: development, learning and instruction, motivation, and evaluation. Part I, on *development,* calls attention to the twin questions of stability and change in student learning. How do students' needs evolve over time? What skills or abilities—and ranges of skills or abilities—can teachers consider typical for a particular age group? These questions face teachers of all grade levels and subject areas, and they face teachers in schools as well as elsewhere. The text deals with the questions by discussing four areas of development in detail—cognitive, language, moral, and social. Multicultural influences are dealt with explicitly in two contexts: once as part of language development and again as part of social development.

Part II shifts the focus to more immediate influences on *learning and instruction.* It looks at behavioral and cognitive theories of learning and theories of memory and transfer, and it suggests how they can be used in a variety of teaching settings. Many beginning teachers will be especially concerned about one particular kind of "immediate influence" on learning and instruction, namely, the handling and preventing of classroom disruptions. If so, they should read Chapter 9, on instructional management. Others may be concerned about how educators can most effectively teach students with special needs; they should see Chapter 10. Neither of these problems, it should be noted, is confined to teaching in schools.

Part III elaborates on the discussion of instructional management by looking at a more positive side of the problem: how to predispose students to learn of their own accord. Theories of *motivation* come in many forms, and they come both attached to and separate from comprehensive psychological theories. A number of these are sampled in Part III and evaluated for their usefulness to teaching.

Part IV examines the subject of *evaluation*. It discusses grading and its alternatives, classroom testing, and nontest methods of evaluation (which teachers working outside schools are especially likely to use). Standardized achievement and ability testing is discussed in detail, on the assumption that teachers of all sorts must understand such tests even if they cannot always control their use completely to their liking.

Features

The text includes several features that should help students in learning the material. Each chapter begins with a *graphic organizer,* a pictorial summary of the chapter's contents. The graphic organizer shows in visual form the most important relationships among topics within the chapter and highlights the chapter's organization and coverage. At the end of each chapter, the graphic organizer is repeated, but added to it are numerous cross-references relating the current chapter's contents to topics in other chapters.

Each chapter also begins with a *narrative* by an experienced teacher, in which he or she describes an important teaching experience or concern relevant to that chapter. The narratives supplement the body of the text by conveying how teaching problems occur in their natural context. In doing so they help show how psychological theories and issues are a part of actual teaching—and not just a part of psychology courses. The narratives, incidentally, all refer to imaginary people and events, even though they are all based on real teaching experiences and concerns.

For similar purposes, each chapter ends with a *case study,* which presents a discussion problem that is related to the psychological and educational issues of the chapter. As with the introductory narratives, the case studies present problems as they normally occur in actual teaching situations. Each case study concludes with questions about the case to stimulate further thought and discussion. Each chapter also ends with an *annotated list of readings* that extend or broaden the topics of the chapter. These often make good beginning points for student projects.

To help students organize and review the text, summary statements of key ideas appear as *marginal notes* throughout the book and each chapter ends with a list of *key points.* Important terms are highlighted in bold when they are first defined; in addition, the text contains a *glossary* of over two-hundred fifty terms.

Ancillary

A *Study Guide* accompanies *Educational Psychology,* to assist students in learning and organizing the content of the text. For each chapter of the text, the *Study Guide* contains a list of learning objectives, a summary of the chapter, a list of key terms to define, exercises on applying key concepts, programmed review questions, and a self-test of multiple-choice items. Since each of these features covers the entire chapter's contents, the features can be used either singly or in appropriate combinations.

Acknowledgments

So many people have helped in preparing this book that mentioning any one of them risks inadvertently ignoring others. I appreciate the several editors who have responded helpfully and patiently to my efforts, and I value the comments of the many students who have braved early versions of the manuscript in order to learn about educational psychology. A number of reviewers made key contributions to the organization and content of the book, most notably:

Eric Bell, The Pennsylvania State University

Charles Bennett, Slippery Rock State College

Jason W. Brunk, Ohio University

Stan Charnofsky, California State University, Northridge

Barbara Heines, Lake Erie College

Thomas G. Holzman, Georgia State University

Steve Lang, University of Georgia, Athens

Edward R. McIntosh, Lamar University

Sue Magruder, Northeast Missouri State University

John Newell, University of Florida

Bernard Rabin, Bowling Green State University

R. Siemoneit, Union College

Ancel J. Tikasingh, Sacramento State University

A special thanks goes to Alice Turman, for her outstandingly fast and accurate typing; by now she must have the book memorized. Finally, I offer a special note of gratitude to my wife, who gestated our second child while I gestated this book, and who remained steadfastly sure of the value of both.

Kelvin Seifert
The University of Manitoba

Chapter 1

THE NATURE OF
EDUCATIONAL PSYCHOLOGY

George Anderson, Grade 10 English teacher: No matter how often I begin a school year, how hard it is for me to prepare for it in a logical way! I browse in this book and that, get an unexpected idea here, hear a suggestion there. My mind ranges around the classroom, thinking of where the furniture and books and other things might go. And I think of the many events that may surround these objects and the students whom I haven't even met yet.

It's all a guessing game. What might a student want to do here? How might I help him with that book there? The possibilities seem so endless that I almost give up planning for them. Should I assign some extra short stories for the students to read? Which ones, is the question. Even our modest school library has more than I can use. And having somehow chosen a few, I have to decide what to do beyond just assigning them. Ask for an essay? Reenact the story? Make drawings based on them? At this point I have an uneasy feeling that I'm not at all clear about what I want my students to learn from me. Or how therefore I will be able to evaluate them later, when marks are due.

Of course, I tell myself that I can't plan too carefully yet because I don't know my students—what they will be ready for and how they will best learn. It's not that planning doesn't pay at all; just that it doesn't pay if I do it too carefully or rigidly. I do have a rough idea of what typical tenth-grade literature students know and how they learn— though sometimes I wish I knew more about that. I guess my expectations will guide me through the first days, and then I hope my students will guide me after that!

DEVELOPMENT

- COGNITIVE
- LINGUISTIC
- MORAL
- SOCIAL

LEARNING AND INSTRUCTION

- THEORIES OF LEARNING
  Behavioral
  Cognitive
- INSTRUCTIONAL APPLICATIONS
  Instructional planning
  Instructional management
- INDIVIDUAL DIFFERENCES AND EXCEPTIONALITY

MOTIVATION

- THEORIES OF MOTIVATION
- HUMANISTIC EDUCATION

EVALUATION

- TEACHER-MADE TESTS
- REPORTING ON LEARNING
  Grading
  Standardized tests

TEACHING others can mean various things, depending on the situation. Sometimes it means a rather specific contact to impart a rather specific skill or piece of knowledge; at other times, it means very general and long-lasting interactions affecting basic motives as well as skills and knowledge. One very common form of teaching, one often found in schools, tries to influence everything: motives, skills, and knowledge. But teachers in schools often lament that they do not succeed equally well at all of these goals. Persons teaching in nonschool situations do not experience this problem to the same extent, since they usually have less time to work with their students, but this fact does not really make their teaching any easier. All education grows out of and reflects a number of general factors; and the more able that teachers are to keep track of these, the more effective they can hope to be.

WHY STUDY EDUCATIONAL PSYCHOLOGY?

This book is a guide to psychology in education: what it is and how it relates to teaching and learning. A lot of education, of course, happens in schools, but not all of it. Nurses, businesspeople, and military personnel all can think of situations in their work that require teaching and learning, and so can parents, for that matter, in their role as child raisers. Nurses sometimes teach patients or members of the community about health-related problems, and businesses frequently need to train new workers to perform new tasks, or even new jobs. Military officers must teach new recruits special skills, all the way from typing to flying an airplane. Even though these educational situations differ in important ways, they all share important psychological features with one another and with the major source of education, namely, school. This book will examine these common features, drawing examples from all types of practical learning situations, although particularly from school classrooms.

useful in a variety of educational settings

Educational psychology is the study of how learning occurs and of how teaching may help learning occur. It includes knowledge about the readiness or development of learners, about how specific behaviors or ideas are actually learned, and about how learners may (or may not) become motivated to learn. And it includes how teachers may apply all of these concerns to teach more effectively and to evaluate learning fairly. To deal with all these topics, educational psychology uses a variety of psychological theories and approaches, all having in common their relevance to either teaching or learning or both.

focuses on key topics for teachers

Psychology has much to give to teaching, and these applications to teaching form the heart of this book. Why do children learn, and how? What are the differences between younger children and older ones? What about handicapped children? Can learning be evaluated fairly—and if so, how? Questions like these, and many others, form the core of psychology as applied to teaching. They are grouped into four main topics in the pages that follow: development, learning and instruction, motivation, and evaluation.

Every one of these topics can help you teach better and enjoy your students more. Take the topic of development: what are the differences between, say, a five-year-old and a fifteen-year-old? Some are obvious, like their physical growth or their language skill. You need not study psychology to know that much. But look a little closer: what particular language skills does one have that the other does not, and how would you as a teacher know them if you saw them? How could you describe them to another teacher, or to a parent, if you saw them? It is here, at this more detailed level, that understanding psychology can make a real contribution to your performance as a teacher and as a human being who knows what people are like.

offers specific, detailed knowledge

Or take the topic of learning and instruction, supposedly the focus of education. You probably have heard that teachers should reinforce students in positive ways. Everyone agrees with this idea, at least in general. But agreement breaks down when we look a little closer. What actually is a reinforcer for a particular student—for one of yours? A smile immediately after she does what you wanted? Or a smile at the end of the lesson, twenty minutes later? A smile on one day and not on others? Or something else entirely? Can you reinforce too often, or not often enough? When does reinforcement become bribery, and when is it simply a healthy incentive to do better? Answering these questions requires both information and good practical judgment by you, the teacher. It requires information because psychologists really have found some important characteristics of reinforcement by observing simple experimental situations lacking the complexities of most real instruction. But applying these results to the hustle and bustle of real teaching also requires good professional judgment by you.

Psychology, then, can help you in teaching, and we hope that the next four hundred pages or so will prove this idea to you. As you read on, keep in mind that psychology cannot know in advance the particular practical problems that you will encounter in your particular teaching, the actual students you have, and their peculiarities. In this sense—but only in this sense—psychology cannot always be relevant; that is, it cannot always predict the tangible pressures and satisfactions of your particular situation. It can, however, offer useful general guidance in meeting these daily surprises, challenges, and pleasures. It will give you a viewpoint for interpreting your teaching experiences. The rest will be up to you, as a professional educator. You will be a practitioner of teaching and, among other things, a practitioner of psychology.

provides general guidelines and viewpoint

Educational psychology gives insight into most aspects of teaching and learn-ing, no matter what the specific setting, instructional goal, or student's age. (Christopher Morrow [*above*]; Martha Stewart/The Picture Cube [*below*])

MAJOR FIELDS OF EDUCATIONAL PSYCHOLOGY

Unfortunately, there is much to learn and too little time in which to learn it. This book assumes that you have many other important things to do besides learn educational psychology. If you are a student, whether in education or in some other field, you will have other courses to take and perhaps practical work to attend to. If you are already teaching, you will be busy keeping a step ahead of your students. In any case, there will not always be enough time to read and digest the many books and articles that have been written on educational psychology.

Under these circumstances, then, what matters the most in psychology for teaching? The chapter titles and subheadings in this book give some answers to this question, but they deserve special explanation. They can be grouped roughly into four categories.

Development

The Concept of Development The area of psychology known as **development** concerns the long-run changes in children over time: their changes in thinking, feeling, and behavior. Obviously, children also grow physically over time as well, but this aspect of development will be noted only as it affects development in the other, more psychological areas. Long-run changes commonly result from a multitude of causes, and unraveling them is part of the study of development. Why, for example, can older children solve more complicated math problems than young children can? Why can some high school students solve algebra problems in their heads, but most elementary children cannot? Why do very young children so often fail at verbal reasoning problems? If a particular older child must "learn by doing," rather than by thinking inwardly, is it for the same reasons that a younger child must do so? If a certain young child can precociously solve algebra in his head, does he understand it in the same way that an older child supposedly does?

long-term permanent changes from many causes

Development pertains to questions like these. Because the answers to them have often led psychologists to propose stages for many areas of development, the chapters ahead will look at several stage theories and their relevance to teaching. All stage theories assume that children go through a fixed sequence of behaviors or skills during their development and that each stage of development incorporates skills from all of the preceding stages. Individuals vary only in how quickly they move through the stages, not in the sequencing itself.

nature of stage theories

As we shall see, stages provide landmarks for teachers in planning experiences appropriate for their children. Suppose, for example, that a developmental theory suggests that children go through a stage of actively

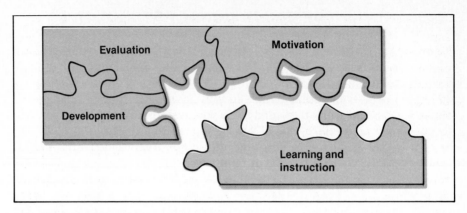

Figure 1–1 How Does It All Fit Together?

manipulating objects before a stage of inner, symbolic thinking. As a teacher, you then will need to plan activities that include a lot of physical action for your relatively young or inexperienced children but that encourage more abstract thinking in the more mature ones. Some slow learners in your class may, in fact, be slow partly because they still are learning at an earlier, doing-oriented stage, not because they need more drill or practice with relatively abstract, language-oriented content. Even some fast learners may need trips back to earlier, doing-oriented stages of learning. Some may understand little of what they learn, simply because they missed out on earlier, more action-oriented learning experiences. You, the teacher, will have to watch for these possibilities in your particular children.

Areas of Development   Chapters 2 through 5 discuss various aspects of child development as they relate to teaching. All in all, these chapters provide ways of knowing where your students fit into the general life cycle. cognitive First comes the theory of Jean Piaget, whose ideas on cognitive growth (the development of thinking) have become very popular among teachers and educators. Some reasons for his popularity will be given in Chapter 2, but so too will some limitations of his theory.

Chapter 3 focuses on language and communication, one of the most important developmental areas for teachers. Since most education consists of talk, teachers should know something about how children learn to talk linguistic and, most especially, about how they learn to communicate with language. Some of this learning seems to occur in spite of anyone's deliberate efforts. Parents do not usually take a course in "How to teach your child to talk," yet most children learn anyway. Nevertheless, many aspects of language can be influenced by teachers—most notably, children's reasons for speaking and their styles of talking for various purposes. These aspects of communication form the bulk of classroom interaction and obligate us teachers to attend to them. How can we help our children communicate effectively?

Chapter 4 considers moral and ethical development in children. Some, but not all, of this information originates from Piagetian ideas. It deals with a fundamental problem of schooling: establishing good character, citizenship, or self-discipline in children and students. What forms of self-control, for example, can teachers reasonably expect from students at different stages of life? How can they foster higher forms of moral development without forcing children to parrot superficially the correct attitudes?

moral

Chapter 5 examines social influences on learning. It begins by describing the major social relationships that children form at different ages and how these affect their ability to learn and to have confidence in themselves. Then it discusses how economic and cultural circumstances can affect the kind of person—and learner—that a child becomes. It ends by considering how gender—maleness or femaleness—influences learning and teaching, and whether in fact it always does.

social

Even though developmental psychology concentrates more on universal changes in children than on differences among them, the chapters on the topic are not meant to imply that the children of any one age all act alike. Five minutes in any classroom will show that individual children differ in many, many ways. Children obviously grow up at different speeds and in different ways. How these differences are acquired is a concern of learning theory, the second essential element of educational psychology.

Learning and Instruction

The Concept of Learning
Learning refers to relatively lasting changes in behavior that result from relatively specific experiences. In educational psychology, learning typically does not refer to physical changes that come from physical experiences, like bigger muscles from lifting barbells. It can, however, include changes in feelings and in thinking: fear can be learned, as can long division. All in all, it includes a rather big piece of life—and a lot of what happens in schools. Learning, in fact, is supposed to be what education is all about, even though rather little of it occurs on some occasions.

lasting changes from specific experiences

Teachers must be careful to distinguish learning from maturation and development, the topics covered in Chapters 2 through 5. **Maturation** refers to the relatively long-term changes in behavior that may be caused by the child's physical growth, possibly in combination with specific environmental experiences. Both maturation and development are beyond the control of any one person, including the child's teacher.

different from maturation and development

Theories of Learning
Chapter 6 looks at **behaviorism**, a theory of learning that focuses on the learner's specific, observable responses and the specific, observable stimuli that lead to them. To the uninitiated, behaviorism often conjures up pictures of rats running through mazes or

behavioral theories

teachers rigidly handing out bits of candy as reinforcers. In practice, or at least in good practice, behaviorism need not be applied this simplistically, and it does indeed seem to explain many classroom events. Different varieties of behaviorist theory, in addition, explain different sorts of events and often do so clearly and concisely.

cognitive theories

Many teachers and psychologists, however, feel that focusing on overt behavior cannot explain the thinking processes that influence learning, the so-called mediating responses. For help with these, they often turn to the so-called cognitive theories of learning. A sampling of these are described in Chapter 7.

Cognitive theories focus on the internal processes of learning. They may explain, for example, how people decide where to pay attention and to whom and how they make sense out of experiences and ideas so that they can remember them and relate them to other experiences and ideas. These thinking processes influence people's behavior, of course, and sometimes lead to quite permanent learning. But compared with behavioral theories, cognitive theories are concerned with the thought leading to behavior as well as with the behavior itself. Although this all sounds very sensible, it has one disadvantage: thinking can be much harder to observe than actual behavior is.

Instructional Applications   Chapters 8 and 9 draw on the previous two chapters to suggest how instruction can be designed and managed as effectively as possible. Philosophically, the two chapters combine behaviorist ideas with cognitive ones. Chapter 8 suggests ways of improving the retention of learning and promoting the use of learning in new situations. And it describes **behavioral objectives**, the use of objectives stated in specific, behavioral terms. Chapter 9 examines **instructional management**, the ways that the many elements of good teaching can be integrated into a smooth and effective style of teaching. Generally, good management involves both preventing instructional problems before they first occur and correcting them after they do. Ideally, too, it means coordinating the efforts of individual teachers so as to benefit their students.

behavioral objectives

instructional management

Individual Differences and Exceptionality   The study of learning must recognize the differences in how students learn, as well as their similarities. In practical teaching, you may actually notice the differences among your students more than you do their similarities. The chapters on development and learning offer some information about individual differences, which are the main topic of Chapter 10, on teaching exceptional children. **Exceptional children** are the ones with very unusual qualities, whether these are physical, mental, or emotional. The unusual qualities themselves are sometimes called **exceptionalities**, and they take many different forms. They include physical handicaps, such as vision or hearing problems or other serious physical abnormalities or conditions. They also include mental handicaps—retardation or specific learning disabilities—as well as extremely high mental capacity—giftedness. And they include emotional disturbance. Some children, of course, may have to cope with more than one exceptionality.

kinds of exceptionalities

Since such children have recently begun to use regular schooling more than in the past, teachers now need to know more about what to expect of them and how to meet their needs. In general, children with special needs often pose the same challenges that other children do: they are individuals and learn best when their individual needs and skills—and limitations—are recognized. At the same time, exceptional children naturally have unique needs that call for responses from their teachers. Chapter 10 samples some of these needs and responses.

Motivation

The Concept of Motivation **Motivation** refers to the tendency to engage in certain behaviors or to the inner arousal that leads to those behaviors. In teaching situations, motivation always poses a challenge to teachers: how can they arouse or excite their students about what they are learning so that they learn the material and alter their behavior accordingly? This problem is most pressing wherever teaching and learning are compulsory: in a required course in public school, perhaps, or in a mandatory training program for new army recruits. It remains a problem, though, even when learning is voluntary, since then the content must compete with other interests and activities. A Sunday morning religious education class, for example, must constantly make its goals seem more important, satisfying, or worthwhile than other ways of using Sunday morning.

Therefore, the fact that a student attends your class faithfully, or even appears to listen, does not prove that he or she is learning. In schools, in particular, students do not ever really have to learn, in spite of the incentives of grades; they only have to attend from day to day. Many would come anyway, and learn eagerly, but not all. Teaching, then, means continually persuading at least some students to learn: persuading them that learning is fun or at least useful in the long run. Chapters 11 and 12 consider how you might tackle this problem, based on the current psychological theories of motivation. Unfortunately (or is it fortunately?), many different theories have been proposed, each one useful for understanding some students, in some situations. Chapter 11 discusses several motives that learners commonly have: to achieve, to affiliate with others, and to gain power. Some motives are intrinsic—coming from within the learner—and others are extrinsic—coming from people or sources outside the learner.

kinds of motives

Each child presents a teacher with a unique developmental level, preferred styles of learning, and particular motives and needs. How best to teach and evaluate the child follows from that unique blend. (Will McIntyre/Photo Researchers, Inc.)

Whatever their source and nature, motives exist in various combinations in all teaching and learning. They can work for good or for ill, and either cooperatively or competitively. Whether teaching in a school or someplace else, teachers have to decide what mixtures of such motives they wish to encourage.

Implications for Teaching   To motivate students we must deal with their feelings about learning, either their interest in the learning itself or their interest in the goals, jobs, or situations that learning can achieve. In most cases, teachers deal with preexisting feelings that students bring to school with them. Often, however, feelings can and should be explored explicitly and incorporated into the teaching program in various ways. Chapter 12, on humanistic education, suggests how teachers might do this. **Humanistic education** refers to a philosophy of teaching and learning that places the highest importance on the needs and wishes of the individual. Such a philosophy can take many forms in actual teaching practice, depending on the age and interests of the students.

Evaluation

The Concept of Evaluation Strictly speaking, schools exist so that students can learn, not so that teachers can teach. Your job success, then, depends less on what you do than on what your students learn. **Evaluation of learning**, therefore, means observing your students in various ways, looking for changes in *their* behavior, not in yours. Chapter 13 offers a number of ways in which you can make such observations. It also analyzes the most popular method for assessing learning, namely, written tests. These have definite limitations as a way to evaluate students, but for important reasons they remain an eternal feature of school teaching. Tests and other observations of students are eventually reported as a grade or mark, a single letter or number that is somehow supposed to summarize the work of an entire course. Various problems and anguish are chronically associated with grades, both in assigning them and in receiving them. Some of these are described in Chapter 14, with suggestions for dealing with them.

Issues in Education Many of the problems of teacher-made evaluations also plague the so-called standardized tests of ability and achievement. How can a child's ability be reported accurately and objectively? Can standardized observations take into account the child's culture and attitudes toward testing? Why bother with standardized tests at all? Issues like these are reviewed in Chapter 14, with such answers as can be given to them. The chapter gives special attention to the concept of intelligence and to IQ tests, the most common standardized measures of general ability. It explains, in particular, what IQ tests do and do not really indicate and how teachers can use the information they do provide.

UNDERLYING ASSUMPTIONS OF THIS BOOK

This book is committed to the need of teachers for a psychological understanding of their children. It is not committed to any one theory of psychology, and it tries wherever possible to present conflicting theories fairly. The book's first priority is to apply each psychological theory or concept to teaching practice, not to reconcile it to its opponents. Theoretical conflicts, in any case, often result more from differences in focus between theories than from their disagreement on key points. Some theoretical loose ends therefore may remain after each chapter, though these should generally not interfere with your using psychology for teaching. If you want to know more about a particular topic, you should consult the annotated bibliographies at the end of each chapter.

Educational psychology is a young science, some say, and hence has not had time to achieve a consensus on many topics. Others—more cynical, perhaps—say simply that psychology is inherently unscientific; after all, how can the study of people be quantified? The author of this book believes that educational psychology does not have all the answers to teaching and learning but that it does have some of them and, maybe more important, that it asks a lot of good questions. Psychology, as we shall see, is not an exact science, though some areas of it are moving in that direction; and some are already rather exact, dependable, and clear. This book will give you dependable information if it exists. If it does not exist, it will give you the best that psychology and professional opinion have to offer. If major disagreements exist, it will describe these with as much fairness as possible to all sides.

Educational psychology is a blend of tentative theories and well-supported ones. Before you go far in studying this field, you will see this mixture. But asserting that educational psychology is sometimes imprecise does not make it only as useful as intuition or common sense. The various theories described in the chapters ahead contain numerous implications for making your teaching better. If you want to help children or young people learn, then psychology does indeed have much to add to your own good common sense, which you will always need as well.

Key Points

1. Educational psychology considers how teaching and learning occur, whether in schools or elsewhere.

2. Four major aspects of educational psychology are development, learning and instruction, motivation, and the evaluation of learning.

3. Development refers to the long-run changes in behavior that result from a multitude of experiences.

4. Learning refers to the relatively long-lasting changes in behavior or thinking that result from relatively specific experiences.

5. One of the many ways that learning theories differ is in the emphasis given to studying behavior rather than thinking processes.

6. Exceptional children have unusual qualities, some of which may be handicaps and some of which may require individual help in learning situations.

7. Motivation refers to the tendency to act and the arousal underlying this tendency.

8. Evaluation of learning refers to observations or tests of how well teaching and learning have succeeded.

9. Since teachers usually serve students rather than theories, this book draws on whatever psychological theories seem useful, rather than on any one of them at the expense of others.

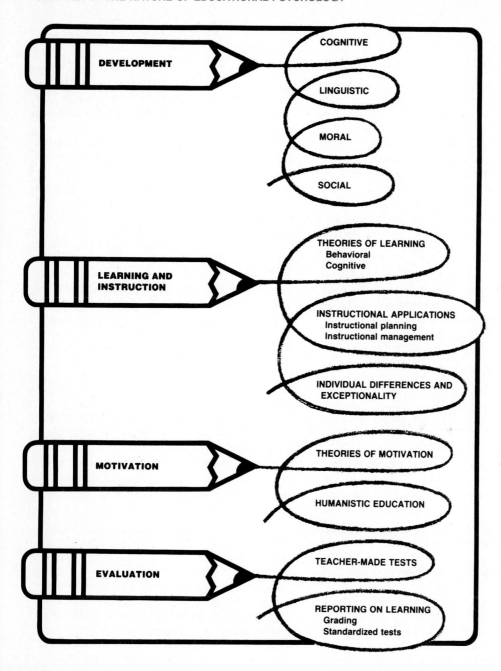

DEVELOPMENT

- COGNITIVE
- LINGUISTIC
- MORAL
- SOCIAL

LEARNING AND INSTRUCTION

- THEORIES OF LEARNING
  Behavioral
  Cognitive
- INSTRUCTIONAL APPLICATIONS
  Instructional planning
  Instructional management
- INDIVIDUAL DIFFERENCES AND EXCEPTIONALITY

MOTIVATION

- THEORIES OF MOTIVATION
- HUMANISTIC EDUCATION

EVALUATION

- TEACHER-MADE TESTS
- REPORTING ON LEARNING
  Grading
  Standardized tests

The graphic organizers that appear at the end of each of the remaining chapters in this book contain cross-references to other chapters in which related topics are covered.

Case Study

Jean Wright Begins Teaching

Jean Wright had planned her first week of her first year of teaching carefully—she thought. She had several sections of junior-high business education. "Be careful," the principal had warned her. "These kids will run all over you if you're not firm with them." Jean certainly did not want to be exploited, she thought to herself, but she also wanted to be a teacher to her students, not a police officer. So she planned her first week carefully, telling herself that good preparation and interesting material would prevent any serious behavior problems in her class.

On the first day, she explained the semester's assignments to her seventh graders: a series of quizzes plus a project to study a local business. "But Mrs. Wright," someone pointed out, "the *other* business teacher isn't making *his* class do a project. Why do *we* have to?"

"Because it's important," Jean replied. It was all she could think of at the moment to say.

"Will we have to read a lot to do the write-up for the project?" someone else asked.

"Well, probably some reading," said Jean, pausing. Several students gave each other exasperated looks but stifled them when they saw Jean looking at them. Their reactions made Jean nervous. On an impulse, she added, "But we'll find lots of time and ways to go over your reading in class before the due date."

She wasn't sure quite what she was promising by this remark. All she knew was that she suddenly had an awful feeling that many of her students might not read very well and might not understand the articles she gave them even if they did read them.

Questions for Discussion

1. What suggestions or advice could you give Jean at this point—after her first day—to help reassure her about her instructional plans and to help her fulfill her promise to "talk about the readings"?

2. Why do you think the student asked the question about reading and the others made faces about the answer? Speculate about how these behaviors could reflect the various elements of educational psychology: the students' developmental level, their ability to learn from written material, their motivations to learn, and their concerns about being evaluated fairly.

3. How could Jean test out your answers to the second question? Suggest some questions or activities that she could use to do so.

Suggested Readings

Kohl, Herbert. *On Teaching*. New York: Bantam, 1977.

Lopate, Philip. *Being with Children*. New York: Bantam, 1975.

Roy, Gabrielle. *Children of My Heart*. Toronto: McClelland & Stewart, 1977.

There are a host of personal accounts of teaching, and these are just three. The first is a critique of current teaching methods and the political pressures on teachers; the second describes the instructional and interpersonal problems of an inner-city art teacher; and the third relates the experiences of a young teacher in a one-room, rural school. Each testifies to the complexity of teaching, no matter what the circumstances.

Lortie, Dan. *Schoolteachers: A Sociological Study*. Chicago: University of Chicago Press, 1975.

Despite its title, this book is a good one for teachers who work outside schools as well as for those who work in them. Much of the book compares the working conditions and pressures in schools with those in other sorts of occupations and professions. Excellent for getting a perspective on teaching.

Ryan, Kevin. *Biting the Apple: Accounts of First-Year Teachers*. New York: Longman, 1981.

This book describes the experiences of twelve beginning teachers of different grade levels and subject areas. Most of them survived their first year, but not without various troubles. The teachers often speak for themselves in this book, and they show the complexity of their job: how it draws on knowledge of development, learning and instruction, motivation, and evaluation—and on more, besides.

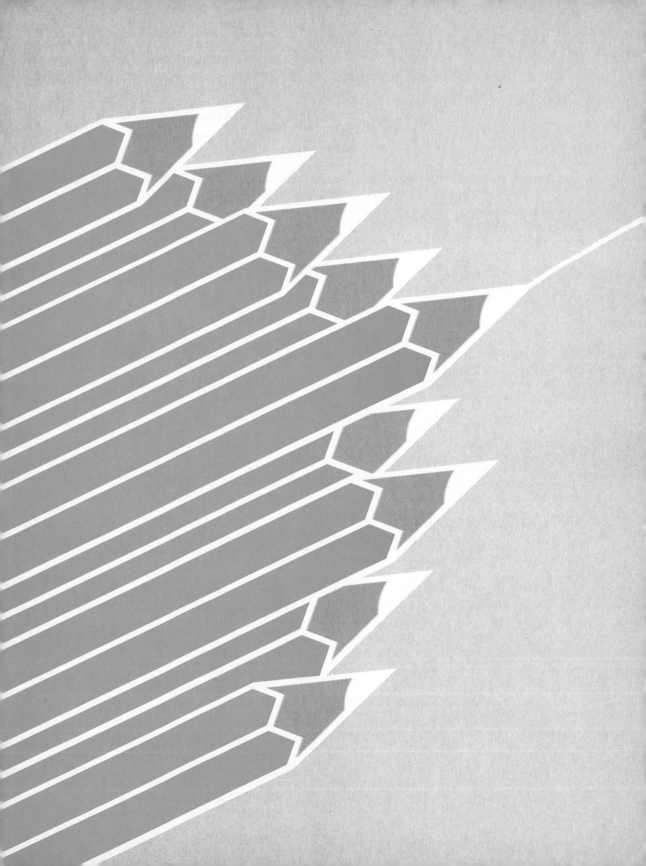

Part I
DEVELOPMENT

Part of teaching requires sensitivity to the differences that age and maturity create among learners. Compared with older children and adolescents, for example, five-year-olds think and learn relatively more by acting on the world. Older children usually handle symbolic representations of their world with far more ease and in a far more organized way. These differences happen for many reasons, including specific experiences that occur before teachers and students ever meet each other. To a large extent, therefore, they are beyond educational influence. But they are not irrelevant to learning and instruction because they provide the framework within which learning and instruction must take place.

Because such differences evolve slowly and lead to relatively permanent changes among individuals, psychologists and educators often label them *developmental*. Teachers may sometimes overlook these trends because the individual differences among their current students may obscure them and because they may feel obliged to concentrate on accomplishing specific curriculum goals. It helps, therefore, to remind ourselves of these differences: to take stock of where current students fit into the overall cycle of human life and into the overall cycle of cognitive growth.

The chapters in Part I discuss several aspects of development. Chapter 2 examines the growth of thinking skills from the viewpoint of a particular theory that is currently popular among educators, that of Jean Piaget. Chapter 3 discusses language development and communication, two processes that form the basis of most learning and instruction in schools and much of it outside schools. Chapter 4 describes how children and young people acquire ethical or moral beliefs and how teachers can influence that development. And finally, Chapter 5 considers how social and economic circumstances can influence individual development, both in school and out.

Chapter 2

PIAGET'S THEORY OF COGNITIVE GROWTH

Barbara Fuller, kindergarten teacher: When I first read about Piaget, I realized that my children had been performing his experiments all along—I just hadn't been paying attention to them! Like Peter, for instance. Whenever we had playdough out, or clay, he would make "bird's eggs": five or six matching little balls in a little nest of clay. But just as soon as he had perfected his creation, he would squish each egg flat, one at a time, and then compare it with the remaining round ones. What was he thinking about while he made and then unmade these eggs? That's what I kept asking myself.

One day my curiosity got the better of me.

"Another nest today, Peter?" I asked as I sat down next to him. He glanced at me briefly but had little time for a smile.

"Yep. Five eggs, all the same. See?" He held one up so close to my nose that I had to look cross-eyed to see it.

"All the same?"

"Yeah, but not any more." And he took one egg out and gave it a swift thump on the table. "Now it's scrambled eggs. My mom says never to touch the eggs at home 'cause they'll break."

"That's true," I said. "They *are* delicate. But what about this one: is there just as much egg in this squished one as in the ones still in the nest?"

He looked at me suspiciously, because he could detect a teacherlike question a mile away.

"Well, I don't know about eggs, but those have more *clay* in them (*pointing to the nest eggs*) than those (*pointing to the squished ones*)."

"Are you sure?" I asked. "What do you mean?"

"Look here," he said. "See—the squished one is lower. But don't worry; I can get the clay back in by making it into a ball again." So he did, and put it back into the nest.

I was impressed by the confidence he expressed in his "wrong" answer and decided to press him just a little about it.

"Are you sure? Somebody else told me the flat ones had just as much as the round ones. What do you think of that?"

"He was wrong," said Peter firmly as he gave another egg a hard thump on the table.

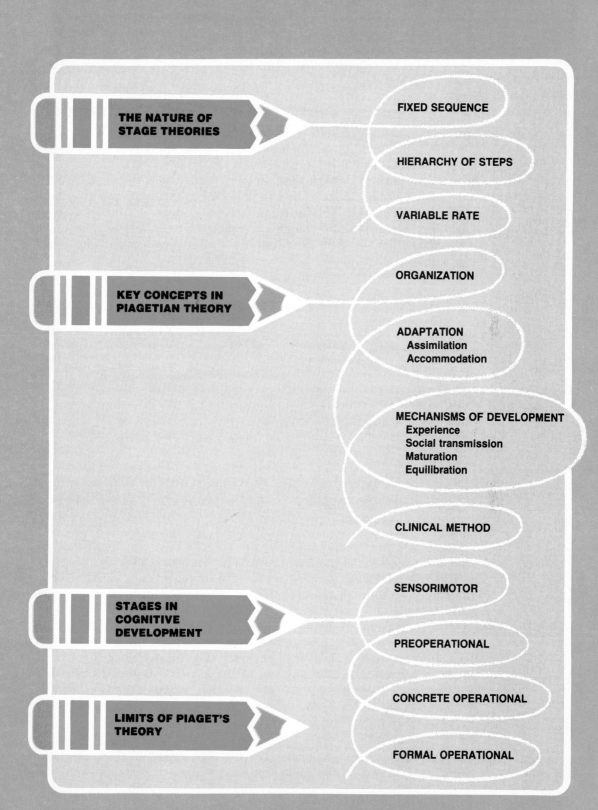

THE NATURE OF STAGE THEORIES

FIXED SEQUENCE

HIERARCHY OF STEPS

VARIABLE RATE

KEY CONCEPTS IN PIAGETIAN THEORY

ORGANIZATION

ADAPTATION
Assimilation
Accommodation

MECHANISMS OF DEVELOPMENT
Experience
Social transmission
Maturation
Equilibration

CLINICAL METHOD

STAGES IN COGNITIVE DEVELOPMENT

SENSORIMOTOR

PREOPERATIONAL

CONCRETE OPERATIONAL

LIMITS OF PIAGET'S THEORY

FORMAL OPERATIONAL

JEAN Piaget has influenced the way that teachers view children perhaps more than any other recent psychologist has. He did so by constructing a theory about how children think and, in particular, about the stages or steps in the development of their thinking. The details of these stages give teachers landmarks to look for when considering their students and planning for their instruction. For example, according to Piaget, children begin life in a period of sensorimotor thinking: learning about objects strictly through their sensory experiences of them and through manipulating them actively. By the time they graduate from high school, however, they may be able to think "formally," that is, to reason about imaginary events without the help of concrete props. Between these two periods are other stages in the children's thinking, each consisting of various thinking skills relevant to the work of teaching.

THE NATURE OF STAGE THEORIES

Piaget's theory is a stage theory.* A **stage** is simply a period or a level in a sequence of development. All stage theories have several general characteristics. First, they contain a **fixed sequence** of attainments. If Piagetian theory (or any other stage theory, for that matter) says that stage A

fixed sequence

must come before stage B, then it means that it will always come in this order—first A and then B. It does not mean that this sequence will occur only sometimes or even usually, nor does it mean that some children may skip stage B, going directly from stage A to stage C. The sequence is fixed—period.

Stage theories also assume that each stage of development incorporates thinking skills from all of the preceding stages; as psychologists sometimes say, they form a **hierarchy**. Stage B incorporates or includes skills learned in stage A, plus distinctly new ones; stage C incorporates skills from both

cumulative hierarchy

stages B and A, plus more; and so on. Piaget's theory assumes that development proceeds in this manner. The high school graduates mentioned in the first paragraph can learn not only through verbal discussions of ideas but also through sensorimotor explorations of materials. Many science labs combine both modes of learning. But the reverse is not true for infants: they cannot learn by discussion (proud parents notwithstanding) but must learn entirely through sensorimotor explorations. Older students may often not use the skills they acquired at an earlier stage, since these may not help them in thinking and acting as much as do the skills they acquire later. Their actual behavior therefore may change dramatically from one stage to the next, even though their capabilities accumulate

*Other stage theories will be discussed in later chapters. Chapter 4 discusses Kohlberg's stage theory of moral development; Chapter 5, Erikson's stage theory of personality development; and Chapter 11, Maslow's stage theory of motivation.

rather than change. Piaget's theory describes in detail how capabilities accumulate in the area of thinking and how their accumulation affects the learning and behavior of children and adolescents.

A stage theory like Piaget's recognizes that the children of any one age differ from one another in many ways. It explains these differences, though, according to how quickly individual children move through the stages of development rather than according to where they are heading in the long run. Indeed, since every child supposedly follows the same route of development, the only way for children to differ is in how quickly they travel along it. This feature of stage theories may contribute to a common, but mistaken, impression that Piaget primarily helps teachers by showing them how to accelerate children through the stages of development. In reality, he intended his findings to help diagnose children's thinking, not to accelerate it; but we shall return to this question later in this chapter.

variations in rates of development

The commitment to finding landmarks in child development has caused Piagetian theorists to emphasize *typical* child behavior somewhat at the expense of unusual or exceptional behaviors. Reading Piaget tells you what to expect of "the child" at key points during childhood, as if every child developed normally. In fact, most children do not exactly follow any normal patterns; yet most grow up to be quite healthy and happy. A few, of course, deviate a lot from the typical path—so much so that they deserve special mention in a later chapter of this book. But in many ways they, too, can grow up as healthy and happy as the others do—just different.

emphasis on typical behavior

If a stage theory like Piaget's is taken too literally, it can make teachers and parents worry unduly about whether or not their own children are on schedule in their development. What if Bill learns to read two years later than do most of the other children his age? Or two years earlier? What if he learns to talk later than the others do? Concerns like these come from many sources, but a large part of them come from interpreting the milestones of stage theories too literally. If the Piaget supporters were to state that infants usually complete their sensorimotor thinking by the age of twenty-four months, then would thirty months be too late? How about twenty-seven months? A careful reading of Piaget and his followers reveals that they specify age limits only to describe development, not to recommend what children should do at different ages. Teachers and parents often do not realize this, but for understandable reasons: unlike Piaget, they must not only understand the behavior of children but evaluate it as well.

KEY CONCEPTS IN PIAGETIAN THEORY

Anyone learning Piagetian theory will immediately confront some unfamiliar terms. Look at the ones below, which are usually considered basic to the theory, and be prepared to return to them as you read on about the

Piagetian stages themselves and their applications to teaching. Many people learn Piaget's theory best by circling back to earlier notions after studying his theory as a whole.

Organization

Piaget was concerned with the tendency of human thinking to become organized as it develops. By **organization** Piaget meant the process of coordinating ideas and actions and making them systematic. Sometimes the results of these coordinations are called **schemes** in Piagetian theory. Schemes can take very different forms depending on the child's level of development. An infant, for example, may organize her manipulations of a toy rattle into a single concept of the rattle as an object; in this case we say that she has developed a scheme of the rattle. A teen-ager, on the other hand, may organize his experiences with and discussions about his best friend into a general concept, or scheme, of his friend. Even though some of the elements of his concept may be far more abstract than those of the infant, they both result from the organization of thinking, and Piaget would refer to each as a "scheme."

increasing organization of thinking

formation of schemes

Adaptation

Human thinking remains organized (in the Piagetian sense) by continually adapting to its environment. **Adaptation** is the process of modifying or changing as a person adjusts to his or her environment, and it can come about in two ways.

continuous adaptation to environment

Assimilation Versus Accommodation   One way is through the process of **assimilation**, in which new experiences are perceived or interpreted according to existing ideas or activities (schemes). A young child might call a dragonfly by the only name he already has for flying objects, perhaps "bird." An adolescent in her teens might react to a police officer in the same way that she reacts to her parents and teachers, the only other authority figures in her life. If she normally receives only minor punishment for talking insolently with her parents, she may do the same with a police officer, but with unhappy results.

interpretation of new experiences according to existing schemes

   Adaptation also includes a second, complementary process called **accommodation**, in which the child adjusts or changes preexisting ideas or activities to fit new experiences. In the examples above, the young child accommodates when and if he encounters enough dragonflies to begin calling them by their right name and to distinguish them from his earlier, more global concept of birds. But the older child above accommodates if and when she learns to respond differently to police officers than she does

modification of existing schemes to fit new experiences

to her parents, and we hope that she will not have to learn the hard way! Note that in both examples, accommodation necessarily occurs slowly, as experiences accumulate; whereas assimilation by definition occurs even on the first encounter.

Integration of Assimilation and Accommodation Note, too, that any one experience really is a combination of assimilation and accommodation. Even the first time that the young child sees the dragonfly and uses a wrong name for it, he may already have noticed its difference from the other winged creatures he has seen and been calling "birds"—even though he may not have words for what he can see. And later, even after he has fully accommodated his thinking to include dragonflies, he still will be assimilating newer experiences to preexisting concepts. Now that the dragonfly is established, he may assimilate other insects to this new name.

The same mingling of assimilation and accommodation occurs with the older child's response to the police officer. Her response must at first be based on whatever social skills she already has (assimilation), but at the same time the demands of this new authority figure force her to begin changing her style (accommodation). Eventually, she learns to deal with the police officer well enough that the situation no longer challenges her as it did at first. Now any further encounters with the police are assimilated to the adolescent's newly learned skills with them, though still more accommodations will always be needed as long as she continues to grow and develop.

Mechanisms of Development

These examples illustrate the combination of mechanisms that Piaget believed account for the actual transition of human thought from earlier to later stages. There are four such mechanisms, though they are not equally important in any particular adaptation.

Experience . First, and perhaps most obviously, children have *experience* with relevant features in the environment. The younger child above, for example, must see dragonflies in order to distinguish them from birds. More generally, all children or adolescents must see, hear, or otherwise sense the objects that they are to think about and adapt to. Some objects of thought, however, are memories and ideas, rather than physical entities. Children's experience in these cases occurs internally, through repeated reflections on their memories and ideas. So instead of necessarily seeing ever more actual dragonflies and birds, the child may sometimes simply remember and ponder his previous sightings of them, and in so doing he may contribute to his adaptation to these two concepts.

encounters with environment

memories of encounters

Cognitive development occurs in part through direct experiences with the environment . . . (Elizabeth Crews)

Social Transmission   *Social transmission* also contributes to adaptation. In order to label dragonflies correctly, the child must somehow find out the term that his society uses for them, usually by simply being told. Or in order for the adolescent to learn how to behave with a police officer, she may have to get help from others—possibly, again, by being told how to conduct herself, but possibly also, in this case, by hearing about or observing others in similar situations. Some adaptations may depend heavily on social transmissions (like learning good table manners), whereas others may depend rather little on them (perhaps learning to judge the amounts contained in two differently shaped pieces of clay).

knowledge conveyed by members of a society or culture

Maturation   But experience and social transmission cannot help a child to adapt without *physical maturation* operating as well. Its influence is most apparent in infants and very young children, who are still rapidly growing physically. The young child above, for example, cannot benefit from experiences with dragonflies if he still lacks the muscles or neural equipment to focus on and watch them reliably. He cannot learn to call them by any particular name—let alone their correct name—if his vocal cords have not yet matured enough to produce recognizable sounds. In adolescence, maturation may continue to influence how much the central nervous system can do and therefore how a person can think; but this idea is controversial at best, and in any case almost impossible to test.

bodily changes resulting from growth, which affect ability to perceive and think

. . . and in part through transmission of knowledge from other members of so-ciety. (Jean-Claude Lejeune/Black Star)

Equilibration All three of these mechanisms contribute to the action of a fourth, which Piaget called **equilibration**. This term refers to the self-regulation of development; or put in other terms, to a tendency for children's thinking to become more stable, general, and in harmony with their environment as they develop. The child differentiating between birds and dragonflies acquires a more general thought pattern than he had before the adaptation: afterwards, he can accurately account for two groups of flying animals, rather than for just one of them. By learning the distinction, furthermore, his thinking becomes more consistent with the facts of nature (there are, after all, more than one kind of flying animal). As a result, after he makes the adaptation, the child has very little incentive for changing back to his former way of thinking. He may, in fact, find it difficult to believe or recall that he ever did use a simpler form of thought—in this case, that he ever used only one classification for two very different animals.

tendency of thinking to achieve stability and harmony with environment

The Clinical Method

Most of Piaget's concepts grew out of studies using semistructured interviews and observations, the so-called **clinical method**. Typically, this method entails interviewing children one at a time with a series of questions on a particular thinking problem or topic. The questions have been planned in advance, but not completely so, since the interviewer can never know ahead of time exactly how the child will answer. The interviewer is allowed some flexibility in following up unexpected replies and clarifying ambiguous ones. Some flexibility, that is, but not complete freedom: the clinical method is partially free, partially structured. In some ways it resembles a job interview or a personal opinion interview; only in this case it asks for a child's beliefs about a particular thinking problem. To many psychologists, this method of observation has seemed too prone to biases and too unsystematic to provide reliable and valid information. Originally, Piaget's work was often rejected on these grounds. More recently, though, carefully designed and experimentally sound studies have tested many of Piaget's clinical findings and, on the whole, have supported them (see, for example, Dasen, 1977, or Flavell, 1977).

STAGES IN COGNITIVE DEVELOPMENT

Piaget proposed that the development of a child's thinking had four main stages. Two of these, and parts of a third, can be observed directly in children of school age. The first stage, the sensorimotor period, occurs well before the school years in normal children; teachers can see only its results, not its acquisition. Even so, it helps explain some of the cognitive

Table 2–1 Basic Concepts and Stages in Piaget's Theory

Basic concepts

Organization: the tendency for thinking to become and remain systematic.

Schemes: the ideas and actions resulting from increasing organization of thinking.

Adaptation: changes in thinking resulting from development.

Assimilation: the interpretation or understanding of experiences according to existing schemes.

Accommodation: the modification of schemes to fit new experiences.

Mechanisms of transition

Experience: encounters with the environment or memories of such encounters.

Social transmission: knowledge conveyed by the members of a child's society or culture.

Maturation: bodily changes resulting from growth and affecting the child's ability to perceive and think about experience.

Equilibration: the tendency of thinking to achieve stability and balance, both within itself and with the environment.

Clinical method: the semistructured style of interviewing a child about his or her reasoning and ideas.

Stage: a period or level in a fixed sequence of development and its particular properties.

Major stages	Age span	Characteristics
Sensorimotor period	Birth to 2 years	Object permanence and imitation begin; circular reactions and a sense of time begin.
Preoperational period	2 years to 7 years	Dramatic play, language, animism, egocentrism, and classification begin; number correspondence begins; collective monologues and parallel play begin.
Concrete operational period	7 years to 11 years	Conservation, multiple classification, and following of rules begin.
Formal operational period	11 years to 15 years	Hypothetical thinking, scientific experimentation, combinatorial thinking, and idealism begin.

changes that come later, during the school years. In reading about these stages, keep in mind the comments made in the previous sections about the nature and limitations of stage theories in general: that children do not change stages suddenly, that the length of stages varies considerably with the child and his or her life circumstances, and that this theory tries only to describe children, not to prescribe what teachers should do about them.

The Sensorimotor Period: Birth to Two Years

learning by sensing and doing

As infants, according to Piaget, children learn mainly through their senses and their own activity. They learn by handling objects, manipulating them, and tasting and biting them. Some actions occur less obviously, such as following an object with the eyes or listening to a sound. Overall, though, their behavior consists of learning by doing, carried to its extreme.

belief in object permanence

Characteristics Through their actions, children gradually construct concepts of their experiences, particularly of the objects around them. By handling a toy duck, for example, in many ways and on many occasions, the child gradually acquires an idea of the duck as an object. Gradually this idea of the duck transcends any particular experience the child has with it, and in this sense it acquires permanence. By about age two or so, children have acquired a belief in **object permanence**, a sense that objects continue to exist whether or not they are immediately visible or within reach. Object permanence marks one of the major achievements of this period of development. From now on, the toy duck will exist for the child whether or not he happens to be holding it and seeing it. To come to this conclusion, the child must somehow represent the duck in his mind. Does he hold an actual picture in his mind, or a verbal label, or some strange sort of mixture? The answer is unclear, but some sort of representation is needed.

circular reactions

Another key characteristic of the sensorimotor period is **circularity,** the tendency of children to repeat specific actions (Piaget, 1952). From the age of about one to four months, children learn to reproduce interesting sights, sounds, and other sensations through what Piaget called **primary circular reactions**. In essence, these are specific behaviors or habits that involve the child's own body and that are repeated, seemingly endlessly. They evolve from the child's own simple and uncoordinated movements. Thumb sucking is a good example. At first the infant moves her hands randomly, but eventually one hand may happen to end up in her mouth, producing new and pleasurable sensations. Gradually she learns to reproduce this experience by repeatedly bringing her hand to her mouth. The process proceeds very slowly at first, however, and it includes much trial and error.

By the end of infancy, children usually acquire the belief that objects—including their own parents—continue to exist even when not immediately visible. (Peter Vandermark/Stock, Boston)

About the age of four to ten months, children apply the same process to objects outside their bodies, at which point the adaptation is called a **secondary circular reaction**. A child may happen to make his crib rattle in an appealing way by shaking his legs. Since he has no way at first of knowing what causes the interesting rattle, he will attempt various movements of his body at random until he happens upon the crucial leg-shaking movement again. If and when he does so, he will probably repeat the reaction. Unlike before, however, he is now beginning to differentiate his actions from the objects and results of his actions. In this sense he begins to show intentions—a separation of means and ends—though his intentions do not exist until he stumbles upon them.

From about ten to eighteen months, infants learn to combine their secondary circular reactions in order to produce interesting, new results on purpose. These combinations are called **tertiary circular reactions**, and they resemble miniature experiments conducted by the child. A child may discover that patting water in her bath produces an interesting new experience—a splash. Although she may originally discover the splashing by chance, she will quickly begin applying her different splashing schemes to the water: patting it in various ways, or with various limbs, or with various toys, or at various angles. Put together, these behaviors constitute curiosity: an interest in novelty for its own sake.

beginning of experimentation

The development of circular reactions also illustrates other aspects of infant development observed by Piaget. For example, as children acquire the means to produce interesting sensations, they also necessarily develop a rudimentary sense of *past* and *future time*. Many circular reactions are expectations of results, as well as recollections of past results. Judging by their behavior, children seem to think, "If I first do X, then Y will happen"; and also seem to think, "X produced Y before, and so I shall try X again." They do not, of course, think these thoughts in any conscious, verbal way. Rather, they act as if they had thought them; their sense of time is intuitive and becomes fully expressed through language only during the preschool and school years.

rudimentary sense of time

Viewed from still another angle, infants' circular reactions also illustrate the beginnings of their *problem solving ability.* After acquiring relatively few relevant secondary circular reactions, they can begin classifying objects and experiences in primitive ways. Some objects, they discover, can be chewed on and others cannot; some grasped and others not; some lifted and others not. And their circular reactions teach them much about the spatial relations between and among objects. They learn which things are "over" which other things, or under them, or behind or in front of them. These understandings allow them, among other things, to look for hidden objects relatively effectively—a basic, but important spatial problem.

beginning of problem solving

During the sensorimotor period, children also develop the ability to *imitate*. At first they copy only behaviors that they themselves have already learned and performed. If they know how to smack their lips, then often an adult can prompt them to copy the adult's version of this same behavior. As they acquire more skills, children become able to imitate (or model) actions that they have never performed before, as long as these actions do not differ very much from their existing repertoire of behaviors. They may attempt to clap their hands after seeing an adult do so, although their first efforts may not succeed very well. Still later in infancy, children apply their interest in novelty, and their skill in producing it, to imitation:

imitation

now they will model sequences of human behavior in a systematic way. They may "brush their teeth" if given a brush when they see their parents doing it, or they may even try to brush their favorite teddy bear's teeth. These behaviors mark the beginnings of dramatic play, which becomes prominent during the preschool and early school years.

Educational Implications   By the end of the sensorimotor period, children have begun to think symbolically as well as through their actions on objects. They believe now that things exist permanently; they know many ways to experiment with them deliberately; and they can begin to model significant pieces of human behavior. All of these adaptations evolve from numerous simple and uncoordinated actions with an assortment of tangible objects and people. Although older children (and adults) take these beliefs and skills for granted, infants definitely do not.

This last fact is a humbling one for those of us who teach children, whatever their ages. Though we may hope and plan for the day when our children can handle relatively abstract ideas and materials, we can get them there only if we accept and encourage their need to do things that do not require much obvious symbolic activity. Though we may hope, for example, that they can some day discuss the differences among the Indian tribes in five major geographical regions in North America, they may learn to do so only through a long series of homely activities: crafts projects, acting out Indian rituals, watching films, and the like. These may not look very academic, and there may be relatively little discussion during them, even though discussion, not action, is our ultimate educational goal. If Piaget is right, these less abstract activities will eventually get our students where we want them to go and do so more effectively than by beginning with abstract discussions. It will do so by helping the students construct concretely the differences among tribes. Indirect and time consuming? Yes, but more effective in the long run, at least if Piaget and his followers are to be believed.

The Preoperational Period: Two to Seven Years

The **preoperational period** is characterized by intuitive, symbolic thinking. The word **operation** in the term *preoperational* refers to thought processes governed by logical rules; the name of this period therefore implies that children have not yet mastered such rules. They do, however, practice their new-found skills at representing objects, even though they have much to learn about how to organize their representations fully.

Characteristics   One form of intuitive, symbolic thinking during this period is **dramatic play**, in which various life experiences are represented

Preschool children make rapid gains in all forms of symbolic activity: language, dramatic play, and thinking tasks. (Sybil Shelton/Peter Arnold, Inc.)

dramatic play

in play. Preschoolers are continually pretending to be mommies or daddies, to drive cars, or to teach school. In Piagetian theory, such play helps children represent many of their experiences symbolically. In so doing it paves the way for the more organized thinking they will achieve later in childhood.

improving language ability

During the preoperational period, young children also demonstrate their growing ability to represent experiences by rapidly expanding their language skills. At age two, most children speak in single words or in short combinations of words. But by six or seven, they can use adult sentence constructions—even if they do not always understand them! The average vocabulary grows from about 250 words at age two to several thousand at age six (Nelson, 1973). In just a few years, their language has gone from baby talk to a good approximation of adult speech.

animism

Children's ability to symbolize (to represent experience) naturally is limited during early childhood. They cannot, for example, always distinguish between living objects and nonliving ones. Followers of Piaget call this **animism**. In one series of studies, Piaget showed that young preschoolers were apt to think that, say, rocks were alive, that trees could think, and that animals could talk like people, at least when adults were not around (Piaget, 1951).

In addition, young children in the preoperational period often fail to distinguish between their own viewpoint and that of others, what Piaget called **egocentrism**. Infants in the sensorimotor stage are egocentric, too: their failure to search for a lost object may imply that they equate the object's existence with their personal experience of it and that they are unaware that others may have their own, different experiences. Although preschoolers probably would not make this particular mistake in their thinking, they still are likely to make other egocentric errors. Numerous studies, both by Piaget and by others, have documented this fact.

egocentrism

1. In one study, young children seemed to think that an arrangement of dolls and toys looked the same across a table as it did from where the children themselves sat (Piaget, 1956).

2. In another study, young children seemed to believe that all natural phenomena were made to reward them personally if they were good and to punish them if they were bad. In essence, they attributed their own feelings and motives to the world around them, and even to the inanimate parts of the world.

3. Transcripts of preschoolers' conversations often contain **collective monologues**—two or more children talking in the presence of others and speaking as if each expects to be heard but not in fact listening to or responding to the others (Piaget, 1976). For example:

collective monologues

Marta: Look at my new shoes.
Carlos: We're going to the store today.
Marta: Brown ones.
Carlos: Do you want to come, too?

4. Similarly, observations of preschool children in group play often show them ignoring one another even when working side by side—in what is known as **parallel play**. They may often do so even when their toys seemingly invite them to interact, as when building with a single puzzle, for example, or when using a doll house containing a single set of furniture. Rather than regarding other children as potential sources of new and independent ideas for play, they may assume (egocentrically) that all ideas must come from within themselves. This assumption gives them little incentive to interact in a truly cooperative way. In none of these examples are children egocentric in the adult sense of "selfish." They are not actually elevating their own thoughts and needs above other people's; they are just confusing theirs with those of others'.

parallel play

At the beginning of the preoperational period, children have difficulty **seriating** objects along a single dimension; in other words, they cannot

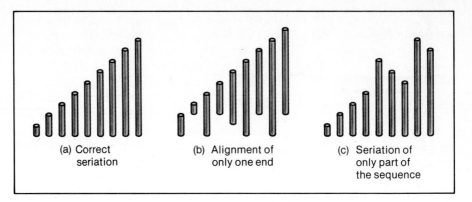

Figure 2–1 Seriation of Sticks

beginning of seriation

place objects that belong in a particular order into their proper sequence. Given a series of sticks that vary only in length, young preoperational children cannot lay them side by side from shortest to longest in stairlike fashion, as shown in Figure 2–1. Toward the end of the period, they may become able to do so, but usually only with much effort and many mistakes. An older preoperational child at this stage may construct a stairlike sequence for only one end of the sticks, neglecting to coordinate the other ends; another one may construct parts of the series but leave other parts undone or out of sequence. The first child fails because he cannot coordinate two perceptions at once—in this case, the two ends of the sticks. The second child fails because she cannot adopt and follow consistent rules to solve the problem—in this case, the rule that each stick must be both longer than the one before and shorter than the one after. Such thinking skills are finally achieved by the next period of development, during the school years.

A similar inability to follow consistent rules affects the preoperational child's ideas of **number**. This term does not refer to verbal counting ability but, rather, to the ability to establish numerical equivalences or *number correspondences* between sets of objects. Given a box of blue beads and a box of red beads, how do children determine whether the boxes contain the same number? They do so by constructing a one-to-one correspondence between the beads in one box and the beads in the other, as shown in Figure 2–2. Young preoperational children, however, use no systematic procedure for doing so: if asked to find the same number in each set, they will simply select items from each until they look about the same. Later on in this period, they may successfully construct a one-to-one correspondence but will easily change their minds if one group of beads is rearranged. Most of the time, they attribute the larger number to the group that then looks larger. Apparently they do not realize that a greater dis-

beginning of correspondence

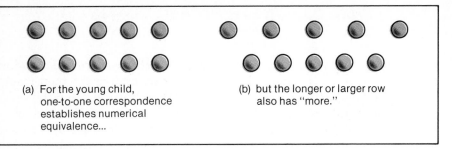

(a) For the young child, one-to-one correspondence establishes numerical equivalence...

(b) but the longer or larger row also has "more."

Figure 2–2 Number Correspondence

tance between individual beads can compensate for the greater overall size of the row. Or put in other terms: they do not realize that physical displacements do not affect numerical correspondence.

Educational Implications   Many children entering kindergarten and first grade still show definite signs of preoperational thinking, and consciously or not, teachers of the very young often make allowances for this fact. First, kindergartens usually allow for dramatic play much more than older grades do, despite notable exceptions. Second, learning to share and to get along with others are frequently stated goals in early childhood education, a reflection of how much young children need to overcome egocentrism. Third, the younger grades usually rely relatively little on purely verbal instructions. Written work sheets, at least the successful ones, include plenty of graphics that help explain the assignment nonverbally; oral instructions from the teacher are kept short and to the point. As children move up through the grade levels, most of these practices shift to ones that rely more and more on purely verbal exchange.

There is some danger in teachers' trying to move their children past preoperational thinking according to some conventional timetable, and not according to the child's personal one. Tradition has it that a child should begin learning to read in Grade 1, at about the age of six. But Piagetian observations of children suggest that many children cannot handle such a skill until a year or two later because of its very symbolic nature. Others seem ready to read well before the traditional starting time (Elkind, 1974). If some day you happen to teach very young children, you will be challenged to diagnose these differences in your children's personal timing and to allow for them in your classroom program. If you teach older children, you may not encounter this particular problem in diagnosis, but you can nevertheless expect others like it: when, for example, can we really expect students to study the national constitution with understanding?

The Concrete Operational Period: Seven to Eleven Years

By the time they reach elementary school, most children are able to think in operations, or logical rules. Fortunately for the children and their teachers, many school activities begin demanding this ability at about the same time that it in fact appears in most children. Piaget called this first operational period a "concrete" one because at this point children apply their new-found logical abilities most successfully to concrete (or real, tangible) objects and events. Only later do they become able to think operationally about abstractions.

Characteristics **Conservation** refers to the ability to perceive constancy or invariance despite certain visible changes. Consider two balls of the same size and shape. If a young, preoperational child is shown these, he will have no trouble agreeing that they contain the same amount of clay. But if one of them is then squished into a hot-dog shape, he may well decide that its amount no longer equals that of the original round ball. Whether it has more or less clay than before will depend on its new shape and on what aspects of the new shape stand out most clearly to the child, but the amount will no longer be the same. Older children, the ones who have reached the stage of concrete operations, are not fooled by this problem. For them, the amount of clay remains the same, regardless of how its shape is deformed. They "conserve" the amount of clay in their minds, despite visible changes that suggest an alteration.

conservation ability

Piaget and other psychologists conducted several experiments like these, and some of them are summarized briefly in Figure 2–3. The results consistently demonstrate that older children (upper elementary-school age) conserve but that young preschoolers do not. Children of school-entering age (kindergarten, Grade 1) often are transitional in their thinking. In general, the conservers seem to base their beliefs on three arguments:

1. *Identity:* since nothing has been added or subtracted, the amount (or length or number of whatever) remains the same as before.
2. *Compensation:* a change in one dimension (say, width) makes up for a change in another (say, height).
3. *Reversibility:* the change in appearance can be undone, at least in principle, thereby proving that it did not affect the amount, but only its appearance.

Children just beginning to conserve probably will not state these reasons in words, and children who do use reasons probably will not state them in these words. But their reasoning contains the same ideas.

The development of thinking in elementary-aged children can also be seen in their growing ability to **classify** objects. Younger children can

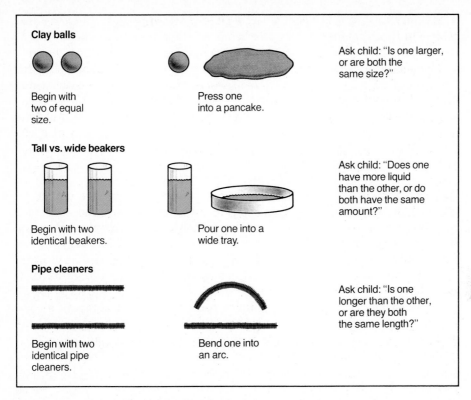

Clay balls

Begin with
two of equal
size.

Press one
into a pancake.

Ask child: "Is one larger,
or are both the
same size?"

Tall vs. wide beakers

Begin with two
identical beakers.

Pour one into a
wide tray.

Ask child: "Does one
have more liquid
than the other, or do
both have the same
amount?"

Pipe cleaners

Begin with two
identical pipe
cleaners.

Bend one into
an arc.

Ask child: "Is one
longer than the other,
or are they both
the same length?"

Figure 2–3 Several Conservation Experiments

group objects according to common single attributes almost as well as older
children can, but they have trouble seeing that two objects might be at
the same time the same in one way and different in another. The younger
ones are more likely to notice either the sameness or the difference, but
not both (Elkind, 1976, p. 93ff).

This development can be seen with a simple experiment in grouping
objects. Show a child a box full of wooden beads, each one painted one of
two different colors, perhaps red and blue. Let her handle the beads if she
likes, to make sure that she understands that the beads are wooden and
that she can name their colors. Suppose, in this particular case, that the
box contains seven red beads and three blue ones—ten wooden beads in
all. Then ask the child two questions: (1) Are there more red beads or more
blue beads? and (2) Are there more red beads or more wooden beads?

Younger, preoperational children and older, concrete operational ones
both tend to answer the first question easily and correctly. The second
question, though, usually proves much more difficult for the younger ones
than for the older children. Why? Because in the first question, the child

*classification
ability*

needs only to group the objects according to one dimension, in this case, color. On that dimension, any two beads can be either the same or different, but not both. Judging which they are requires only simple perception.

The second question, though, poses a more difficult problem. Here the child must keep in mind two dimensions at the same time, rather than one—in this case, the dimensions of color and woodenness. To succeed, she must realize that two beads might be both the same (both wooden) and different (red and blue); they must be matched in two ways at once. She cannot let her mind focus on just one dimension or the other, as the younger child seems to do.

Educational Implications   Children's ability to conserve definitely affects how they can be taught. Nonconservers usually are more swayed by how problems are presented and explained. Seemingly small changes in drawings or graphics may strike a nonconserving child as very important. Likewise, seemingly insignificant changes in wording, either written or oral, may matter more to a nonconserving child than we adults first realize.

implications of conservation ability

This last problem points out a key assumption of most Piagetian conservation experiments: in general they all assume that the children understand the language of the task in more or less the same way that adults would and that small changes in procedures or wording will not affect the results of the experiment. This assumption reflects the basic Piagetian conviction that language functions as a tool of thought, and rather little as a director of it: hence Piaget's seemingly casual attitude toward how to ask for information from children.

Some psychologists and educators, though, object to this attitude. In their view, the Piagetian tasks test children's language ability, and not just their thinking. Therefore, they argue, why not simply teach the children the right answers to a problem like conservation, and perhaps they then would understand conservation. This suggestion has been made frequently by skeptics of Piaget. Since it deserves further consideration, we shall return to it later in this chapter.

implications of classification ability

Elementary teachers find that many school tasks require the kind of classification or grouping ability described earlier in this section. Three of these tasks are work sheet problems, reading, and following rules. The first, work sheets, may ask a child to use extensively his grouping and matching abilities. He may be asked to "find the word that begins with *L* and that belongs with the word *vehicle*." In this case the child must examine all the words arrayed on the work sheet for two kinds of relationships, one to a certain letter and the other to a class of objects. Two dimensions must be held in mind at once, just as in the wooden beads experiment. Such a task should not be difficult for a concrete operational child, but a child may not have reached this level of development when he first enters school. He may be able to tell which words begin with *L*,

work sheets

and even which words "belong with" vehicle. But asking him to do both at once—a double-barreled question—may just cause confusion.

Many reading tasks, too, require children to make comparisons in several ways at once. Knowing how to pronounce a strange word requires knowing not only how sounds correspond to letters but also how they correspond to places and sequences in typical words. Figuring out a new word requires formidable, and multiple, classification skills; knowing just a few sound-letter relationships will not be enough. Again, the concrete operational child can cope, or at least hope to cope, with the multiple demands of the task; but many children cannot do so during their first year or two or three in school, simply because of developmental slowness.

reading

The third task requiring classification ability is following rules, both those of the children's own making and those from adults. During grade school, children seem for the first time to relish games with rules. Sometimes they even seem more interested in creating and changing the rules to their games than in playing the games themselves (Sutton-Smith, 1974, chap. 11). For the first time, too, they can reliably follow the classroom rules set by their teachers, although they can argue about what constitutes infringement. Games and classroom management require classification skill: for both, children must constantly ask whether a particular behavior follows a rule or violates it. They must, in essence, mentally pigeonhole behaviors as either legal or illegal.

following rules

In one form or another, all these examples suggest that children in school must be able to classify fairly well: they must understand relationships between the whole and its parts and among alternative ways of grouping objects. In general they must be able to know how two things can be the same and different, not just the same or different. If they can, they will be much better prepared to survive the demands of elementary schooling than if they cannot.

Notice also that all of these examples use concrete experiences, objects, or events that the children experience directly. Concrete operational children cannot yet imagine hypothetical events, ones that might occur but do not. This ability requires more experience in living and in thinking. Eventually, children must begin to treat thoughts themselves as objects of experience; they must begin to manipulate ideas. When they can do so, they are entering the next stage of cognitive development, formal operations.

The Formal Operational Period: Eleven to Fifteen Years

In this stage, young people (hardly children any longer!) can think logically, not only about the concrete, immediate present, but also about abstract and **hypothetical ideas**. These are ideas that exist only in the human mind, like the idea of a "man from Mars" or the idea that "$2x + 3y = z$." Because of this new ability, young people can at last begin to shift their attention from what is to what might be. This change has significant implications for their behavior and the way they can learn and be taught.

hypothetical thinking

Characteristics   Because formal operational thinkers can reason about the possible, they can now experiment with ideas, in the true, scientific sense of the term. Piaget used the following study to observe formal operational thinking. A young person is shown a table with rods that will bend mounted on the side. The rods also vary in length and in thickness. She is also given a pile of washers that vary in thickness and that cause the rods to bend down until they touch the table (see Figure 2–4). The experimenter asks her a few questions about the setup: What circumstances or factors will cause the rods to bend until they just barely touch the table? How can she prove her theory?

scientific experimentation

To solve this problem, a person must use **combinatorial thinking**, a formal operational skill in which each relevant factor is systematically combined with every other relevant factor. This experiment has four such relevant factors: the length and thickness of the rods and the length and thickness of the washers. Every possible combination of these elements must be tried to ensure finding a solution. To make sure she is systematically combining the factors, the person working the problem must treat each factor as a mental (or hypothetical) object, imagining all possible combinations and keeping mental track of which ones remain to be tested. This skill, incidentally, also is the basis of the scientific method.

combinatorial thinking

Though the ability to manipulate thoughts per se frees adolescents to think more broadly than before, it also condemns them to **idealism**: an insensitivity to the practical limits of ideas. A young person may criticize his parents, not necessarily because they are really so terrible, but because they do not—cannot—live up to his concept of perfect parents. Or adolescents may fall in love—and out again—more on the basis of ideal images of lovers than on the real qualities or behaviors that their partners have shown. The ability to imagine what might be outstrips the ability to test what is, at least during the early part of the period of formal operations, and it is both a blessing and a curse.

idealism

Educational Implications   Teachers of students in the formal operational period can now finally teach relatively abstract ideas like democracy or gravitation or even cognitive development and have some hope of their students' understanding them as adults do. Before this period, such ideas often have to be converted to more concrete, graphic forms or else are not taught at all. But high school students are beginning to be adults, and the senior high school often reflects this fact with more emphasis on

greater abstract content

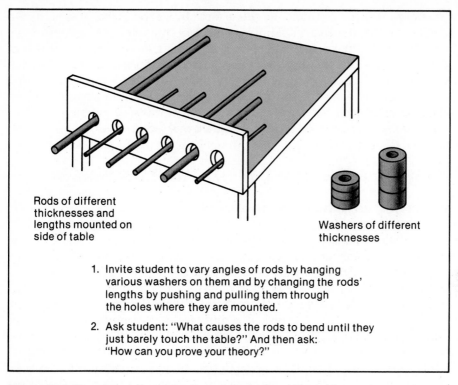

Rods of different thicknesses and lengths mounted on side of table

Washers of different thicknesses

1. Invite student to vary angles of rods by hanging various washers on them and by changing the rods' lengths by pushing and pulling them through the holes where they are mounted.

2. Ask student: "What causes the rods to bend until they just barely touch the table?" And then ask: "How can you prove your theory?"

Figure 2–4 Experiment Requiring Formal Operational Thought

ideas. Even vocationally oriented programs require several credits in thought-oriented subjects like English, math, and social studies; and the college preparatory programs may focus almost exclusively on formal operations. The teaching methods, too, reflect a greater verbal emphasis: students in high school are expected to sit, listen, read, and write much more than in Grade 1. High school deals much more in faraway people, places, and abstractions; and compared with elementary school, it expects its students to understand just how faraway these ideas are.

greater verbal emphasis

This kind of teaching and learning runs the risk of overlooking a key idea of developmental stage theories, including Piaget's theory: that development proceeds by adding abilities, not by replacing them. Though many adolescent and adult students now can use language and thought more powerfully then they could in early childhood, to a great extent most still learn by concrete experience and active manipulation of materials. Most people, for example, cannot learn to drive a car safely just by being told how or by reading a book on the subject. They usually require some actual experience as well, no matter how old they are and no matter how advanced in the formal operational period. In fact, some psychologists

danger of forgetting active basis of learning

(including Piaget) account for these facts by arguing that a majority of adults never really achieve formal operational thinking. Even many adults, they point out, have real trouble solving problems that require abstract thinking, like the bending rods experiment described earlier in this section. Whether or not such facts really show a lack of formal operational ability, they do show the importance of an active basis for learning. When teaching goes well with adolescents and adults, it tries constantly to relate abstract content to the students' familiar, real experiences.

LIMITS AND CAUTIONS ABOUT PIAGET'S THEORY

Is Piagetian Theory Scientific?

Plausible as Piaget's stages seem, the theory has been criticized, among other reasons, for lacking scientific rigor. The clinical method, in particular, allows different wordings and emphases to be used in questioning different children, and some psychologists have argued that this unaccounted-for variation makes the results of Piagetian studies ambiguous. If the questions had been asked a different way, would the child have answered differently (Ginsburg & Opper, 1979, p. 91ff)?

ambiguous
research methods

Many reports of Piagetian studies, in addition, have been rather casual about describing the actual conduct of the study. How many children were actually interviewed? Did the results report on all of the interviews, or only a sample of them? How were the children introduced to the interview? These questions may affect the results, some psychologists say; yet the original Piaget research seems to ignore them. Overall, Piagetians sometimes give the impression of caring more about constructing a reasonable theory than about proving it rigorously through scientific methods. As pointed out earlier, in recent years this criticism has prompted more rigorous, scientifically sound studies of the theory. On the whole they have confirmed the major aspects of it; but many others remained untested, and some have been confirmed only under special circumstances.

inexact reporting
of results

need for more
rigorous
confirmation of
results

Can Stages Be Accelerated?

This question has been asked so many times in the United States and Canada that Piaget dubbed it the "American question." For reasons that apparently reflect North American culture, many educators react to hearing about cognitive stages by wondering how to speed them up. How, they ask, can we teach stages of thinking to children so that they can be accomplished more quickly? Can we help slow developers to catch up, and fast ones to move ahead?

Even learning that uses abstract, formal thinking benefits from—and sometimes requires—active learning as a basis. (Susan Lapides)

possibility of
accelerating
specific skills but
not general stages

Piaget and his followers, however, caution against efforts to accelerate children's development through cognitive stages (Kamii & DeVries, 1974; Stendler-Lavatelli, 1970). Why? Because, they say, the stages represent general abilities that cannot be broken down into smaller, more teachable parts. Hurrying up a cognitive stage is like hurrying up spring: both express themselves in so many ways and are caused by such a multitude of factors that no merely human efforts can greatly affect them. On the other hand, just as specific plants can be forced by special gardening efforts, so specific cognitive skills can be accelerated. The result, however, is not an earlier arrival at a general stage of development but an earlier acquisition of a specific skill.

The only reason for accelerating, then, might be if we teachers could identify selected, specific skills that merited the special efforts needed for doing so. But Piagetian theory does not identify such skills as unusually important; it identifies only general stages. Contrary to one popular impression of the theory, the experiments like those described earlier in this chapter are only examples of stages. They are not—repeat, are NOT—the stages themselves (Furth & Wachs, 1972). Pouring water from a tall beaker into a wide one, for instance, is not considered any more important than any other activity that leads to conservation, though by the same token, neither is it considered any less important. As teachers, we may want to identify specific skills to teach in our curriculum, but we will have to do so without any help from Piaget.

Décallage: Are Stages Really General?

Piaget intended to identify general stages in cognitive development. The usual description of, perhaps, conservation therefore sounds as if that ability is gradually acquired as a whole and that observing any one sign of it demonstrates that other signs may be lurking about, so to speak, ready to be observed as well. If conservation really is a general developmental ability, then a child who conserves amounts of clay should also conserve amounts in other conservation problems.

Common sense and various research studies both support and contradict this prediction. Some studies find that the conservations illustrated in Figure 2–3 do tend to appear at somewhat the same time, but never exactly at the same time (Siegler, 1981). Some psychologists do not feel that they appear close enough in tandem to be called a "general" stage (Smedslund, 1977). Common observation, in addition, shows that children do not always conserve on the same task every time they are asked to do so, especially when that task is first being acquired. They may succeed on one day but not on the next, or at one moment and not an hour later. In practice, then, a teacher or other observer can never feel sure that he or she has really seen the ability in the child.

These differences in timing are called **décallage** by the Piagetians, literally, a gap or lag. Children are thought to develop through general stages, but the stages nevertheless are manifested at slightly different times according to what task is used and the circumstances of the observation. A stage therefore is really acquired over a range of time; it is not a single point in time. In essence, décallage gives the theory a way of fudging on its basic notion, the acquisition of general stages.

lags in stages

As a teacher, you may wonder how much décallage you can allow in Piagetian stage theory before it loses its usefulness to you. How close in time should a child show concrete thinking skills in order for Piaget to be believable? How close in time should abstract skills appear in adolescents? If, in your opinion, specific skills show up too far apart or too unreliably, you may well question the wisdom of Piagetian theory. But its stages are useful to teachers precisely because they are general: they allow prediction, that is, from children's specific expressions of a stage to other specific behaviors. But if no predictions are really possible, then you might as well dispense with stages as a way of organizing your thinking and try to observe children without them.

Does Language Shape Thinking?

Piaget believed that children's increasing language ability reflects, rather than causes, their increasing **thinking ability**, the ability to represent experience that was almost lacking during infancy. Note that by making language follow thinking development, Piaget differs from many other psychologists and educators. Many others give language and thought a more equal role in cognitive development: new, more complicated sentences prove the existence of new, more complicated ideas; but the appearance of new language also helps direct thinking toward new ideas. For some psychologists and educators, in fact, language and thought are considered identical: language equals thought because one cannot be observed without the other.

Most of the Piagetian experiments assume that children understand the questions they are asked. Language is taken as given, and the thinking behind the language becomes the mystery being studied. The exact wordings used in an interview matter rather little in this perspective, as do the exact wordings of the children's replies. Hence Piagetian experimenters feel that they commit no scientific crime by allowing variations in a procedure from one child to the next or within a single interview, for that matter. Likewise, the children's replies are analyzed for their underlying content, not for their subtle differences conveyed by small changes in phrasing.

Some psychologists and educators, however, have argued not only that children's thinking may not be as alien as Piagetians claim it to be but also that children's language, not their thinking, deserves more careful observation. From this perspective, errors on Piagetian tasks may translate into errors of language use, and not necessarily of thought processes.

effects of wording on thinking tasks

In a conservation problem, a child may define *amount* as a kind of visual appearance, rather than in the adult sense of quantity. One beaker of water may have more in it than another does if it appears taller than the other—by definition. If so, then simply teaching the child the correct definitions of terms should make his or her thinking suddenly seem more mature or developed. "Teaching the answers" to Piagetian tasks, in fact, has been tried, with what some consider success and others consider failure (Beilin, 1977; Kamii & Derman, 1971). Generally, the experiments have improved performance on specific tasks, but the improvement has not generalized fully to other comparable tasks.

teaching the answers to tasks

Notice that to teach Piagetian tasks directly, you must assume that children can in fact process the language instruction more or less as adults do. They must, for instance, learn new verbal definitions by grouping and regrouping old and new terms into categories of meaning, a form of classification. And they must do so on a heavily verbal level, without significant objects or props to help. There is little room in such language learning for the active manipulation of materials at a concrete level, as Piaget might suggest. In essence, making language the focus of instruction forces the teacher or child-observer to take the child's thinking abilities for granted—just the opposite of Piaget's viewpoint. Given how closely related language and thinking are, no easy ways out of the dilemma exist: studying one seems to require assuming that the other already functions in an adult, fully formed way. Since the issue continues to arouse disagreements among people who study children, we shall discuss it more fully in Chapter 3.

Key Points

1. A stage theory describes a fixed sequence of attainments that form a cumulative hierarchy, that emphasize typical behavior, and that children achieve at different rates.

2. Piaget's theory is a stage theory of cognitive development.

3. Piaget's theory is concerned with how human thinking gradually becomes more and more organized and how thinking and behavior gradually become better adapted to the environment.

4. Adaptation consists of an interplay between assimilation (interpreting the new in terms of the old) and accommodation (modifying the old to fit the new).

5. Cognitive development occurs through four

mechanisms: experience with the physical and mental environment, social transmission, maturation, and equilibration.

6. Piaget studied cognitive development in children by using semistructured interviews and observations, a style sometimes called the clinical method.

7. Piaget distinguished four major periods of cognitive development: sensorimotor, preoperational, concrete operational, and formal operational.

8. In the sensorimotor period, the infant acquires object permanence and a number of so-called circular reactions, as well as basic problem-solving and imitative abilities.

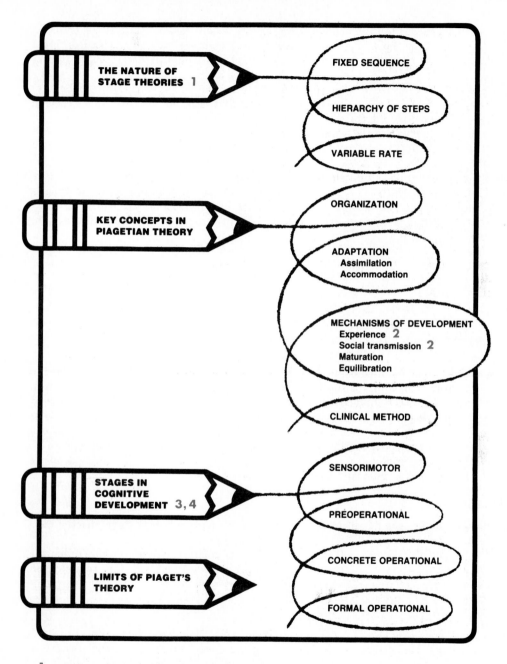

THE NATURE OF STAGE THEORIES 1

FIXED SEQUENCE

HIERARCHY OF STEPS

VARIABLE RATE

KEY CONCEPTS IN PIAGETIAN THEORY

ORGANIZATION

ADAPTATION
Assimilation
Accommodation

MECHANISMS OF DEVELOPMENT
Experience 2
Social transmission 2
Maturation
Equilibration

CLINICAL METHOD

STAGES IN COGNITIVE DEVELOPMENT 3, 4

SENSORIMOTOR

PREOPERATIONAL

CONCRETE OPERATIONAL

LIMITS OF PIAGET'S THEORY

FORMAL OPERATIONAL

1 Other stage theories (Chapters 4, 5, and 11)

2 Learning and instruction (Part II)

3 Learning to structure knowledge (Chapter 7)

4 Making instruction more effective
(Chapter 8)

9. In the preoperational period, the young child develops extensive dramatic play skills, language abilities, and rudimentary seriation and number skills.

10. The preoperational child is limited by a belief in animism and by egocentrism in several forms.

11. In the concrete operational period, the child consolidates his or her logical abilities and shows this development through a belief in conservation and through classification skills.

12. The concrete operational child is limited to reasoning about real, concrete objects.

13. In the formal operational period, the adolescent can finally reason about hypothetical, imaginary, and contrary-to-fact ideas.

14. The formal operational person can sometimes overestimate the importance or power of his or her newly found hypothetical thinking ability, and teachers may be tempted to forget that formal thinking still has its basis in concrete, active learning.

15. Piagetian theory has been criticized for lacking scientific precision, though recent research has supported many aspects of it.

16. Piagetian theory does not imply that children should be accelerated through cognitive stages of development.

17. Various specific expressions of a stage may appear at somewhat different times, making it sometimes difficult to identify the presence or absence of a particular stage; these differences in timing are called décallage.

18. The exact language used in Piagetian experiments may affect children's performance in them.

Case Study

Anne's Variation on Piaget

Anne, a kindergarten teacher, tried two versions of the conservation task, which entailed pouring water from a tall, narrow beaker into a short, wide one. In one version she let the child see the beakers while the child herself poured the liquid from one to the other, and she and Anne discussed whether and how the amount may have changed. In the other version, Anne put a large cardboard barricade between the child and the beakers so that the child could not see the beakers, and Anne poured the liquid instead of letting the child pour it. While she did so, she explained in simple terms what she was doing. She tried each version on half the children in her class, though she did not use both versions on any one child. She wondered how the barricade would affect the judgments that the children made about the amounts of liquid.

Questions for Discussion

1. What results do you think Anne found? More belief in conservation with the barricade? Or more belief without it? Speculate about why you think the barricade had an effect.

2. Suppose that some of the children in Anne's class conserved more with the barricade but that others conserved more without it. Think of reasons why the barricade may have affected individual children differently.

3. In your opinion, would the results of either the first or second question imply that conservation may not really be a sign of the concrete operational stage after all? Explain.

Suggested Readings

Ault, R. L. *Children's Cognitive Development: Piaget's Theory and the Process Approach.* New York: Oxford University Press, 1977.

Flavell, John. *Developmental Psychology of Jean Piaget.* New York: Van Nostrand, 1963.

Ginsburg, H., and S. Opper. *Piaget's Theory of Intellectual Development.* 2nd ed. Englewood Cliffs, N.J.: Prentice-Hall, 1979.

These are three thorough presentations of Piaget's ideas and of many of the experiments that support them. The first book applies the theory more explicitly than the others to child rearing and teaching. The Flavell book is the most rigorous of the three in its descriptions and discussions of Piaget's theory. The third book gives a shorter account than does Flavell, but nevertheless a very complete one.

Donaldson, Margaret. *Children's Minds*. London: Croom Helm, 1978.

Here is a stimulating and readable critique of Piagetian theory, along with descriptions of some relevant studies that challenge its validity. If you are feeling skeptical about Piaget, this book is a good starting place.

Elkind, David. *Child Development and Education*. New York: Oxford University Press, 1976.
Elkind, David. *The Child and Society*. New York: Oxford University Press, 1979.

Elkind has a well-deserved reputation as an interpreter of Piaget to teachers and other educators. These books show why. The first one contains more than many Piaget books do about curriculum analysis and other practical implications for teaching. The second one goes well beyond the classroom to comment on other settings: home life, psychotherapy, church influences, and society's influences. It draws heavily on Piagetian ideas but is not limited to them.

Chapter 3

LANGUAGE AND

COMMUNICATION

Joyce Walmer, community health nurse: This year I've been visiting families with newborn babies. What surprises me the most is how much I have to figure out about each child and parent in so short a time. It's easy enough to give advice, but the advice doesn't matter if I express it wrongly or in ways that are hard to understand.

Families with other children—mostly preschoolers—challenge me the most. You have to talk on two or three levels at once: as an adult for the parents, of course, but in the very next sentence, more as a child! I'll be telling a mother about the well-baby clinic in the neighborhood. Meanwhile, her three-year-old is commenting to me about her toy animal or her newborn sibling. I want to include everyone in my visits, so I have to shift gears for the child: compliment her on her toy, or on her baby brother, or whatever. Then, it's back again to talking with her mom or dad.

Without knowing a family very well, it's hard to gauge just how much language a small child knows and can use. I remember one time, for example, when I thought a child was less mature than he really was. He looked about two years old and was mostly silent during our visit. When he finally did speak, he just said, "Jean!"—that was his new sister—and pointed to her. So I said, "Jean smile?"—meaning, "Can your sister Jean smile at people?" The brother just stood there looking at me, silent. I was sure he was still learning to talk. But he fooled me. When I was going out the door, he said, "Sometimes she smiles, but she's not smiling now." A pretty long sentence for a two-year-old! I found out later he was really four.

That made me realize how different language ability can be from language use. The ways a child *can* speak may not be the ways he *does* in fact speak. That's true of the parents I visit, too; in fact, probably of most adults. Some of the parents talk incessantly during my visits, and others are almost silent. But the quiet ones are not necessarily inarticulate; they may just not believe in using language for chit-chat.

I must admit, though, that it helps me in my work if both parents and children talk a fair amount. It lets me get acquainted faster, and I feel more effective in the advice I give if I can gear it to needs that people actually express in words. I sometimes wish I knew more ways to draw quiet families out when I visit, without making them feel self-conscious about it.

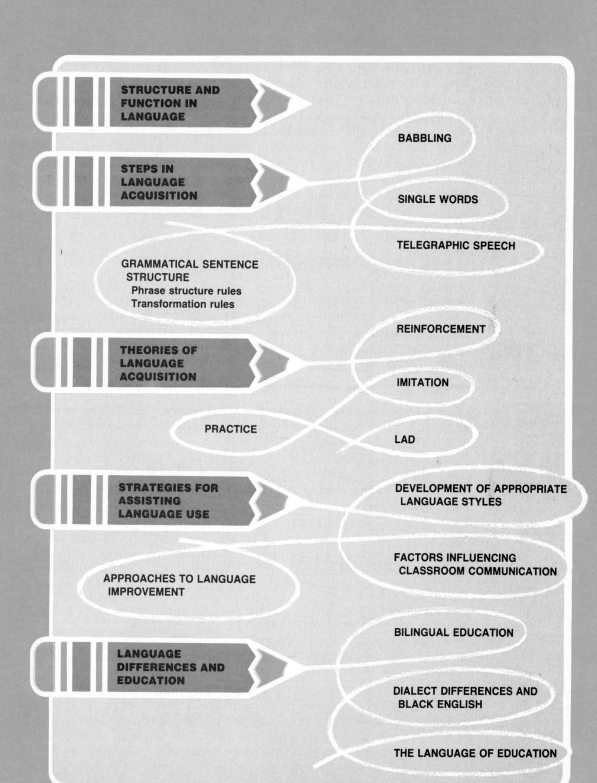

STRUCTURE AND
FUNCTION IN
LANGUAGE

STEPS IN
LANGUAGE
ACQUISITION

BABBLING

SINGLE WORDS

TELEGRAPHIC SPEECH

GRAMMATICAL SENTENCE
STRUCTURE
    Phrase structure rules
    Transformation rules

REINFORCEMENT

THEORIES OF
LANGUAGE
ACQUISITION

IMITATION

PRACTICE

LAD

STRATEGIES FOR
ASSISTING
LANGUAGE USE

DEVELOPMENT OF APPROPRIATE
LANGUAGE STYLES

FACTORS INFLUENCING
CLASSROOM COMMUNICATION

APPROACHES TO LANGUAGE
IMPROVEMENT

BILINGUAL EDUCATION

LANGUAGE
DIFFERENCES AND
EDUCATION

DIALECT DIFFERENCES AND
BLACK ENGLISH

THE LANGUAGE OF EDUCATION

SCHOOLS have always relied heavily on language and talk. Why? Partly because schooling, as opposed to education in general, occurs out of context. Going to school means sitting in some special place at some special time and talking about topics that may be abstract or at least not immediately visible. Much schooling, in fact, can occur without visual aids, but none of it can occur without language. Teachers are expected to understand and use language reasonably well, and perhaps even more important, they are expected to understand and help the language and communication of their students. Because language and communication affect teaching so much, this entire chapter is devoted to them.

STRUCTURE AND FUNCTION IN LANGUAGE

structure versus function

Language can be studied for how it is put together—its **structure**—or for how it is used—its **functions**. **Language structure** refers to the nature of language itself: its sounds and their combinations into "words," the words themselves, and how words are combined into utterances or "sentences." **Language function**, on the other hand, refers to the effects of language on the world: the purposes of language and its influence, whether intended or accidental.

emphasis on language functions in school-aged children

Children develop skills in both areas of language, though their uses of language may become apparent to teachers during the school years, since by mid-elementary school they have acquired most of the basic structures of adult language (Cazden, 1972). Knowing how children use language may therefore be more important to school teachers than understanding the details of their grammar and pronunciation. This chapter reflects this bias, though as will become evident, the two areas cannot be fully separated. Children may, for example, learn certain grammatical phrases to make certain impressions on their friends—learning a structure for a function. This chapter, then, will look at language from the standpoints of both structure and function, but with more emphasis on the latter.

STEPS IN THE ACQUISITION OF LANGUAGE

Children acquire language in several distinct steps. These do not, strictly speaking, form "stages," such as those defined in earlier chapters. They do *not,* for example, develop in a completely sequential, hierarchical order, and each step is not necessarily qualitatively different from the ones before it. They do, however, tend to emerge in the order described below and in Figure 3–1, and they seem to apply to nearly all children, despite wide variations in the early language experiences of individual children.

The Babbling Period (Four to Nine Months)

Children first use language by **babbling**, the seemingly random sounds of infants. At first these sounds have little relationship to the sound that children will later need to speak their native language, and these sounds are, in fact, remarkably similar in many different language cultures (DeVilliers, 1978). During this earliest period, parents can influence how much their children babble by praising and smiling at the right times, but not the particular sounds they make. Partly for this reason, some observers of children argue that human beings have an inborn ability to learn to speak: all babies seem to have the same equipment, and they all are predisposed to use it.

wide range of early sounds

Before the age of twelve months, however, infants are already narrowing their initial babbling to a relatively small number of meaningful sounds that their native language or dialect uses in adult speech. These units of sound are called **phonemes** by linguists. Spanish, for example, uses a *b* phoneme that has a sound that is part way between an English *b* and an English *v*. Many versions of black English rarely use the *th-* phoneme of standard English, and so a word like *think* sounds like *tink*. These differences are already contained in infants' speech by their first birthday, even though their parents may not notice them or may not recognize their own influence in creating them. The most dramatic evidence of parental influence at this period of development, however, is shown in studies of infants born deaf: these children babble at first as other babies do but eventually give up doing so at about the time that normally hearing children begin using words (Lenneberg, 1967). Like all babies, deaf ones seem "programmed" to experiment with sounds through babbling. But because they cannot hear, they cannot make use of the language influences of their parents and other adults and eventually give up using language.

phonemes

The Single-Words Period (Nine to Eighteen Months)

Somewhere between the ages of one and two, the child begins combining particular phonemes into meaningful units, which linguists call **morphemes**. Though most morphemes are essentially words, a few are not. The *-s* added to many words to create the plural, for example, is a morpheme. It carries its own meaning by causing quite a few other morphemes to refer to many of something, rather than to just one of something. Yet it cannot stand alone in ordinary speech. Morphemes mark an important turning point in language acquisition because, for the first time, the child can form utterances that communicate to others verbally. Several years later, verbal communication will form the basis for much of the child's education.

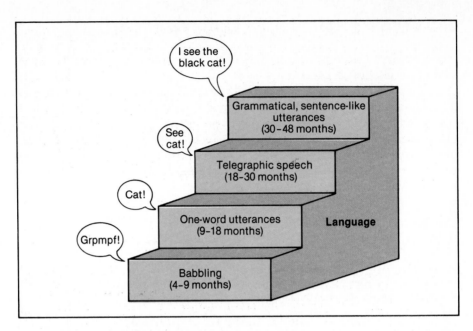

Figure 3–1 Steps in Acquiring Language

At first the pronunciation of many morphemes may leave much to be desired: pointing to the family cat, a toddler may say "kitzh" (kitty), or something like that. At first, too, a single word functions as a whole sentence—a **holophrase**, in linguistic terms. "Kitty" may mean "See the kitty" or "Come here, kitty" or "I like the kitty." The child's parents may understand a holophrase surprisingly well, though, because it often occurs in a familiar context, one in which the child's intentions seem relatively clear from everything else that is going on. Most beginning talkers, in addition, simplify their early pronunciation in ways that parents, at least, quickly recognize and allow for, as if the child were speaking to them with a foreign accent. Toddlers tend to simplify initial consonant clusters— *broom* becomes *room, sparrow* becomes *parrow,* and so on. They sometimes use the same "word" of their own for more than one adult word: *tata* might be used for *table,* but also for *teddy bear* and *toilet.* Any words with several consonant phonemes usually are modified to use just one of the consonant phonemes: *mother* (three consonant phonemes) becomes *mama,* for example (DeVilliers, 1979).

Vocabulary begins growing during this period and continues growing for the rest of the child's life—literally. At twelve months, some infants may still not have produced a single word, but others may be correctly using up to a dozen, and a few may even have a vocabulary of over 40

qualities of first words

words. The size of the vocabulary seems to depend not only on the child but also on how the vocabulary is measured (Snyder et al., 1981). By age two, most children can use somewhere between 50 and 300 words, and by age three somewhere between 100 and 1,000 words. By age six, when they begin school, they can use over 2,500 basic words (Bloom, 1973). These estimates do not include derived forms of words, like the ones made by adding -*ing* or -*ed*; counting these as additional items greatly multiplies the child's vocabulary. The estimates also refer only to words that children can produce and use; throughout development, they can correctly understand a larger vocabulary than they can produce (Bates et al., 1979).

vocabulary size

The Period of Telegraphic Speech (Eighteen to Thirty Months)

As their vocabularies grow, children begin to use words in simple combinations. These first "sentences" are often called **telegraphic speech** because they lack the small connecting words of adult language: the prepositions and articles and auxiliary words that indicate relationships among words and that make adult language seem complete. Toddlers make up for these omissions partly, as in infancy, by relying on the situation to convey meaning, but partly now—for the first time—by using word order to convey meaning. Many of their early sentences may put the agent or "doer" first, followed by the doer's action, followed by the object of the action:

Agent	*Action*	*Object*
Mama	cooks	breakfast.
Doggie	wags	tail.

The Period of Grammatical Sentence Structure (Thirty to Forty-eight Months)

In using this and other common word orders, children begin showing an understanding of **grammar**, a system for relating words within a sentence to one another according to particular rules. By their nature the rules affect the meaning of both individual words and the sentence as a whole. During early childhood and well into the elementary school years, most children perfect their grammar in two important ways: by learning new, acceptable sentence structures and by learning to convert these structures from one form to another in ways that sometimes change language use but not essential meaning. Children need both kinds of learning because of the nature of language and of its relationship to thought.

nature of grammar

The language of preschool children suggests that they actively infer the grammatical organization of adult language. (Michael Weisbrot and Family)

Phrase Structure Rules   A lot of grammar consists of rules for grouping words into larger units, the so-called **phrase structure** of sentences. Linguists often analyze phrase structure in diagrams that look like trees:

phrase structure
of sentences

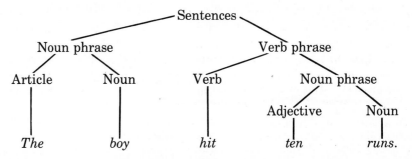

A diagram like this can also be written as a series of rules for rewriting phrases into their constituent parts. In the above sentence, the verb phrase (VP) consists of a verb (V) plus a noun phrase (NP). Linguists often express this rule with an →, like this: VP → V + NP. Here the arrow means that the left-hand expression (VP) "consists of" or "can be rewritten as" the group of expressions on the right. In learning grammar, then, young children in part learn a long list of phrase structure rules. More precisely, they learn to *use* them, without knowing that they are doing so.

Language specialists have traced many of the details of the acquisition of phrase structure rules. They have found, for example, that young children overgeneralize or regularize such rules when they first learn them (Cazden, 1968). A young child says, "I goed to the store" instead of "I went to the store," or "two foots" instead of "two feet." These mistakes seem to come from an overzealous use of certain rules for constructing sentences— the addition of *-ed* to form the past tense, for example, or *-s* to form plurals. Children seem more ready to learn the rules than to learn the exceptions, at least at this point in their development.

overgeneralization

Transformation Rules In addition to phrase structure rules, children learn certain rules for transforming certain sentences into others that contain mostly the same words and that carry much the same basic meaning, but that may function differently in ordinary conversation. Consider these two sentences:

transformational grammar

The boy patted the dog.
The dog was patted by the boy.

Although the sentences convey almost the same idea, they have very different phrase structures: one is NP *(The boy)* + V *(patted)* + NP *(the dog)*, and the other is NP *(The dog)* + auxiliary *(was)* + V *(patted)* + prepositional phrase *(by the boy)*.

This kind of difference in phrase structure has led many linguists— most notably, Noam Chomsky (1978a, 1978b)—to distinguish two levels of structure in sentences. The **surface structure** refers to the actual string of words uttered, and the **deep structure** refers to the words' underlying or essential meaning. In linguistic terms, the two sentences above have different surface structures but the same deep structure. As young children grow, they learn certain *transformation rules* for converting essential meanings or ideas into a variety of acceptable surface structures.

surface structure versus deep structure

Evidence that transformation rules take time to acquire comes from some of the language errors that young children make. Many preschoolers do not hear the difference between the active and passive transformations of a sentence. If you ask them to illustrate each of the following sentences with a toy car and truck:

The car hit the truck.
The car was hit by the truck.

they will probably respond to *each* by hitting the truck with the car. Apparently the second, passive sentence means the same to them as the first, active one does.

But if you ask preschoolers to find at least two meanings in this sentence:

They are bouncing balls.

they may not see the ambiguity in it. In one meaning the sentence refers to a type of ball (the bouncing sort), and in the other meaning, it refers to something "they" are doing (bouncing, not doing something else). The two sentences have the same surface structure but different deep structures, and young children may not yet sense them. Eventually they can, however, and this fact has important implications for how to assist children to use language, as we shall see later in this chapter.

THEORIES OF LANGUAGE ACQUISITION

A psychologist once said that to explain why children learn language, he favored the "miracle theory." Indeed, the acquisition of language does rival the most difficult achievements of adults. In just a few years, children acquire most of the grammar that adults use in normal conversation and almost half the vocabulary they will ever use in ordinary speech; they will take decades to learn the other half. Overall, young children learn their first language more skillfully and painlessly than any adult can ever learn a second language. Most other skills can be learned more easily by older individuals than by younger ones; yet language goes against this pattern. How do children acquire such a unique and important ability? Psychologists and educators have proposed several answers to this question, some of which account for more facts than do others.

Reinforcement

Do children learn language by being praised or otherwise encouraged for speaking? As plausible as this idea seems, little evidence of it has been found. One study analyzed the conversations of parents and children and found that parents approved of their child's utterances for being factually true, rather than for being grammatically correct. Conversely, they disapproved of utterances that were factually false, not ones that were badly formed (Brown et al., 1969). Another study found that mothers who corrected their infant's pronunciation had children who acquired language more slowly than usual, *not* more quickly (Nelson, 1973). Other research points to the same conclusion: that praise contingent on using emerging skills has little effect on language acquisition and may even be harmful. In any case, most parents are apparently just too tolerant of their child's linguistic mistakes to use such reinforcement consistently. A very large part of the child's reward for acquiring language skills must therefore

no evidence that praise affects language development

come from the process of acquisition itself. To a large extent, "breaking the code" must be its own reward.

Imitation

One common-sense reason that children learn to speak is that they imitate those around them. In some way this must be true: children growing up in an English-speaking environment learn English words and phrases, not Chinese or some other language. Without language models, they could not hope to learn their native language. Imitation seems to occur when children repeatedly ask for the names of new objects—"What's that?"—or for the reasons for events—"Why?" After being told the names or reasons, they repeat them as best they can, though sometimes silently or at a later time.

role of language models

In imitating, though, they may be less interested in actual names or reasons than in learning the verbal *forms* by which names or reasons are expressed, forms like "It's a . . . " or "Because. . . . " They may imitate the *way* an answer is given, as well as its content. In any one case, however, their verbal priorities may be difficult to determine, since children may not actually imitate the model out loud or at a time when adults are listening.

The overgeneralizations of grammatical rules, which were mentioned earlier in this chapter, suggest that learning to talk requires more than imitation. Consider this dialogue between a parent and child:

limitations of imitation

> She said, "My teacher holded the baby rabbits and we patted them."
> I asked, "Did you say your teacher held the baby rabbits?"
> She answered, "Yes."
> I then asked, "What did you say she did?"
> She answered, again. "She holded the baby rabbits and we patted them."
> "Did you say she held them tightly?" I asked.
> "No," she answered, "she holded them loosely."
> (Gleason, 1967, p. 1; in DeVilliers, 1979)

In this case the child heard and understood the adult form, *held,* but persisted in using her own, more regular form of the past tense, *holded.* Situations like these presumably give children ample opportunity to hear and imitate language in the "right" way; yet at certain points in their development, they steadfastly refuse to do so.

Practice

In addition to imitation, practice would seem to help children learn language, just as it might help in learning to play the piano or knit a sweater. Research on this possibility, however, has produced confusing results. One study found that children understand sentences with frequently spoken words better than they understand sentences with more rarely occurring words (Ervin-Tripp, 1966). Does this difference show a lack of practice with uncommon words? Perhaps, though it may just as easily show a complete ignorance of them. Another study showed that brief instruction in the meanings of uncommon words allows children to use them about as well as they can common ones (Olds, 1970; in Cazden, 1972, pp. 94–95). Is this because instruction gives them practice with the words or because it gives them a relatively sudden increase in knowledge about them? The answer has implications for encouraging language in classrooms and other educational settings: if practice does in fact help, then teachers should provide the time for it in their programs.

uncertain benefits of practice

Much of the problem of evaluating the benefits of practice is in judging how much children really practice speaking in the same way that other skills are practiced. Unlike many other skills, language can be practiced at almost any hour of the day or night, and it can be practiced silently as well as out loud. As a result, adult observers cannot be sure when and how much a child has rehearsed any particular bit of grammar or vocabulary. Parents of young children will confirm that their children babble words, sounds, and sentences at all hours of the day—during play, before sleep, and even during sleep. Even though this talk often makes little sense at the time, it certainly looks like practice: the rehearsal of new combinations of word meanings, sounds, and grammatical constructions.

role of listening

But children may improve their speaking ability simply by listening to language, an activity that by definition may go unnoticed. The precise benefits of listening cannot be proved easily, since children may sometimes listen when we adults fail to notice, or they may fail to listen sometimes when they look as though they are. Teachers and parents must presume that listening involves some silent practice of language, a plausible presumption, if not really provable.

Language Acquisition Device (LAD)

The difficulty of reinforcing language learning and the active roles that children take in it have prompted some psychologists to propose that children are innately programmed to learn to speak (Chomsky, 1972, 1980). How else, they argue, could young children learn such a complex skill more quickly and perfectly than most adults can? Some have even proposed that all languages have the same underlying structure and that children all over the world are born predisposed to learn it. For convenience, many linguists have called this predisposition the **Language Acquisition Device**, or LAD for short. For them, studying language acquisition includes searching for **language universals**, features or grammar that exist in all possible languages and that all children seem to acquire on

innate predisposition

their way to full language competence. Some advocates of this idea believe that they have found one such universal in the agent-action-object construction mentioned earlier in this chapter (Brown, 1973). This basic pattern for sentences seems to occur in a wide variety of languages and in quite a bit of early child language. It remains to be proved, though, that it occurs in *all* languages, or in *all* children (Erreich et al., 1980).

The child's LAD relies on a variety of cognitive skills, but external reinforcement plays little role in it. Skill in associating names meaningfully with objects, for example, seems necessary in order to use the agent-action-object sentence pattern. And, perhaps more fundamentally, this pattern assumes that the child can mentally separate objects from the actions involving them. This distinction resembles Piaget's idea of object permanence discussed in Chapter 2, and the child may learn to make this distinction through play and the manipulation of objects.

STRATEGIES FOR ASSISTING LANGUAGE USE

Even though children's initial language learning cannot be influenced directly, their later uses of it can often be guided in various directions by the adults and peers in their lives. Children learn when certain comments are expected or are frowned upon and the effects that various phrasings of a sentence have on people. They learn, furthermore, not to talk to certain people (like strangers) and always to talk with others (like parents).

Development of Appropriate Language Styles

Most important for teachers, children learn **language styles**: unstated rules about when and how they should talk. The style appropriate for a classroom has several features familiar to anyone who has successfully attended school. One of them is that individuals should not speak out of turn but that they should always respond if a teacher asks a direct question. Another is that they should usually choose informal but correct-sounding language when they speak, especially if other students can hear them.

Language style differences are illustrated by the following three sentences, only one of which would normally be considered appropriate in class:

About Right for Class: "Mr. Smith, how do you do the problems on page 100?"

Too Casual: "Hey, teach, what's with the stuff on page 100?"

Too Formal: "Mr. Smith, sir, would you be so kind as to explain how I might solve the problems on page 100?" (spoken with respect, not sarcasm).

Even though there doubtlessly are students and classrooms in which the second and third alternatives are used, the first style is probably the one used most often in ordinary public school classrooms. The slangy tone of the second alternative is a more appropriate style among peers outside class, but less so with a teacher in class.

Skill with these language styles comes partly from attending school for a number of years and thereby observing and copying others' language use, but much of it also comes from children's increasing thinking abilities, which allow them to notice more and more subtleties in classroom verbal interaction. In any case, as children grow older, they gradually become better able to adjust their language to the various situations that life presents to them. As a result, their use of language becomes more varied in practice, even if not always during class.

the teacher's role
How can teachers help their students gain competence in the use of language? Let us look at two ways: first, by encouraging students to communicate more in class and, second, by arranging for certain specific interactions to occur.

Factors That Influence Classroom Communication

Topic Selection   Studies of communication have found, perhaps not surprisingly, that children will talk more about one topic than about another (Waterson & Snow, 1978). Some children may talk more about a

topics of interest to students
picture of a birthday party than about a picture of a car, or some may talk more about a real toy than about a picture of the same thing. They may not necessarily, please note, use more complex language structures; they may simply talk at more length.

Common sense, of course, suggests that students will respond more to one topic than to another: that is why we teachers are always urging ourselves to "use the students' interests," or some such idea, in the hopes of stimulating more discussion in class. Supposedly students will talk more, and therefore learn more, if the content involves them personally. This presumably is good advice, though two cautions must be noted about it. We can, first, make our discussions *too* personal—sex education can be

some limitations
fascinating, but not if your own actual behavior is used for classroom examples. And second, adjusting the topic of discussion may not always be easy to do or particularly helpful to every student: if students in chemistry become bored learning the Periodic Table of the Elements, how can you "change the topic" to generate more interest? No doubt experienced chemistry teachers learn how to do just this, but in the end they still may not please all students: after all, learning the names and properties of chemical elements is still work, especially for students not interested in science.

The language style appropriate with friends is not necessarily appropriate for the classroom—and vice versa. (Elizabeth Crews)

Task Selection Both common sense and research studies suggest that the amount or complexity of language depends on *what* children are asked to do, as well as on what they are asked to talk about. One study found that children actually made up longer stories about a series of pictures if they did *not* look at the pictures while they were talking; the sight of them seemed to distract the children from their story and instead encouraged simple description rather than story making (Brent & Katz, 1967). Other studies found that some children will talk more if given highly structured, specific directions about what to talk about but that others will talk more if *not* given such directions (Cazden, 1970). In these studies children and students did not vary in the topic of conversation, but in the *way* that they were asked to handle it.

Finding the right way to pose a topic, in fact, presents teachers with one of their major challenges in fostering communication in the classroom. In the chemistry class mentioned above, a teacher may find that some students discuss the subject more if, say, they can build models of chemical compounds from sticks and clay but that the others discuss it more if they can use the real compounds to do an experiment. Finding the right method for each student depends, among other things, on accumulating experience

assign tasks that stimulate conversation

with students as individuals, as well as keeping in mind psychological principles like those described in this book.

Within reasonable limits, teachers may be able to vary the tasks of individual students in order to encourage more communication and learning. Just as in hunting for better topics, though, finding more appealing tasks may not always be easy. What if a student must learn about certain chemical compounds, but all he wants to do is play football? Ways can probably be found to reconcile the conflict, but it may challenge even the best of teachers.

Listener Expectations   To whom children talk also affects their way of speaking. As mentioned earlier, children from one American Indian tribe tended not to say much to their teachers, who presumably were considered authorities, but they did speak fluently with their freinds, who were presumably their equals in status (Phillips, 1969). Several studies of language use have found that children and adults adjust the complexity of their talk to the age of the listener and to what they think is his or her language ability. The younger the listener is, the simpler the speaking will be; and the older the listener is, the more complex the speaking will be. Even three-year-old children talk more simply to one- and two-year-olds than they do to adults (DeVilliers, 1979). Does a listener trigger simpler language by his or her behavior? Or do people expect some listeners— and especially children—to understand less and therefore offer them less language? Without definitive research to settle this question, a safe and plausible answer must include both possibilities: some listeners "ask" for less language than others do, and some speakers offer less as well.

As professionals, however, teachers should probably strive to expect and get more from students, not less. In general, students should gradually talk better and think more wisely, and one hopes that they would do so because of, rather than in spite of, their conversations with teachers. The best level of language complexity may therefore be one just a little harder than the level that students use with each other, but not one so hard that the teacher talks "over their heads." Choosing a reasonably, but not overly, hard level conveys an important expectation to students: that the way they currently talk is good but that a slightly more sophisticated way might be even better.

converse with students at slightly higher language level

Three Approaches to Language Improvement

Many educators have published ideas about how to help children with language and speech in the classroom. For our purposes, however, we shall concentrate on only three approaches which have a relatively clear basis in psychological principles.

Simplification Strategies The first approach was originated by Marion Blank and her associates over the past fifteen years (Blank, 1973; Blank et al., 1978). Her goal is to enable all children, no matter what their background, to develop an "abstract attitude" in using language, an ability to engage in "sustained sequential thinking." Blank assumes that most school children have the ability to use complex language forms but that for various reasons some children do not habitually choose to do so. She recommends brief tutorial sessions with these "underthinkers," as they might be called, using an assortment of techniques to stimulate stronger habits of logical, sequential thinking. Table 3–1 lists a few of these techniques, as well as examples of when they might apply. All of the techniques, please note, entail simplifying, but not removing, the cognitive demands on children whenever they make a wrong response. Simplification of the teacher's language is supposed to lead, paradoxically, to greater complexity of the children's language and thought in the long run. It does so presumably by building the children's commitment to using language for "sustained sequential thinking" and by preventing them from entirely giving up this use of language.

The tutorial sessions recommended by Blank resemble Piaget's clinical method of interviewing: one-to-one contact, semistructured questioning, and following up on "mistakes." They differ from Piagetian interviews, though, by their intention to influence children's behavior and by their focus on specific language shortcomings. In the choice to intervene lurks a basic disagreement with Piaget about the relationship of language and thought: unlike Piaget, Blank believes that improving language will stimulate thinking, and not just the other way around. For her, language is an object of study and an important cause of other developments in childhood; it is not just a pipeline into the child's thinking.

Encouraging Logical Uses of Language Some of the same attitude underlies the work of Joan Tough in Great Britain, who with her associates has evolved some suggestions for helping children with their language use (1974, 1976, 1977a, 1977b). As with Blank, Tough finds that some, but not all, children need help in making a habit out of using language logically. Her research suggests that some children scarcely ever use language to predict events, to empathize with the experiences of others, or to imagine unusual or unlikely events. Instead, some children use language in the classroom only to maintain their own needs or to direct the actions of others (1977). Tough proposes a number of ways that teachers can encourage the more thinking-oriented functions of language, some of which are illustrated in Table 3–2. As with Blank's techniques, these are also intended for conversations with individual children; but unlike Blank's, they are meant to be incorporated into the regular flow of daily activities.

Table 3–1 How Teachers Can Simplify Their Use of Language When Necessary

1. **Delay**

   Sample problem: Teacher says, "Pick up the. . . . " Child starts grabbing objects.

   Simplification: Teacher says, "Wait a minute. Listen to what I want you to pick up."

2. **Focus for attention**

   Sample problem: Teacher says, "Go to the sink and get me the pot." Child goes to the sink and reaches for the first thing she or he sees, which is a glass.

   Simplification: Teacher asks, "Do you remember what I asked you to bring?"

3. **Repeats demand**

   Sample problem: Teacher says, "Put your coat on the chair next to the table." Child puts the coat on the table.

   Simplification: Teacher says, "No, not on the table. Put it on the chair that's next to the table."

4. **Synonymous rephrasing**

   Sample problem: Teacher says, "Lift the box off the floor." Child does nothing.
   Simplification: Teacher says, "I mean I want you to pick it up with your hands."

5. **Partially completes task**

   Sample problem: Teacher asks, "What is a pail for?" Child says nothing.

   Simplification: Teacher says, "It can carry w———."

6. **Restructures task to highlight specific components**

   Sample problem: Teacher asks, "Why do you think we couldn't get this sponge into the |too small| cup and we could fit the marble?" Child says, "Because it's a sponge."

   Simplification: Teacher says, "Okay, I'll cut this sponge into two. Now it's still a sponge. Why does it go into the cup now?"

7. **Offers relevant comparisons**

   Sample problem: Teacher asks, "Where did the ball go?" Child says nothing.

   Simplification: Teacher says, "Well, let's see. Did it go under the table or did it go under the chair?"

8. **Didactic presentation of information**

   Sample problem: Teacher asks, "Could you go over there and get me the strainer?" Child goes to table and looks bewildered.

   Simplification: Teacher asks, "Do you know what a strainer is?" Child shakes head. Teacher says, "Look, this one is a strainer."

Table 3–1 How Teachers Can Simplify Language (*cont.*)

9. **Relating unknown to known**

   Sample problem: Teacher says, "Now the spaghetti is hard. How do you think it will feel after it is cooked?" Child says, "I don't know."

   Simplification: Teacher asks, "Well, do you remember when we cooked the potatoes? How did they feel?"

10. **Directed action to recognize salient characteristics**

    Sample problem: Teacher asks: "How is the ice different from the water?" Child says, "I don't know."

    Simplification: Teacher says, "Well let's see. Turn over the cup of water and turn over the tray of ice."

11. **Focus on relevant features**

    Sample problem: Teacher asks, "Why did you pull your hand away from the stove?" Child says nothing.

    Simplification: Teacher asks, "Well, how did the stove feel?"

Source: Reprinted by permission of Marion Blank, *The Language of Learning* (New York: Grune & Stratton, 1978), pp. 95–96.

Table 3–2 Some Strategies for Promoting Logical Uses of Language

Situation: a conversation between teacher and child about a bird's nest

Orienting strategies: to begin a conversation that uses reasoning
   "Why do you think the bird needs a nest?"
   "Why do you think the nest is in the tree?"
   "And how do you think the bird made it?"
Enabling strategies: to encourage reasoning once it has begun
   "How does the bird keep safe?"
   "Are there any animals that might go after the bird?"
   "Feel this; does it feel like stones?"
Informing strategies: to give information when needed to continue reasoning
   "The bird would have to fly up with bits of dry grass in its beak."
   "Some birds build their nests on the ground."
   "Here's a picture of a meadowlark's nest."
Sustaining strategies: to reinforce the child's verbal efforts
   "That's a good idea."
   "Anything else?"
   "Yes, indeed."
Concluding strategies: to help finish a conversation
   "You do know a lot about birds. Have you seen the bird book in our library?"
   "Let's put back the nest now for others to look at."

Source: Based on Joan Tough, *Talking and Learning* (London: Ward Lock Educational, 1977), pp. 30–33.

Structured Tutoring (DISTAR)   A third approach to language improvement, called DISTAR, was developed by Siegfried Engelmann and his associates (1965, 1974, 1978). The initials of the program stand for Directed Instruction in the Teaching of Arithmetic and Reading, and it relies on fast-paced, tightly structured drills in language skills and language-related skills. The program comes out of the behaviorist tradition in psychology, which we shall discuss in Chapter 6 and which relies heavily on providing specific cues and reinforcers to increase the frequency of specific desired behaviors. In the case of DISTAR, these cues are mainly comments and commands from the teacher; the reinforcers are mainly praise from the teacher; and the desired behaviors are mainly specific language forms. Teachers follow a carefully planned program—some would call it a "script"—that shows exactly how they should conduct each lesson and what responses they should expect from each child. Figure 3–2 is an example of one of the language lessons. Although some teachers find this approach constricting, others feel that it ensures that learning occurs and that children practice key language structures in a logical order. At its best, the atmosphere of a DISTAR lesson is like that of a pep rally, and many children seem to find this exhilarating.

Assisting Language or Assisting Thought?

The existing theories of language and educational practice have not yet discovered how language and thought are, or are not, related. Obviously some kind of thinking can occur without language: a baby probably thinks when he stacks one block on top of another, even though he cannot say much about it. Most higher animals, including dogs and cats, probably think in some sense of the term, but with little or no language in the human sense. On the other hand, it is harder to imagine language occurring without thought. The clearest example might be the rote parroting of language, as when, literally, a parrot talks without knowing what it says. Children and adults sometimes also speak without understanding: some Americans may recite the Pledge of Allegiance, for example, without knowing what they are saying.

relationship between language and thought

In between these extremes lies the great bulk of human talking and thinking: thoughts that require at least some words and words that reflect at least some thought. In this middle ground, how are the two processes related? Psychologists have taken various positions regarding the problem without being able to reach a consensus. Piaget, as we mentioned in Chapter 2, favored a thought-first position. For him, language could be taken more or less for granted during child development. Improvements in language reflect gradual improvements in children's thinking as they grow up, but these improvements in no way cause changes in thinking (Piaget, 1955). Most other psychologists, however, have attached more importance to language. Bruner (1975) and Vygotsky (1962), for example, both argue

Praise the children for correct responses. Correct mistakes immediately.

Task 4 Teaching **Next to**
Group Activity

a. Point to the dog. We're talking about the dog. What is the dog next to?

The cat.

Where is this dog? Everybody, say the whole thing.

This dog is next to the cat.

What is the cat next to? *The dog.*
Say the whole thing.

The cat is next to the dog.

b. Point to the cat. We're talking about the cat. What is the cat next to?

The bird.

Where is this cat? Everybody, say the whole thing.

The cat is next to the bird.

What is the cat next to? *The bird.*
Say the whole thing.

The cat is next to the bird.

Individual Activity

c. Point to an animal. Where is this _____? Say the whole thing.

Now go to Book B.

Figure 3–2 Example of a Structured Language Lesson
Source: From DISTAR® Language I by S. Engelmann, J. Osborn and T. Engelmann. © 1969, Science Research Associates, Inc. Reprinted by permission of the publisher.

that children's speech serves to direct their thinking and that the growth of logical thinking during childhood in part reflects the logical structure of language itself. In their view, learning language should help in learning to think, as well as the other way around.

At first sight, the Bruner-Vygotsky position seems to offer more support for teachers than the Piaget position does. Teachers, after all, purposely talk with children every day in order to help improve their thinking. Closer scrutiny, though, suggests that this assumption may be too simple. A lot of classroom talk seems to have little to do with thinking in the sense of analysis or logic. Instead, if often meanders, diverges, expresses feelings, and otherwise fails to follow logical patterns. Does such language help students improve their thinking? Probably only if thinking is defined broadly to include reflection on feelings and relatively aimless mental play.

In the end, as we pointed out in Chapter 2, comparing the roles of language and thought turns into a chicken-and-egg problem (Smedslund, 1977). In order to observe children thinking, we must usually ask for at least minimal speech or verbal understanding. But to observe their language ability usually requires asking children to think as well—they must at least think about what they are supposed to say. In school, for all practical purposes, knowing means talking and talking means knowing, and the two abilities are often assumed to be closely tied. Their closeness gives children an advantage in school if they already can speak the language of instruction well, and it puts an extra burden on those children who normally speak some other dialect or language. For these latter children, the equation of language ability and thinking ability does not hold. In the next section we shall examine this problem more closely, as well as helpful ways that teachers can respond to it.

LANGUAGE DIFFERENCES AND EDUCATION

Bilingual Education

Significant minorities of children bring languages other than English to school with them. In the United States, the most common non-English language is Spanish, spoken by about fifteen million people, or about 5 percent of the population (Epstein, 1977, chap. 4). There are numerous other language communities as well, even in a country as seemingly monolingual as the United States is: there are several native Indian tongues, for example, as well as most of the world's major languages. In Canada, about seven million people speak French as their first language.

How much instruction should the children from these groups receive in their original language, and how much should they receive in English? Except in French-speaking Canada, the public schools have traditionally favored an English-only policy. Yet many educators have questioned its effectiveness and have advocated much more use of native and non-English language for instruction. The issue has generated quite a lot of controversy, since there are important positive arguments on both sides.

The two major positions on the problem might be called the *native language approach* and the *direct method* (Engle, 1975). Both assume the need for bilingual children to acquire and use two languages, but they give different emphases to English for instructional purposes. Proponents of the native language approach argue that teaching children in their first language gives them the same advantage in school learning that English-speaking children have—except, of course, in learning to use English it-

native language education

Experts disagree about how much and when to use bilingual children's native language as part of their education. (Elizabeth Crews)

self. In addition, since children's language is a major expression of their family background and culture, using it for instruction can show respect for them as persons and as members of their culture. Teachers can, they point out, introduce English into the curriculum at appropriate times, but they can limit the rate and amount to whatever their students can assimilate and to whatever they actually need for functioning in the dominant, English-speaking language. Reading instruction, in particular, should probably be given first in the *native* language so that its potential difficulties do not become tangled with the added challenge of learning a second oral language. Only after children are reading well in their first language, according to this view, should they be introduced to reading in English. Doing so would also, presumably, benefit the children by opening their family's culture to them still further, through its written tradition.

Educators who favor the direct method assert that delaying instruction in English may make it harder to learn and may prevent the children from fully perfecting their use of it. As a practical matter, curriculum materials in minority languages are often unavailable or inappropriate. Borrowing materials from foreign countries (for example, Spanish curricula from Latin America) is a logical alternative, but the style and content

direct teaching of English

of such materials have often seemed inappropriate for North American schools. For the least well known languages, in addition, teachers fluent in the language are difficult to find, at least if they must meet normal certification requirements.

As for the teaching of reading, advocates of the direct use of English believe that oral English and written English need not be learned together. Instead, early in their schooling, children can receive oral training in English, and then later, after they have reached a suitable level of oral competence, they can begin instruction in written English. Their teachers, therefore, need not have the intimate familiarity with their language and culture that the native language approach calls for, although they should certainly know something about both of them.

social influences on language education

The influence of English in the United States, compared with that of minority languages, has greatly affected discussions of bilingual education. Most non-English–speaking parents want their children to learn English in order for them to participate on an equal footing with other members of society. At the same time, they also want their children to know their family's language and culture and to feel proud of it. The first motive has lent support to the direct method of bilingual education, and the second, to the native language approach.

In the United States, being bilingual has often carried a stigma, since non-English speakers historically have included immigrant and other groups that have not participated fully in society—or at least have not yet. The effort of such groups to overcome the stigma of bilingualism has, paradoxically, contributed to both the native language and the direct method viewpoints of bilingual education: both ways are seen as leading ultimately to higher self-respect for bilingual children, as well as to more social respect for the non-English language by society at large.

Dialect Differences and Black English

dialect variations

Although so far this chapter has referred to English as if it exists in only one form, in fact many varieties—called **dialects**—are spoken. On formal, public occasions, for example, most people will use **standard English**: the "proper" style heard on network news broadcasts and used in most school classrooms. In casual speech, however, many English speakers adopt other styles. They may choose more slang and colloquial terms, like *ain't* instead of *isn't* or *biffy* instead of *toilet*. They may change their pronunciation of certain words, like dropping the *-g* in *talking*. And they may even change certain grammatical constructions, as in *You going?* instead of *Are you going?* The particular dialect variations depend on many factors, such as the speaker's geographical region, ethnic background, occupation, and economic level.

A common and educationally controversial dialect is **black English**, so called because it is spoken by many (but by no means all) black people in the United States. This dialect contains elements of general southern English dialect, as well as African and Caribbean influences. The history of slavery and racial prejudice in the United States probably contributed to the impression, once common, that black English is a more primitive or inferior version of standard English. Recently though, linguists have discredited this idea by demonstrating that the dialect can in principle be used for all the same purposes that the standard dialect can, that in fact it has more similarities to standard English than differences from it, and that speakers of black English cannot therefore be considered verbally or intellectually deficient on account of their dialect (Labov, 1972). Other research shows that in any case many black people do not use the dialect and that if they do, they often use it only in selected situations (Dale, 1976). The majority of black adults and children shift their speaking style to fit the circumstances, just as everyone else does.

black English

Just as with bilingualism, dialect differences have created a controversy about how best to educate those children who do use nonstandard dialects, most notably, the ones who speak black English. And as with bilingual education, educators disagree about whether teachers should use standard English as the exclusive medium of instruction. Does using black English for instruction promote better learning, increased self-respect, and increased social status for the speakers of that dialect? Or does it interfere with these goals by isolating children from the mainstream language longer than necessary?

A reasonable alternative is to use both the standard and the black dialect in teaching such children, but educators and parents continue to debate the proper patterning, timing, and emphasis of the two dialects (Shuy, 1972; Somervill, 1975). The same advantages and disadvantages apply to using black English for instruction as apply to using a non-English native language. Two-dialect speakers differ from bilingual ones, though, in using a form of language that can usually be understood by other English speakers. In that way they may therefore seem less handicapped linguistically. But in another way they may face a more difficult language problem, since their problem pertains more to the social stigma associated with their non-standard dialect. As a result, therefore, some educators feel that the schools by themselves should not be expected to resolve the issue of dialect differences; a full solution, they say, awaits economic and social reforms that will create more equality in society (Jencks, 1973).

bidialectical education versus direct teaching of standard English

The Language of Education

Because most children easily learn their first language, it may be surprising that educators devote so much effort to developing language in all sorts of ways. Should not the initial ease of learning mean that teachers can simply take their students' language abilities for granted and turn their attention elsewhere?

Apparently they cannot, and apparently not because schools rely on a particular version of language that all children do not learn equally well as preschoolers. It might be called the *language of education*. It uses vocabulary, grammatical forms, and even pronunciations that may not coincide with those used in a particular child's home or among his or her

continuing need for language development

particular friends. And the language of education has certain features of style, informal rules of how and when to speak and for what purposes. These qualities, too, must be learned. Many, or perhaps most, children and youth must learn at least some of these aspects of school language in order to function well in that setting. Significant minorities may need to learn most, or even all, aspects of the language of education, including the basic vocabulary and grammar of English itself. Whether children have a lot of this language to learn or only a little, they deserve to learn it in a way that respects their language background. Given this obligation and given the continuing reliance of education on a particular form of language, educators will probably continue to create and improve programs for language development.

Key Points

1. Language has both structure (its organization) and function (its uses and purposes).

2. Language is acquired through a series of steps: babbling, single-word utterances, telegraphic speech, and grammatical sentences.

3. The grammar of children follows phrase structure rules and transformation rules, but these may not correspond exactly to adult grammar.

4. There are several theories about how language is acquired: reinforcement for speaking, imitation of language models, practice of language structures, and an innate Language Acquisition Device.

5. Of these theories, reinforcement for speaking has less evidence supporting it than the others do.

6. Acquiring an appropriate classroom language style is important for school-age children and youth.

7. Teachers can help motivate students to communicate more and better in class by varying their selection of topics and tasks and conveying expectations that students can and will communicate well.

8. Three methods for improving language and communication are simplification strategies, encouraging logical uses in conversation, and structured language drill.

9. Techniques for fostering language and communication probably also foster better thinking, but the exact relationship is unclear.

10. Bilingual children can be taught the language of the majority (in North America, this is English) by either the native language approach or the direct method.

11. Bidialectical children (the ones who speak a nonstandard version of English) have many of the same language and communication problems that bilingual children do and can also be taught by either the native language approach or the direct method.

12. In the United States, one significant nonstandard dialect is black English.

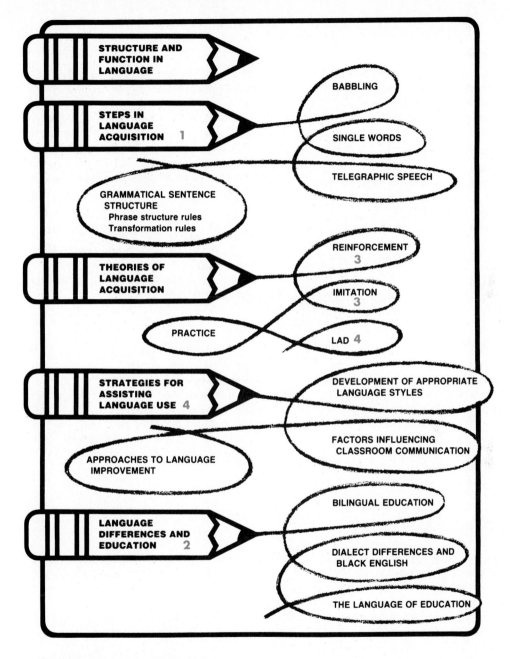

STRUCTURE AND FUNCTION IN LANGUAGE

STEPS IN LANGUAGE ACQUISITION 1

BABBLING

SINGLE WORDS

TELEGRAPHIC SPEECH

GRAMMATICAL SENTENCE STRUCTURE
Phrase structure rules
Transformation rules

THEORIES OF LANGUAGE ACQUISITION

REINFORCEMENT 3

IMITATION 3

PRACTICE

LAD 4

STRATEGIES FOR ASSISTING LANGUAGE USE 4

DEVELOPMENT OF APPROPRIATE LANGUAGE STYLES

FACTORS INFLUENCING CLASSROOM COMMUNICATION

APPROACHES TO LANGUAGE IMPROVEMENT

LANGUAGE DIFFERENCES AND EDUCATION 2

BILINGUAL EDUCATION

DIALECT DIFFERENCES AND BLACK ENGLISH

THE LANGUAGE OF EDUCATION

1 Other stage theories (Chapters 2, 4, 5, and 11)

2 The social context of learning (Chapter 5)

3 Learning as behavior change (Chapter 6)

4 Learning to structure knowledge (Chapter 7)

Case Study

Teresa's Nursery Class

Teresa Holtsman, a nursery school teacher, witnessed this conversation between two children in her class, Jenny and Karen. Jenny was four years old, and Karen was two and one-half. They were listening to music.

Jenny: I'm dancing!
Karen: Dancing too.
Jenny: Look, Karen; go like this. *(Hops on two feet.)*
(Karen stares, does nothing.)
Jenny: Hop! *(Hops again.)*
(Karen attempts to hop.)
Jenny: That's it. Hop! Hop, hop, hop. *(Continues hopping.)*
Karen: I hop. *(Hops clumsily.)*
Teresa: Oh how nice. You're teaching Karen to dance.

Karen: Hot, hop, hop, hot. Hot, teacher. Hot foot!
Teresa: Hot? *(Looks at Jenny for help interpreting.)*
Jenny: She said, *hop* on your feets. *Both* feets. *(Demonstrates.)*
Karen: Hot, hop, hod, hot. You hot, too? *(Looks at teacher and hops.)*
Teresa: Hop? I can't now because I have to visit some other children. But you go ahead. You hop.
Karen: *(smiling)* I hot.
Jenny: Say *hop,* Karen; not "hot"!
Karen: Hop *(hops)*; hot *(hops)*; hod *(hops)*. Hop! *(Hops very high.)*
Jenny: *(exasperated)* Oh, Karen. *(then, to teacher)* Isn't she silly?

Questions for Discussion

1. How does Karen's language illustrate the steps in language acquisition discussed in this chapter? Look especially for example of telegraphic speech.
2. How, if at all, does this dialogue illustrate the mechanisms of language acquisition discussed in this chapter? Consider these three in particular: reinforcement, imitation, and practice.
3. Does this dialogue support, contradict, or ignore the proposal that children have an innate

"Language Acquisition Device" (or LAD)? Explain your opinion.
4. a. How did Jenny and the teacher each assist Karen's language development in this example? Be as specific as you can.
   b. How could they follow-up or extend their assistance further? Again, be as specific as you can.

Suggested Readings

Cazden, Courtney, ed. *Language in Early Childhood Education.* Rev. ed. Washington, D.C.: National Association for the Education of Young Children, 1981.
   Cazden has collected essays by various experts on how the language needs of young children, ages three through about eight, can best be served in preschool and school-based programs. One especially helpful chapter analyzes the relative advantages of two dozen early childhood curricula currently available that encourage language and communication. Many of them are intended for children who speak English as a second language or who speak nonstandard dialects of English.

DeVilliers, Peter, and Jill DeVilliers. *Early Language.* Cambridge, Mass.: Harvard University Press, 1979.
   This is an excellent, short discussion of how language develops during infancy and the preschool and elementary school years. It emphasizes the development of grammatical structures

more than the development of language functions, though it recognizes the connections between these two areas.

Dickson, W. Patrick, ed. *Children's Oral Communication Skills*. New York: Academic Press, 1981.

This is a thorough compilation of information about how children develop communication skills and what teachers and other adults can do to help the process. Some of the articles are difficult to understand because they summarize somewhat technical research studies, but they are well worth the effort. As we pointed out in Chapter 3, communication skill affects, and is affected by, thinking skills.

Henley, Nancy. *Body Politics: Power, Sex, and Nonverbal Communication*. Englewood Cliffs, N.J.: Prentice-Hall, 1977.

Lakoff, Robin. *Language and Woman's Place*. New York: Harper Colophon Books, 1975.

These two books take the stand that language and communication tend, in various ways, to keep women in subservient roles in society. You may or may not agree with this idea, but the authors present a good argument for it, and it makes fascinating reading. The first book emphasizes the importance of nonverbal methods of communication—facial expressions, gestures, and body language—as well as methods of verbal communication, such as those emphasized in this chapter.

Chapter 4

MORAL BEHAVIOR

AND DEVELOPMENT

Andrea Friesen, Grade 9 biology: In my first year of teaching, my purse was stolen. I had been working in the room after school and left my purse on the desk in front. I was in the back, setting up some equipment for the next day. When I turned around, it was gone! I knew that a couple of kids—Billy and Jack—had been out in the hall just before, but I really couldn't prove anything. They were gone when I looked for them.

When I told the principal, he was convinced that Billy and Jack had done it. "I've had trouble with those two before," he said, sounding both angry and weary. "Don't worry, I'll get your purse back." He called Billy and Jack into his office after I left and apparently "grilled" them about the incident. And sure enough, by the next day, he brought me back my purse—soaking wet! The boys had hidden it in the water tank of one of the toilets. Everything was there, even the money, and Billy and Jack even apologized—rather awkwardly. I suppose the principal had made them do it.

Well, I was glad to get my purse back, but the whole thing left me rather uneasy. Why would the boys have wanted to steal? Maybe, I thought, they wanted to test each other's courage against the authorities. The money itself should not have mattered very much, since they both came from fairly well-to-do families. Their loyalty to each other is what really impressed me: they cared a lot about each other's opinions. "If only they would care that much about the rest of us!" the principal remarked to me.

And the principal's conduct bothered me, too. I couldn't prove it, but I suspected that he did not follow what most courts would consider "due process" when he got my purse back for me. I was uncomfortable with how he had zeroed in on Billy and Jack before he had any real evidence to suspect them. He apparently just went by their reputations—because they had done wrong before, therefore they must be doing wrong again. It sounded unfair to the boys: good or bad, they were being hassled by the principal! What if they had been innocent this time? What would that have done to their self-esteem and their attitudes toward stealing? Probably solidified their commitment to each other, I thought, and hardened their hearts toward theft. I wished there had been a better way to solve this crime, but I didn't know what it was.

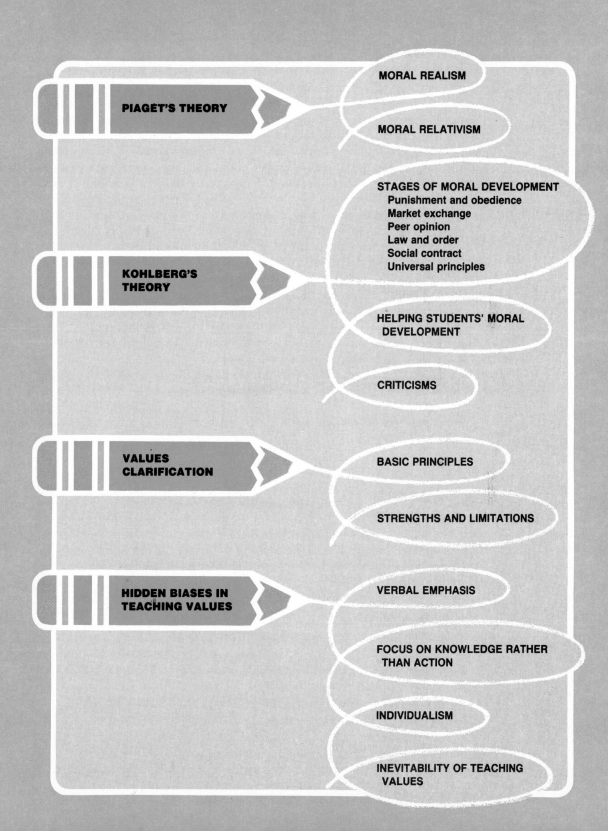

PIAGET'S THEORY

MORAL REALISM

MORAL RELATIVISM

KOHLBERG'S THEORY

STAGES OF MORAL DEVELOPMENT
  Punishment and obedience
  Market exchange
  Peer opinion
  Law and order
  Social contract
  Universal principles

HELPING STUDENTS' MORAL
DEVELOPMENT

CRITICISMS

VALUES CLARIFICATION

BASIC PRINCIPLES

STRENGTHS AND LIMITATIONS

HIDDEN BIASES IN TEACHING VALUES

VERBAL EMPHASIS

FOCUS ON KNOWLEDGE RATHER
THAN ACTION

INDIVIDUALISM

INEVITABILITY OF TEACHING
 VALUES

TEACHERS in schools have long been expected to teach good citizenship in addition to clear thinking. When they have completed their education, children and young people are supposed to have acquired habits of self-discipline, initiative, fair play, and service to others. Even trainers and educators outside the public schools usually hope to influence character in desirable directions. Camp counselors, for example, usually try to develop social cooperation and ecological care, as well as to instill knowledge about the woods or improve specific camping skills. Training programs offered by corporations usually attempt to encourage good business ethics as well as business skills, even when ethics is not an explicit focus of the training. In all cases, teachers who want to develop character in their students face a double challenge: they must consider their students' maturity and experience at the same time that they look for specific techniques for implementing such goals.

This chapter will speak to both needs. To compare levels of character development, we shall rely heavily on a theory of moral development originated by Lawrence Kohlberg (1975), which built on earlier work in this field by Piaget. In suggesting ways for developing good character, we shall refer to both Kohlberg's theory and a body of literature and techniques often called **values clarification** (Raths, 1966, Simon et al., 1978). Both theories focus on how children or young people form ideas about right and wrong and good and bad. This concern may not cover all of what teachers usually consider ethics and citizenship, but it does cover much of it.

PIAGET'S TWO-STAGE THEORY

The Cognitive-Developmental Approach

As part of his studies of thinking, Piaget observed the development of ethical ideas in preschool and school-age children. He did so by posing to them certain ethical dilemmas contained in pairs of brief anecdotes. One story in the pair would illustrate an accidental action that caused a lot of damage, and the other would illustrate an intentional action that caused only a little damage. Here is one such pair of stories:

Accidental, but large damage:

A little boy once noticed that his father's ink pot was empty. One day when his father was away he thought of filling the ink pot so as to help his father, and so that he should find it full when he came home. But while he was opening the ink bottle he made a big blot on the table cloth. (Piaget, 1932, p. 122)

Intentional, but small damage:

Once there was a little boy. His father had gone out and the boy thought it would be fun to play with father's ink pot. First he played with the pen, and then he made a little blot on the table cloth. (Piaget, 1932, p. 122)

Piaget asked individual children which child in the pair of stories behaved more wrongly, and he discussed with them their reasons for their judgments.

Moral Realism Versus Moral Relativism

From their responses, Piaget observed two main types, or stages, of moral thinking. In one of these, which Piaget called **moral realism**, the child judges wrongdoing by how much physical damage is done, regardless of the wrongdoer's intentions. In the stories above, a moral-realist child thought that making a big ink blot was worse, even though it happened by accident, than making only a small ink blot on purpose. Such children also seem to believe that ethical rules are fixed by some sort of higher authority (like God or parents or teachers), and so they cannot change under any circumstances. On the whole, moral realists tend to be preoperational in their thinking.

moral realism

As children develop, they shift gradually to what Piaget called **moral relativism**. Here the child considers personal intentions in evaluating ethical behavior; in the stories above, the moral relativist judged the small, intentional ink blot as worse than the large, accidental one. In other ways, too, the relativists seem to be the reverse of the realists. They believe that ethical rules result from mutual agreement rather than authoritative decree, that rules therefore can be modified by mutual consent, and that rules are guidelines rather than rigid dictates. On the whole, moral relativists rely on concrete or formal operational thinking.

moral relativism

Educational Implications

These observations regarding ethical beliefs may seem pessimistic to some teachers, as they indicate that classrooms for the very young cannot and should not function as democratically as do classrooms for older children. With the very youngest, it seems, classroom management would have to rely heavily on teachermade rules. Although such a style may seem dictatorial, it need not be if used benignly and in moderation. In most school classrooms, certain rules can almost always be turned over to the group for discussion, even if others cannot. Even kindergarten children may have useful suggestions for when and how to share toys, even if they may not have them for serious stealing or hitting.

The distinction between moral realism and moral relativism does not directly address the needs of teachers of adolescents and adults. What happens to young people, ethically, beyond late elementary school? Common sense says that they continue to grow and develop and that moral relativism is not the last and best kind of ethics that human beings ever acquire. Adults can easily imagine situations in which moral realism seems more ethical or mature, even though Piaget considers it less so. Suppose that a child's friends mutually agree to steal candy from a drugstore, even though the child's parents have forbidden it. Here, stealing may be morally relativistic, and abstaining may be morally realistic, but which seems more ethical by adult standards? This kind of question has led to the expansion of Piaget's ideas described below.

KOHLBERG'S SIX-STAGE THEORY

Lawrence Kohlberg's work evolved out of earlier, related work on moral development by Piaget and in fact uses similar methods of study. Kohlberg observed children's ethical ideas by posing certain ethical dilemmas contained in anecdotes and then explored their responses in semistructured interviews. Here is one dilemma that Kohlberg has often cited as an example of his work:

> In Europe, a woman was near death from a special kind of cancer. There was one drug that the doctors thought might save her. It was a form of radium that a druggist in the same town had recently discovered. The drug was expensive to make but the druggist was charging ten times what the drug cost him to make. He paid $200 for the radium and charged $2000 for a small dose of the drug. The sick woman's husband, Heinz, went to everyone he knew to borrow the money, but he could only get together about $1000, which is half of what it cost. He told the druggist that his wife was dying and asked him to sell it cheaper or let him pay later. But the druggist said, "No, I discovered the drug and I'm going to make money from it." So Heinz got desperate and broke into the man's store to steal the drug for his wife. Should the husband have done that? Why? (in Hersh et al., 1979, p. 54)

For the benefit of younger children, Kohlberg and his associates have also created a series of filmstrips that present dilemmas in simpler terms. Here is one:

> Holly is an eight-year-old girl who likes to climb trees. She is the best tree-climber in the neighborhood. One day while climbing down from a tall tree she falls off the bottom branch but does not hurt herself. Her father sees her fall. He is upset and asks her to promise not to climb trees any more. Holly promises. Later that day, Holly and her friends meet Shawn. Shawn's kitten is caught up in a tree and can't get down. Something has to be done right away or the kitten may fall. Holly is the only one who climbs trees well enough to reach the kitten and get it down, but she remembers her promise to her father. (Selman & Kohlberg, 1972; in Colby, 1975, p. 137)

Kohlberg and his associates transcribed and analyzed the replies of various ages to dilemmas like these (Kohlberg, 1976; Kohlbert & Turiel, 1971).

The results resemble the interviews that Piaget reported on many other topics, and they have both the richness and the ambiguity of the Piagetian findings studied in Chapter 2. The stages Kohlberg proposes, however, seem very plausible, and they are supported by Kohlberg's own research.

A Hierarchy of Moral Development

Kohlberg described six major periods of moral development, which form hierarchical stages in the sense described in Chapter 2. The stages of development always occur in the same fixed sequence; each stage incorporates the skills from all the preceding stages; and the individuals in them vary in how fast they move through the stages, but all progress along the same route.

The First Two Stages   In stage 1, a child decides what is right and wrong by the rewards and punishments involved. The right or good thing to do is whatever is rewarded, or at least is not punished, and the wrong or bad thing is whatever is punished. In evaluating the first dilemma above, such a child might consider only whether Heinz, the husband, will be caught for stealing and show little awareness of whether the circumstances might make stealing acceptable in this particular case. Likewise, in evaluating the second dilemma, the stage 1 child would consider only whether Holly would be punished or rewarded for saving the kitten.

stage 1: ethics of punishment and obedience

Notice, incidentally, that a child's way of thinking defines his or her stage of ethics, not the final decisions about specific dilemmas. Some stage 1 children may conclude that Holly should climb the tree, others, that she should not. In both cases, if the children have reached their conclusion because of possible or actual rewards and punishments for concrete actions, then it qualifies as stage 1 thinking.

In stage 2, children decide on rightness and wrongness on the basis of whether an action gives mutual advantage to them and to whoever else is affected. Their thinking is still guided by a simple pursuit of pleasure and avoidance of pain, but contrary to when they were in the first stage, they now distinguish clearly between their wishes and others'. Ethical choices now are like market exchanges of goods and services. In the first dilemma above, a child may decide that Heinz and the druggist should have worked out a compromise: perhaps Heinz should have mortgaged his home to the druggist to pay off the extra money or offered to work for him for nothing. In the second dilemma, perhaps Holly should have found someone to lie, just that once, about her climbing the forbidden tree, in exchange for some later favor. Again, the content of the solution itself does not define this stage as much as how the solution is thought through does.

stage 2: ethics of market exchange

At the preconventional level of ethics, children might consider stealing fruit to be "good"—or at least not "bad"—as long as they were not caught and punished. (Marcia Weinstein)

At both of these first stages, ethical judgments have little to do with the intrinsic goodness of behavior and much with its external consequences. Children in the first stage may believe in saying "please" and "thank you" *not* because doing so is good intrinsically but because they are rewarded for these behaviors by parents and others. In stage 2, they may still believe in these courtesies, but for different reasons: perhaps they now observe them to ensure that sharing and other considerate behaviors will come their way in return. In essence, courtesies become items in mutually beneficial exchanges.

limitations of stages 1 and 2

Since short-run considerations dominate ethics in these earliest two stages, children can easily go astray from time to time. If their families and friends reward them for "acting tough," for example, they may indeed come to value needed qualities of independence and assertiveness. But at times they may also get into some unnecessary conflicts and scraps with other children and consider it good or right to do so. In the same way, if their families and friends reward them for quiet, submissive behavior, they may come to value these behaviors in ways that are both helpful and harmful: they may, perhaps, be good teammates but at times let others take unfair advantage of them.

Likewise, stage 2 ethics can lead to ethical mistakes as well as to ethical solutions. Although some exchanges of favors may genuinely benefit both children by leading to a sharing of materials, skills, and behaviors, other exchanges may well harm one or both parties. Despite the mutual advantages, is it good for two children to trade an expensive toy truck for a large handful of candy? Or twenty-five cents for the privilege of not being hassled by the school bully? Children do make such exchanges, especially those thinking in terms of stage 2 ethics. To avoid the mistakes of this type of thinking, children eventually must evaluate right and wrong in ways that take into account the long-run consequences.

The Third and Fourth Stages   Children do begin to consider long-run consequences during the next two levels of ethical development. In stage 3, they distinguish between right and wrong by how much their actions please those around them and by how much those actions support the existing codes of behavior of their peers. Stage 3 children may decide that stealing a candy bar is wrong if it displeases their friends to do so, but they may just as easily decide that it is right to do so if it pleases them. Accordingly, in Kohlberg's dilemmas above, both Heinz and Holly should do whatever satisfies the largest number of people in their respective situations. The potential contradictions of this sort of ethics show up clearly in Heinz's case: if most of his family and friends would rather that he *not* steal the drug, should Heinz then just let his wife die? In spite of such difficulties, though, stage 3 ethics at least recognizes and respects the wishes of others more than the earlier stages do. Eventually the contradictions may become noticeable enough to move the children on to the next stage of moral development.

stage 3: ethics of peer opinion

By stage 4, children become less concerned with the approval of their immediate peers and more with upholding the general moral and legal codes of their community or society, what Kohlberg calls a "law and order" mentality. Standards shift from the children's immediate peer and family groups to the larger community or society at large. Stealing a candy bar now may be considered wrong, not because the children's friends may disapprove, but simply because it is against the law. In evaluating Kohlberg's story of Heinz, children at this stage would often refer to laws and conventions. Perhaps Heinz should not steal the drug because stealing violates the law, or on the contrary, perhaps he should in fact steal it

stage 4: ethics of law and order

because society believes that spouses should support each other. Even though the latter idea may not exist in any actual law, it holds a lawlike place in the minds of most citizens, and children at this stage may invoke it in judging right and wrong.

In most situations, the ethics of stages 3 and 4 lead to "good," in the sense of conventional behavior. By definition, the children or young people in these stages now believe in pleasing others as much as possible and in living by the laws and conventions of the land. But since they lack any notion that common beliefs, laws, and conventions can change under certain circumstances, their ethics may sometimes seem rigid. Should, for example, girls ever pay the cost of a date? A stage 4 person might disapprove because such behavior contradicts the usual rules for dating in our society. But a stage 3 person might either approve or disapprove, depending on whether the girl's friends rejected her brashness or admired her feminine liberation. All such evaluation assumes that laws and conventions are fixed, now and for eternity, and here and in all places.

limitations of stages 3 and 4

The Fifth and Sixth Stages   At stage 5, children (now actually adolescents or young adults) begin to regard right and wrong as products of a **social contract**, the set of legal and legal-like rules of procedure for settling basic disagreements that are created and followed by society. Good or right actions now consist of adhering to these ground rules in deliberating about issues; conversely, bad or wrong actions conflict with these rules. For those in stage 5, the specific opinions that individuals hold during disagreements and debates are no longer "good" or "bad" in and of themselves, as long as the individuals express their opinions and influence others only in socially accepted ways.

stage 5: ethics of social contract

A simple example: whereas children may not have believed earlier that driving on the left-hand side of the street could be right, they can believe now that it may be acceptable under certain conditions. It can, in principle, become acceptable, they now see, if the proper discussions, voting, and other preparations are made so that everyone agrees to the new arrangement. Likewise, Kohlberg's dilemma regarding Heinz might be resolved in stage 5 by calling attention to how society can change its laws and conventions, but it has not. Perhaps, according to this sort of ethics, Heinz would benefit from different laws regarding stealing or from different economic customs regarding pricing drugs, but for now he must adhere to the existing laws and customs.

At stage 6, the final point of development, young people define right and wrong according to personally held, abstract principles. They supposedly have decided on these by pondering competing ethical principles during the preceding stages, especially stage 5. By thinking about how society may change its rules, they eventually reach their own conclusions about ethics that have universal truth. The conclusions that they reach may or may not coincide with generally accepted social standards, and they may

stage 6: ethics of universal principles

Individuals at conventional levels of moral development judge right and wrong according to existing laws. But a person at a postconventional ethical level would be likely to disobey these signs if someone's life were at stake. (Michael Weisbrot and Family)

or may not coincide with the conclusions of other stage 6 persons. They may decide that killing is *always* wrong, including in war—even though their nation forces them to enlist in the army or even though their best friends, also in stage 6, disagree with them. If they apply such a principle to Kohlberg's story of Heinz, they may decide that Heinz should save his wife's life at any cost, even if he has to steal the money for the drug or forcibly take it from the druggist.

Even though stage 5 and 6 ethics may seem to be the most developed or mature of any stage, many adults never seem to achieve them. Kohlberg and others have found that about two-thirds of the adults in North American society, and even higher proportions in certain other societies, never use personally held, abstract principles to determine their ethical beliefs; they rely instead on the conventions learned from society that feature so heavily in stages 3 and 4 (Kohlberg & Turiel, 1971; Rosen, 1980). Part of the reason for this finding may come from the difficulties that adults have with formal, abstract thinking in general. In addition, though, abstract ethical thinking can be easily confused with the conventional thinking of the preceding stages. Why? Because many personally held beliefs just

difficulty of reaching stages 5 and 6

happen to coincide often with social conventions about right and wrong. An individual may become personally committed to saving human life (stage 6 ethics), but if his society also forbids murder and promotes the saving of life (stage 3 and 4 conventions), then his principled position may be indistinguishable from a merely conventional one. Only the reasoning leading up to his principle will clearly identify his stage, but for the highest stage of ethics, such reasoning becomes difficult to analyze reliably. For these reasons, among others, some psychologists remain skeptical of Kohlberg's assertion that most adults do not become ethically autonomous and principled (Simpson, 1974).

Table 4–1 summarizes the six stages and their definitions. Note that Kohlberg has often grouped the six into three more inclusive groups, according to how well they uphold society's conventional rules of ethics. The middle pair of stages, the "conventional" ones, characterize most school-age children and youth. Since many adults as well may rely on these stages, the following suggestions are based on students with middle-level

Table 4–1 Stages of Moral Beliefs According to Kohlberg

Preconventional level

Stage 1:	Ethics of punishment and obedience	Good is what follows externally imposed rules and rewards and which avoids punishment.
Stage 2:	Ethics of market exchange	Good is whatever is agreeable to the individual and to those to or from whom he or she may give or receive favors; there is no long-run loyalty.

Conventional level

Stage 3:	Ethics of peer opinion	Good is whatever brings approval from friends as a group.
Stage 4:	Ethics of law and order	Good is whatever conforms to existing laws, customs, and authorities.

Postconventional level

Stage 5:	Ethics of social contract	Good is whatever conforms to existing procedures for settling disagreements in society; the outcome of the settlement is not necessarily good or bad in itself.
Stage 6:	Ethics of universal principles	Good is whatever is consistent with personally held, abstract moral principles.

ethics: on the whole they judge rightness by its effect on their peers and by how well it coincides with existing laws and customs.

Helping Students Move Through Moral Stages

Because these moral stages form a hierarchical sequence, students must somehow or other proceed through them in the order just described. Kohlberg believes that teachers can help students along, both directly in specially designed activities and indirectly through the overall organization of the classroom and school. The direct, intentional intervention consists of presenting students with moral dilemmas like the ones presented earlier in this chapter. Kohlberg suggests that teachers respond to students' solutions of such problems at a level just *above* the students' current level of thinking: a student with a peer-group orientation (stage 3) might be encouraged to think about the consequences of mercy killing for the general stability of society (stage 4 ethics), rather than considering only the consequences for the individual and his or her immediate circle of friends. Some studies using this discussion technique concluded that students *prefer* to hear moral arguments just above their own level of development, even though they can *understand* arguments at all lower levels just as well or even better. Hearing the higher-level ethics, Kohlberg argues, supposedly motivates students to overcome the contradictions of the lower stage and in that way moves them on to higher levels (Mosher & Sullivan, 1976; Rest, 1974).

discussion of dilemmas

As Kohlberg and others have pointed out, the examination of dilemmas can also be used with much of the material ordinarily studied in people-oriented subjects like English, social studies, history, or government (Beyer, 1976; Purpel & Ryan, 1976). Many works of literature, for example, are constructed around moral dilemmas that students can analyze and evaluate. Likewise, most current events contain a host of ethical issues underlying the particular conflicts and events of the day. By discussing examples like these, teachers can integrate moral education into their existing teaching programs and therefore try to make them more relevant (Duska & Whelan, 1977; Hersh, 1979).

ethical implications of curriculum

In addition to the intentional discussion of dilemmas, Kohlberg believes that moral education can occur indirectly through the overall organization of the classroom and school (Kohlberg, 1970). Sending a tardy student to the principal, for example, may imply to the students a stage 4, law-and-order morality. But discussing the effects of being late, both with the student and the rest of the class, may demonstrate that ethical decisions must be constructed by consensus and due process (stage 5 ethics). The discussion of such real incidents duplicates, in effect, the technique of discussion of moral dilemmas, but in the context of real school events.

ethical implications of school life

Needless to say, reviewing real classroom incidents may sometimes require real changes of school and classroom policy, as well as good will among teachers and students.

Criticisms of Kohlberg's Methods and Theory

Not everyone agrees with the methods of moral education that Kohlberg proposes. Why? Because, some say, discussions of moral dilemmas may require more sensitivity than most teachers have. To handle a discussion of ethics well, teachers have to make accurate judgments of their students' present levels of development and at the same time figure out what sorts of arguments constitute the next higher stage. In addition, the teachers have to allow somehow for the individual differences that inevitably exist in groups: a two- or three-stage spread would not be unreasonable to expect in a single classroom. All of these judgments require familiarity with Kohlberg's stages, with a variety of dilemma examples, and with the students themselves (Fraenkel, 1976). Identifying the highest stages would seem especially difficult, considering how easily they can be confused with lower, more conventional stages. Since Kohlberg himself has claimed that most people never go beyond stage 3 or 4, presumably most teachers have not, either. If so, then they cannot understand the highest stages well enough to move their students into them, even if they wanted to.

In addition to their concerns about its methods, psychologists disagree about how accurate or universal Kohlberg's stages really are. Kohlberg and his associates have presented moral dilemmas to children in several different cultures and believe that their results show the sequence to be universal (Kohlberg, 1975; Kohlberg & Elfenbein, 1975). Critics, though, point out that their findings apply only to the middle stages, stages 2, 3, and 4. The extreme stages, they say, do not occur often enough to observe them reliably. Even the sequence of the middle stages may be affected, for example, by the content of the dilemma, by the source of moral authority in the dilemma, and by the sex of the child being interviewed (Henry, 1980; Roberts & Dunston, 1980).

Perhaps even more significant for teachers, some research suggests that Kohlberg's universal sequence does not really constitute a set of hierarchical stages, but simply a trend or tendency of development (Rest, 1980). Like any trend, it includes many exceptions: in this case, some children develop their ethics in the "wrong" order, or in no identifiable order at all (Fraenkel, 1976; Simpson, 1974). As a teacher, such individuality among students may challenge you as much as their common abilities do; yet Kohlberg's stage theory has relatively little help to give in understanding and dealing with exceptional cases. In this respect, it differs little from the other major stage theories of development.

Behaviorally oriented psychologists, the ones who study specific, ob-

heavy demands on teachers

questionable universality

existence of exceptions

servable behaviors, have expressed skepticism about whether truly general stages exist for moral development (Mischel, 1974). Peer-oriented and legalistic morality may appear around school age simply because school life rewards the behaviors and beliefs needed for these ethics. As they spend more time in school, children may be rewarded more and more by their friends for supporting peer ethics and by their teachers and parents for supporting law-and-order ethics. Eventually they may learn so many elements of these two ethical orientations that they will seem to have acquired a general, ethical philosophy. But for most of their school years, their ethical beliefs will really consist of only bits and pieces of these orientations, not of any general, stagelike orientation.

influence of behavioral rewards

This explanation is consistent with one of the classic studies in moral thinking and behavior, *Studies in the Nature of Character,* conducted by Hartshorne and May in 1928. About three thousand students were observed and tested with regard to both their moral beliefs and their actual conduct in situations involving moral issues. In general, little relationship was found among specific beliefs or behaviors, such as a stage theory like Kohlberg's would predict. Children might believe that a certain kind of cheating was wrong and yet be observed to commit that very form of cheating in another situation. Even their beliefs lacked consistency: children might believe cheating was acceptable in one situation and not in another.

ethical inconsistencies

Despite appearances, however, this study may not really disprove the existence of stages of moral development. First, Kohlberg's theory does not claim to deal with moral action but, rather, focuses on knowledge of or *beliefs* about right and wrong. In real life, of course, all of us must eventually accompany our actions with beliefs, and our beliefs with actions. But Kohlberg cannot really be faulted for limiting his purpose to the smaller and more manageable study of beliefs only. Second, despite the Hartshorne and May findings, stages of moral belief may in fact exist if children are helped to explain their ideas at some length. The notion of honesty, for instance, can be translated into various specific ideas and therefore can lead to the appearance of inconsistency within and among children on tests that allow only short, relatively superficial responses. But by talking at length about a problem concerning honesty, children can express a more complete, stable version of the idea and can show how it fits in with their other moral ideas. Kohlberg's method of clinical interviewing does just that, which may explain why he has been able to find stages that other researchers have not always been able to identify.

ethical stages versus specific beliefs

THE VALUES CLARIFICATION APPROACH

During the last decade or so, an approach called *values clarification* has been popular in the schools and elsewhere (Simon et al., 1978). Some of its success may come from its relatively strong practical emphasis—stronger, for instance, than Kohlberg's. The method in its usual form relies on several dozen specific techniques or exercises that can be conducted easily by teachers or other leaders of groups.

Basic Principles

valuing as a process

The creators of the values clarification method base their techniques on a number of general principles. They begin by assuming that a _value_ is a process, rather than a sort of mental object or idea, and they identify several elements in the process of **valuing**:

Choosing: 1. freely
　　　　　2. from alternatives
　　　　　3. after thoughtful consideration of the consequences of each alternative
Prizing:　4. cherishing, being happy with the choice
　　　　　5. willing to affirm the choice publicly
Acting:　 6. doing something with the choice
　　　　　7. repeatedly, in some pattern of life

(Raths et al., 1966, p. 30)

As a teacher, you will need ways to know when these rather general behaviors have actually occurred in your students. When, for example, has a student really chosen freely? Not necessarily because you, the teacher tell her that she is free, not because she claims to be free. She may react as did the student in a permissive, progressive school who asked, "Teacher, _must_ I do what I _want_ to do today?"

indicators of values

The creators of the values clarification approach recognize that identifying values in students can never be done with complete certainty, but they do suggest several behaviors that indicate their presence. Although any of these behaviors may also indicate relatively trivial concerns, they do tend to reflect the true, basic valuing process outlined above:

1. Expressions of goals or purposes: What is the student wanting to accomplish over the short- or medium-run?
2. Aspirations: What does he want to accomplish in the long-run, "in his wildest dreams"?
3. Attitudes: What is the student for or against?
4. Interests: What does he like to talk about or spend time on?
5. Feelings: What does he like or dislike?
6. Beliefs and convictions: What does he consider right or wrong?
7. Activities: How does he use his time?
8. Worries, problems, obstacles: What concerns or hassles him?

(Raths et al., 1966, pp. 30–32)

Any one student, of course, may not indicate his values in these exact words. He may or may not ever say, "My goal is to do X" or "I aspire to do Y," but instead express the same ideas in other words, or even nonverbally. By the same token, he may use these words to state rather minor concerns that do not deserve to be called values; he may say, "I believe in the New York Mets," when in fact the statement has nothing to do with values as usually understood.

In one way or another, each of the values clarification techniques tries to draw out these indicators of personal values. One exercise asks students to list twenty things they love to do and then to analyze the list in specific ways that force them to set priorities among these things. In the process, they have to express their value indicators, their beliefs, aspirations, and the like. In another exercise, called "Alligator River," students are asked to evaluate the behavior of several unsavory characters, each one of which does something bad to disrupt a love affair. The students rank the characters in order of their "badness," and in so doing they must sort out a variety of attitudes, beliefs, and concerns with the other students doing the same exercise. ("Alligator River" appears as part of the case study at the end of this chapter.)

These activities are guided by various comments and questions from the teacher. The original book on values clarification lists thirty *clarifying responses* that teachers can use with students. Each of them, of course, is supposed to be used only when it is appropriate to the discussion; if it is overused, it quickly will seem phony and lose its effectiveness. Here is a sample of the thirty:

1. Is this something that you prize?
6. Was that something that you yourself selected or chose?
11. Where would that idea lead; what would be its consequences?
16. What are some good things about that notion?
21. How can I help you do something about your idea? What seems to be the difficulty?
26. Do you have any reasons for saying (or doing) that?

(Raths et al., 1966, pp. 56–62)

All these questions encourage open-ended replies from the students. In doing so, they encourage students to elaborate on their values, however confused they may be, and to reach their own conclusions. The values clarification approach itself, therefore, values certain things—for instance, solving problems for oneself—but it takes no moral stand on any particular issue. It also assumes, with Kohlberg, that values (or morality or ethics) can be dealt with through special activities designed for the purpose, and not only in the context of normal living and its array of ethical choices. Some psychologists do not agree with these assumptions (Stewart, 1975), but it often seems necessary and convenient for teachers

clarifying
responses

to make them. After all, teachers must work in classrooms and usually cannot participate in the rest of their students' lives.

Strengths and Limitations of Values Clarification

Probably one reason for the popularity of values clarification is its emphasis on practical help for teachers. The major works on the subject contain numerous activities that supposedly promote moral development, or at least clarity of values, and these can be used more or less as printed. The book *Values Clarification,* for example, contains detailed directions for each of seventy-nine clarifying activities, helpful notes to the teacher, and in many cases suggestions for extending or varying the original activity (Simon et al., 1978). Most of the activities can be used with widely varying ages with only small changes. For teachers busy with the pressures of school and large classes, these are indeed strengths.

usefulness to teachers

In several important ways, values clarification resembles Kohlberg's approach to moral development. Both try to build the students' ability to judge issues; both encourage them to do so for themselves; and both encourage consistency of belief. Compared with Kohlberg's theory, though, values clarification shows more concern with issues that would have to be called merely personal, as opposed to moral. One activity, called "values voting," asks students to answer various questions in front of the group, including the following:

emphasis on both personal and moral values

Do you think that children should work for their allowance?
Have you ever gone skiing?
Do you think you are racially prejudiced?
Do you like Yogurt?

(Simon et al., 1978, p. 38ff)*

By promoting self-knowledge, all the questions help reveal personal values. Only the first and third seem to pertain to moral issues as such—issues of right and wrong or good and bad.

In general, values clarification aims to increase the students' awareness of what they believe, want, or feel. Unlike Kohlberg's theory, it does not try to make students differentiate between what they *do* value and what they *should* value. This omission has been severely criticized by some educators and psychologists (Colby, 1975; Stewart, 1975). Values clarification, they say, inadvertently creates the impression that all values are

relativistic views of values

*Reprinted by permission of A & W Publishers, Inc., from *Values Clarification: A Handbook of Practical Strategies for Teachers and Students* (New Revised Edition) by Sidney B. Simon, Leland W. Howe and Howard Kirschenbaum. Copyright © 1972; Copyright © 1978. Hart Publishing Company, Inc.

equally good, for instance, that liking yogurt and believing in racial equal-ity are equally desirable values. The method implies, they assert, that there is no way to evaluate the relative importance or desirability of com-peting values, despite an obvious need to do so. Is the courage of a bank robber, for example, as valuable as the courage of the police who capture him? In practice, so the argument concludes, teachers unintentionally sneak their own moral values into the values clarification exercises, since no one can ever be expected to be truly value-free.

The debate has not been settled yet. Advocates of values clarification admit to the charge of "relativism" (Kirschenbaum, 1976) but protest that the approach should not be criticized for not accomplishing what it did not set out to do. Although teachers do indeed have various biases, the values clarification approach minimizes them by purposely avoiding any partic-ular ethical viewpoint. The fact remains, furthermore, that values clari-fication offers considerable practical help to teachers. As a remedy for its relativism, in fact, some have suggested combining the approach with Kohlberg's (Colby, 1975).

HIDDEN BIASES IN THE TEACHING OF VALUES AND ETHICS

Both of the approaches to moral education discussed in this chapter share certain qualities that contribute to their success in roughly the same ways. Call them either biases or strengths, depending on your viewpoint.

Verbal Emphasis

Both Kohlberg's theory and the values clarification approach rely primar-ily on verbal exchange—discussion—as a learning medium. To benefit from either program, the students or children must be able to put their ideas into words skillfully and quickly, and they must do so when, and as much as, a group activity demands. But as we pointed out in Chapter 3, not all students can meet these expectations. Children who speak little English, for example, may be quickly lost in any discussion requiring them to express themselves in English. And in general, very young children cannot reasonably be expected to explain themselves verbally at any great length. Selman and Kohlberg (1972) have created special activities to use with children as young as eight years old, but teachers of still younger children may find even these materials inappropriate for their classes. Some adult-oriented values clarification exercises include versions modi-fied for elementary children (including "Alligator River" mentioned above).

emphasis on language

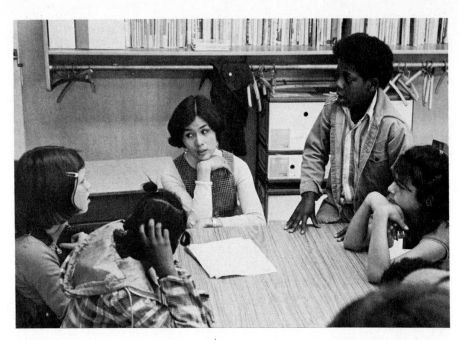

Like Kohlberg's suggestions for values education, the values clarification approach relies heavily on discussions and give-and-take about ethical issues. (Elizabeth Crews)

But if Piaget is right, such a modification still may not help the youngest children in schools: the youngest will still need to learn first by doing and only secondarily by talking.

How can morals and values be taught without words? Presumably through a combination of modeling good behavior for children and encouraging them to practice it in their school work and play. In Kohlberg's terms, this probably means shifting young children's concerns from the more self-centered ethics of rewards and market exchanges to the more community-oriented ethics of peers, laws, and social conventions. This shift, however, must be shown and acted out, rather than discussed. Although such teaching is prominent in the work of many individual teachers, it is not prominent in the literature on either values clarification or Kohlberg's stages.

Focus on Knowledge Rather Than Action

In addition to an emphasis on verbal skill, both Kohlberg's theory and values clarification emphasize knowing one's personal values or ethics, somewhat at the expense of acting on them. Though both approaches may sometimes use situations or dilemmas taken from the students' own lives, they tend on the whole to confine themselves to ensuring clarity and insight, rather than actual moral behavior. Both programs assume that insight will lead the students to various kinds of good deeds, good either for themselves or for others. As educational programs, of course, perhaps neither one could do otherwise. In our society, children's schooling occurs separately from the rest of their personal lives. Because of this fact, schooling must often rely on discussions of events rather than on the events themselves, and on knowing rather than doing. Or at least it must do so in reference to the complex problems of living, including the development of morals and values.

ethical beliefs versus ethical actions

Preference for Individual Values over Communal Needs

In one way or another, the two approaches support the individual person as an authority regarding values. External forces like parents, the community, or religion are considered less legitimate sources of values, unless, of course, the values that they propose are honestly and freely espoused by the individual. Values clarification expresses this attitude especially clearly in its introductory statements (see page 95). Elsewhere, one of the authors examines the role of the individual in the approach:

individual choice

> The values-clarification approach does not aim to instill any particular set of values. Rather the goal of the approach is to help students to utilize the above seven processes of valuing in their own lives; to apply these valuing processes to already formed beliefs and behavior patterns and to those still emerging. (Simon et al., 1978, p. 19)*

Kohlberg's stage theory also favors individualism, even though some of the stages also consider community needs and norms. By discussing moral dilemmas, the students are supposed to reach their own conclusions about the nature of good and bad. They are supposed to do so no matter how primitive or advanced their own ethical ideas may be and no matter what the ethical notions are that other people propose to them. Even if they adopt a community-oriented ethics (like stages 3 or 4), they do so—or should do so—by their own free choice. Furthermore, in the long run, they should give up even convention-directed ethics in favor of the self-direction of stage 6, the one based on autonomous moral principles. According to Kohlberg, then, ethics derived from external sources are only a temporary way of thinking, gradually overcome as children develop.

*Reprinted by permission of A & W Publishers, Inc., from *Values Clarification: A Handbook of Practical Strategies for Teachers and Students* (New Revised Edition) by Sidney B. Simon, Leland W. Howe and Howard Kirschenbaum. Copyright © 1972; Copyright © 1978. Hart Publishing Company, Inc.

The emphasis on individual values and ethics certainly supports one of the basic goals of North American education, namely, to help all children and students develop to their fullest potential. It does not, however, directly support another basic goal of education, namely, to help children and students get along despite their diverse backgrounds and interests—and values. Values clarification might argue that a reconciliation between self-values and community values will inevitably occur if students can become clearly enough aware of their personal valuing processes. Some psychologists and educators, though, do not agree that self-knowledge always leads to a greater commitment to community needs, as opposed to simply a more refined form of selfishness (Lockwood, 1975; Stewart, 1975).

Other psychologists and educators believe that Kohlberg, as well, values community commitment less than personal development (Fraenkel, 1976; Peters, 1975). Too, they believe that Kohlberg should emphasize more the middle, convention-oriented stages in his practical suggestions to teachers. Most school children and students are moving into these stages during their school years; at most, they will have recently arrived at them. **priorities among stages** Very few, if any, are at or near the highest, more principled stages. Teachers therefore need plenty of suggestions about how to strengthen their children's commitments to rules per se (stage 4 ethics) or how to improve their children's tact and diplomacy (stage 3 ethics). Some of the techniques used by values clarification seem promising in this regard, but as pointed out earlier, many of them do not relate to questions that are specifically ethical. Other techniques for helping the middle stages might be borrowed successfully from schools in other societies. Some writers have described the educational systems in the Soviet Union and China, for example, in which teachers rely heavily on groups as a device for motivating and managing students (Bronfenbrenner, 1970; Kessen, 1976).

The Teacher's Role: Value-free or Value-able Education?

Moral education and values education will continue to challenge teachers as long as teachers retain their major role in introducing children and students to the society in which they will be living. As a classroom teacher, you can expect your children or students to vary in their ethics and values **awareness of ethical diversity and similarities** just as much as they vary in other ways. In some ways, of course, their variety may simply cover up underlying common principles or values: everyone may believe in cooperation, for example, even if individuals disagree about how to show cooperation specifically. Teachers therefore should know both the common ethical ground of and the differences among their students, and they must do so despite the limited time and competing demands on their attention.

In a way, teachers who teach in schools may have an especially large responsibility for fostering their students' moral development. Such teachers work with the young, who presumably have more to learn about what society considers right and wrong than do adults. Such teachers also have an especially large amount of time to work with their students, more than in most other instructional situations and sometimes even more time than the students have with their own parents! And as is not the case with many other teaching and learning settings, society requires all young people to attend the classes offered in schools. Society does so, in part, because it deems the contents of school instruction to be ethically good for all individuals, and not merely useful or practical.

These are heavy responsibilities for school teachers to bear, but they are actually not confined to the schools. Teachers in business or military training programs often consider it part of their job to convey some sense of ethics to their students: how things *should* be done in that particular corporation or military unit, as well as how things actually *are* done. Nurses who teach patients about health care usually do so from some ethical basis that they hope their patients will also acquire. They may believe that staying healthy is a very important value, important enough, in fact, to be worth some inconvenience at times in using certain medications or following certain treatments.

Sometimes, no matter what institutional setting they work in, teachers are too pressed for time to deal with questions of values as explicitly as Kohlberg and other educators recommend. Instead, they may incorporate ethical issues into other curricular activities or even try to avoid dealing with such questions altogether. But this does not, however, alter the responsibility that most teachers have for developing ethical beliefs of some sort in their students.

Given the pressures of teaching, you, too, may be tempted to avoid concerning yourself with ethics. After all, you may say, by remaining neutral on questions of values, do you not show the greatest possible tolerance for your students' ethics? Unfortunately, as some writers mentioned earlier have pointed out, no merely human teacher may be able to respond to students in a truly value-free way. Even if you could, you would not really be showing your tolerance of fully formed ethical positions but, rather, your tolerance of your students' incomplete ones.

moral education in different settings

inevitability of teaching values

Key Points

1. Piaget identified two stages of moral belief, moral realism and moral relativism.
2. Moral realists are more aware of and responsive to rules set by parents, teachers, and other authorities, whereas moral relativists are more aware of and responsive to rules set by peers.
3. Lawrence Kohlberg has identified six stages of moral belief, which span a wider range of de-

velopment than do Piaget's.
4. According to Kohlberg, in the first stage of moral development, children judge right and wrong on the basis of punishment, reward, and obedience to external rules.
5. In the second stage of moral development, they do so on the basis of fair or marketlike exchanges.

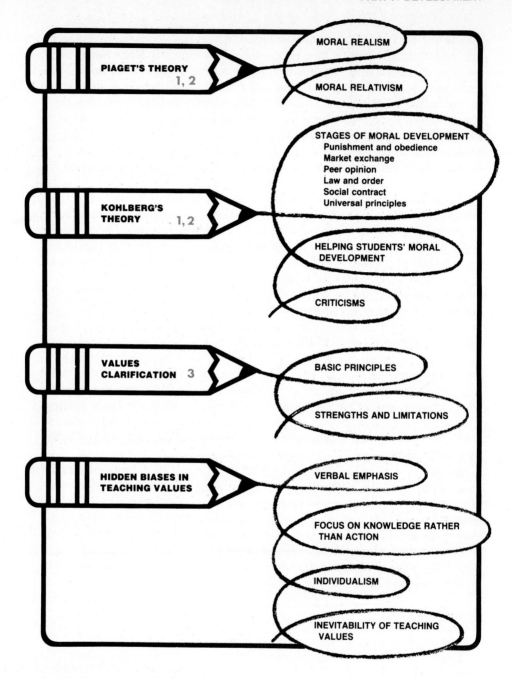

1 Piaget's theory of cognitive growth
   (Chapter 2)

2 Other stage theories (Chapters 2, 5, and 11)

3 Motivation (Part III)

6. In the third stage, they do so on the basis of peer opinion.

7. In the fourth stage, they do so on the basis of law and order.

8. In the fifth stage, they do so on the basis of social contract.

9. In the sixth stage, they do so on the basis of universal ethical principles.

10. Each stage (except the sixth) contains inherent limitations that help lead people to the next higher stage of ethical thinking.

11. Teachers can help students move through these stages by posing ethical dilemmas to them and then discussing solutions at one stage higher than their existing stage of ethical thinking.

12. Kohlberg's theory of moral development has been criticized for placing overly heavy demands on teachers to diagnose and respond appropriately to stages, for having questionable universality, and for not considering the effect of specific reinforcements on specific ethical behaviors.

13. Values clarification is an approach to fostering moral development that consists of responding to certain indicators of values, using certain clarifying responses to those indicators, and leading various group exercises related to values.

14. Values clarification consists primarily of practical activities for teachers and other group leaders, and it is not based on a large body of developmental research.

15. Both Kohlberg's theory and values clarification emphasize verbal skill in discussing ethical issues.

16. Both focus on beliefs about right and wrong, rather than on actual deeds or behavior.

17. Both favor individually held values rather than communally determined ones.

18. Teachers should be aware of both the diversity and the similarity in their students' values.

19. Moral education differs somewhat according to the setting in which it occurs, but it shows certain universal qualities in all settings.

Case Study

Alligator River and Moral Development

Joe read the following story to his twelfth-grade class. He found it in the book *Values Clarification:*

> Once upon a time there was a woman named Abigail who was in love with a man named Gregory. Gregory lived on the shore of a river. Abigail lived on the opposite shore of the river. The river which separated the two lovers was teeming with man-eating alligators. Abigail wanted to cross the river to be with Gregory. Unfortunately, the bridge had been washed out. So she went to ask Sinbad, a river boat captain, to take her across. He said he would be glad to if she would consent to go to bed with him preceding the voyage. She promptly refused and went to a friend named Ivan to explain her plight. Ivan did not want to get involved at all in the situation. Abigail felt her only alternative was to accept Sinbad's terms. Sinbad fulfilled his promise to Abigail and delivered her into the arms of Gregory.
>
> When she told Gregory about her amorous

escapade in order to cross the river, Gregory cast her aside with disdain. Heartsick and dejected, Abigail turned to Slug, with her tale of woe. Slug, feeling compassion for Abigail, sought out Gregory and beat him brutally. Abigail was overjoyed at the sight of Gregory getting his due. As the sun sets on the horizon, we hear Abigail laughing at Gregory. (Simon et al., 1978, pp. 291–292)*

Afterwards Joe asked his students to respond in writing to the story, concentrating on the question, "Which character behaved the most badly and why?" The question sparked a lot of interest, and Joe later had quite a lively exchange with his students. Here are a few of their responses:

*Reprinted by permission of A & W Publishers, Inc., from *Values Clarification: A Handbook of Practical Strategies for Teachers and Students* (New Revised Edition) by Sidney B. Simon, Leland W. Howe and Howard Kirschenbaum. Copyright © 1972; Copyright © 1978. Hart Publishing Company, Inc.

Arlene: I don't know who was worst, but I think Ivan was the best of the five—or at least the "least worst." He managed to avoid a conflict with the others. The rest of them each must have made *somebody* mad by what they did, but not Ivan. Even though it doesn't say so, I bet he had the best chance of coming out as everyone's friend.

Bill: I think Abigail behaved the worst because she should have known that she might be caught for playing around with Sinbad. It's really her own fault; if you sleep with someone when you're not supposed to, you're bound to get punished somehow—by getting pregnant if not by being discovered.

Carrie: I think Slug was the worst for having assaulted Gregory. In real life that kind of attack is against the law. Sinbad's bargain was pretty underhanded, too, but, strictly speaking, it isn't against the law if Abigail consented. And it isn't even all that unusual, either, in this day and age.

David: I can't decide whether Sinbad or Slug was worse. Slug was certainly bad because he hurt Gregory physically—which I can never approve of. But Sinbad may have been just as bad if his unpleasant bargain mentally hurt Abigail in some permanent way. His bargaining may have been a kind of "rape," even though it looked like a free choice by both of them.

Evelyn: I really cannot decide who is the worst in this story. I suppose that Sinbad should not have made Abigail sleep with him. But on the other hand, she was always free to refuse him; so they both made a bargain. Also, Abigail managed to get back at Gregory by having Slug beat him up. So everyone came out even in the end, didn't they?

Frank: Slug was the worst, because his assault clearly broke the law—although I can sympathize with his behavior. It's too bad that somebody cannot change the laws to help Abigail, though. Maybe if they all could be miraculously transported to the capital, they could persuade the lawmakers and the public to prohibit what Sinbad did as well as what Slug did. So Sinbad did not really do anything wrong.

Questions for Discussion

1. Try classifying each response according to Kohlberg's six stages. Explain your reasons for each classification. If you think any responses can belong sensibly to more than one stage, explain why.
2. If you were the teacher of these students, how would you respond to what each one said? Try formulating your responses at levels just higher than each student's apparent level of ethical thinking. If you think any student belongs to Kohlberg's stage 6, how would you respond helpfully to him or her?
3. Devise a few activities or discussion topics to follow up on this values clarification activity. Try to design them so that they help students confront higher stages (in Kohlberg's sense) of moral thinking. Note that none of these has to apply to the needs of all of the students equally well, since their needs presumably vary.
4. Suppose you taught third-grade children instead of twelfth-grade youth. How could you modify the story to make it appropriate for the age of your children? Try revising it first yourself, then check *Values Clarification,* pages 292–293, for a version that its authors wrote for just such a purpose.

Suggested Readings

Arbuthnot, J. B., and D. Faust. *Teaching Moral Reasoning: Theory and Practice.* New York: Harper & Row, 1981.

Hersh, R. H., J. P. Miller, and G. D. Fielding. *Models of Moral Education: An Appraisal.* New York: Longman, 1980.

Windmiller, Myra, N. Lambert, and E. Turiel, eds. *Moral Development and Socialization.* Boston: Allyn & Bacon, 1980.

These are three general discussions of the issues and problems of moral education and moral development. In one way or another, each book compares Piaget, Kohlberg, and values clarification, as well as other significant approaches to this topic. Each book also discusses ways that teachers can encourage moral development in students.

Bronfenbrenner, Urie. *Two Worlds of Childhood: U.S.A. and U.S.S.R.* New York: Pocket Books, 1973.

The author describes some major differences in child rearing and education in the United States and the Soviet Union and how these differences may influence the character or ethical sensibilities of children and youth. The descriptions of teamwork in the Soviet Union are helpful in evaluating the advantages and problems of the more individualistic ways of North America.

Kohlberg, Lawrence. *The Philosophy of Moral Development: Essays in Moral Development.* New York: Harper & Row, 1981.

This book is probably the single most comprehensive presentation of Kohlberg's stage theory of moral development. It is part of a series of three volumes planned for publication during the next few years. Later volumes are supposed to focus somewhat more than this one on the educational applications of the theory.

Simon, Sidney, L. W. Howe, and H. Kirschenbaum. *Values Clarification: A Handbook of Practical Strategies for Teachers and Students.* Rev. ed. New York: A & W Publishers, 1978.

This book, which was quoted several times in this chapter, contains many practical suggestions for activities that stimulate and develop ethical awareness in children and youth. For similar suggestions intended specifically for helping handicapped children, see Simon, Sidney, and O'Rourke, *Developing Values with Exceptional Children* (Englewood Cliffs, N.J.: Prentice-Hall, 1977).

Chapter 5

THE SOCIAL CONTEXT

OF LEARNING

James Fenton, business leadership trainer: I've been teaching leadership courses privately now for several years. Mostly to small businesses. Their managers want to improve their effectiveness or boost the staff morale. So they contract with me for workshops or courses—like the one in "assertiveness," or in "public relations skills."

It's sure different from teaching high school! I used to teach business in high school, so I know. My students are real adults. They're serious about achieving all they can in their businesses, and about making a real contribution to the local community. I like that a lot—except that sometimes it puts me on my toes. I can't lecture *them* about "what a business career is like," because they already know. My high school students, as I remember, were still making up their minds a lot of the time.

I have to be pretty careful about any practical suggestions I give to adult students. For instance, one time I led a discussion where I kept urging them to build workers' self-confidence by expecting good results from the workers. I thought it was a pretty good idea, but when I started getting really eloquent about it, one of my students squashed my enthusiasm. He was a manager, I think, in a small department store. "I tried that positive expectations idea last year," he said, "but it didn't work. My people just thought I was faking it. You've got to be sincere about what you expect."

Overall, though, my courses usually succeed. I think it's partly because I get very special students—pretty well established financially and already believers in education. That helps a lot. But they aren't all alike, either, not by any means. I know one fellow, for instance, who really bungled my assertiveness training course by being *too* aggressive all the time, instead of just moderately assertive like you're supposed to be. When I talked to him afterwards about it, he agreed that he overdid it but said he thought he needed to. "Where I came from," he said, "you had to push—or be pushed!"

Sometimes I wonder what makes one student so different from another—so much more aggressive, or more articulate, or whatever. I suppose part of it comes from differences in ability; but then, where do *those* differences come from? A person's social experiences *must* matter somehow: his family and what they value, what his education was like, and that kind of thing. I bet it matters a lot, too, how much people really care about you as you grow up.

But those influences all get so tangled up in real, live students! That's something I learned from *both* high school and adult students. The best students are *not* all alike. They never are in their backgrounds, either. They can be rich or poor, male or female, black or white. What counts is their uniqueness, at least in my classes.

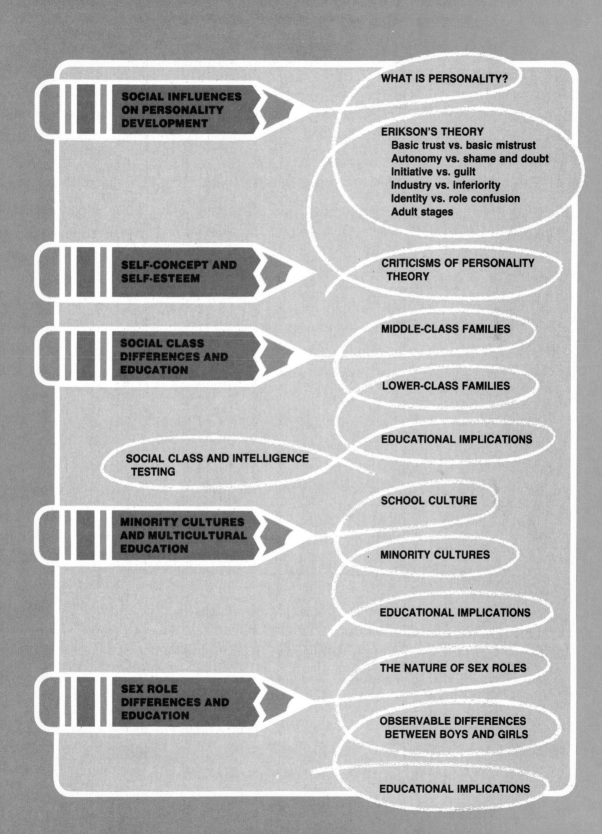

SOCIAL INFLUENCES ON PERSONALITY DEVELOPMENT

WHAT IS PERSONALITY?

ERIKSON'S THEORY
Basic trust vs. basic mistrust
Autonomy vs. shame and doubt
Initiative vs. guilt
Industry vs. inferiority
Identity vs. role confusion
Adult stages

SELF-CONCEPT AND SELF-ESTEEM

CRITICISMS OF PERSONALITY THEORY

SOCIAL CLASS DIFFERENCES AND EDUCATION

MIDDLE-CLASS FAMILIES

LOWER-CLASS FAMILIES

EDUCATIONAL IMPLICATIONS

SOCIAL CLASS AND INTELLIGENCE TESTING

MINORITY CULTURES AND MULTICULTURAL EDUCATION

SCHOOL CULTURE

MINORITY CULTURES

EDUCATIONAL IMPLICATIONS

SEX ROLE DIFFERENCES AND EDUCATION

THE NATURE OF SEX ROLES

OBSERVABLE DIFFERENCES BETWEEN BOYS AND GIRLS

EDUCATIONAL IMPLICATIONS

PEOPLE, of course, usually live and grow in the midst of other people and usually organize themselves in certain political, social, and cultural ways. This seemingly obvious statement has important implications for teaching and learning, and so this chapter will examine some of them. It will look first at how society helps create particular qualities and needs in all individuals at certain points in their lives; then, at how experiences (especially schooling) can influence self-respect; third, at how economic and cultural circumstances can affect students' readiness and motivation to learn; and fourth, at how sex roles may (or may not) determine what children think, feel, and do. None of these social influences has a simple, direct effect. But they all indirectly influence development and learning, whether the students are young or old or are learning in a public school or some other place.

Teaching and learning always happen in a social context: among people, in a certain society, and for certain cultural reasons. Instructors have to take this context into account if they hope to teach effectively. By affecting whom individuals become as people, social influences also affect whom they become as students. Public school teachers may see such influences especially clearly, since they often work with a cross section of students for relatively long periods of time. But social influences also affect short-term teaching and learning: in business and military training programs, for example, or in recreation programs attended by the community. In all cases, the students reflect the community from which they come, or more precisely, they reflect their particular aspect or segment of society.

SOCIAL INFLUENCES ON PERSONALITY DEVELOPMENT

What Is Personality?

Personality is a person's enduring, unique qualities—the attitudes, feelings, and typical style of behaving that distinguish that individual as a person. Often, though not always, the term *personality* includes cognitive traits like intelligence or special thinking skills. But it usually does not include bodily features, like being overweight or having red hair, even though these may sometimes indirectly affect behavior. Throughout life, personality grows at least partly out of a person's social relationships, though at the same time it contributes to these and even determines which relationships a person is willing to foster at any particular time. To the extent that teaching and learning are social experiences, then, the personalities of teachers and learners will affect their nature and success.

Psychologists have proposed various theories of how personality develops and functions (Hall & Lindzey, 1979), but not all of these theories have been equally useful for teachers in their work. Classical psychoanalysis,

personality defined

for example, as originated by Sigmund Freud and his followers, proposed that children go through stages that are motivated by sexual drives and by the children's unconscious efforts to disguise their sexuality in socially acceptable forms. The theory has proved useful for many psychotherapists trying to understand and help individuals with personal problems. But it has never achieved widespread popularity among educators, possibly because teachers usually deal with children's conscious processes (their thinking and choosing, for example, rather than their hidden or unconscious motives). Classical psychoanalysis, in addition, seems to neglect children's social relationships, which figure heavily in classroom life.

limitations of psychoanalytic theory for educators

Erikson's Theory of Personality Development

One theory of personality development that has responded to these criticisms is that developed by Erik Erikson (1963). He proposed eight stages in the development of the child's social relationships which account for the formation of the child's personality (see Figure 5–1). Four or five of these stages normally occur during the school years. The others, especially the two preschool stages, help put the school-age developments in perspective. Each stage requires that the child choose between new, relatively risky ways of acting and feeling and older, safer, but essentially unprogressive ones. Most children resolve these crises by adopting a mixture of older and newer behaviors, with the balance preferably leaning toward the newer ones. Each crisis, in addition, must be resolved by the combined efforts of the child and the other people in his or her life: in this sense, Erikson's theory depends on social relationships. In other ways, though, it shows the unmistakable influence of classical Freudian psychoanalysis. For example, several of the stages in Erikson's theory parallel the stages that Freud proposed for the development of personality. And Erikson's ideas do not deny the importance of sexuality or unconscious processes in human development; instead they broaden this classical focus in two ways. First, Erikson's theory emphasizes conscious motives and is more apt to accept them at face value, and second, it gives more importance to what happens between children and those around them.

eight stages of personality development

Crisis 1: Basic Trust Versus Basic Mistrust   During the first year of life, children must somehow convince themselves that their world, including the people in it, is dependable. They must come to believe that they will be fed when they are hungry or be comforted when they are tired or lonely. But because their needs during infancy are unpredictable, their parents may have a hard time proving themselves worthy of their baby's trust!

basic trust

A few children, in fact, never do learn to depend on others adequately. If you encounter any of these children in your class, you may find yourself

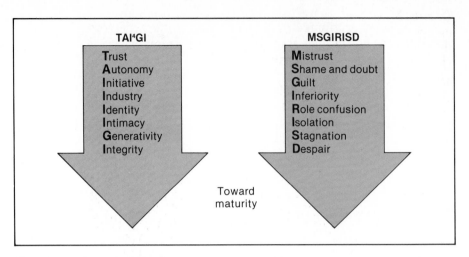

Figure 5–1 Stages of Development According to Erikson

proving over and over to them that you genuinely care about them *personally,* and not just their performance. With luck, you may be able to do this without showing undue favor to these children or otherwise violating your standards of fairness in the class. But until they can somehow trust the important people around them, the relationships that they form will remain distorted.

Crisis 2: Autonomy Versus Shame and Doubt   As children become toddlers, their concern shifts to the issue of autonomy. How, they now ask, can I begin to assert my own will without jeopardizing the closeness with my parents that we all have worked so hard to establish? Their first expressions of independence may come as a surprise to their parents: refusing to eat certain foods they usually enjoy, perhaps, or urinating at

autonomy   the wrong time or place. Somehow, according to Erikson's theory, parents must allow their children to make these choices without undermining either their confidence in doing so or the continuing love between and among the family members. This can be difficult if children assert their autonomy by endangering their safety (what if they insist on playing with matches?), or if the parents had a hard job establishing rapport in infancy and therefore feel rejected by this declaration of independence.

Teachers, too, may encounter such problems with students who have never resolved the crisis of autonomy. These students may, for example, insist on breaking class rules apparently just to see if it can be done or just to assure themselves that they still have minds of their own. In extreme cases, you may be so busy recovering from these bad incidents that you have little energy left to value these students as persons. Your relationship with them may then deteriorate seriously.

Crisis 3: Initiative Versus Guilt

By the preschool years, children usually have assured themselves that they can in fact influence some of the decisions that affect their lives. They then begin to explore the limits of this control by initiating a variety of actions, behaviors, or "projects," as they now might be better called. Unlike the previous crisis, in which children could only approve or veto activities that others determined for them, children can now actively construct simple plans for themselves: they may choose to get a chair, for example, stand on it, and help themselves to a cookie. Their parents may welcome some of this initiative and dread other parts of it. Even though they may want to encourage their children to take action, they will also need ways to limit these initiatives so that they do not hurt themselves or interfere with the rights of other family members. They must find a balance, and they must do so without spoiling their rapport with their children or their children's willingness to continue taking initiatives.

initiative

Table 5–1 Erikson's Eight Stages of Development

Positive aspect of stage or crisis	Versus	Negative aspect of stage or crisis
Basic trust: mutual harmony, regulation, and satisfaction with care-taking person.		*Mistrust:* lack of mutual harmony, regulation, and satisfaction with care-taking person.
Autonomy: confidence in one's own right to make decisions.		*Shame:* fear and dislike of one's own willfulness.
Initiative: confidence in one's own particular plans or actions.		*Guilt:* self-blame for one's own particular plans or actions.
Industry: motivation to perfect certain skills and confidence in one's own ability to do so.		*Inferiority:* indifference to and lack of confidence in perfecting certain skills.
Identity: belief in one's own continuity as a personality.		*Role confusion:* uncertainty about one's own continuity as a personality.
Intimacy: motivation and confidence to become close to others.		*Isolation:* indifference to and lack of confidence in becoming close to others.
Generativity: motivation and confidence to contribute significantly to society.		*Stagnation:* indifference to and lack of confidence in contributing to others.
Integrity: belief in the essential rightness of one's life work and relationships.		*Despair:* uncertainty and fear regarding the rightness of one's life work and relationships.

By the time they have reached this crisis, children are well into the preschool years and may even have entered school. Unlike the previous two stages, then, some teachers may encounter the crisis in its normal form, and not only among children who have carried it over from failures at some earlier point in development. If you teach very young children, you may need to ask yourself how you might encourage them to try a variety of new activities, but in ways that keep them from causing undue grief to you, the other children, or the materials in the classroom.

Crisis 4: Industry Versus Inferiority   During the elementary school years and often into high school, children move from a concern for whether they can carry out activities of their own choosing to a concern for perfecting certain specific skills or competencies that they deem important. No longer is it sufficient simply to try out new activities; now, in addition, *industry* they must be done well. Playing baseball or pounding the piano, for example, no longer produces enough satisfaction; now batting skills must help win games, or piano playing must sound like real music. This attitude, which Erikson calls industry, amounts to a form of achievement motivation, and it pervades much of children's school life as well as their home life. Their parents and teachers are challenged to help them succeed in ways that both give them a feeling of accomplishment and avoid any discouragement from undue failure (Erikson's "inferiority").

Teachers of children in this stage need to set standards high enough to challenge them, but not so high as to prevent them from succeeding. Finding that balance, in fact, is one of the main problems of teaching every-*inferiority* where. But we should remember that educational standards may have to be different for each student. What they achieve, according to Erikson, does not matter as much at this stage of development as their feeling of accomplishment.

Crisis 5: Identity Versus Role Confusion   Assuming that children, with help from their parents and teachers, succeed in building genuine competencies, their attention eventually will shift to the long-term meaning of their own skills and temperament. By adolescence, instead of wondering whether they will ever be good at math, say, or baseball or *identity crisis* playing the piano, they will begin to wonder what kind of people they have become and can expect to become. Children in this stage ask, "Who is the 'I' or 'me' underlying all of my daily activities and daily changes in moods?" The process of facing this question is what Erikson sometimes refers to as the **identity crisis**.

Children's parents, teachers, and friends can help them resolve this crisis, but they will not usually do so quickly or smoothly, given the complexities and ambiguities that most young people experience in their own behavior. Teachers, in particular, can offer a special perspective on young people's identities and goals, one more detached than the parents' and

Forming a stable and positive self-identity can be a major concern for many adolescents, whatever their particular life circumstances. (Karen Rosenthal/Stock, Boston)

more mature than the children's peers'. Often they are familiar with young people's school interests and abilities: yet unlike parents, teachers have less need to see their children use their talents in particular ways.

Crises 6, 7, and 8: Adult Stages   Erikson's theory covers the entire life span, and the last three stages tend to occur after most children have completed their public schooling. In the next stage (crisis 6, "intimacy versus isolation"), young adults shift their attention from their own identities to how they might form close relationships with another person or with a few others. At the same time, they fight the danger of becoming permanently cut off from all deep personal relationships. This crisis may be resolved by marriage for many young people, but by no means all of them. In crisis 7 ("generativity versus stagnation"), adults, now middle aged, become concerned with how to contribute to society's welfare in genuine, meaningful ways—whether through a job or family rearing, or in some other way. If they can find no genuine way to contribute, they run the risk of stagnation, or finishing a life that adds up to "nothing." In the final crisis (crisis 8, "integrity versus despair"), older adults must sort

intimacy

generativity

out their accomplishments and mistakes, realize that there is no way to turn back the clock in order to relive their lives, and accept having lived their lives as well as possible in the existing circumstances. Erikson calls such acceptance **integrity**; without it, the individual may resolve the crisis through despair.

integrity

These stages have important implications for teachers of adult students. Adult students already know who they are and where they are headed better than many adolescents and most children do, and they may even have acquired lifelong personal commitments to spouses, children, and other relatives. Under the right circumstances, this all may motivate adult students very effectively. A particular adult may approach a course in, say, auto mechanics with truly admirable confidence because he knows from long experience that he has talent for that subject. And he may approach the course with considerable drive because he believes that it will contribute to his competence at work or because it will allow him to earn more money for his family. By the same token, the same factors can sometimes make certain older students virtually impossible to motivate. The course in auto mechanics, for example, may not appeal to certain students because they know—again, from experience—that they lack the aptitude for it or because they suspect it will lead their career in directions that may spoil their family life. In general, adult students can make such decisions more firmly and finally than adolescents and children can.

relevance to teaching adults

Indirectly, Erikson's later stages of personality development can also help teachers of adolescents and children because they explain some of the needs and motives of the parents and grandparents of these younger students. Parents must, for example, feel that their lives matter to someone and that they have somehow contributed to society over the long run. Their children, however, may be too young to appreciate their parents as individuals or as workers, or they may be too bent on achieving their own independence to admit whatever respect they do feel. In this situation, teachers can help by not taking children's indifference to and criticisms of their parents at face value. Their direct contacts with parents often show them to be human beings, too, contrary to the impressions that their children may sometimes convey.

relevance to understanding parents

As their children approach adulthood, many parents find themselves taking stock of the child rearing that has kept them so busy for the past fifteen or twenty years. They may find themselves wondering whether they, as parents, really did do the best they could have done. Again, their own children may hardly be the best people to answer such a question. Others—notably spouses, mature relatives, friends, or counselors—may be far more helpful. Although teachers generally play a relatively small part in this process, they should at least remain aware of and sympathetic to its existence. Some day, after all, they too may wonder whether their own lives have been well spent.

Criticisms of Personality Theory

Many psychologists have criticized personality theories, including Erikson's, for their basic assumption: that individual people really do have enduring traits (Mischel, 1973). In Erikson's theory, children seem to be building permanent qualities as they move from one crisis to the next: during infancy, they acquire a trustful quality (we hope), followed by the abilities to act autonomously, with initiative, and industriously. Or so it seems. As children successfully resolve each crisis, they add a new permanent quality or trait to their personalities, which, the theory implies, they can use repeatedly in their daily living. In this way, apparently, their "selves" emerge.

As sensible as this picture may seem, it may exaggerate the consistency of real human behavior. Suppose that children do successfully resolve Erikson's first crisis in favor of basic trust: can we count on them to behave in a trusting way forever after? Common sense says no; it says, in fact, that all sane, healthy children should sometimes behave cautiously (*without* trust), no matter what their official stage of development—for example, when walking down a dark street at midnight.

lack of consistency in human behavior

A lot of research supports this common-sense observation of variability in behavior (Mischel, 1973). In one study, high school students were given special training for a few weeks in a subject area, but the training was arranged so that some of the students were successful, whereas others failed or else received no information at all about their performance. Later they were allowed to choose between a relatively small reward for simply having taken the training and a larger one that they would receive only if they had succeeded at another task similar to the ones done during training. Those students who had previously been successful chose much more often to "take a chance" on the larger reward. The effect, in fact, overshadowed any opinions they had had about their chances for success at the start of the training program; even pessimistic students suddenly became optimistic about their prospects (Mischel & Staub, 1965). Any general quality of "industry" did not have much to do with how they reacted to the situation. In this situation, therefore, knowing students' stages—and therefore their personal qualities—could not have helped teachers predict the outcome very well.

Erikson and other personality theorists, of course, might argue that general personal qualities, like those described in his theory, refer to tendencies or dispositions to act a certain way. After all, no one would be foolish enough to propose that a person's behavior never varies. Children who have acquired basic trust, for example, may indeed sometimes behave cautiously, but their underlying tendency consists of trusting behaviors. And the high school students described above may well respond to particular success experiences in unusual ways, ways that are out of character

significance of personality tendencies

for some of them. Nevertheless, personality theorists argue that they will behave more or less industriously or ambitiously over the long run, regardless of any exceptions to the trend. Resolving the crisis of industry and inferiority really means showing such a trend, not behaving industriously every time.

For us teachers, the important question about personality theory may come down to how well it actually helps our teaching and what dangers it poses for oversimplifying our students' behavior. Stages of personal development like Erikson's do offer useful notions for organizing our general expectations and plans for students. Some of the implications of Erikson's theory have already been mentioned above.

General stages may not be so useful, though, in diagnosing and planning a detailed program of study for an individual student. At this practical level, the overall developmental process is quickly obscured by the daily actions and interactions of a student's behavior that make it seem so variable—and unique. Take those students supposedly moving between crisis 3 (initiative) and crisis 4 (industry). Could you plan *all* of their activities as if they had acquired the ability to take initiative in *every* possible situation but were still preoccupied most of the time with proving their competency? To do so would probably miss many of the subtleties and inconsistencies of your students' daily behavior and would probably reduce your effectiveness as a teacher. Your problem, then, is to keep in mind your students' general needs, while being able to recognize those complications that contradict the trends.

danger of oversimplified view of daily behavior

SELF-CONCEPT AND SELF-ESTEEM

As children become adolescents, they gradually develop ideas and feelings about themselves as people—their **self-concept** and **self-esteem**, respectively. They may think of themselves as likeable, intelligent, friendly people—or as being the opposite sorts of people. Because their behavior may include contradictions, they may also try to reconcile conflicting experiences into some deeper, more enduring assessment of themselves: they judge themselves to be "rather friendly," for example, meaning friendly most of the time but not always. In general, their evaluations of themselves—their self-esteem—becomes tightly woven into their knowledge of themselves. Knowing that one can fix mechanical things, for example, can hardly be separated from having an opinion about whether this ability is good, bad, or mixed. This evaluation may not correspond to the ones that other people may make, but a person will make one, nevertheless.

self-concept and self-esteem defined

The concept and esteem we each have of ourselves depends on both our own choice of what facts about ourselves to consider significant and the reactions of others to these facts. Two students may both have mathematical talent, but for various reasons, only one of them may consider this talent an important fact about herself, that is, a part of her self-concept. Or two students may be about equally friendly, but for various reasons, the quality may be noticed by others in only one of them. In either case, the same personal trait may lead to different self-concepts or self-esteem.

Self-Esteem and School Achievement

Several research findings suggest that students' senses of self-worth affect their motivation in school (Covington & Beery, 1976; Purkey, 1978). Students who feel good about themselves set relatively high goals for themselves, yet not so high that they do not have a reasonable chance of reaching them. But students with lower self-esteem may set goals that are either unrealistically high or else extremely low. They do so, apparently, because going to extremes protects them from the anxiety of failure: an extremely high, difficult goal is "safe" because success seems so unlikely: "nothing ventured, nothing failed," in this case. Because these motivational patterns can profoundly affect students' educational careers, they are discussed again in more detail in Chapter 11. The effects of low self-esteem can, unfortunately, accumulate: as failure-avoiding students move through school, they have fewer and fewer successful experiences, and failure avoidance becomes more and more a part of their lives.

relationship between self-esteem and motivation

By their nature, and without intending to, schools may indirectly widen the gap between students with high self-esteem and those low in it. Why? For one thing, schools sometimes prevent students from setting their own goals, goals that might maximize their personal feelings of achievement, and therefore their self-esteem. Instead, some teachers may feel obliged to complete designated pieces of curriculum during designated time periods ("Let's finish long division by Christmas"). Although teachers usually try to match these goals to the abilities and interests of their students, they probably cannot be expected to do so for every student in every class. Unfortunately, such students are likely to be evaluated by the same tests and standards as are the students who better fit the teacher's expectations and therefore may be reminded repeatedly of their "limitations." This is especially likely to occur if the teacher's grading system relies on competition or its varieties—only so many A's, gold stars, or whatever—so that one student's success automatically means another student's loss.

Although some students respond with enthusiasm or even vigor to these facts of school life, others may reach various negative conclusions: that success is beyond their personal control, that the effort to learn benefits only the teachers and not the students themselves, that the rewards of learning have nothing to do with the subject matter, or that the rewards of learning depend rather much on luck. For such students, the achievement values of school do not capture their attention as much as its "dark side" does, that is, the constant threat of failure.

Enhancing Self-Esteem Through Teaching

Even though high self-esteem and high achievement motivation are related, it is not easy to say which one causes the other. Presumably students' feeling good about themselves will give them confidence to attempt school work, as well as to reduce whatever anxiety they feel about failing. On the other hand, consistent and genuine success at school work should improve students' feelings about themselves, since school success is so widely respected in our society. As teachers, we can intervene at either point in this relationship, and with a variety of techniques. Some of these are discussed more fully in Chapter 12, but here we shall study a few, as well. For still more information, see W. W. Purkey, *Inviting School Success* (1978).

Using Positive Expectations   In various ways, you can convey to your students that you believe they can do well, though to be effective, your belief must be sincere. After one group of educators found that three very different curricula for young children created equally good academic improvements (Weikart, 1972, 1981), they concluded that they must have done so because of the teachers' generally high morale and positive expectations. The ways that such expectations influence students seem subtle and complex, but they are nonetheless real.

Unfortunately, one of the most well-known studies of the effects of expectations, that by Rosenthal and Jacobson (1968), was later shown to contain serious flaws in its methodology. Their study seemed to show that schoolchildren's achievement is dramatically improved when their teachers are misled into believing that their students have exceptional ability. This "self-fulfilling prophecy" effect received considerable publicity and was nicknamed the "Pygmalion effect," after a play by George Bernard Shaw that was constructed around the same theme. Subsequent efforts to repeat the study in its original form, however, have generally failed—though even this finding might be interpreted as the self-fulfilling prophecy of skeptical psychologists (Wilkins & Glock, 1973).

effects of self-
fulfilling
prophecies

Despite the failure of the Rosenthal and Jacobson study, a careful review of expectation research in general suggests that through their behavior, teachers do convey expectations about student performance, even though these expectations do not always lead to simple or dramatic effects on student performance (Braun, 1976; Willerman, 1979, pp. 195–199). In some cases, teachers may call on favored students more often than on others, respond more positively to their comments, or even smile more often and broadly at them (Ensor, 1976; Palfrey, 1973).

Conversely, teachers may unconsciously ignore certain students even when the students try to contribute to class discussions or activities, or teachers may criticize the errors of some students more than they do others. Or they may "save" favored students until last during a recitation (question-and-answer session), thus giving the favored ones the advantage of hearing earlier attempts at answering the teacher's questions. Less favored students then must deal with classroom questions without having as many clues—a more difficult task and therefore more likely to lead to failure and criticism. One research study even found that teachers' stereotypes regarding children's names affected the rapport that teachers and children established: children with more "desirable" names, as rated by the teachers, eventually established more positive relationships with their teachers than did children with less desirable names (Garwood, 1976).

By their very nature, such behaviors cannot be controlled easily, but their importance to students makes it essential for teachers to try. As a first step, teachers can make themselves aware of their own expectations in the classroom.

Ensuring a Pattern of Success   In addition to communicating positive expectations, as a teacher you can arrange as many learning experiences as possible to ensure that everyone in your class experiences reasonable amounts of success. To be valuable, this success must come from genuine and reasonable levels of effort. As pointed out earlier, success on very easy tasks does not enhance self-esteem, since the student merely thinks, "Anybody can do that." On the other hand, success on very hard tasks may be discounted, especially by low achievers, as mere luck or a gift from the teacher, rather than an actual achievement. You will need, therefore, to learn what tasks give a "middling" challenge to your students—the kind that creates the greatest feeling of success and therefore the biggest gains in self-esteem. Chances are, again, that your students will vary among themselves in what achievements they consider genuine, and you will have to be alert to these differences.

encouraging sense of genuine achievement

Encouraging a Climate of Cooperation   In general, the research suggests that both self-esteem and achievement improve in classrooms in which students often cooperate with one another and interact among themselves (Johnson, 1981). Teachers can encourage such a climate by avoiding negative criticisms in their conversations with students and by not reinforcing such criticisms when they occur between students. In addition, teachers can consider using criterion-referenced tests (see Chapter 13), evaluations based on absolute standards rather than comparisons among students. Or they can experiment with the various methods of discovery learning (see Chapter 12), to allow students to regulate the pace and difficulty of their own tasks. Teachers can also reward students for helping one another, perhaps through group projects or other joint efforts.

These suggestions should not be taken to mean that there should never be any competition in schools, but only that it should be tempered with more humane or cooperative techniques when it becomes excessive. In fact, students sometimes actually demand the chance to compete with one another and look for signs of status where none really exist (for instance, "How many comments did the teacher write on *your* paper?"). To work

creating a healthy mix of competition and cooperation

well, though, their competition must meet two assumptions. First, the students must begin with roughly the same abilities, skills, or advantages; and second, they must not take the outcomes too seriously, lest they refuse to participate at all in the future. In most classrooms, these assumptions may indeed be met some of the time, but they are probably also violated often enough to cause real grief for some students—and to lower their self-esteem. The suggestions above are intended to help you keep a healthy mix of cooperation and competition in your class whenever you feel that they are getting out of balance.

SOCIAL CLASS DIFFERENCES AND EDUCATION

In spite of our society's democratic ideals, families vary considerably in personal wealth, and their economic differences have indirect, but important, implications for teaching and learning. As a rule, people at particular places on the economic scale develop particular ways of life that justify calling them a **social class**. Because its economic situation and lifestyle are related, social class sometimes also goes by the name of **socioeconomic status**, or SES for short. Social scientists often define and study several social classes. Educators, however, have usually concerned themselves with the differences between two broad SES groups, the middle class (who earn middling incomes) and the lower class (who earn very little). Members of the second group are sometimes considered to be *disadvantaged,* since for various reasons they participate in society with a handicap. What are the essential differences between the middle and lower classes, and how do these differences affect teaching and learning?

*social class and
SES*

Middle-class Families and Their Children

Compared with lower-class families, families with middle incomes tend to concern themselves more with their future material and personal development. A father is more likely to consider his work to be a career rather than a job—a long-run, permanent investment in his and his family's welfare and one that will eventually pay off handsomely in both personal and material rewards. A mother who works may also regard her work as a long-run career, and even when she does not work for pay, she may engage in volunteer activities that have many of the same qualities that a career has. Both parents are apt to encourage their children to take an equally responsible, long-run concern for their education; in a sense, schooling becomes the children's career—a sometimes painful but worthwhile investment in their future (Leslie, 1979; Piotrkowski, 1979).

future orientation

Compared with members of the lower class, middle-class parents more often involve themselves with other people and groups—and sometimes

Children learn important skills and attitudes at home which affect their success in school, either for better or worse. (Christy Park/Monkmeyer Press Photo Service)

quite a bit more. Their contacts can occur through either work (business contacts, for example) or volunteer activity (parent-teacher groups, for example). Their children may parallel this involvement by participating in extracurricular activities of their own—community sports teams, special music lessons, social clubs, or the like. Again, this involvement is determined in great part by the encouragement—and chauffeuring—of the parents.

involvement with community

Middle-class family members value independence and individual initiative in their children relatively highly, although not to the exclusion of obedience. Parents reflect this mix of attitudes when, for example, evaluating their children's misdeeds: compared with lower-class parents, they are more likely to consider their children's intentions along with their actual misdeeds (Wright & Wright, 1976). The value placed on independence may also be seen in another peculiarly middle-class custom, that of giving every child in the family his or her own room, or at least allotting the fewest possible children to any one room. Presumably this practice gives each child a haven from the crosscurrents of group living and helps reinforce some sense of his or her individuality. Fortunately, middle-level incomes usually allow purchasing or renting the relatively expensive housing needed to implement this practice.

independence training

Lower-class Families and Their Children

Those individuals at the bottom end of the economic scale are too preoccupied with their immediate survival to make long-range plans for their future. Making ends meet becomes relatively more important: ensuring continued employment, a place to live, or even sufficient food (Macarov, 1980). Such concerns leave little time or money for involvements in the
survival
orientation
community, let alone for involvements of children in clubs or lessons. Residents of disadvantaged communities may want the good things of life—education, security, success—just as much as anyone else does. But they may not know how to procure them given their circumstances, and they may not actually believe that society wants or will allow them to succeed even if they try (Coles, 1968–1977; Ogbu, 1974).

The circumstances of poverty, some have argued, also lead members of the lower class to value obedience in their children relatively highly. As adults, they frequently find themselves needing to follow other people's rules carefully, whether made by landlords, employers, welfare workers, or even their children's teachers. Training children to mind their elders is a good preparation for these later experiences. Unfortunately, it may sometimes also make certain disadvantaged children seem "dull" in school by discouraging them from taking the initiative and acting independently even when their teachers expect it.

Educational Implications of Social Class

Use of Language   One of the most important implications of social class involves language use. At home, disadvantaged children are less likely than more favored ones to use language to solve school-like problems or to carry on school-like discussions (Karnes & Zehrback, 1977). By the time such children enter school, their language style may not fit classroom requirements very well. For example, instead of giving reasonably elaborate answers when questioned, they may volunteer only short phrases
class-related
language styles
or even single words; or instead of speaking in turn, they may not hesitate to speak whenever they want. Compared with middle-class youngsters, lower-class children may use more slang and obscene language, and they may be relatively awkward about using language courtesies ("Could I please have one?" versus "Give it to me!"). If they are bilingual or if they speak a nonstandard dialect of English, these differences in style may be even more noticeable. By the standards of careful, classroom English, their language may seem "deficient." Nevertheless, as pointed out in Chapter 3, nearly all children have good language ability and speak some language or dialect quite well; they differ mostly in how well their language and language style fit conventional classroom expectations (see, for example, Tough, 1977).

Performance of Learning Tasks Social class differences affect, though not in any simple way, how favored and disadvantaged children perform on learning tasks. One study illustrated this idea well by comparing children's success on several different tasks, all of them reminiscent of school activities (Yando et al., 1979). One task was simply reading sentence cards; another was balancing various small objects on a box while walking; and still another was thinking of unusual uses for a teaspoon. Comparisons of middle- and lower-class children showed different patterns of achievement for each group, but no consistent advantage for either one. The verbal skills of middle-class children helped them do better on the reading task, as might be expected, but they showed much less confidence than the disadvantaged group did on the balancing task. The latter group also did better at thinking of unusual uses for a teaspoon, in the sense of producing more ideas easily, fluently, and confidently. Their responses, however, were not as original as the middle-class responses were, according to judges who did not know which children belonged to which social class.

class-related patterns of problem solving

Based on these and other results, the study suggested that middle-class children do not really always have an advantage in problem solving. As a group, many of them seemed overly concerned with achieving and rather anxious about failing. Compared with the disadvantaged children, middle-class children seemed more likely to hesitate if they did not think their answers or performances would be "right," and they asked for help less often if they got bogged down in their solutions.

Social Class and Intelligence Testing

The Nature of Intelligence Tests Disadvantaged children have consistently scored lower than middle-class children have on tests of general ability or "intelligence" (see, for example, Willerman, 1979). This fact may not really conflict with the findings of the Yando study described above, however, because of the nature of general ability tests. Typically they demand verbal skill and the ability to find single correct answers—both qualities that Yando found more frequently in middle-class children. A few questions from one well-known intelligence test, the Stanford-Binet, are listed on page 415.

The items on such tests are selected to predict success in school: children who get them right also tend to earn high grades, and children who get them wrong tend to earn low grades. To an extent, then, intelligence tests sample those thinking skills that children most often need to succeed academically, although they do not intentionally sample the actual content of school curriculum. The procedures for testing vary with the test, but typically, easy items come first and hard ones come later, until a point arrives at which the child cannot (or will not) answer any more questions

prediction of school success

correctly. The results are interpreted in standardized ways which are ex
plained in Chapter 14. Whatever other information the test provides, i
always also gives a single number, the **IQ score**, that reflects how well
child performed compared with other children of his or her age.

The Heredity-Environment Controversy Psychologists and th
general public have argued about how much IQ scores reflect inborn, ge
netic differences among individuals and how much they reflect the effect
of different learning environments. Evidence for both kinds of influenc
comes from a variety of kinship studies. Identical twins, for example, ten
to have IQ scores that are more similar than those of fraternal twins
Identical twins are, by definition, completely alike genetically, wherea
fraternal twins are no more alike than ordinary brothers and sisters are
The greater similarity in IQ for identical twins must therefore come from
their shared heredity. This idea is further supported by studies of adopted
children. These children tend to have IQs more similar to those of their
biological mothers than to those of their adopted mothers.

On the other hand, identical twins reared together also have more similar IQs than do identical twins who, because of special circumstances,
were reared apart. Since in this case both groups are equivalent genetically, the greater similarity in IQ for the "together" twins must come from
their shared life experiences.

Psychologists have found similar trends for other combinations of relatives and living situations. In general, IQs tend to be more similar for
relatives who by definition share more heredity, and less similar for relatives who share less (siblings versus second cousins, for example). Furthermore, IQs tend to be more similar for combinations of relatives or
individuals who live together than for the same combinations that live
apart (Rice et al., 1980).

Using certain statistical techniques on these kinship studies, psychologists have tried to estimate the relative contributions of heredity and
environment to IQ scores, but for various reasons they have not reached
a consensus on this issue. A few estimates have claimed very high genetic
contributions (for example, Jensen, 1969), but most have considered the
genetic influence less important than the environmental one, or else impossible to determine (Bouchard & McGue, 1981). One difficulty in making
such estimates is the scarcity of certain kinship situations—there are not
many twins reared apart, for example. Another difficulty is separating
genetic and environmental influences; for example, siblings share many
experiences as well as many genes. Still another difficulty is the impos-
sibility of knowing whether the typical environments of individuals really
affect their IQs as much as an ideal, or best, environment might: it is still
possible that ideal learning conditions might greatly outweigh genetics in
determining IQ, but educators have not yet devised such conditions.

No matter how this controversy is resolved, teachers will still have

evidence for both
influences

current opinion
about sources
of IQ

much to do in providing the best possible experiences for their students. A good bit—and possibly most—of verbal, analytical thinking skill appears to come from the experiences that children have. Since, however, children clearly have not had equal amounts of experience when they enter school and since thinking skills may not be the only form of intelligence, teachers face two related questions. First, how can they help individual children make up for their lack of particular thinking skills? And second, how can they ensure that their curriculum draws on those thinking skills that all children, including disadvantaged ones, do have? These questions will be discussed further—and, we hope, answered—in Chapters 7 and 8. Chapter 7 examines the varieties of cognitive learning that all students engage in, and both Chapters 7 and 8 suggest how teachers can systematically plan instruction for these varieties.

MINORITY CULTURES AND MULTICULTURAL EDUCATION

Students' motivation and preparation for school are affected not only by their economic backgrounds but also by their cultural backgrounds. A **culture**—the entire pattern of behaviors and beliefs of a group of people—often includes a particular language or dialect (see Chapter 3), but it includes other elements as well: ways of becoming and being a friend, for example; attitudes about the comparative importance of the past, present, and future; or customs about how to participate in a group activity. Cultural patterns vary with particular **ethnic groups**: groups with common national or racial origins. They also vary with the region of the country that a group lives in, and with its economic level. These facts make most modern societies—including that of the United States—truly *multicultural*. These facts also often create confusion between the notions of culture and economic class (Lewis, 1978). Members of some minority cultural groups live at economic levels significantly below national averages, but their culture or way of life is not necessarily equivalent to or determined by their depressed incomes.

factors affecting cultural patterns

Conflicts Between School Culture and Minority Cultures

In a number of ways, life in schools is a culture in the sense defined above. In the United States and Canada, this school culture closely resembles the culture favored by the majority of their societies' members. For better or worse, this culture sometimes conflicts with those of various minorities, and in order to teach effectively, educators must respond helpfully in these situations.

Elements of School Culture   Educators have identified several aspects of school culture that have particular relevance to nonmajority students (Maehr, 1974; Trueba et al., 1981). Here is a sampling of them:

1. Although there are many differences among schools, teachers, and students, all schools tend to encourage individual accomplishment and its frequent partner, competition. Group projects or activities do occur, but they usually are not the main basis on which students are evaluated. As both a cause and an effect of this emphasis, schools also tend to value individual freedom quite highly, and sometimes at the expense of loyalties to friends or relatives. Students sense this aspect of school culture most clearly and painfully when, for example, they try to maintain ties with friends with whom they must also compete on tests or in major sports events. Sometimes the ties can survive these pressures, but often individuals feel forced to choose between an important relationship (for example, a boy friend or girl friend) and school success.

2. School culture values efficient use of time and "keeping busy." Very few classrooms (perhaps even none) make relaxed, quiet, and inward-looking behavior a major part of their day. Many allow for quiet times on a limited basis: for example, many have unsupervised, silent reading periods (sometimes nicknamed "USSR"), and often nap times occur in nursery or kindergarten rooms. But these usually form only a minor part of the school day, and they tend to be regarded as means to other educational ends.

3. School life distinguishes between work and play—often sharply. Certain activities are regarded by the teacher and the students as "work" (for example, reading lessons) and others are regarded as "play" (for example, recess time). The distinction exists in spite of continual efforts to combine the two forms of activity by making work fun. Students learn early to recognize when teachers expect them to work and how to conduct themselves differently when they do.

4. School culture, like the majority culture in general, looks upon nature as something to control and use through technology rather than as something to contemplate and respect. Even efforts to create respect for nature (the ecology movement) often end up by recommending more technology as an antidote to existing technology (reducing smog by inserting emission control devices in cars, for example, rather than by encouraging less driving in the first place). Whole professions such as engineering have grown up to implement society's belief in technology, and schools prepare individuals for these professions by teaching mathematics, science, and various vocational subjects. Through the study of these subjects, even the majority of students who do not become actual implementors of technology learn to understand its basics and to value its use.

Elements of Minority Cultures   Generalizations about minority cultures must be made cautiously because cultures differ among themselves as well as from the majority culture. Within any minority, furthermore,

[margin notes:]
individual accomplishment and competition

efficient use of time

distinction between work and play

control of nature through technology

some individuals may participate much more fully than others in the ways and beliefs of that minority, and some members of a minority may participate more fully than others in the majority culture. Teachers must be sensitive to these variations and respond to students as individuals rather than as stereotypes.

differences within and between cultures

Nevertheless, for every value described in the previous section, minority cultures exist that foster opposing values in its members. The belief in individual effort and freedom, for example, runs counter to what many Mexican-Americans favor for themselves and their children (Ramirez & Castenada, 1974) and counter to the practices of many North American Indian groups (Mohatt & Erikson, 1981). These cultures often expect individuals to help one another far more than does the mainstream society, and they may value and reward group achievements and teamwork more highly than individual achievements.

group efforts valued

Such attitudes can affect when and how individual students choose to participate in class. Students from these cultures may restrain themselves from raising their hands during class discussions for fear of standing out from the group too much. Yet they may participate enthusiastically during individual, private encounters with the teacher, or during group or committee projects. Teachers unfamiliar with the attitudes underlying these patterns may misinterpret the students' behavior as laziness or incompetence, rather than as expressions of group solidarity or concern for others.

Compared with school culture, furthermore, some minority cultures do not value efficient, overt activity especially highly, nor do they foster it in their children. One study of meetings and everyday conversations in a particular Indian band showed that these encounters occurred at what most Anglo-American teachers would consider a very leisurely, slow pace (Fox, 1976; cited in Mohatt & Erikson, 1981). Even the pauses between individual comments were much longer than normal by usual school standards.

slower pace of interactions

Similar tendencies toward slow, "inefficient" interactions have been reported for other minority groups (Hymes, 1974), though by no means for all or for all individuals within any one culture. Perhaps as a result, one study of a Mexican-American classroom (LeComte, 1981) found that the teachers spent considerable energy reminding the students of the timeliness of activities ("It's not time to do that now") and of the inherent scarcity of time in school ("Pretty soon we'll have to go on").

Some cultures do not distinguish as clearly between work and play as school culture tends to do; instead, all activities are thought to have some qualities of both. A study of Hawaiian children concluded that many of these students underachieved in elementary reading because they often did not perceive traditional reading instruction as "work." As a result, they did not take the teachers' efforts seriously enough; and although they did learn to some extent, they did not achieve as well as expected on the basis of early evaluations of their abilities. Teachers often stereotyped

blending of work and play

these children as "unmotivated," but these evaluations were right only from the perspective of conventional school culture. Conventional remedies, such as new curriculum materials or behavioral reinforcement, worked rather poorly. The solution for these children consisted instead of helping their teachers to conduct themselves in ways more in keeping with Hawaiian culture: treating reading as a form of group storytelling, for example, and emphasizing the mutual participation of teacher and students in reading activities (Au & Jordan, 1981).

While some minorities encourage more social sensitivity in their children than does the majority culture, other minorities encourage respect for and sensitivity to the physical world and its organization (Maehr, 1974; Witkin, 1977). The ecological sensitivity of the latter groups may be especially high: their sense that the world consists of many interacting and mutually dependent parts. Such an orientation may question the value of studies based on a technological point of view, at least if that point of view focuses too narrowly on specific technological problems and therefore ignores their broader relationships. Studying the biology of the forest may be good, for example, but *not* studying how to cut down trees most efficiently for lumber production, especially if cutting them down destroys the forest.

respect for physical nature

Educational Implications

Teachers can make instruction more effective by responding to the features of minority cultures described above. In doing so, however, they must keep in mind that individual minority students belong to their cultures to varying extents. Some may have very individualistic or competitive attitudes even if their culture does not encourage it, just as some majority culture members may have very group-oriented attitudes. These individual differences make the suggestions below more beneficial for some individuals than for others. Since, however, the suggestions generally encourage diversity of content and teaching methods, they are helpful for every teacher and classroom.

Cultural Content   One obvious way to make instruction more multicultural is to include, wherever practical, minority cultural content in the curriculum: to commemorate holidays as minorities do or to study historical events and leaders important to minority cultures. Teachers unfamiliar with such content should make themselves more knowledgeable about it, either through academic study or through in-service training, preferably provided by members of minority cultures. The exact content to be learned depends on the cultural composition of the local community and on the subject where the content is to be included.

teaching about cultures

Because a culture encompasses the entire lives of its members, making education truly multicultural requires more than just turning cultures

Whenever possible, teachers should include in the curriculum aspects of diverse cultural backgrounds. (Nancy Hays/Monkmeyer Press Photo Service)

into objects of study. Wherever possible, students must become immersed in a culture and its characteristics; only by doing so can they really get the feel of the culture and of how it creates a broad pattern for living. For this reason, among others, school staffs should include members of minority cultures in schools where the students come from those cultures in significant numbers. For this purpose a staff consists not only of teachers in charge of classrooms but also of other teaching-related personnel such as teacher aides, bus drivers, and school secretaries. Given the history of discrimination against some minorities, finding qualified minority staff— and especially university-trained ones—can pose a problem, but finding them can be (and has been) done.

hiring members of cultural groups

Such individuals can provide links between minority and school cultures. Ideally, they understand both worlds well enough to help students begin understanding both worlds, too. Sometimes such understanding consists literally of understanding and using two languages—English and a minority language. Even when minority students do not need linguistic translations to get along in school, though, they may still benefit from cultural translations: comments and responses from experienced minority members that help in interpreting the unfamiliar school culture in terms of the familiar minority culture.

Classroom Monitoring   Teachers who do not belong to a minority culture, however, can also help make multicultural learning possible and effective. One way consists of monitoring classroom **participation structures**: the patterns of who gets to participate in activities and discussions, and under what circumstances (McDermott & Gospodinoff, 1979). Simple checklists can supplement the teacher's own memory in making such monitoring effective (see Chapter 13 on informal observations); the checklist can record which students initiate or respond during discussions, for example, or during free work times. Written anecdotes about what students actually say and do during these times can fill in some additional details and can also serve as a supplement to the most valuable resource, the teacher's own informal memories.

observing the structure of participation carefully

Altogether, such monitoring can give clues about when and how minority students prefer to participate—and for that matter, about how all students prefer to participate. In some cases, the teacher can respond by giving individual students more of the participant situations they seem to prefer. In other cases, however, the teacher may respond by devising ways for students to practice and become comfortable in new, relatively untried forms of participation (Au & Jordan, 1981). The right mixture of strategies will depend on the needs of the particular students.

Diverse Modes of Instruction   Studies of thinking styles suggest that different cultural groups may emphasize different sensory modes for solving problems. The ability to visualize spatial relationships, for example, was found to be especially strong among Chinese-American children (Stodolsky & Lesser, 1967) and among several American Indian groups (Kleinfield, 1973). Compared to Anglo-American children, these children could solve complex jigsaw puzzles relatively easily. The advantage did not, however, apply equally to all individuals from these groups.

These facts suggest that good multicultural teaching may mean providing a diversity of teaching methods wherever possible (Cazden & Leggett, 1981). Mathematics problems, for example, might be presented in several different ways: as word problems (verbally), as pictures or diagrams (visually), and perhaps also as objects to manipulate (tactually). As it happens, the general reliance on variety in teaching supports what other

presenting problems in several ways

educators and psychologists have suggested for making instruction more effective for all children (see Chapter 8).

Allowing for Differences in Cognitive Style   A body of research suggests that individuals differ in how much they mentally divide the physical world into specific pieces (Witkin, 1974, 1977). Individuals who tend to think in this way perform relatively well when they must find a simple figure within a more complex one. Their skill is sometimes called **field independence**, and its opposite is sometimes called **field dependence**. Individuals with the latter quality are not necessarily less skillful people; other research has found, for example, that field dependent individuals tend to be more socially sensitive and skillful with people.

Some studies suggest that certain minority cultures may foster field dependence comparatively more than does the majority culture (Ramirez & Price-Williams, 1974). These results have prompted educators to devise educational programs that capitalize on the strengths of field dependent individuals and that compensate for their relative limitations. One of these plans (Ramirez, 1974) encourages the formation of relatively personal relationships between the teacher and students while also encouraging the teacher to provide more than the usual amount of organization to the educational program. The first strategy presumably takes advantage of the field dependent students' skill at forming and profiting from close social relationships, and the second strategy presumably provides them with more of the structure in their thinking that they supposedly need. As students become more field independent, the teacher is supposed to modify strategies accordingly: in particular, he or she is supposed to expect increasing amounts of self-planned learning from such students.

compensating for cognitive styles

Some educators have criticized this approach to multicultural education (for example, Cazden & Leggett, 1981). For one thing, they point out, the qualities of field independence and field dependence constitute only tendencies within large groups of individuals; basing an entire educational program on them therefore risks stereotyping members of minority cultures almost as badly as traditional beliefs have done in the past. Any particular Mexican-American, for example, may be hardly more likely to show "field dependence" than to show any other type of stereotypical behavior. Teaching programs, the critics argue, should be based on individual differences, not on cultural differences.

Furthermore, some argue that the strategies for teaching field dependent individuals do not really constitute multicultural education. Instead, the strategies simply advocate suggestions often made for good teaching in general. Fostering personal relationships is a mainstay of humanistic education (Chapter 12), and structured teaching is favored in some form by most cognitively oriented educators and psychologists (Chapters 7 and 8).

SEX ROLE DIFFERENCES AND EDUCATION

The Nature of Sex Roles

Our society has many ideas about the differences between boys and girls. One sex (can you guess which?) is supposedly more warm and nurturing, whereas the other is supposedly more assertive and aggressive. Girls co-operate and follow; boys compete and take initiative. Girls need things fixed; boys fix them. And so on: the list can become quite lengthy, especially when it refers to our society's impressions of the two sexes, rather than their actual behaviors. These impressions, together with the behaviors that sometimes correspond to them, constitute our **sex roles**: the behaviors that we attribute to one another on account of our sex.

In many ways, sex roles have served valuable purposes, both now and in the past. For example, they give members of both sexes some widely accepted guidelines by which to conduct their lives. A woman adhering to her traditional role would give child rearing and family management a high priority in her life, and a man would give earning a living a high priority in his. Neither would need to devote time and energy to question-ing these priorities; they would simply get on with living their lives.

Furthermore, traditional sex roles reveal one obvious and eternal phys-ical difference between the sexes, namely, that only women can give birth to children. In older societies, in addition, the greater physical size and strength of men may have helped them with their breadwinning functions, such as hunting and certain aspects of farming. For that matter, greater size and strength still helps in many present-day occupations (for example, lumbering), and such occupations are still largely dominated by males. These physical differences between men and women may in turn contrib-ute to the stereotyped differences in the behavior of the sexes: more quiet nurturing in women, for example, and more aggressiveness in men. In the minds of many individuals, these patterns of behavior may seem quite sensible, natural, and inevitable—perhaps even inborn.

Although many people today still find clearly defined sex roles valuable and necessary, others have come to criticize them as constrictions from an earlier, less democratic era. Women, some have argued, can learn to assert themselves in ways traditionally associated with men, and men can learn to care and nurture personal relationships, as women have traditionally done. Individuals of both sexes should feel free to ignore conventional sex roles in order to be and become themselves; such an attitude, it is argued, simply applies democratic principles to questions of gender. Teachers pre-sumably should, therefore, encourage their students to liberate themselves from conventional role expectations.

These changing attitudes have created new confusion about what, in fact, now constitutes the female and male roles in our society. Teachers should recognize this confusion as much as should any other professionals who work with people, no matter how they as individuals might evaluate

sex-role stereotypes

support for and criticism of sex roles

the matter. Do sex-related traits really exist any more, and if so, which ones and how much? And supposing that differences do exist, then how should teachers deal with them? Suppose that it turns out that boys have more mathematical skill than girls do: then should teachers emphasize math with boys because they may profit from it more, or should they emphasize it with girls because they need the extra help? Both of these questions deserve answers, though psychology can speak to the first, more factual one more easily than to the second, more value-laden one.

confusion about sex roles

Observable Differences Between Boys and Girls

Maccoby and Jacklin reviewed hundreds of studies of sex differences (1974) with the intention of discovering the accuracy of such differences. They found that many of the common impressions of the sexes had little or no basis in fact or that such differences occurred only under very specific conditions. All of the following, for example, had research support:

1. Both girls and boys seem equally sociable, although they may express this quality differently.
2. Both girls and boys have equally high self-esteem.
3. Both girls and boys perform simple repetitive tasks equally well.
4. Both girls and boys are equally well motivated to achieve, although girls in fact express their motivation more consistently than do boys.

observed similarities

But Maccoby and Jacklin also found that several common stereotypes were well supported by research. They found, for example, that females of all ages show greater verbal ability than males do, but especially during adolescence and adulthood. In general, females tend to use language better, both for difficult purposes like verbal reasoning and for easy ones like speaking fluently. Males, however, tend to excel at "spatial reasoning"— the ability to put puzzles together, for example, or to find their way through a difficult maze. Beginning in adolescence, males also hold a slight edge in mathematical skills, even though they do not think more logically on the whole. And perhaps most noticeable of all, at least for teachers: males show more aggression of all kinds, whether in play fighting, verbal teasing, or outright fisticuffs—and they do so at all ages. Because this difference appears so early in life and because it can be seen across all cultures, Maccoby and Jacklin suggest that it may be biologically programmed at least to some extent.

observed differences

A large number of sex-role stereotypes, according to Maccoby and Jacklin's review, either have not been studied well enough for any conclusions to be drawn, or else the findings from research studies have been rather mixed. For example:

1. Are girls more timid and fearful than boys? They are if asked to report on their own feelings, but not if an outsider observes their behavior: then they act just as bravely.

conflicting evidence

2. Are boys more active than girls? Apparently not in general, though they may be more so in some situations, especially with other boys.

3. Are boys more competitive than girls? Sometimes, but then again, sometimes not.

4. Do boys tend to dominate girls? Not necessarily, because during most of the school years the sexes tend voluntarily to remain separate. In these segregated groups, boys show more concern about dominating one another; in mixed groups, the pattern is unclear.

5. Do girls show more nurturing or maternal behaviors than boys do? Little information exists to answer this question one way or the other, in part because there have been few studies of nurturance in boys and men. Among adults, the existing studies suggest that sometimes men are more kind and helpful, and at other times women are, depending on who needs help and the kind of help that is needed.

Educational Implications of Sex Role Differences

General Trends Versus Individual Differences   Since all of these findings refer to trends rather than individuals, teachers should consider both and treat them with a bit of skepticism. Even though females may perform less well than males do in math, for example, individual females may actually do outstandingly well in this subject. Or even though males and females may have similar levels of self-esteem, individual males or females may show rather low levels of it. Teachers must respond to individual differences, not to the trends that dictate what their students ought to be. At the same time, these trends can help teachers understand the general nature and extent of sex differences and help them guide their relationships with students accordingly.

But because there are some sex-related differences, even though they are not equally strong in all children or in all areas of behavior, how should teachers deal with them? For any particular teacher, the answer depends partly on the importance that he or she assigns to promoting sex-role equality and partly also on the importance that his or her students assign to it. Most teachers do not favor an extreme or rigid division of roles, however much they may joke about it. But many may allow or even encourage students to divide themselves along traditional sex-role lines if the students themselves seem to wish it. One girl may insist on becoming a secretary, even though she has outstanding math and science skills; another boy may refuse to express his feelings in front of his friends. Certain children of both sexes might delight in stereotyped stories like "Cinderella." Ordinary tolerance requires teachers to accept these traditional expressions of roles, even if they think students are overdoing them.

A more difficult question is whether to promote sex-role equality actively: should teachers try to lead students to new, more egalitarian viewpoints even if they do not demand it? Although the answer will vary

tolerating student attitudes

Teachers can enhance children's self-esteem by encouraging them in whatever activities they do well, even if these do not coincide with traditional sex roles. (© Kit Hedman/Jeroboam, Inc. [*left*]; Jean-Claude Lejeune [*right*])

among individual teachers, a majority would probably answer, "Yes, with moderation: many students would profit from new insights into sex roles." Two areas of teaching that may provide such insights are curricular materials and program guidance.

promoting greater
sex-role equality

Sex Typing in Curricular Materials   Many surveys have shown that textbooks at all levels of schooling often exaggerate the differences between males and females (for example, Pottker, 1977; Sprung, 1978; or Trecker, 1971). In general, girls and women are portrayed as staying closer to home, needing help, and following the initiative of others, who are likely to be males. In general, boys and men have more exciting adventures and seem to have more varied characters. These differences have been noticed even in mathematics texts, which do not usually tell stories as such but often do convey bits of social information in the course of presenting math problems (Jay, 1977). And differences also have been found among the toys of children of various ages, beginning in the preschool years (Queen, 1978). Such differences go well beyond those usually found in real life.

Countering such prestereotyped materials in your classroom may be difficult, though not impossible. Distortions of a character's role, for example, can sometimes become the object of discussion for your students, rather than simply an assumption underlying the discussion. Some toys

counteracting stereotyped classroom materials

for elementary children, in addition, can actually be used with either sex (a toy train set? a doll?), despite their sex-typed packaging or advertising. And in the long run, you can also keep your eyes open for more sexually even-handed tests and curricular materials; there are more on the market now than in the past. Finding them, however, does not mean that they will immediately be adopted by your school, since older materials often are used for many years, despite the biases they might contain. For instance, some older reading texts may show traditional divisions of the sex roles, but presumably they have taught a lot of children to read, anyway.

Program Guidance Research has shown a large imbalance in the help given to young men and women, including high school students, as they begin to think about careers. The problem seems to apply to both the official guidance that students receive from school counselors and the many informal conversations that they have with school staff, including classroom teachers. One study showed that adolescent women who inquired about engineering as a career received many more negatively biased comments from their counselors than did men inquiring about the same field (Pietrofesa & Schlossberg, 1970). The counselors were more likely to say, "The status of women is higher in teaching," for example, instead of, "There is more prestige in becoming an engineer." Or they might say, "One normally would think of this as a man's field," instead of, "There is no such thing as a man's world any more." Another study suggested that at least some of this bias resulted from the counselors' being uninformed about the current employment trends, especially those for women (Bingham & House, 1973): uninformed counselors may believe that career aspirations for women are more unusual than they really are.

reducing bias in career counseling

Such biases may not show "bad counseling" but, rather, the result of our society's long history of sex-role divisions. Boys and men traditionally have had a wide range of careers from which to choose, of which both counselors and classroom teachers have traditionally made themselves aware as much as possible. Girls and women, though, have traditionally had far fewer choices among paying careers, as well as one very common option, homemaking (Adams & Laurikiets, 1976). Males traditionally have had a lot of freedom in how to work, but not in whether to work; whereas females traditionally have had more freedom in whether to work than in how to work. Promoting sex-role equality, then, may mean helping males set other goals in life besides earning income, as well as helping females think about careers more seriously and realistically.

Key Points

1. Personality refers to an individual's enduring, unique qualities, and it therefore can affect the nature and success of learning in important ways.

2. A theory of personality development useful to educators is that originated by Erik Erikson, which consists of eight stages: basic trust, autonomy,

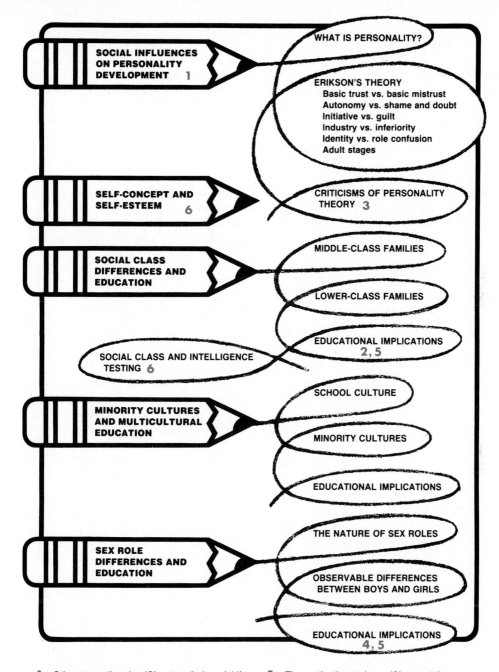

SOCIAL INFLUENCES ON PERSONALITY DEVELOPMENT 1
- WHAT IS PERSONALITY?
- ERIKSON'S THEORY
  - Basic trust vs. basic mistrust
  - Autonomy vs. shame and doubt
  - Initiative vs. guilt
  - Industry vs. inferiority
  - Identity vs. role confusion
  - Adult stages
- CRITICISMS OF PERSONALITY THEORY 3

SELF-CONCEPT AND SELF-ESTEEM 6

SOCIAL CLASS DIFFERENCES AND EDUCATION
- MIDDLE-CLASS FAMILIES
- LOWER-CLASS FAMILIES
- EDUCATIONAL IMPLICATIONS 2, 5
- SOCIAL CLASS AND INTELLIGENCE TESTING 6

MINORITY CULTURES AND MULTICULTURAL EDUCATION
- SCHOOL CULTURE
- MINORITY CULTURES
- EDUCATIONAL IMPLICATIONS

SEX ROLE DIFFERENCES AND EDUCATION
- THE NATURE OF SEX ROLES
- OBSERVABLE DIFFERENCES BETWEEN BOYS AND GIRLS
- EDUCATIONAL IMPLICATIONS 4, 5

1 Other stage theories (Chapters 2, 4, and 11)
2 Language differences and education (Chapter 3)
3 Learning as behavior change (Chapter 6)
4 Making instruction more effective (Chapter 8)
5 The motivation to learn (Chapter 11)
6 Reporting on learning (Chapter 14)

initiative, industry, identity, intimacy, generativity, and integrity. TAI"61

3. Each stage in Erikson's theory involves a crisis or transition in the social relationships of the
individual and in his or her personality.

4. Erikson's stages help in understanding the
motives and needs of students and sometimes also
of their parents.

5. Some research suggests that behavior is much
more changeable from one situation to another
than Erikson's theory implies.

6. Self-concept and self-esteem refer to individuals' ideas and evaluations of themselves, and
they are heavily influenced by the opinions and
feelings of others.

7. Students high in self-esteem set high, but
realistic, goals for themselves.

8. Teachers can promote high self-esteem by using positive expectations, ensuring a pattern of
success for students, and encouraging a climate
of cooperation.

9. Social class indirectly affects students' attitudes toward school.

10. Middle-class families tend to have a future
orientation, to be involved in the community, and
to train their children early to be independent.

11. Lower-class families tend to have a strong
concern for survival and to train their children
to obey specific, explicit rules.

12. Students' social classes affect their language
style, usually to the advantage of middle-class
students and the disadvantage of lower-class ones.

13. Although lower-class students tend to have
a disadvantage with verbal and written tasks in
school, they have advantages with certain other
skills, including some school-related ones.

14. Lower-class students tend to score relatively
low on intelligence tests, but a large part of this
difference can be attributed to disadvantaged
preparation for such tests.

15. School culture tends to value individual effort, competition, and the efficient use of time.

16. School culture also distinguishes between
work and play and values scientific control of the
environment.

17. Some minority cultures foster values that
conflict with major aspects of school culture, although minorities also differ among themselves
in important ways.

18. Schools can respond to cultural differences by
including more cultural content in their programs and by hiring minority members as staff.

19. Teachers can respond to cultural differences
by monitoring classroom participation carefully,
by providing diverse modes of instruction, and by
allowing for differences in cognitive style.

20. Sex roles refer to the behaviors that we perform and that are attributed to us on account of
our sex.

21. Sex roles have served useful purposes in the
past and, for some people, still do in the present.

22. The differences observed between males and
females do not necessarily correspond to the stereotypes commonly held by society.

23. Teachers should recognize and respect the individual differences among their students in regard to how much they adopt conventional sex
roles.

24. If teachers wish to promote greater sex-role
equality, two places to do so are in the school's
curricular materials and the program guidance
given to students.

Case Study

Diana

Today Diana drew a flower again. It was full of
the sun and sky, in bright pastel-chalk colors.
And with lots and lots of petals, a kind of daisy-
chrysanthemum. She worked for a good hour to
make it and then patiently lettered her name:
DIANA.

Diana draws many pictures, each full of intricate details and bright colors. Drawing seems to
be her medium, and for her, small is definitely

beautiful. Lots of five-year-olds, of course, make
lots of drawings, but Diana's stand apart because
of their complexity and because of Diana's way
of working on them.

She sits silently, head bent intently over the
paper, oblivious to her surroundings. Today, for
example, she sat between Jean and Maria—though
she never knew it. Jean and Maria chattered
steadily over her head: "Where's the red?" "My

mum took me to the doctor's yesterday." "Look what I made!" And so on and on. For them, drawing was a social event.

Meanwhile Diana drew her flower. She could have been alone, on a deserted island. Last week, in fact, she did use a table far away from the others. She made a house that time, in five colors. But working alone didn't matter to her: people or no people, the drawing was her concern, not the company. And her product showed it.

Questions for Discussion

For each of these questions, explain your opinions.

1. **a.** According to Erikson's theory of personality development, what stage or stages does Diana show evidence of in this case study?
   b. Can Diana be accurately classified according to Erikson's theory?
2. Judging by the information given in this chapter, does this incident suggest that Diana's classroom has been encouraging or discouraging her self-esteem?

3. Some education students who read this incident asserted, "Based only on what is written here, there is no way to guess Diana's social class." Do you agree or disagree?
4. **a.** How does this incident confirm or deny popular stereotypes regarding sex differences?
   b. How does it confirm or deny current research findings about sex differences?

Suggested Readings

Cedoline, Anthony. *The Effect of Affect: Over 100 Classroom Activities to Develop Better Relationships, Self-esteem, and Decision Making.* San Rafael, Calif.: Academic Therapy Publications, 1978.

Clark, Carolyn. *Assertiveness Skills for Nurses.* Wakefield, Mass.: Contemporary Publications, 1978.

Two short but practical books for building confidence; one intended for nurses, and the other intended for teachers and students.

Coleman, Richard, and Lee Rainwater. *Social Standing in America: New Dimensions of Class.* New York: Basic Books, 1978.

Keniston, Kenneth. *All Our Children: The American Family Under Pressure.* New York: Harcourt Brace Jovanovich, 1977.

Both of these books are discussions of the influence of social circumstances on individual life. The first book provides a more precise description than possible in our chapter on social class and related concepts. The second book is especially relevant to teachers of children and youth.

Lips, Hilary. *Women, Men, and the Psychology of Power.* Englewood Cliffs, N.J.: Prentice-Hall, 1981.

Tavris, C., and C. Offir. *The Longest War: Sex Differences in Perspective.* New York: Harcourt Brace Jovanovich, 1977.

There are numerous books about sex roles and their effects; these are two. Both look at how men and women influence each other in accordance with their sex roles, in a variety of settings: in the family, at work, in politics, and as individuals.

Pasternak, M. G. *Helping Kids Learn Multi-cultural Concepts.* Champaign, Ill.: Research Press, 1979.

Tiedt, P. L., and I. M. Tiedt. *Multi-cultural Education: A Handbook of Activities, Information, and Resources.* Boston: Allyn and Bacon, 1979.

These two books briefly discuss the need for multicultural education and then devote considerable space to ideas for implementing multicultural ideas in the classroom.

Sheehy, Gail. *Passages: Predictable Crises of Adult Life.* New York: Bantam, 1976.

This book describes many of the social influences on development during adulthood—from about age eighteen onward. It has many examples to illustrate its ideas and the stages it proposes.

Part II
LEARNING AND INSTRUCTION

Learning refers to any fairly long lasting change in behavior or thinking that results from a relatively specific experience. Instruction refers to any systematic efforts to cause learning to occur. The chapters in Part II examine how these two processes relate to each other—and sometimes fail to relate. Learning and instruction each can occur without the other: students sometimes pick up knowledge on their own, and teachers' efforts do not always result in learning. Teachers usually welcome the first process, but not the second one.

In order to make instruction successful, teachers need to understand the nature of learning. Chapter 6 considers this question and then focuses on those kinds of learning that consist of changes of behavior. We shall look, in particular, at how the association of stimuli can lead to new behaviors, how reinforcement can do so, and how observation and imitation can do so. Chapter 7 studies learning as thinking, as changes in ideas and their relationships that occur within the learner. Chapters 8 and 9 then discuss several implications of the nature of learning for designing instruction. Chapter 8 suggests ways of systematically planning instruction and making it more effective once it is under way. Chapter 9 examines the problems of coordinating the many demands on teachers who work with groups of students—including how to manage problem behaviors. Chapter 10 looks at the needs of exceptional students and at what their special needs imply for regular classroom instruction.

Chapter 6

LEARNING AS BEHAVIOR CHANGE

Joan Hammond, dental assistant: The dentist I work for tried an experiment that really surprised me: he paid some of our patients for having clean teeth. Actually he gave them a small refund on the cost of their visit if their teeth showed less than a certain amount of plaque—that "tooth fuzz" you get from not brushing and flossing.

Paying them made a real difference in their habits. Most of the people who knew they might get paid obviously made an effort to clean their teeth the way I had shown them when they first came in. Before the experiment, I had gotten pretty tired of explaining the right ways to brush and floss. It seemed that people just didn't listen, and I got tired of their not caring.

One of the patients said he thought paying people seemed like bribery. I suppose that in a way it was. The incentive came from outside the person and not from inside him. But not completely, because I still had to teach patients how to brush and floss effectively, just as I always did. So they still had to listen to me and care enough to earn their refunds. Anyway it worked, and that's important.

I must admit, though, that I'm still not sure that any of these people will keep up their new habits if we stop paying the refunds. The patients will *say* they'll keep them up, of course, but heaven knows they've promised that before.

I did discover one problem I hadn't expected. A few patients did not earn their refunds, and two of them suspected that I had purposely not inspected their teeth properly just to save money for the dentist! They were not convinced even when I showed them how I did it, with those "disclosing" tablets that stain your teeth and with careful probing with mirrors.

I guess they had a point—it's hard to convince people you're being fair about the refund if your own finances are affected by how many refunds you give. It's funny: this experiment is supposed to make more teeth clean, but now the dentist and I have a financial reason for welcoming teeth that are dirty! I guess somebody else should give out the rewards, to get us and the patients both out of this bind. I heard about another dental clinic that got a government grant to try this same idea, and apparently it worked better there.

142

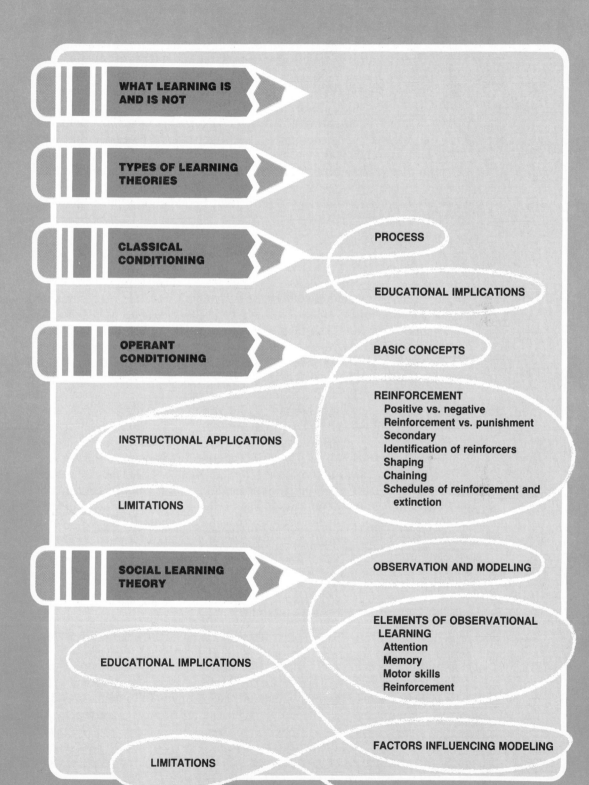

WHAT LEARNING IS
AND IS NOT

TYPES OF LEARNING
THEORIES

CLASSICAL
CONDITIONING

PROCESS

EDUCATIONAL IMPLICATIONS

OPERANT
CONDITIONING

BASIC CONCEPTS

REINFORCEMENT
Positive vs. negative
Reinforcement vs. punishment
Secondary
Identification of reinforcers
Shaping
Chaining
Schedules of reinforcement and
extinction

INSTRUCTIONAL APPLICATIONS

LIMITATIONS

SOCIAL LEARNING
THEORY

OBSERVATION AND MODELING

ELEMENTS OF OBSERVATIONAL
LEARNING
Attention
Memory
Motor skills
Reinforcement

EDUCATIONAL IMPLICATIONS

FACTORS INFLUENCING MODELING

LIMITATIONS

THIS chapter begins with a discussion of the nature of learning and how it differs from other sources of behavior change, such as instincts, maturation, habituation, or fatigue. We then shall describe the broad types of learning theories. In general, accounts of learning differ in their emphasis on changes in specific, observable behavior, compared with the relatively abstract and inaccessible thought processes that presumably lead to new behaviors. In the remainder of the chapter we shall examine three behaviorally oriented theories of learning: classical conditioning, operant conditioning, and social learning theory. For simplicity, those learning theories oriented to thought processes are left to the next chapter.

WHAT LEARNING IS AND IS NOT

Because schools are supposed to be for "learning," we teachers presumably ought to know what we mean by this term. Like a lot of other basic terms in psychology, though, the idea seems to be easier to use than to define. A child learns to behave, a parent learns about child rearing, or a worker learns to operate a new machine: the same verb describes them all, or tries to, as though the thinking and behaving needed for one were the same as for the others. But common sense says that learning comes in various forms and that these may differ widely—so widely, in fact, that they might really deserve separate names and explanations. Settling this question, however, leads to philosophical and psychological questions beyond the scope of this book. Thus this chapter, and the ones that follow, will take a moderate stand by assuming that some one phenomenon called learning does exist, even though it comes in a number of different forms.

learning defined

Most definitions of **learning** go something like this: learning consists of any relatively permanent change in behavior that is caused by some particular experience or by repetitions of an experience (see, for example, Hilgard & Bower, 1975). This definition, please note, rules out changes that occur by means of instincts, maturation, habituation, or physical fatigue.

learning versus instincts

Instincts are natural or innate behaviors that are not affected by learning or experience. Instincts are common to all members of a species—the behaviors of a bird, for example, in building a nest or feeding its young. Because instincts do not result from any particular experience, they do not qualify as learning. For most species, and especially for human beings, there are few, if any, pure expressions of instincts. More often, these expressions are heavily modified by learned behaviors. Students may flirt with each other (the sexual instinct), for example, but they have *learned* how to do this effectively; they were not born with the skill. Or they may eat, but only at certain times and places and with certain people and food—all of which have been learned. What stands out in these behaviors is not the instinctive element, but the learned one.

Students may also change their behavior from fatigue, but this change does not qualify as learning either. The first time that students listen to a teacher talking, for example, they may show a lot of curiosity about the teacher's behavior and style of teaching. If, by some misfortune, the teacher simply talks on and on and on, however, the students may eventually stop listening. They have not done so from learning, but from habituation—from experiencing too much of the same thing. They may not think, "This teacher is boring, and so I'll now start thinking about other things"; instead they just start doing so without quite realizing what is happening. The effect can be interrupted, of course, by any novel stimulus or significant change in situation. Someone's dropping a book on the floor may bring the students back to life, or better yet, the teacher may vary his or her style to hold their attention indefinitely.

learning versus habituation and fatigue

For teachers, maturation is the source of behavior change that is most easily confused with learning. **Maturation** here refers roughly to development, the topic covered in Part One. It usually refers to those relatively long term changes in behavior that are caused by either the child's physical growth or a multitude of specific environmental experiences (for instance, Piaget's conservation). In either case, the changes are beyond the control of any one person, including the child's teacher. Psychologists of development usually concentrate on the common changes in children, somewhat to the neglect of the reasons for their individual differences. But psychologists who study learning often emphasize individual differences somewhat more, though believing at the same time that common mechanisms of learning underlie the variety among individuals.

learning versus maturation

Some of the ways that teachers see maturation (or development) occur have already been discussed in earlier chapters. Children who cannot speak well when they enter kindergarten can talk fluently at the end of Grade 2. How much credit do their teachers deserve for helping this change occur? Probably some, but probably also not all, if part of their improvement depended on physical growth. Or consider this example: a Grade 7 student cannot understand the basic experimental methods in his science class, but by the time he enters college he can use them well. How much has he directly "learned" the experimental method from his classes, and how much has he simply grown into the knowledge, through some sort of mental maturation?

Since developmental changes often require important basic skills, we teachers would often like to take credit for having taught them. But an honest look at our efforts in some of these cases makes it difficult to point to particular times and ways that we caused a child to grow, develop, or mature. Perhaps we did contribute, but the evidence is hard to specify. We may remember a few special, "teachable" moments when we felt sure that we made a basic difference to a student, rather than only a small difference. But these moments are noteworthy partly because they rarely occur.

Most of the time, teaching consists of making many small differences to our students—perhaps that is why it can be hard work. We shall call these relatively small differences *learning,* remembering that they actually come in many different forms.

In Part Two, we shall consider several theories of how such learning occurs and how they might be used by teachers in their daily work. As a rule of thumb, you can expect different theories to be useful in different ways, and your choice of which to use will depend on your particular purposes. Over the long run, your purposes may be so varied that you will get some use from all of the theories.

TYPES OF LEARNING THEORIES

behavioral and cognitive theories

Learning theories can be divided into two broad groups, which this book will call "behaviorist" and "cognitive." These groups are divided according to a number of important issues, all related to their importance to studying the observable behaviors and conditions of learning, as opposed to the thinking that underlies most learning; hence the names *behaviorist* and *cognitive*. **Behaviorist theories** are concerned with the stimuli that immediately precede the learned behavior and often also with the consequences of the behavior, which are called reinforcements. **Cognitive theories** are concerned more directly with the less visible processes of human learning: memory, attention, insight, organization of ideas, and information processing. These terms are listed in Table 6–1, and all of the terms and people there are discussed somewhere in this book.

behaviorist focus

In general, the behaviorists would focus our attention on any relatively direct relationships between what we provide for our students and how they respond. By concentrating on their observable behaviors, we hope to be spared the need to form subjective judgments about why our students learn or fail to learn. It may be more important, for example, to know that your reprimands inadvertently cause a certain student to talk out of turn

Table 6–1 Behavioral and Cognitive Theories Compared

Theory	Terms	Theorists
Behavioral	Stimulus	Pavlov
	Response	Skinner
	Operant	Bandura
	Reinforcement	
	Conditioning	
Cognitive	Memory	Bruner
	Attention	Piaget
	Insight	Ausubel
	Organization of ideas	
	Information processing	

than to know why he responds to you in this way. Or it may be more important to know that one student works harder if you smile at her than to wonder why this might occur. These relationships among observables are the essence of teaching. Or so the behaviorist theories say.

A lot of student behavior, of course, cannot be easily explained by the relatively simple relationships among observed behaviors. One student, for example, may throw tantrums now and then for no apparent reason. Another student may work well on some days, but not on others, and depend rather little on whether you reward him with a smile. Worse yet (from the viewpoint of behaviorism), students may from time to time seem to achieve insights into their work: "Aha! Now I understand" or "This story really shows us how to learn from our mistakes, doesn't it?" These responses cannot be related easily to any particular rewards or stimuli from the teacher, only to the general behavior of students who are offered curricular materials and a learning environment. Nor do insights seem to bring any specific reward, except perhaps the reward of greater knowledge. Instead of meeting the requirements of behaviorism, then, insights seem to require some kind of unseen, internal processing ("thinking"?) and to lead to more structure or organization in behavior. The nature of such thinking and structure forms the core of the cognitive theories of learning.

cognitive focus

Even this characterization, though, is oversimplified, as we shall show in the next few pages. Every theory of learning must somehow come to terms with *all* the facts, even if they differ in how to interpret them. For teachers, these facts include relationships among various specific behaviors, as well as a large amount of seemingly unpredictable but organized behavior by students. Every learning theory agrees that both kinds of behavior occur, but the theories differ in how much they explain these by observing the actual behaviors, rather than the thinking or meaning behind them. One way or another, regardless of theoretical biases, every learning theory must answer certain questions about learning. How and when do practice and repetition help? When and how do rewards work? Why do people (including students) forget things, and can anything be done about it? These kinds of questions plague teachers everywhere, though usually not one at a time, as they occur in this book. The rest of this chapter will focus on three behavioral theories, and the next two chapters will examine several cognitive theories of learning.

concerns common to all learning theories

CLASSICAL CONDITIONING

Classical conditioning refers to learning in which a behavior that originally followed one event is made to follow a different event. Psychologists often refer to each "event" in this definition as a **stimulus**, and to the behavior that follows them as a **response**. Stated in these terms, then, classical conditioning refers to learning in which the response that originally followed one stimulus is made to follow a different stimulus.

This kind of learning was first studied by a Russian scientist, Ivan Pavlov (1927). His experiments began with **reflex connections**: stimuli and responses that occur together simply by virtue of how an animal (or person) is physically constructed. Blinking an eye is a reflex response to the stimulus of a puff of air, and moving the lower leg is a reflex response to the stimulus of a light tap on the knee. Through classical conditioning, Pavlov showed how these responses can be made to follow other, nonreflex stimuli.

The Process of Classical Conditioning

classical
conditioning

Consider this example: at the sight of food, a hungry dog inevitably salivates. If the food is repeatedly presented together with a neutral event— one that has no previous or intrinsic relationship to the salivating—then eventually that neutral event will make the dog salivate. In one of his original experiments, Pavlov used a bell as the neutral event. After repeatedly pairing the bell with the food, he made the dog salivate simply at the sound of the bell almost as well as it did at the sight of the food.

The process can be diagrammed like this:

Before conditioning: Food ⟶ Salivation

                          Bell ⟶ No response

During conditioning: Bell & food ⟶ Salivation

After conditioning: Bell ⟶ Salivation

In the end, the dog substituted the bell for the food as a stimulus to salivate.

Conditioning theory has names for the food, bell, and salivation according to their function in the learning process:

Food = Unconditioned stimulus (UCS)

Bell = Conditioned stimulus (CS)

Salivation (before conditioning) = Unconditioned response (UCR)

Salivation (after conditioning) = Conditioned response (CR)

Notice that the salivation changes its name after conditioning occurs, to describe its new function, even though the behavior itself remains basically the same. In theoretical terms, then, classical conditioning gives us the following model of learning:

Before: UCS ⟶ UCR   Food ⟶ Salivation

         CS ⟶ No response   Bell ⟶ No response

During: CS + UCS ⟶ UCR   Bell & food ⟶ Salivation

After: CS ⟶ CR   Bell ⟶ Salivation

The strength of the conditioned connection between stimulus and response will depend on how often the CS is paired with the UCS and how closely together they are actually presented during learning. After the UCS is removed, furthermore, the connection will eventually disappear again, a process that behaviorists call **extinction**. In the example above, the dog will eventually stop salivating to the bell alone, or in technical terms, it will extinguish its response to it.

extinction

Educational Implications of Classical Conditioning

Classical conditioning helps explain much learning in which one stimulus is substituted for another. One important example of this process is the learning of emotional attractions and fears. Suppose that a teacher strikes fear into the hearts of her children by shouting at them frequently, that a policeman does the same by (literally) pushing around the people on his beat, or that a nurse does so by continually giving unwelcome injections to her patients. All of these behaviors create responses of fear and anxiety in the people under their care. The situation is then ripe for conditioning these fears to otherwise neutral stimuli:

Teacher shouts (UCS) $\longrightarrow$ Fear and anxiety in child (UCR)

Policeman pushes threateningly (UCS) $\longrightarrow$ Fear and anxiety in citizens (UCR)

Nurse gives injections (UCS) $\longrightarrow$ Fear and anxiety in patients (UCR)

Any neutral stimulus that repeatedly occurs together with these stimuli is apt to become a conditioned stimulus (CS) to these fear responses. If a teacher always looks at a child before criticizing him, then simply looking at him without criticizing may cause him anxiety. At the extreme, the child may come to associate so many behaviors of the teacher and the classroom with his fear and anxiety that he develops a generalized **phobia**, or illogical fear of, school. In the same way, citizens can develop general phobias of police officers, and patients, of nurses.

conditioned fear

But positive responses can also be classically conditioned. If a teacher praises a student frequently after calling on her, then that behavior may eventually elicit positive responses from the student, even when she is not actually praised. In the long run, this process can build rapport in the classroom. It is the same for the police officer, nurse, or any other person who works with people: stimuli that reliably elicit positive responses can be conditioned to other, neutral stimuli and thereby increase the ways that these people can develop positive feelings in their clients.

conditioned rapport

Stimulus substitution can help even in certain learning processes that do not contain a strong element of feelings. Such learning is not strictly

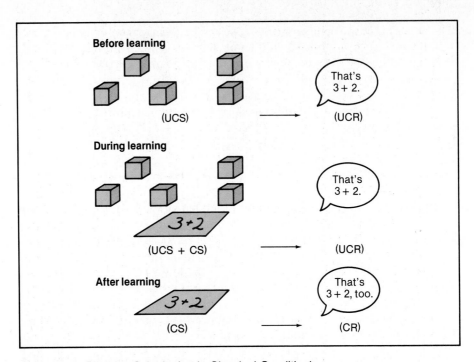

Figure 6–1 Stimulus Substitution in Classical Conditioning

classical conditioning, however, since it does not require reflexes as a start-ing point. Some psychologists prefer to call it **contiguity learning**, since it simply requires that two previously unrelated stimuli occur together in the presence of a response to one of the two stimuli. If a child has learned how to add using small unit-blocks, then these stimuli can be paired with their more abstract, written equivalents until the written version alone produces the correct response (see Figure 6–1). Unlike the earlier exam-ples, the response here does not originally have an automatic, reflex qual-ity, but like them, it becomes associated with a new stimulus, one that was originally neutral to the child.

contiguity learning

OPERANT CONDITIONING

The most widely known variety of behaviorism, operant conditioning, was evolved by B. F. Skinner over several decades. By studying simple behav-iors of animals, usually kept in boxes for observation, Skinner worked out an entire theory of learning based on a process called *operant conditioning,* which he proposed could explain even complex human behaviors, includ-ing classroom behaviors. **Operant conditioning** is a process by which the

consequences of behavior

consequences of certain behaviors influence the chances of those behaviors being repeated in the future. A pigeon, for example, will usually peck at a lever more often if doing so releases food for it to eat, or a student may work harder at an assignment if doing so earns him or her praise or a good grade.

Basic Concepts

In operant conditioning, the behavior that increases in frequency is often called an **operant**, presumably because it "operates on," or in some sense produces, its consequences. The consequences themselves are referred to as **reinforcements** if they succeed in increasing the frequency of the operant. But they need not occur after every instance of the operant behavior to do so, although they must occur at least some of the time and *never* occur if the operant also never occurs. The pigeon need not get its food every time to be reinforced by it, but it must get it at least sometimes and never get it if it never pecks the lever.

In operant conditioning, in addition, certain surrounding stimuli may affect the likelihood that an operant response will occur, without itself "causing" the response, as in classical conditioning, and without itself being reinforced to the behavior. A pigeon may learn to peck at a lever if, and only if, a nearby light is turned on, but the light itself neither directly causes the pecking nor reinforces it once it happens. Likewise, children may work in class only if their teacher is visible somewhere in the room, but his or her presence may not threaten or reward them so much as simply signal that the school work, will, at that particular moment, produce real reinforcements—praise, perhaps, or permission to do some favorite activity when they have finished. In operant theory, such a signal is often called a **discriminative stimulus**. Its place in the model and the places of the operant and of reinforcement are illustrated in Table 6–2, along with other examples. Not surprisingly, the model itself is often called *operant conditioning,* in order to distinguish it from the classical, stimulus-substitution conditioning discussed earlier.

The Nature of Reinforcement

Positive Versus Negative Reinforcement Skinner's basic formulation of the theory (1953) distinguishes between positive reinforcement and negative reinforcement. In **positive reinforcement**, some sort of reward, desirable object, or event is given as a consequence of the operant being performed. In Skinner's original experiments on animals, positive reinforcers most often consisted of basic creature comforts, usually food, water, or sex. These were reinforcers not because of their intrinsic

[margin notes:]
operant behaviors

reinforcement

discriminative stimulus

positive reinforcement

nature but because they caused the operant behavior to happen more often: food for an overfed dog (or child), for example, does not reinforce in the Skinnerian sense. In Skinner's studies with people, the positive reinforcers more often were nonphysical rewards: praise for children in a classroom or a commission paid to salespeople in certain businesses.

In **negative reinforcement**, some sort of aversive object or event is removed or prevented from occurring. If a dog can escape an electric shock by jumping over a hurdle, it is being negatively reinforced. Or if children can avoid being nagged by their teacher if they hand in their assignments on time, then they are being negatively reinforced. In each case, the probability of the behavior increases because of its consequences: that is why the consequences are defined as "reinforcing." Negative reinforcement therefore functions in the same way that positive reinforcement does, except that it works by removing undesirable items instead of adding desirable ones.

negative reinforcement

Reinforcement Versus Punishment   Whether teachers work in schools or elsewhere, they should be able to distinguish positive and negative reinforcement from a third important consequence of learning, *punishment*. Unlike reinforcement, **punishment** actively suppresses behavior, usually by adding aversive stimuli: a pigeon in a Skinner box may quickly stop pecking for food if it is shocked mildly for doing so, or a child in a class may stop talking if he or she is criticized often enough for doing so. In recent years, operant-conditioning psychologists have studied punishment almost as avidly as they have positive and negative reinforcement. When used in most practical settings, such psychologists have found that punishment does *not* influence behavior as effectively as reinforcement

Table 6–2 Elements of Operant Conditioning

Term	Discriminative stimulus	Operant	Reinforcement
Function	Signal of availability of reinforcement	Behavior to be learned	Consequences that increase future probability of operant
Examples	Patient seems awake.	Nurse looks directly at patient when talking (rather than away).	Patient smiles and converses more.
	Computer indicates it is ready for instructions.	Bank teller types computer instructions slowly (rather than hurriedly).	Computer responds correctly.

does (Walters & Grusec, 1977, chap. 6). Although behavior can be changed or stopped by negative consequences, most research shows this effect to be more temporary than learning by reinforcement is. Punishment, furthermore, may sometimes inhibit positive behaviors related to the one being punished: a child criticized too harshly for wrong answers may stop giving *any* answers. Punishment remains a problem for teachers, especially for ones who work in compulsory settings like public schools and with immature learners like children. For this reason we shall return to it later, in Chapter 9.

limitations of punishment

Secondary Reinforcement As elegant as the operant model may be, it is not a very useful one for teachers as long as reinforcement must consist only of primary creature comforts—food, water, and sex (these are known as **primary reinforcements**). If we have to use these to make learning occur in our classrooms, then we are in trouble (though the trouble might be interesting while it lasts!). We shall have to find other reinforcers to make this theory work in education.

primary reinforcement

Fortunately, operant-conditioning psychologists argue that other reinforcers do exist—many of them, in fact. In particular, any stimulus that happens to occur together with a primary reinforcer will eventually acquire reinforcing properties of its own (this is known as a **secondary reinforcement**). A pigeon pecking a lever, for example, may be reinforced with only food at first, but if a bell is rung together with the presentation of food, the bell itself will eventually suffice for increasing the bird's pecking behavior. In a sense, the pigeon acts as if it pecks in order to ring the bell, rather than to get food. Studies have shown secondary reinforcements to have most of the same properties as do primary reinforcements, though they must be paired with primary reinforcements from time to time for their continued existence (Rachlin, 1970, chap. 3; Skinner, 1953).

secondary reinforcement

Many behaviorist psychologists, including Skinner, believe that the idea of secondary reinforcement accounts for many of the reinforcers that people, including children, rely on in real life. Money, for example, becomes a powerful secondary reinforcer for most of us because it is associated with so many things and activities that reinforce (satisfy) us in more basic ways—including food, drink, and sex. To a lesser extent, school grades function in the same way. Even verbal praise from a teacher can be seen as a secondary reinforcer. You need only to assume that in the past, praise was generally associated with more basic needs, possibly because a child's parents smiled and praised the child for eating, for example, way back in the old days. Over time, then, praise became associated with food and acquired its own reinforcing properties.

widespread occurrence of secondary reinforcers

Identification of Reinforcers in Practice To be able to use the ideas of operant conditioning, then, teachers must be able to identify true secondary reinforcers, whether positive or negative. This job, however, turns out to be one of the most difficult problems in applying the theory

Praise and attention are among the most important reinforcers that teachers control. (Joe DiDio/National Education Association)

to ordinary instruction. It will not do simply to draw up a short list of stimuli that we teachers think always work, or ought to work: smiles, let us say, or gold stars or free time after class. The trouble with a list like this is that none of the items seems to work all, or even most, of the time. One student will like gold stars, but another will be reinforced only by free time; worse yet, the same student may like gold stars on one day but not another, or for one learning activity but not another. In practice, adding to our list of reinforcers does not help, since very soon we will be coping with a long list instead of a short one, searching for the right reinforcer for a particular situation and child.

How, then, can we define reinforcement for practical teaching if we cannot point to any stimuli or states that always (or even usually) work? David Premack (1965) has suggested a useful solution, though it requires assuming that the child (or animal) values some activities more than others. If we agree to this assumption, Premack argues, then any response of **Premack principle** higher value can be used to reinforce any response of lower value, but not the other way around. Suppose that eating a sandwich is more valuable to a child than reading a book, which is in turn more valuable than doing math problems. In that case eating a sandwich could be used to reinforce either reading a book or doing math, and reading a book could reinforce doing math; but the math problems could not be used to reinforce either of the other two activities.

This proposal frees teachers from using any preconceived group of reinforcers that may not work reliably in practice. Instead, they can reinforce with whatever responses from their students seem to have high value, even if these are different for each student or for each learning situation. The one remaining problem: how do teachers determine if a response (or activity or state) really has a high value for a child? In practice, many teachers will probably just ask their students, "What do you most like to do?" Doing so, of course, breaks the behaviorist rule of not using students' inner thoughts to arrange their learning experiences, but it has the advantage of being supported by common sense.

Asking students does have a more serious difficulty, however, in that some students may not always be conscious of their true values (see Chapter 4 on values clarification), or they may be unable to articulate them in words. The latter problem may be especially prevalent in young children, who may lack experience in talking about their feelings. Such children may still be made to indicate their preferences in other ways—for example, by choosing among toys in a free-play situation. The choices they make are likely to reflect their most valued responses or activities—and therefore the ones most useful as reinforcers. A kindergarten child, for example, may be invited to play with a truck, a sand table, several books, and a record player. If she freely chooses the truck over the other, equally available toys, her teacher may assume that the truck will be the most powerful reinforcer of the four items.

Another way to allow for the individual differences in reinforcers is to set up a *token economy*. Instead of being reinforced by specific valued objects or events, students in a **token economy** are reinforced with general tokens—poker chips, for instance, or play money—which they can later exchange for those items or activities that each values. One student might exchange his tokens for free time, whereas another might exchange hers for the chance to use a computer terminal; still another might prefer a candy bar. The teacher must therefore make available a suitable array or "menu" of choices for his or her students. Doing so is no simple matter, but it may be easier than predicting how each individual student should be reinforced.

token economy

With time, the tokens can become associated in the students' minds with a variety of reinforcements, and as they do, they become more and more powerful in controlling behavior. In the process, too, token economies can come to resemble society's money economy: like real money, the token becomes a **generalized reinforcer**, one leading to many other, more primary reinforcers. Token economies have been successful in a wide range of settings and with a wide age range of people, from homes for delinquents to school classrooms to summer camps (see Allyon & Azrin, 1968; or O'Leary & O'Leary, 1977, for reviews).

generalized reinforcers

Shaping No matter how flexible our reinforcers are, teachers will not be able to apply them if the responses they want to reinforce do not occur.

What if a teacher wants to reinforce a usually noisy student for reading silently in class, but the student is never quiet long enough to do so? In that case the teacher is stuck: he cannot begin operant conditioning because he has nothing to reinforce. The student continues being noisy, and the teacher continues feeling frustrated and eventually may get tired of looking for nonexistent silent reading behavior to reinforce.

Operant conditioning offers a way out of this dilemma by means of the concept of response differentiation, or **shaping**, as it is more frequently called. Instead of waiting for the desired behavior itself to occur, you try reinforcing approximations of the behavior, however distorted they may seem at first. Even though the noisy student may never sit quietly reading for, let us say, a full fifteen minutes, he may do so for one minute from time to time, or even for thirty seconds. This approximation to your goal can be increased in frequency, if not in length, by reinforcement. As the student's short reading spells become established, you can then raise your standards a little, since slightly longer silent reading periods will now be more likely to occur among the one-minute spells. Soon you may be able to reinforce for three-minute periods or five-minute ones. Eventually (you hope) you may work him up to periods as long and as frequent as those of the other students. But if you had waited for the final behavior to occur before starting to reinforce, you might never have reached this point.

Many classroom behaviors seem to be shaped from gradual approximations to their final forms. Some of these behaviors can hinder the overall learning effort of your class, as when a student gradually learns how to get on your nerves by clowning in more and more aggravating ways and is reinforced repeatedly by your attention to her. Other behaviors, though, can be shaped for constructive purposes, as in the example in the preceding paragraph. Teachers should be alert to both good and bad uses if they hope to guide the process to primarily constructive goals. According to behaviorists, shaping will occur in our classrooms in any case, and the only choice is whether or not to use it. If so, then your motto for teaching might be: "Accept Approximations!"—at least for behaviors that you consider constructive.

Chaining   Some actions cannot be approximated easily but can be constructed from a series of simpler behaviors, in a process called **chaining**. This idea has been used successfully by animal trainers to produce very complicated performances. A dog, for example, might be trained to pick up a ball, carry it across the room, and then drop it carefully into a basket—all for one dog biscuit as a reward. The performance is too complicated to shape as a whole, and so instead the actions are trained one at a time, beginning with the last item in the sequence. In this case, the dog is first trained to drop the ball into a basket, using ordinary operant-conditioning methods. When this behavior is well established, the dog is then trained to carry the ball across the room to the basket. This time, though, its reinforcement is only the opportunity to carry out its earlier

differentiation of
responses

chaining of
responses

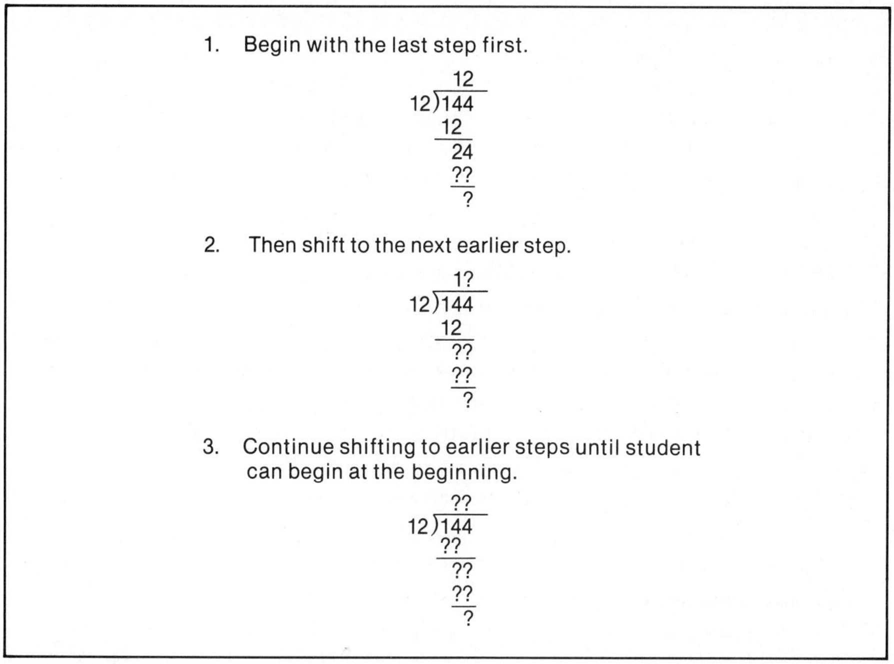

1. Begin with the last step first.

$$
\begin{array}{r}
12 \\
12\overline{)144} \\
12 \\
\hline
24 \\
?? \\
\hline
? \\
\end{array}
$$

2. Then shift to the next earlier step.

$$
\begin{array}{r}
1? \\
12\overline{)144} \\
12 \\
\hline
?? \\
?? \\
\hline
? \\
\end{array}
$$

3. Continue shifting to earlier steps until student
    can begin at the beginning.

$$
\begin{array}{r}
?? \\
12\overline{)144} \\
?? \\
\hline
?? \\
?? \\
\hline
? \\
\end{array}
$$

Figure 6–2 Steps in Building a Chain of Responses

learned behavior of dropping the ball into the basket. The discriminative stimulus from the first behavior—the sight of the basket and the feel of the ball in its mouth—now functions as a reinforcer for the new action. When this one also is well established, the trainer can add the third action, picking up the ball before crossing the room. For that matter, several more actions can be added as well, thereby producing seemingly very difficult performances by the dog, who now may even qualify to join the circus.

In classrooms, chaining may work best in situations that can use clearly recognizable steps. An important part of chaining is working *backward,* not forward, through a series of steps. Consider the problems of teaching the steps in doing long division. The principles of chaining would suggest that the teacher begin by presenting the students with the *last* step in this procedure, that is, with nearly complete problems and then reinforce them for finishing. As the last steps become established, the teacher can begin giving the students problems with the last two steps still undone. The students' reward for doing the next-to-last step is the chance to do the very last step, which may bring them the still more powerful reinforcer of approval from the teacher. In like manner, the teacher can gradually work backward through all of the steps of long division until the students can chain together all of them. The overall procedure is diagrammed in Figure 6–2.

working backward

Note that if you teach the steps forward instead of backward, you may have to reinforce each new step as it occurs and then afterward to accustom the students to being reinforced only at the end ("fade" the middle reinforcements, as some behaviorists say). As a busy teacher with many other students needing attention at the same time, you will probably appreciate the "backward" method, since it requires less constant attention from you.

Schedules of Reinforcement and Extinction   Children (and animals) need not be reinforced every time they perform a desired behavior, at least after the behavior has been learned. Every few times or every so many minutes usually works almost as well. Skinnerian psychologists have studied in detail these patterns of reinforcement—which they call **schedules of reinforcement**—hoping to find in them some clues to the laws of learning. They have indeed discovered a number of interesting patterns, some of which seem relevant to classroom instruction (Harzem & Miles, 1978).

In general, one of the most important findings concerns the permanence of **partial reinforcement**—reinforcement only some of the time. This schedule seems to make responses last longer, even after the reinforcers are no longer given. Figure 6–3 illustrates this phenomenon in a simple lever-pressing experiment with a pigeon, but the effect has been shown in many experiments, including some with children. Partial reinforcement causes the correct behavior to take longer to build up in frequency, but afterward it takes longer to disappear, or extinguish, as behaviorists say.

greater permanence of partial reinforcement

This finding may explain why many behaviors of students (and other people) persist long after they have lost their usefulness. One student may act like a clown in class, for example, because at some earlier time he was reinforced for doing so—perhaps last year or with his family. But he may have been reinforced only some of the time (partial reinforcement), a situation that seems quite possible in human affairs. If so, then he will take longer to extinguish his clowning behavior than if he originally was reinforced at every occurrence. At its extreme, the clowning behavior may even seem permanent, even though this may seem so only because the extinction is moving so slowly. Much of the stability in student behavior (and in ours, too) may be explained in a similar way. We teachers reinforce students in various ways and for behaviors both good and bad, but since we are human, we succeed in doing it only some of the time. So the behaviors become resistant to change—which is good news for constructive behaviors and bad news for destructive ones.

Instructional Applications of Operant Conditioning

In the 1950s, B. F. Skinner urged the widespread application of operant-conditioning principles to teaching and learning (1954).

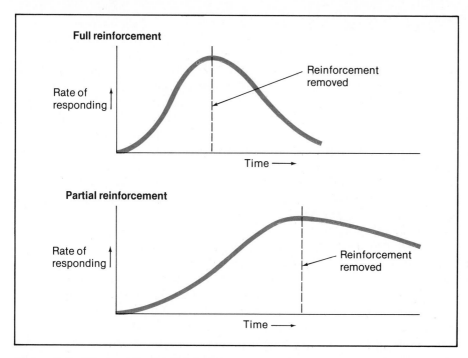

Figure 6–3 Effects of Partial Reinforcement
Although partially reinforced behavior takes longer to establish, it also takes longer to extinguish.

Programmed Instruction   Skinner's writings and research on operant conditioning led to the eventual popularity of **programmed instruction**, a method of instruction with three important features:

1. Content is presented in carefully sequenced steps.
2. The student is required to respond actively.
3. The student is given immediate feedback regarding the success or fail-
    ure of the response.

The small steps in a program were often called **frames**, and they contained
a brief introductory orienting comment followed by a question for the
student requiring a specific response. If the program was printed in book
form, the answer to a frame might appear on the next page, in a separate
answer column, or in another separate, but readily accessible, place.

features of
programmed
instruction

   Not surprisingly, therefore, programmed instruction resembled the operant-conditioning model of learning:

Discriminative
stimulus   Operant   Reinforcement
(orienting   ⟶   (student's   ⟶   (immediate information
comment and   response)   about correctness)
question)

By carefully designing the frames, educators ensured that most of the students could correctly answer most of the frames and therefore receive ample reinforcement.

During the 1960s and 1970s, programmed instruction became quite popular with many educators, and it underwent many refinements beyond Skinner's original conception of it. Because those programs that allowed only one sequence of frames (**linear programs**) were often inappropriate for certain students, more flexible ones (**branching programs**) were constructed that directed individuals to different frames in the program depending on their success or failure along the way. Students who already knew some of the content could therefore skip ahead to new material, and those who had trouble with a specific frame could be referred elsewhere in the program for further review.

linear versus branching programs

Computer-assisted Instruction   Programmed instruction received a further boost in the 1960s when computers began to be used to administer instructional programs. With such **computer-assisted instruction** (or CAI for short), the student sits at a computer terminal, usually a large typewriter, and responds to questions and information posed by the program. CAI has several important advantages over the older methods of programming. A computer terminal can present television pictures and audio recordings, as well as the more usual printed material of instruction. And it not only can easily store complicated branching programs, but it also can analyze their results almost as soon as students respond to them. And a computer can "supervise" numerous students at once and even compare their results with one another on request.

CAI

Despite these enticements, however, CAI remains a relatively expensive form of instruction for many schools to use. But this obstacle may disappear as the newer *microcomputers* become more widely available: small, self-contained units no larger than a good-sized electric typewriter, which can store, administer, and analyze instructional programs almost as well as the older, larger computers can. Even lower cost, though, may not make computers and programmed instruction useful for certain kinds of learning: content that requires a lot of global, integrated thinking, for example, or that calls for social interaction among students. Reviews of programmed instruction and of CAI find it successful in many learning situations, but by no means in all (Kulik et al., 1980; Jamison, 1974; Tennyson, 1981).

The Limits of Operant Conditioning

Accounting for Individual Differences in Behavior   Even though operant conditioning explains many bits of classroom learning, it does not really tell practicing teachers why some of these bits seem to be learned much more easily than others are. Why would one student easily be shaped to quiet reading behavior, but another would resist shaping in this direction—even though both started from the same point? Or why would one student respond well to reinforcement for doing math problems, but not for doing reading work? Common sense would tell us that these differences reveal something about our students as individuals: their motivations, attitudes, and abilities, which together affect their behavior in complex ways. Such common sense, however, violates the behaviorists' advice to confine our attention to our students' actual behaviors. From the behaviorists' viewpoint, individual differences in behavior originate largely in the students' histories of reinforcement. The one who shapes easily to quiet reading behavior, for example, must have been reinforced for quiet reading some time in the past, whereas the other one has not or has even been shaped to do the opposite. The student who responds to reinforcement for math work must have been reinforced well in the past for doing it. If the same student does not respond for reading work, perhaps he or she has been reinforced for *not* reading or has even inadvertently been punished for it ("Stay after school and read your book").

complex individual histories of reinforcement

Such explanations support the theory of operant conditioning, but they do not really help teachers in their work with children. It does not matter whether students fail to learn because of their "motivation" or because of their "previous reinforcement history": in either case the teacher must speculate about the probable cause. Such speculation, remember, is supposed to be made unnecessary by behaviorism's emphasis on observing only overt behavior. The trouble seems to be that students experience a great number of overt behaviors and reinforcements before they even arrive in class on the first day of the year, and teachers cannot reasonably be expected to know about all of this. As a result, teachers must make many inferences about the behavior of their students, since in practice much of it bears little obvious parallel to either the stimulus-response-reinforcement model of operant conditioning or the stimulus substitution model of classical conditioning.

As a practical result, then, behaviors are not equally available for learning, despite the impression that the Skinnerian psychologists may give. Studies with animals have found analogous results, though for animals the differences in their ability to learn may also relate to their physical differences or predispositions. A rat, for example, can be trained rather easily to press a lever, but a gerbil will learn only with some difficulty. Among children and students, too, some differences in potential may depend on innate dispositions: can a teacher as easily shape a child to smile as to frown? Can a young child be reinforced as easily for sitting still as for running and jumping?

Accounting for Language and Other Thinking Processes   Many psychologists have criticized operant conditioning for its strict exclusion of the "inner person" (or the inner pigeon or rat, as the case may be) from any explanation of behavior. Thinking processes generally have no place in the theory but, instead, are reinterpreted as the indirect result of reinforcement histories for various combinations of behaviors. This includes the most logically structured and "human" of human activities, language: Skinner calls this activity "verbal behavior" and has even written a book that explains it in these terms (1957).

thinking and behaviorism

Language and thinking, however, may not be easily analyzed from a strict behaviorist point of view. By their nature, these activities rely on organization and structure. But Skinnerian behaviorism often seems to lose sight of these qualities by focusing on relationships between specific responses and reinforcers—as though individual thoughts or utterances can exist in isolation from others. Less-strict behaviorists, including most teachers, would probably reject this idea in such an extreme form, preferring instead to regard language and thought as part of some larger, structured whole. But this larger structure (should it be called the "human mind"?) cannot be observed directly.

Even the supposedly objective quality of terms like stimulus, response, and reinforcement may not be objective in actual practice. In particular, some psychologists and educators argue that the significance of behavior comes not from what is seen of it but from the *meaning* that a child or student attaches to it (Lindfors, 1980). Having a teacher approach the child in the classroom, for example, could mean that she is pleased and likes the student, that she is angry and threatening him, or something else entirely. The reinforcing effect of the teacher's behavior will depend very much on which of these three meanings is actually operating, even though they all are "objectively" based on the same behavior. The teacher and child, in fact, may differ in the meaning they give to the behavior, in which case the student's meaning, not the teacher's, will determine its effect as a reinforcer.

meaning and behaviorism

This sort of disagreement over the meaning of behaviors, some psychologists say, may account for many classroom behaviors' seeming to be impossible to condition: a teacher may think that he is reinforcing a student for doing something, but the student may not be seeing it that way (Bandura, 1965). This problem can be illustrated by the old story of a behaviorist teacher who handed out a piece of candy for every page of math problems that her children completed. One child dutifully did all her work, making a careful line of uneaten candies along the top of her desk as she finished each page. When she had accumulated quite a long row of them, she asked, "Teacher, do I *have* to eat these things?" What the teacher assumed meant "reinforcement" in this case did not agree with what the child meant by the term; instead the child's real reinforcers were elsewhere—perhaps in the school work itself.

The need to assume the existence of inner thinking processes is seen very clearly in the way human beings—including students—use language (Chomsky, 1971; Piaget, 1978). Many utterances can be understood only if the student responds to its underlying structure or meaning rather than its surface form. Take the sentence *They are eating apples.* In one inter-

language and behaviorism

pretation the sentence specifies what "they" are doing: eating; in another, it specifies what kind of apples "they" are: eating apples. To choose correctly between these two interpretations, a student must respond to the sentence's underlying grammatical structure (the deep structure discussed in Chapter 3) rather than just to the words as they appear. The student must also respond to the sentence's overall context, which often can be rather diffuse. One meaning of the sentence would probably be appropriate for a conversation at the fruit center of a grocery store, at which several kinds of apples are displayed, including eating apples. The other meaning probably would be more appropriate for a picnic, at which many kinds of food are available, but only one kind of apple.

Since students (and other humans) seem to interpret sentences like this correctly, they must often be responding to the language's underlying organization, as well as to the general context in which language is used. Skinner might argue that in principle the child has been reinforced for responding to the language's deep structure rather than its surface features and that the child also has been reinforced for responding to the broad context of the language's use. Other psychologists, though, find this explanation somewhat far-fetched and prefer to assume that the child possesses some sort of internal language-processing ability (see Chapter 3). This assumption admittedly coincides with the common-sense requirements of teachers, who in any case do not have the time to trace down complicated reinforcement histories.

Ethical Dilemmas of Using Operant Conditioning Skinner has argued repeatedly that concepts like "freedom" and "choice" have no place in understanding human behavior (see, for example, his book *Beyond Freedom and Dignity,* 1971). Excluding such concepts, however, puts a special ethical burden on teachers, who must make many daily decisions that pertain to these ideas. In essence, conditioning theory argues that freedom and choice are illusions, that the only real classroom events are the ones that can be seen concretely, and that these inevitably will be controlled through reinforcement. Behavior control can be done accidentally or intentionally, and it can be done efficiently or clumsily, but it cannot be avoided. Carried to its extreme, their ability to control behavior seems to put teachers completely in charge of what students do—and *should* do—during school, since presumably the teachers control most of the reinforcers. Many educators have rejected behaviorism on these grounds, asserting that it comes too close to asking that teachers play "God" (Rogers & Skinner, 1956). There would be little room left for humane ideals, they say, if operant conditioning were taken seriously. Teachers cannot foster individual potential or use self-guided learning or even democratic classroom control, since these all amount to euphemisms for "behavior control."

The humanistic teachers have a point, but they may also be overlooking the extent to which problems of behavior control really do confront teachers. Much of teachers' daily energy goes, for example, to quieting down

behaviorism and freedom

students at the beginning of a class or lesson, to organizing them to move from one activity or place to another, and to maintaining order whenever things begin to fall apart. All this has been called "crowd control" by cynics and "instructional management" by optimists, but by either name it is a prominent fact of school life. Because operant conditioning has much to offer to this general area of teaching, we shall return to it again in Chapter 9, as part of the general discussion of instructional management. Reinforcing overt behaviors may not solve all of a teacher's problems, but it does seem to work in many classroom situations, especially when doing rather than thinking is involved.

usefulness in classroom management

SOCIAL LEARNING THEORY

The above critique of operant conditioning does not really prove that the theory is wrong but only that it may be difficult to apply in teaching practice. After all, it is still possible in principle for a psychologist with lots of time and perseverance to track down the individual reinforcement histories of a classroom of students and thereby to account for much of their unpredictable, spontaneous behavior. Our criticism would be more serious if it showed that a major part of ordinary classroom behavior really resulted from some systematic mechanism of learning, one that acted independently of operant and classical conditioning.

modeling

Social learning theory believes it has found such a mechanism in the process of *modeling* or *observational learning,* and it has attempted to modify the extreme behavioristic operant conditioning to include this process. Its most prominent exponent, Albert Bandura, pioneered an area of research showing just how much these processes affect human learning (1963, 1977), though he never denied that operant and classical processes may occur as well. In his research, Bandura freely assumed that children and students use internal processes of thinking while they learn. Social learning theory therefore impresses some people, including many teachers, as being more down to earth and commonsensical, but also as less tightly organized than is operant-conditioning theory.

The Process of Observation and Modeling

According to social learning theory, the process of reinforcement through shaping occurs too slowly to explain the appearance of many complex behaviors. As a supplement to reinforcement, therefore, this theory calls attention to **observational learning** and **modeling**, processes that most teachers notice in their classrooms from time to time: one child observes another doing something and then at some later time performs a version of the behavior himself or herself. Since the copied version usually does not duplicate exactly what the child actually observed, some psychologists

modeling versus imitation

These air force cadets are probably learning much of their role by being reinforced for correct behavior, as well as by modeling themselves after fellow cadets and superiors. (Owen Franken/Stock, Boston)

prefer to call this process modeling rather than imitation. An elementary
school student, for example, may observe his teacher day after day in her
role as teacher; then, during a free time, he may himself "play teacher."
His version of the role, though, will likely differ from the real one (often
painfully!). At a more sophisticated level, a new staff member of a business
may model many behaviors of her supervisors—including, among others,
forms of speech, statements about company goals, and choice of clothes.
In most cases, though, these behaviors do not duplicate but merely resemble the behaviors being modeled. In general, an observer modifies the
model to make it his or her own: observational learning is not playing
"copy cat" (Bandura, 1971).

   Modeled behavior appears too quickly to be explained easily by ideas
of shaping and secondary reinforcement. Usually, in fact, it appears fully
formed on the first occasion, rather than coming in small steps that gradually work toward the final product. One teen-ager hears a new slang
expression from another and at some later time begins using it. Or one

*sudden
appearance of
modeled behavior*

student sees another roughing up somebody and later inflicts more or less the same aggression on someone else. Or conversely, a person observes an act of kindness or consideration and later does the same when the occasion presents itself. As with conditioning, then, observational learning can either help the teaching effort or hurt it. But unlike conditioned learning, modeled behaviors appear rather suddenly, though not unexpectedly if the chance to observe a model is accounted for.

Observational learning does not prevent conditioning from occurring as well. A student who models an act of kindness, for example, may then increase the frequency of such acts because of the reinforcement he or she receives. On the other hand, a student who models aggression may also be shaped toward further aggression, though presumably from peers rather than teachers. What observational learning gives is a new way to understand the *first* appearance of complex behaviors, a way that shortens the more laborious process of operant conditioning. Once a behavior has appeared, though, operant processes may also apply to it.

Elements of Observational Learning

four elements

According to the observational learning theory, learning through observation consists of four elements, two of which require significant compromises with Skinnerian behaviorism.

Attention Observational learning first assumes that students can and will focus their *attention* and that from time to time this attention will be directed to a model. This somewhat common-sense idea has no place in extreme behaviorism, as it assumes the existence of an internal thought process that cannot be observed but that serves to direct attention to a particular person or action.

Memory As its second element, observational learning assumes that students can *remember* behaviors that they have seen well enough to perform them again at a later time. Presumably a mind of some sort must do the remembering, though it cannot be seen directly, as Skinnerians would require.

Motor Skills The other elements of social learning theory do not in and of themselves conflict with the Skinnerian philosophy of behaviorism. To perform an action that they have observed, children must possess the *motor skills* needed for the action, and these usually require overt practice rather than covert observation. Watching someone drive a car, for example, usually does not ensure perfect driving when you take the wheel for the first time: you need "hands on" experience as well. Or watching a fine performance of a piano sonata will not lead to a successful imitation unless the observer already has the intricate motor skills needed to play the piano well. For this element of observational learning, "practice makes perfect," a dictum that operant conditioning would certainly support.

Reinforcement The fourth element of observational learning is *reinforcement*. As already pointed out, this process can augment the effects of modeling, but it also does more. It can call attention to particular behaviors or models or inform a student whether a particular behavior is valued and therefore worth performing. Consider the student described earlier who accumulated her candy rewards without eating them. Social learning theory might argue that she had in fact been reinforced in the broad sense of the term, even if not in the Skinnerian sense. The candies may have reinforced her with information if not food, information about whether she was doing well and whether the teacher considered her effort worthwhile.

These cognitive functions of reinforcement can be seen clearly in *vicarious reinforcement,* a process that has been extensively studied by social learning theorists (Bandura, 1971). In **vicarious reinforcement**, the observer watches the model receive reinforcement (or fail to receive it), without directly receiving any himself or herself. In class, one student may watch another be praised for answering a question correctly, or conversely, he may see the student be ignored for doing so or, in some cases, even punished. As might be supposed, vicarious reinforcement increases modeling more than vicarious nonreinforcement does, or more than vicarious punishment does, for that matter. Although none of these findings contradicts the possibility that reinforcement operates directly on some behaviors, they all suggest that a student may also think about the reinforcements he or she receives and respond to their meaning.

vicarious reinforcement

Factors Influencing Modeling

Various factors have been shown to affect the extent to which modeling occurs. High-status models, for example, tend to be modeled more often than low-status ones are. In a school, this suggests that a popular teacher may be modeled more often than a student is and that the student body president may be modeled more often than an unpopular student is. Nurturant models also tend to be modeled more, and so a warm, caring teacher should produce more observational learning than a cool, uncaring one should. In general, a model is modeled more if the observer considers that person similar to himself or herself: a live person is modeled more often than one on film is, for example. Note, though, that at least when they are young, children do not necessarily model the same sex more often than they do the opposite sex (see Chapter 5, on sex roles).

status models

nurturant models

similarity between models

Hostile or agressive behaviors also have been studied in social learning theory, and the results reveal that children often model such behaviors. In a typical study, young children may watch a person or another child

"Playing teacher" may be learned first through observation and modeling, even though reinforcement may further modify or extend this behavior. (Harvey Stein)

aggression

"beat up" a big punching-bag doll; then later the children are given a chance to play with various toys, including the same punching-bag doll. Under many (but not all) variations of this experiment, these children will fight the doll more often than if they had not observed the same behavior earlier. How much aggression they show, though, depends on the qualities of the model described above, whether vicarious reinforcement is observed, and whether any direct reinforcement is received. The largest amount of hostile behavior is modeled after observing a high-status model who is warm, similar to the observer, and well rewarded for modeling hostility. The same effects also occur, though, for constructive behaviors, like kindness or generosity (Mussen, 1977). Like most findings in learning theory, the effect can be used for good or ill, and only the teacher, not the theory, can promote desirable uses.

Educational Implications of Observational Learning

Social learning theory can help teachers in their work only if they gain control of the elements of observation and modeling, described earlier.

Directing Attention to Appropriate Models Teachers must find ways to direct their students' attention to behaviors or models that they would like their students to imitate. Presumably doing so helps students see the right way of doing problems, stating ideas, or using tools—or whatever the learning goals may be. If done sensibly and humanely, calling attention to standards need not prevent students from having reasonable leeway to learn in their own way.

Teachers encounter a perennial dilemma in directing attention to model behavior without implying undue criticism of those students who have not yet learned the "right way." By using themselves as models, however, teachers may partially solve this problem: "Look how I do it" may seem to criticize the students less than "Look at how _____ does it." The first technique is safer than the second one because students rarely expect to outperform their teachers. Singling out a student, though, can accentuate any competitive pressures in the class, since students frequently compare themselves with one another, despite the teacher's efforts to the contrary. Directing students' attention, in any case, requires more than telling them verbally whom to look at and when. Further suggestions for doing so are discussed in Chapter 8.

teacher as a model

Helping Students Remember Likewise, social learning theory suggests that teachers must look for ways to help students remember what they learn. This entails more than the old army adage, "Tell them what you will say, tell it to them, and tell them what you said." There are many other techniques besides the "sledge-hammer" approach of improving memory—though this one works well in some situations. These are explored in Chapter 7, along with suggestions for improving motor skills. And reinforcement? Much can be learned from operant conditioning about the application of reinforcement, as described earlier in this chapter, though to these direct uses of reinforcement should be added its vicarious uses. We shall examine in the next chapter the information value of reinforcement.

The Limits of Observational Learning

In many ways, social learning theory is a middle-of-the-road approach, trying to combine the best of the cognitive theories of learning with the best of analytical behaviorism. This combination has much to recommend it to teachers, whose commitment lies with human beings more than with a particular philosophy of education or psychology.

combination of learning theories

Multiple Models and Observers Nevertheless, the support for this blend of approaches is far from universal among educators. One of their questions is, even if children do learn by observing models, can a teacher really sort out the effects of modeling during their daily teaching? In a

A classroom contains many potential models—and some of them may not al-ways foster learning among students. (Elizabeth Crews)

classroom, instead of one observer and one model, the teacher confronts a room full of observers and models, a veritable cast of characters both seeing and being seen. In that situation, where does observing end and modeling begin? Ask yourself this question whenever your students get out of hand.

identification of
models You may get the distinct impression that clowning behavior, for example, snowballs through observation and imitation or that a rash of obscene language begins in the same way. But where does the process begin? To make social learning theory work for you, you will need to find the source or sources of undesirable behavior, however ambiguous they might be. Only by doing so can you hope to use observational learning to help man-age your class.

Conflicting Models   Critics of social learning theory also point out that teachers' influence on observational learning depends very much on their underlying rapport with their students. If the rapport is good, teach-

importance of
teacher-student
rapport ers can have much influence as models: after all, they are powerful and (we hope) warm members of their classes and therefore are more observed and modeled than any other persons in them. But if understanding and respect breaks down, the students may look for other models. Instead of aspiring to the teacher's standards of good work, for example, they may aspire to follow the other students' ideals, and these may fall well short of the teacher's. To some extent, of course, all students follow their peers rather than adults like teachers. But sometimes the problem goes deeper. Even the best teachers encounter individual students, or even an entire class, where peer standards seem to be paramount, and the teacher's standards seem to be ignored. The problem is encountered most often when particular students have values and goals very different from their teachers', and so the teachers must spend a lot of time reconciling themselves to this gap, rather than modeling desirable skills or behaviors. How, for example, can a teacher use observational learning with a student whose chief desire is to leave school at the first possible chance?

LEARNING AS MORE THAN BEHAVIOR CHANGE

Behaviorally oriented theories of learning account for much of what teachers notice about everyday student learning. They illustrate how one event can sometimes substitute for another as a stimulus, how the consequences of an action may affect the frequency and nature of that action, and how observation and modeling may determine whether certain complex behaviors will occur at all. Taken together, behavioral theories suggest how teachers can make instruction more effective. We discussed some of these suggestions in this chapter and shall offer others in Chapters 8 and 9, which examine the planning and conduct of instruction.

According to many psychologists and educators, behaviorist theories of learning do not explain one large sort of learning, namely, changes in thinking and in the organization of student knowledge. Even behaviorists themselves have often found it convenient to assume that unobservable mental processes profoundly affect learning. The observation and modeling processes in social learning theory, for example, depend on this assumption. Certainly, in the daily practice of teaching, most teachers find it convenient to supplement behavioral explanations of learning with ones focused more on thought processes and the organization of knowledge. The next chapter will look at some of these and at what they imply for instruction.

Key Points

1. Learning refers to any relatively permanent change in behavior caused by a relatively specific experience.

2. Some learning theories focus their attention rather exclusively on changes in overt behavior, but others focus more on the internal, unobservable thinking processes that lead to and result from behavior.

3. The three behaviorally oriented theories of

learning described in this chapter are classical conditioning, operant conditioning, and social learning theory.

4. Classical conditioning explains how one stimulus can come to substitute for another in causing a particular response.

5. Classical conditioning may account for the learning of likes and dislikes regarding school and instructors, and an analogous process of

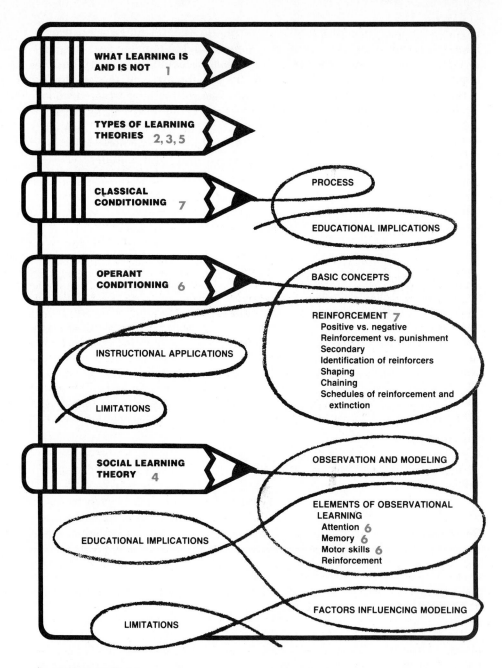

WHAT LEARNING IS
AND IS NOT 1

TYPES OF LEARNING
THEORIES 2, 3, 5

CLASSICAL
CONDITIONING 7

PROCESS

EDUCATIONAL IMPLICATIONS

OPERANT
CONDITIONING 6

BASIC CONCEPTS

REINFORCEMENT 7
  Positive vs. negative
  Reinforcement vs. punishment
  Secondary
  Identification of reinforcers
  Shaping
  Chaining
  Schedules of reinforcement and
    extinction

INSTRUCTIONAL APPLICATIONS

LIMITATIONS

SOCIAL LEARNING
THEORY 4

OBSERVATION AND MODELING

ELEMENTS OF OBSERVATIONAL
LEARNING
  Attention 6
  Memory 6
  Motor skills 6
  Reinforcement

EDUCATIONAL IMPLICATIONS

FACTORS INFLUENCING MODELING

LIMITATIONS

1 Development (Part I)

2 Piaget's theory of cognitive growth
   (Chapter 2)

3 Moral behavior and development
   (Chapter 4)

4 The social context of learning (Chapter 5)

5 Learning to structure knowledge (Chapter 7)

6 Making instruction more effective
   (Chapter 8)

7 The motivation to learn (Chapter 11)

stimulus substitution may account for certain kinds of academic learning.

6. Operant conditioning explains how the consequences of a behavior may affect the frequency of that behavior occurring at later times.

7. Reinforcement is the term used in operant theory to refer to the consequences of a behavior that increase the frequency of that behavior's occurrence.

8. Positive reinforcement refers to the application of positive consequences following a behavior, and negative reinforcement refers to the removal of aversive or unpleasant consequences.

9. Punishment is the application of unpleasant consequences after a behavior.

10. Secondary reinforcement is the process by which a previously neutral stimulus acquires reinforcing properties.

11. In teaching practice, reinforcers differ from one child to another and even from one occasion to another.

12. Shaping is the process of reinforcing approximations of a behavior until the behavior finally resembles a desired outcome.

13. Chaining is the linking of behavior sequences using reinforcement procedures.

14. In order to be effective, reinforcement need not be given every time a desired behavior occurs.

15. In addition to being used to help manage classroom behaviors, operant conditioning has found extensive applications in programmed learning and computer-assisted instruction.

16. Operant conditioning has been criticized for neglecting internal thought processes, for not accounting well for structured processes such as language, and for violating ethical standards in dealing with learners.

17. Social learning theory explains the influence of observation and modeling on learning.

18. Observational learning requires that the learner attend to particular modeled behavior, remember the observation for a later time, have the appropriate motor skills to reproduce it, and (sometimes) be reinforced for modeling.

19. A person is most likely to imitate a model who has high status, who is nurturant, and who resembles the observer in certain ways.

20. Teachers can use the modeling process by directing students' attention to appropriate models, by helping them remember desirable modeled behavior from earlier occasions, and by reinforcing desirable modeled behavior.

21. The modeling process can pose complex problems for teachers because classrooms, by definition, contain many potential models and observers.

Case Study

George's Token Economy

George Bennett had set up a token economy in his classroom at the start of this year. It was his first year of teaching, and he had been given a Grade 6 room. During his teaching training he had become enthusiastic about token economies after seeing a film about them and talking about the idea with a teacher-friend he knew. So when his teaching began in September, he bought a pile of play money at a local toy store and announced his plan to his students.

"You can do a lot of things in my room in exchange for this pretend money," he said, showing them the play dollar bills. "If you work on your math problems for the last half-hour of the afternoon, for instance, I will 'pay' you one 'dollar' for it."

"A *real* dollar?" someone asked excitedly.

"No, a *pretend* dollar," George emphasized, "Later you can turn the dollar in for something else that you want or enjoy doing. So we need to talk first about how you can earn these dollars, what you can cash them in for, and when." George showed them a list of activities that he would pay tokens for and how much each was worth. Then he showed them a list of how the students could cash in their token dollars and under what circumstances. Here are parts of his lists:

Ways to earn tokens

1. Do math for last half-hour ($1).

2. Read extra novel and report on it ($2).

3. Clean chalkboard for three days ($1).

4. All assignments in on time for five days ($2).
5. Clean hamster's cage for two weeks ($1).
6. Perfect score on three math papers ($1).

Ways to spend tokens

1. Last half-hour free time (cost = $4).
2. Use computer games (cost = $2).
3. Keep hamster at home for weekend (cost = $3).
4. Treated to lunch and ice cream by the teacher (cost = $3).
5. Permission to visit the library alone (cost = $2).
6. Note of congratulations home to parents (cost = $4).

Many of the students looked very interested in the whole plan, although none really said very much or challenged the values that George had assigned to the tasks or rewards. "What if I don't earn enough tokens to do anything good?" someone said. "You will," said George firmly.

But now, three months later, the plan was not working as well as George had expected, and he was feeling frustrated by the whole business. One of his students, Susan, did not seem to care whether or not she earned token dollars. She did a reasonable number of the tasks and assignments from the "Things to Do" chart, but half the time she forgot to collect her tokens for them, and George felt awkward reminding her to do so. One time he saw her give some of her token dollars to a classmate. "She needs them," she said. "Isn't that what friends are for?"

Another student, Bill, was concise about his opinion. "It's stupid," he said. "Why don't you just give us the things on the reward list directly, instead of bothering with the tokens?" George sometimes wondered this himself, though he also noticed that Bill exchanged his tokens for different rewards each week, and George could never predict what he would choose next.

Margaret worked diligently for her tokens but periodically asked for new tasks to be added to the chart. "How about watering the plants by the windows? Shouldn't we get paid for that?" The first time she made a request like this, George agreed to it, but almost immediately she asked for another task to be added. So George now was less sure that he should agree to them. Recently Margaret complained that George had set the pay for watering the plants too low.

But there was a bright side. A number of students—notably Frank, Kathy, and Dave—were managing themselves better than their former teachers had thought possible. These teachers had remarked to George how the three students had become "different people" this year—less inclined to disrupt classes or assemblies, for example. George was proud of these comments and secretly felt that he had interrupted some potentially harmful self-fulfilling prophecies by the teaching staff. He had not yet, however, figured out how to "wean" the three students away from their pretend-dollar rewards. "Perhaps," he told himself, "I do not need to have all the answers about token economies this year."

Questions for Discussion

1. If you were George and had to report to the local school board as to whether or not token economies should be promoted throughout the school district, what would you say?
2. How can George make his particular token economy work more effectively? What intrinsic limits, if any, do you think there will be on its eventual success?
3. To what extent do you think Susan actually lacks motivation to earn tokens? What, if anything, do you think George should do about it?
4. What would you say to Bill? Why not, indeed, just reward students directly—by-passing the tokens?

5. How should George respond to requests like those made by Margaret?
6. How much credit can George claim for improving the behavior of Frank, Kathy, and Dave? What else besides the reward system may account for their change? Go beyond the obvious in your comments, but also be reasonable.
7. This token economy is far from complete, at least judging from the account of it given here. What advice would you give George to make his system more precise and complete? You may want to check one of the references in the annotated bibliography for ideas in answering this question.

Suggested Readings

Bandura, A. *Social Learning Theory*. Morristown, N.J.: General Learning Press, 1977.

Rachlin, H. *Introduction to Modern Behaviorism*. 2nd ed. San Francisco: W. H. Freeman, 1976.

If you want to learn more about behavioral theories, these are two books that will help. The first book examines observational learning, and the second one combines thoroughness with relative brevity.

Kazdin, A. E. *The Token Economy: A Review and Evaluation*. New York: Plenum, 1977.

Rimm, David C. *Behavior Therapy: Techniques and Empirical Findings*. 2nd ed. New York: Academic Press, 1979.

Walker, James, and Thomas Shea. *Behavior Modification: A Practical Approach for Educators*. 2nd ed. St. Louis: C. V. Mosby, 1980.

These books discuss three different ways that behavioral principles can be applied to learning. The first book reviews token economies in general, whether they occur in schools or in other institutional settings (for example, psychiatric hospitals). The second book explores the application of behavioral principles to psychotherapy, and the third relates these ideas to the classroom.

Skinner, B. F. *Beyond Freedom and Dignity*. New York: Knopf, 1971.

Stolz, S. B. *Ethical Issues in Behavior Modification: A Report of the American Psychological Association*. San Francisco: Jossey-Bass, 1978.

If you feel uneasy about the moral issues surrounding behaviorism, read these two books on the subject. The one by Skinner is written very clearly, and as you might expect, it concludes that behaviorism has been wrongly accused of authoritarian ethics. The book by Stolz states the official position on the problem of the American Psychological Association, a major professional group of psychologists.

Chapter 7

LEARNING TO STRUCTURE KNOWLEDGE

John Keating, Grade 10 history teacher: It's taken me years to do it, but I think I'm finally learning just how varied my students are in how they learn—even for supposedly the same material. Take my unit on the Civil War. Cathy seemed to view the whole topic as a collection of facts—dates of battles, names of people and towns, and so on. But José went for the generalizations—trends and underlying causes, similarities among historical incidents, and that sort of thing. It showed on the test, too. Cathy did best on the objective questions, which focused on recalling information, but José wrote better essay questions. I like José's approach better: I wish all my students could integrate information the way he does. But perhaps he was helped by studying the same topic last year in another course. Maybe that's where he went after the facts.

How am I supposed to take into account differences like that? Larry can remember practically everything from the films we have; if I tested my class just on films, I bet he'd be at the top. But Bill is the opposite: he has to be told in words or else read it somewhere. It doesn't seem fair to give him and Larry the same test—or José and Cathy, for that matter. It's as though they're each learning a different subject—a different version of the Civil War in this case. Or as though they're paying attention to different experiences in class and making sense of them differently.

Well, I like that variety, except I'm not always sure how to provide for it. There's not time enough to teach and evaluate every student completely in his or her favorite style, even if I were a good enough teacher to do it. I can't just show movies every day or just lecture every day or just do any one thing every day. I can't just teach only facts or only general ideas, even if that would help a certain student. My students all are so different that I feel compelled to give a balance. I call it my "mixed salad."

Mind you, I *do* believe in individualizing instruction, as they used to tell me when I was at university. And I succeed at it, I guess, to some extent. I helped Larry do a project on films on the Civil War, for instance, but Bill wrote a long essay for me. And I gave different supplementary readings to different students: José got a pretty abstract article about the role of slavery in the war, and I found Cathy a short story about essentially the same topic. But I was stumped for a reading for Larry. Another teacher showed me an article on photography during the Civil War, but it looked sort of academic in style, and sure enough, Larry wasn't very excited by it.

That's the trouble with that "individualizing instruction" idea. They tell you it's good for the students—and I agree—but half the time, nobody gives you the materials you need to individualize well. But my students keep on learning in diverse ways anyhow.

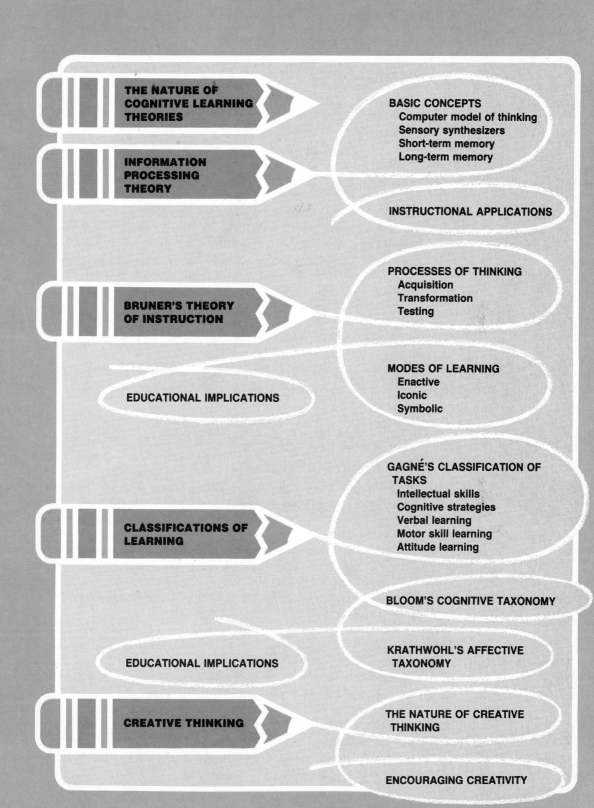

THE NATURE OF
COGNITIVE LEARNING
THEORIES

INFORMATION
PROCESSING
THEORY

BASIC CONCEPTS
Computer model of thinking
Sensory synthesizers
Short-term memory
Long-term memory

INSTRUCTIONAL APPLICATIONS

BRUNER'S THEORY
OF INSTRUCTION

PROCESSES OF THINKING
Acquisition
Transformation
Testing

EDUCATIONAL IMPLICATIONS

MODES OF LEARNING
Enactive
Iconic
Symbolic

CLASSIFICATIONS OF
LEARNING

GAGNÉ'S CLASSIFICATION OF
TASKS
Intellectual skills
Cognitive strategies
Verbal learning
Motor skill learning
Attitude learning

BLOOM'S COGNITIVE TAXONOMY

EDUCATIONAL IMPLICATIONS

KRATHWOHL'S AFFECTIVE
TAXONOMY

CREATIVE THINKING

THE NATURE OF CREATIVE
THINKING

ENCOURAGING CREATIVITY

To a large extent, students learn by acquiring and organizing knowledge. This process may not produce immediate or obvious changes in their behavior, but it often sets the stage for such changes. The acquisition and organization of knowledge make individuals more flexible and free and thus more able to choose their responses and courses of actions. Such a view of learning assumes that human beings contain more than just what we can see of them: that they also contain thinking and memory, and perception and motivation. All of these factors must be inferred from what people say or do, rather than observed directly. Since they constitute a major part of what most teachers consider the process of education, they deserve special attention and a detailed discussion. Different types of knowledge, for example, call for different types of educational goals and methods. These do not necessarily conflict with the behaviorist methods of association, reinforcement, and modeling, but they often do view instruction differently and set different priorities for it.

THE NATURE OF COGNITIVE LEARNING THEORIES

concern with acquisition, memory, and relation of information

The last chapter ended by describing how social learning theory has shifted its emphasis toward greater attention to inner thinking, as opposed to overt behavior. When this emphasis is carried further still, the result is often called a **cognitive theory** of learning. Such theories share several features, though in widely different amounts. They look at how human beings acquire information and knowledge, how they remember it, and how they relate ideas and concepts to one another. The achievement of insight (sudden understanding or perception) often figures heavily in these theories, as do the activities that underlie such achievement. In this sense, Piaget's theory of development (Chapter 2) qualifies as a cognitive theory of learning, even though it may be more vague regarding instruction than many teachers may wish. In all cognitive theories, the outcome or per-

concern with internal, organized thought

formance of learning matters relatively less than in behaviorist viewpoints. What matters more are the internal, organizing processes of thought that lead to performance.

three cognitive theories of learning

This chapter will examine several cognitive theories of learning. The first of these, the so-called **information-processing theory**, models learning after the operations of a modern high-speed computer. Another, originated by the psychologist Jerome Bruner, combines information about child development with information about human learning and points out the difficulties of constructing a systematic theory of teaching. A third approach, originated by Robert Gagné, organizes learning into general types, most of which require cognitive skills. All three theories recognize the importance of structuring knowledge in order to learn it, though they disagree about what this idea means for teaching methodology. Bruner, in particular, emphasizes discovery learning (see also Chapter 12, on humanistic education), by which he means the active involvement of students with learning materials that will lead them to form their own ideas and insights. Gagné, on the other hand, gives a more visible role to telling as a method of teaching, as long as the telling is well organized and suited to the students' true learning needs. These differences and similarities, however, reflect matters of emphasis; they are not, please note, all-or-nothing dichotomies. The chapter presents two other classifications of learning: one by Benjamin Bloom that describes cognitive learning and one by David Krathwohl that describes affective (feeling-oriented) learning. The chapter concludes with a discussion of creativity.

INFORMATION-PROCESSING THEORY

Basic Concepts

Computer Model of Thinking   Information-processing theory divides human thinking into elements that resemble the features of a modern high-speed computer (Newell & Simon, 1972). Psychologists differ in precisely what elements they include in this model, but most usually include specific mental operations, temporary states of mind, long-term storage facilities, and general rules for processing new information. The analysis can be represented in a chart such as that in Figure 7–1, which shows what happens to information from the moment it comes to a person to the moment it is either stored or acted upon.

Elements of Thinking   Each box in Figure 7–1 refers to some feature of human thinking and learning. The layout of the boxes is definitely not meant to imply that those features are somehow arranged in a physically similar way in actual human brains. What matters in the model is its analysis of thinking: the steps in thinking that it identifies and their relationships. The model in Figure 7–1 should be understood as a system—a set of related elements that, in this particular case, describe how thinking occurs.

According to the model, thinking begins with experiences, in the form of sensations, perceptions, and information. These enter the system (or human mind) through so-called **sensory detectors**—our eyes, ears, nose, mouth, and skin. In order to think about or make sense from these experiences, they must usually be combined in certain simple ways. Children may easily experience a sensation of blue color, for example, but they cannot think about the experience effectively unless they can also combine it with other experiences. If they also experience white patches along with

sensory detectors

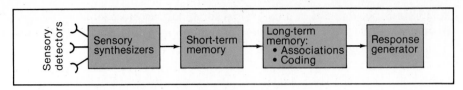

Figure 7–1 Model of Human Information Processing

sensory synthesizer

the blue color and receive the information that the time is 12 noon then they may be able to synthesize the three experiences into one interpretable whole. Perhaps blue color plus white patches plus 12 noon may combine into the single, more meaningful experience called "a view of the sky." In the information-processing model, the process of combining is sometimes called **sensory synthesis**, and the feature or aspect of human thinking that does the combining is sometimes called a **sensory synthesizer**.

short-term memory

Synthesized experiences are then sent (figuratively, not literally) to short-term memory, which acts as a kind of blackboard or working space for true information processing. **Short-term memory** refers to the many events of thinking that human beings retain only briefly. When you look up a telephone number that you call only rarely, you may store it in short-term memory only long enough to dial the number. Within seconds after you have finished dialing, you will probably have forgotten it.

long-term memory

coding

A lot of information that reaches short-term memory is simply forgotten, but some may be related to other, permanently stored information in various ways so that it, too, may be retained for long periods of time. The storage of relatively permanent ideas and information is called **long-term memory** in the information-processing model. New ideas and information enter it by being associated with old ideas and information or by sorting and classifying processes sometimes called **coding**. Long-term memory often uses short-term memory to help code information. Permanently memorizing the address of a friend, for example, may require recalling temporarily a picture of his house and street (using short-term memory) and then associating this rather fleeting memory with the name of the street. Or it may require other temporary steps that rely on short-term memory.

response generator

A few ideas or thoughts cause overt responses—real, observable actions such as those on which behaviorist psychologists focus their theories. Because causing such actions to occur is itself a thinking process, the information-processing model gives a name to it; in Figure 7–1, it is called a **response generator**, the feature of thinking that creates or generates responses. This feature, along with the other terms in the model, is summarized briefly in Table 7–1.

By systematically separating the elements of human thinking, information-processing theory identifies particular processes of learning that may concern teachers. Consider the simple activity of counting a small number of beads on a table. The theory offers several important ideas about this task, ideas that may seem obvious—and yet are often neglected:

1. The children must see the beads ("detect" them).
2. They must perceive them to be beads ("synthesize" their sensations) and not mistake them for other things (like splotches on the table).
3. They must have previously acquired a mental routine for counting them.
4. The routine must be stored and accessible (in long-term memory).
5. The routine must be activated by the perception of this particular group of objects.
6. Other routines must be activated if any overt response (like pointing, sorting, and the like) is expected.
7. These routines must lead to correct behavior in response (cause the response generator to operate correctly).
8. The result of the counting must be remembered permanently (coded for long-term memory) if the children expect to use the result at some later time.

specific processes of learning

If any step of this list fails to occur, the children will seem not to know how to count the beads, at least on this occasion. According to information-processing theory, learning resembles a puzzle with more pieces in it than we first imagine. Actual teaching, however, often is concerned only with the routine for counting (step 5) and takes for granted the other parts of the process. To be effective, though, instruction must plan for all the steps. The sections below suggest ways of doing so—and for tasks more complex than counting a few beads.

Table 7–1 Key Terms in Information-Processing Theory

Information: sensations, perceptions, or knowledge that enters the human mind and does so in a form capable of being coded or processed.

Processing: a systematic sequence of actions or changes regarding information; together the sequence constitutes human thinking.

Coding: the process by which new information is associated with existing categories, ideas, or other information in order to facilitate its permanent storage in long-term memory.

Sensory detectors: the sense organs—eyes, ears, nose, mouth, and skin.

Sensory synthesizers: the feature of human thinking that combines basic sensations into meaningful units suitable for further processing.

Short-term memory: the feature of human thinking that provides a temporary working space for information processing.

Long-term memory: the feature of human thinking that contains the permanent store of ideas and knowledge in a meaningfully coded form.

Response generator: the feature of human thinking that causes overt behaviors to occur.

Instructional Applications of Information Processing

Getting and Keeping Attention Before children can deal with the experiences their teacher gives them, they must pay attention to them and, furthermore, pay attention to those aspects of them that are important. In school, as everywhere else, children are bombarded with far more stimuli than they can process. This fact presents a management problem for teachers: although children can listen to their teacher or read a page in their books, they can also notice various noneducational matters instead. They can watch the flies on the ceiling, study the good looks of another student, or listen to noises out in the street. If it is just before lunch, they can even listen to their empty stomachs—literally!

Ways must be found, therefore, to get and hold students' attention to the tasks that relate to their education. One way is to vary the stimuli given to students (Keele, 1973). Instead of using just one method of presentation (say, discussions), try intermingling it with others—say, lectures

variety in presentation of material

and individual work. Or within a particular mode of presentation, try providing variety as well: some studies suggest that students attend and learn better if their instructors vary their gestures, intonation, and bodily movements (Rosenshine, 1971). When carried far enough, such variety is usually construed as enthusiasm, a quality that most students admire in their teachers. Written and printed material can follow the same principle by varying the graphic layout of words on the page, making some larger or smaller than usual, or by changing the print or even its color (see Figure 7–2). Even the teacher's blackboard writing can be varied in these ways to some extent, as by interspersing printing with script or using differently colored pens for an overhead projector.

The language of teaching can also affect students' tendencies to pay attention. Up to a point, students will listen better if teachers use words that arouse them or that evoke vivid images. Slang often does the same,

use of colorful language

as long as it is current and does not date the teacher. Feeling words or expressions—*murder, love, cry,* for example—often do both. The use of colorful language, though, can also be overdone and thereby lose its impact, or it can be used sparingly but in poor taste, as when slang verges on profanity. Students have varying thresholds of good taste and varying expectations regarding casual language, to which teachers should be sensitive.

In general, any stimulus that differs from the ones near it can attract attention more effectively than one that duplicates the others. Interspersing a joke in a serious discussion can help attention (Kaplan & Pascoe,

averting habituation

1977), as can varying the difficulty of a series of math problems (easy, hard, middling, and back again) or introducing a topic that does not fit the students' existing knowledge ("Ever hear of a man-eating plant?"). All of these techniques help fight **habituation**, or just plain boredom, as teachers

Figure 7–2 Illustrations of Graphic Variety

are more likely to call it in practice. None of them however, ensures that learning in and of itself will occur but only that learning can begin. Adding bells and whistles to a teaching performance guarantees only that students will watch the performance—not that they will understand it.

Improving Short-term Memory and Transfer   Whether or not we intend it, most of us forget most of what we do pay attention to. Most stimuli go in one ear and out the other, as the saying goes—or into short-term memory and out again, in information-processing terms. For better or for worse, the principle applies to school learning as well: students forget most of what they hear teachers say or see them do. The reasons are varied but relate at least in part to students' difficulties in relating their learning to knowledge and experiences that they already have or expect to have. This is the problem of *transfer,* which is so important in teaching that it will be discussed separately in the next chapter.

Most learning that lacks transfer value is forgotten. When persons learn three-letter nonsense syllables, for example, they often can recall, only a few minutes later, less than a quarter of what they learned (Guilford, 1952, p. 408). More meaningful kinds of verbal material (prose and poetry) are recalled better than nonsense is, presumably because the learners can relate it to preexisting, more permanent knowledge. A challenge in teaching, then is to make the curriculum meaningful in various ways, by connecting it whenever possible with the students' existing knowledge. According to psychologist David Ausubel: "If I had to reduce all of educational psychology to one principle, it would be this: The most important single factor influencing learning is what the learner already knows. Ascertain this and then teach him accordingly" (1978, p. iv).

rapid forgetting of nonmeaningful data

Aiding Long-term Memory   Long-term memory is the part of the mental system that attempts, among other things, to relate new knowledge held in short-term memory to already existing knowledge, usually stored in long-term memory. The job usually is to relate the new to the old: compared with existing knowledge, new ideas or terms must be seen as the same or different, as more specific or more general, as larger or

meaning as an aid to memory

Learning the same material in several different ways helps to improve its transfer to other situations. (Elizabeth Crews)

smaller, but in some way related. By making the new material meaning-ful, these relationships help in remembering it, as well as in recalling it later. As a rule, students probably have fewer resources to draw on than do their teachers in forming such relationships between the old and the new, which may be another way of saying that they have less knowledge and thus are apt to find learning less intrinsically meaningful. Studying a map of the world may mean rather little to children who have never even left their home town and who lack the notions about politics, climate, and geography that give the map its importance.

With help from their teachers, however, students can find meaning in their studies. They can consciously look for **mediators**—familiar terms or devices that link new, unfamiliar ones. This traditional poem of young children is a mediating device: "Thirty days hath September, April, June, and November; All the rest have thirty-one; Save February, which stands alone." The familiar rhythms and vocabulary of English help associate the unfamiliar and arbitrary information about the lengths of the months. By the same token, of course, the device does *not* mediate very well for chil-dren lacking skill with standard English—notably bilingual children and perhaps some bidialectical children.

use of verbal mediators

In general, any way of organizing information seems to help students recall it later. Some psychologists favor a *hierarchical organization* wher-ever possible (Ausubel, 1978; White, 1974): more specific concepts should be related to more general ones that include them, and vice versa. A number of research studies support this idea. In one, college students had to memorize four undifferentiated lists of twenty-eight words each (Bower, 1970). One list might have looked like this:

hierarchical organization as an aid to memory

perch	bobolink	eagle
beetle	bee	rhinoceros
shark	pickerel	owl
deer	dragonfly	kangaroo
(and so on)		

Another group of students in the study learned the same information from a tree-diagram like the one below:

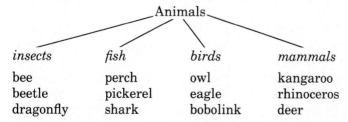

insects	*fish*	*birds*	*mammals*
bee	perch	owl	kangaroo
beetle	pickerel	eagle	rhinoceros
dragonfly	shark	bobolink	deer

When both groups were tested later for recall, the group with the organ-ized presentation performed much better than the other group did: by their third trial at recalling the names, in fact, they remembered all 112 words perfectly!

Teachers can use this finding whenever they can organize content into general categories that contain specific concepts or ideas. Memorizing the Periodic Table of the Elements, for example, may be done more easily by grouping the elements into their general types—metals, neutral gases, radioactive elements, and the like. Or, remembering the structure and functions of government may come more easily by grouping the structures and functions into several general categories—executive, legislative, and judicial, for example.

Some content, of course, cannot be easily grouped into hierarchical structures: how, for instance, could you group the names of all the U.S. presidents? For such a motley assortment, a structure must be imposed. They can be grouped by chronology—all those before 1800 in one group, 1800 to the Civil War in the next, and so on. Or they can be grouped by their region of origin—all the northern presidents in one group, all the southern ones in another, and so on. Or in various other ways as well. These really are hierarchical organizations imposed on the information, however imperfectly they may fit some of the facts. Which grouping is best depends on how well it helps the students learn the information and on what the teacher expects the students to do in the long run with the information.

Limitations of Information-Processing Theory

As with other theories of learning, information processing can be criticized on several grounds. Modeling human thinking after a computer, for example, impresses some psychologists and educators as rather arbitrary (Hilgard & Bower, 1975). Why, they ask, divide human thinking into particular parts (as shown in Figure 7–1 at the beginning of this chapter)? One feature that seems arbitrary is the implication that the processing of information must be in a long series of steps, one at a time. But real-world problem solving often requires doing several steps at once and then combining the results at the end. Shopping for several items in a store may require keeping one's eyes open for all the items simultaneously, without a commitment to finding them in any particular order. This may in turn require receiving and storing a variety of perceptions at the same time. Some revisions of the information-processing theory, the so-called parallel processing systems, have tried to remedy this situation by postulating several short-term memories or processors, rather than just one. Unfortunately for practical people like teachers, such revisions of the model can quickly become unwieldy, since no one of them can account for the variety of real-world problems that humans can normally solve.

In addition, the information-processing model has sometimes been crit-

real thinking
processes
oversimplified

icized for using machine-like language to rename familiar, human activities that teachers have been concerned about for a long time. In practice, sensory detectors seem to mean eyes and ears; sensory synthesis seems to mean perception or recognition; short-term memory seems to correspond to conscious attention; and long-term memory seems to contain the ideas of memory, thinking, and their many variants. Using computer language for these eternal phenomena may help cognitive psychologists analyze them in new ways. But it is not clear that it helps teachers, who must usually respond to student thinking immediately, rather than after the next psychological study is completed.

familiar processes
renamed

Nevertheless, information-processing theory does provide a healthy emphasis on the *analysis* of human thinking and how individuals may combine information in organized ways to result in learning. Whether or not the theory's particular dissection of the mind has merit, its general belief in doing so certainly does and has been shared by other cognitively oriented theories of learning. And so the next sections of this book will consider other prominent examples of this approach.

BRUNER'S THEORY OF INSTRUCTION

Jerome Bruner has written extensively about human thinking and how it occurs—and should occur—during instruction. His writing on education shows Piaget's philosophizing tendencies and is a rich fund of ideas, though with somewhat less emphasis than usual on the experimental proof of each idea. Compared with the other theories of learning in our book, Bruner's is less tightly organized, to the point, in fact, that some even question whether his deserves to be called a theory. A number of themes run through Bruner's writings, however, that suggest a definite point of view, one that shows a cognitive slant (see Table 7–2).

Basic Concepts

Three Processes of Thinking   Bruner thinks of learning as a mixture of three processes: acquisition, transformation, and testing of adequacy (1966, 1971, 1973). These are steps in an individual's active organization of knowledge, the hallmark of cognitively oriented theories. To an extent, Bruner's processes parallel the analysis of learning made by information-processing theory. Acquisition looks a bit like sensory reception and synthesis; transformation looks something like the routines that long-term memory applies to new information; and testing looks a little like response generation. Bruner's second and third processes also resemble Piaget's ideas of assimilation and accommodation, respectively. Transformation and assimilation both refer to changing information to fit

acquisition

testing and
transformation

preexisting knowledge (or Piagetian schemes), and testing and accomodation both change old knowledge to fit new information. Bruner does not, however, intend any explicit parallels between his theory and these other points of view.

simultaneous processing

Bruner's three processes of learning happen at virtually the same time: children cannot acquire knowledge without transforming it and testing it almost in the same breath. In learning that water freezes into ice, for example, children will almost immediately compare the idea with their own previous experiences of water and ice (testing) and at the same time extend and apply the idea to new situations (transforming). In transforming, they may wonder whether other liquids also freeze into ice—how about alcohol, milk, vegetable oil? Notice, though, that the children in this example must first have been taught something about water and ice in order for transformation and testing to occur. In Bruner's model of learning, society, including teachers, has a responsibility to give information and skills to children as well as to allow them to process it. In this way Bruner differs from Piaget, who sometimes gave the impression that children must discover the raw materials of learning completely on their own.

enactive learning

Three Modes of Learning Bruner also believes that learning can occur in any of three ways or *modes:* enactive, iconic, or symbolic. **Enactive learning** bears a striking resemblance to Piaget's sensorimotor

Table 7–2 Key Terms in Bruner's Theory of Instruction

Three processes of thinking

Acquisition: the receiving of perceptions and knowledge from experience.

Transformation: the changing of new perceptions and knowledge into more meaningful forms.

Testing: actions designed to assess the adequacy or accuracy of existing knowledge.

Three modes of learning

Enactive: learning by means of the active manipulation of objects.

Iconic: learning by means of mental images or representations of sensory experiences.

Symbolic: learning by means of arbitrary representations of experience (such as language) that bear no physical resemblance to the experience itself.

Other terms

Spiral curriculum: a program of studies that returns periodically to the same topics in revised or more advanced form.

Discovery learning: learning that relies on the student's motivation to learn and his or her ability to formulate questions of study and to pursue them.

The enactive mode of learning described by Bruner resembles Piaget's sensorimotor period of development: both refer to learning and thinking through actual
physical behaviors. (Jean-Claude Lejeune/Stock, Boston)

intelligence: it means learning by manipulating objects—doing things rather
than conceiving of them. Children may know how to jump rope ("enact"
the skill), but not how to describe the activity in words, nor even how to
picture it in their minds. **Iconic learning** is pictorial; in this mode, chil-   iconic learning
dren represent knowledge through mental images, which can also come
in a series much like a slide show for representing more complex activities
or memories. Children may be able to picture their family's Christmas
tree in their minds, even though they cannot explain that picture very
well in words. **Symbolic learning**, as its name implies, requires arbitrary   symbolic learning
or abstract representations of knowledge, and as such, it resembles Pi-
aget's formal operational thinking. Because the most prominent system
of abstract representation is human language, children cannot think symbolically very well until they have achieved fluency in talking. Even then,
however, they may not process all learning in a symbolic mode. Adults—
even those good with language—may still not be able to explain in words
how to jump rope or how their Christmas trees look each year. Acquiring

the ability to use each mode does not guarantee its actual use in every situation. As a result, teachers may still have much work to do with students of all ages, to help them use each mode of representation more effectively.

Educational Implications of Bruner's Theory

Bruner's theory of instruction explains when and how learners can process information most effectively in these three modes of representation. Unfortunately for teachers, his ideas offer few practical suggestions for doing so but, rather, several general ones about what to include in a fully worked-out theory. Significantly, Bruner entitled one of his major works *Toward a Theory of Instruction* (1966), reflecting not only his belief that no complete, usable theory yet exists but also his emphasis on the process of learning rather than its products. Bruner's discussion of instruction, like that of learning generally, is more of a search for answers than a presentation of the search's final results. In any case, Bruner believes that any theory of instruction should include the following elements:

elements of a useful theory of instruction

1. *Information about how to create favorable intentions and goals among students.* A usable theory of instruction must recognize that learners have active purposes of their own, that these may not coincide with the teachers', and that teachers must persuade their students to *want* to learn. In some ways, this idea parallels Robert Gagné's concern with attitude learning, discussed later in this chapter, as well as the concerns of most educators with motivation, examined in Chapter 11. How, for example, can teachers generate interest in the causes of the American Civil War, in the titration of an acid, or in socialized medicine? Students must want to learn about such topics before they will in fact do so, and any theory of instruction must somehow deal with this fact.

understanding students' purposes

2. *Organizing knowledge to aid learning.* The form that knowledge takes in advanced presentations of it (for example, at a conference of professors) does not necessarily coincide with the forms that can be learned most efficiently by comparative beginners. Educators, including teachers, must transform the subjects they teach to usable—learnable—forms for their students. Any theory of instruction that is supposed to serve teachers must therefore reconcile subject matter with the psychology of learning: reconcile what students need to know with how they are able to know it.

appropriate organization

3. *Sequencing knowledge to aid learning.* This part of Bruner's theory of instruction refers to the developmental theme discussed in Chapters 2 through 5 of this book: how to present information in a way that allows for long-run changes in the learner. Bruner is optimistic about teachers' being able to do so. In a widely quoted passage, he writes, "Any idea or problem or body of knowledge can be presented in a form simple enough

sequencing knowledge

As Bruner points out, successful teaching depends on generating interest in a topic. (Helen Nestor/Monkmeyer Press Photo Service)

so that any particular learner can understand it in a recognizable form" (1966, p. 44). Although some educators have criticized this idea as simplistic, it contains an element of truth. Advanced algebra, for example, cannot be taught to kindergarten children in the abstract way it is often taught to high school and university students. But some basic algebraic notions may be taught if they are converted from symbolic forms to the enactive or iconic modes more suited to young children. At appropriate points later in their education, children can return to these concepts in new forms and new contexts.

This doubling back of instruction on itself over time, Bruner calls the **spiral curriculum.** Concepts, topics, and whole subject areas, he believes, should return again and again to the student, in increasingly complex frameworks each time. Algebra may begin in kindergarten as an active discovery of numerical correspondences among tangible objects in the room; it may return later in elementary school as rules and procedures for visualizing specific numerical relationships; and it may return still later in

spiral curriculum

high school as abstract principles that govern numerical relationships in general, independent of the specific numbers involved. This last version approximates *algebra* as adults understand the term, but the first and second ones belong to the study of algebra just as much.

4. *The roles of success, failure, reinforcement, and punishment.* Reinforcement and punishment have been studied extensively in behaviorist theories of learning, though often without enough emphasis on complex learning situations to suit the needs of teachers. Bruner believes that in complex situations—including classrooms—reinforcement and punishment function as information about success and failure, rather than as direct influences on behavior. Such information reinforcement can come from the learners themselves, or from others. Somehow a theory of instruction must allow for these real-world complications.

5. *Motivating learning in school settings.* How, in other words, can we put more vim and vigor into students' learning? This element of Bruner's theory of instruction is closely related to the first one, about understanding students' purposes. Bruner focuses here on the results of their purposes: how teachers can get students to initiate their own learning. One way, according to Bruner, is through **discovery learning** (see Chapter 12); that is, teachers should stimulate their students to investigate learning materials and information on their own, and students should form their own ideas and concepts from these investigations.

To illustrate discovery learning, Bruner (1966) developed a social studies curriculum for elementary school children called *Man: A Course Of Study* (MACOS). The program teaches child-rearing practices, group relationships, and several aspects of socialization and culture. Rather than simply giving children information about these topics, however, MACOS invites them to form their own ideas about them. They can do so by comparing information from several different sources: Eskimo society, for example, baboon troups, and prehistoric society. The curriculum contains information about each of these groups, but it expects the students to do the real work of synthesizing it. How? First, it contrasts practices in one group with those in another; second, it encourages speculation and guessing about the reasons for such differences; third, it asks students to look actively for information to test out their speculations; and fourth, it encourages students to think carefully about their ways of gathering information.

As the curriculum shows, Bruner values the process of learning quite highly (as opposed to its outcome), and he has faith that children will rise to the challenge of active, personally directed learning. Contrary to a popular belief, though, he is not committed to this method of teaching as the only way (see, for example, Bruner, 1960, chap. 2). To some extent, learners must also be given knowledge to manipulate, especially through the

(margin notes:) information as reinforcement; discovery learning; MACOS; emphasis on process of learning

medium of language. They do not always have to reinvent the wheel if their teacher can show them how to make one. In general, such acquisition of knowledge matters less to Bruner than the production of it, at least for typical classroom learning.

Limitations of Bruner's Theory

As stimulating as Bruner's ideas are, they can be frustrating to anyone who seeks precision and clear organization in a theory. His ideas on learning and instruction are scattered among a number of published sources (two of the best are Bruner, 1966 & 1971), and therefore the precise relation of one topic to another sometimes becomes obscure. Bruner himself is interested in a tremendous variety of psychologically related studies, from objective, experimental studies of thinking to speculative essays about creativity and the unconscious (Bruner, 1979). His breadth of interests gives his writings on education some added perspective—educational issues take their proper places in the larger issues of life itself (Bruner, 1982). But the breadth may also prevent him from focusing on the details of daily instruction as most teachers and students experience them under typical conditions.

diffuse terms

Bruner's wide-ranging style reflects another aspect of his theory that is sometimes criticized: his emphasis on *how* learning occurs, at the expense of *what* is actually learned. The process of education (as opposed to its contents) figures heavily, for example, in his notion of discovery learning. What really counts here is how students learn, namely, by using their own strategies and guidance. Some educators, however, argue that Bruner neglects the problem of how students acquire self-guidance in the first place. Some, such as Gagné (see the next section), believe that self-guidance strategies are based on simpler intellectual skills practiced over long periods of time and on huge varieties of learning tasks (Gagné, 1977, 1979, chap. 4). If so, then the bulk of instruction should probably be given in relatively structured forms. Perhaps most instruction should teach content and simple thinking skills to students and use the Bruner kind of freedom to learn in only selected, and somewhat advanced, learning situations.

neglect of learning as content

GAGNÉ'S CLASSIFICATION OF LEARNING TASKS

Robert Gagné bases his ideas on both the behaviorist and cognitively oriented theories of learning (1977). He distinguishes several types of learning, which are listed in Table 7–3 along with a brief definition and example of each. Most of the categories classify what teachers ordinarily would call "thinking," although Gagné conceives of these categories more as outcomes of learning than as processes by which learning occurs. The distinction may have little relevance to the daily use of his theory, but it does reflect its behaviorist influence, with its focus on overt performance rather than the internal processing of information.

Gagné believes that many forms of learning are based on conditioning processes like those described in the last chapter: the reinforcement of specific behaviors, the chaining together of responses, and simple verbal associations. Although these processes continue to affect learning throughout a student's educational career, they also combine into or contribute to more complex processes like those listed in Table 7–3. The next several pages will examine the nature of each of these processes and what each one implies for instruction.

Table 7–3 Five Major Categories of Learned Capabilities According to Gagné

Learned capability	Definition	Example
Intellectual skill		
Discrimination	Noticing differences between two objects.	Distinguishing printed *m*'s and *n*'s.
Concept	Relating or identifying a group of objects or other concepts.	Correctly naming two or three examples of a cat or defining a mammal.
Rule	Applying a class of relationships among a class of concepts to a particular instance.	Demonstrating a sentence's agreement in number of subject and verb.
Cognitive strategies	Finding methods for making thinking and learning effective.	Using an efficient way to recall names.
Verbal information	Stating labels, facts, or the essential meaning of verbal knowledge.	Reciting the names of European countries or stating the essence of the Gettysburg address.
Motor skill	Performing an action according to certain standards of perfection.	Swimming, handwriting.
Attitude	Choosing to act one way rather than another or choosing a certain class of actions.	Choosing to study an assignment rather than to go to a movie.

Intellectual Skills

In Gagné's theory, the most concrete kind of intellectual skill is **discrimination learning**: distinguishing objects by their visible, tangible properties. Young children learn discrimination skills when, for example, they learn to tell the difference between red objects and pink ones or between the letter *p* and the letter *b*. High school science students learn discrimination skills when they learn to distinguish a blood vessel from an artery during a laboratory dissection or when they learn to distinguish a warbler from a sparrow from observing actual specimens. To be sure, older students may improve their discrimination ability by using various verbal rules, but these cannot replace the perceptual ability they will need for actual identifications.

discrimination learning

Concepts consist of mental groupings of objects or events that relate to one another in some way. Children have acquired the concept of "fish," for example, if they can use the term to refer to all—and only to all—the objects that swim in the water, have gills and fins, and so on. In using such a concept, of course, children may not be able to state the definition itself, as teachers often discover from giving vocabulary tests that ask for verbal definitions. Adults, too, often experience the same limitation at more sophisticated levels: you may be able to identify examples of dinosaurs without being able to define them accurately or fully.

concepts

This problem highlights a distinction that Gagné makes between "concrete" concepts and "defined" concepts. Concrete concepts refer to classes of real objects (*fish, car, pencil,* and so on). Defined concepts, on the other hand, are relationships among groups of other concepts. Usually these relationships are expressed verbally. *Democracy, intelligence,* and *thinking* all are defined concepts, even though each term may sometimes also refer to some particular concrete object or event.

Concepts also relate to one another by statements that Gagné calls **rules**. Young children learn such rules when, for example, they always raise their hand in class before speaking or when they invariably add *-s* to words that refer to more than one object. As with concepts, they need not know how to state a rule in order to use it. Much of children's and adults' intuitive behavior may depend on using rules that they cannot articulate. A teen-ager may know not to cross his dad when he gets a certain unpleasant look on his face, without being able to say why he knows. Rules can, in principle, combine into complex forms—rules about rules, or higher-order rules.

rules

Educational Implications Even though these skills range from logically simple to logically complex, they do not form a developmental hierarchy in the way that, say, Piaget's stages do. Except possibly for young preschoolers, students of all ages can, in principle, acquire and use every type of intellectual skill, from discriminations to higher-order rules and cognitive strategies.

Learning any particular skill, though, may depend on having first learned its simpler components. Gagné's classification of intellectual skills can help teachers analyze complex skills into their logical prerequisites, and in so doing it can help them sequence particular units of instruction. Following such a procedure, however, may not always reflect the steps in learning without instruction. One study found that students learned the complex general task of ordering numbers in ways that resembled, but did not duplicate, Gagné's analysis of the task (Airasian & Bert, 1975). The results implied that teachers would do well to analyze intellectual skills, as Gagné has, but that they should remain ready to modify their instructional sequencing to fit the actual learning behaviors of their students.

sequencing of instruction

Cognitive Strategies

Rules can also pertain to procedures for finding out knowledge, rather than contain or convey knowledge itself. Gagné calls such search-oriented rules **cognitive strategies**. They resemble the processing rules mentioned in the information-processing model of learning, and they seem also to refer to much of what Bruner considers important in learning. Cognitive strategies guide the search for knowledge, rather than constitute the results of it. A university student may use a strategy like this one: "When confronted by an assignment of type X, look up the rules for completing it on page 000 of the textbook. If these rules make no sense, then ask the instructor to clarify them before beginning work." Elementary school children may use cognitive strategies to help them read difficult material. They may follow a rule like this: "When confronted by an unfamiliar word in print, recall the rules that we previously learned about how letters and sounds correspond." This strategy itself does not help them sound out the word, but it does help them find rules that will help them do so. Indirectly, then, using this particular cognitive strategy can help children recognize many new words in print—without ever having been explicitly taught their spoken equivalents.

cognitive strategies

As with intellectual skills, students may not state their cognitive strategies in so many words but simply act on them intuitively. In the examples above, the college student may not actually articulate this way of figuring out an assignment but instead may just go ahead and look up the appropriate place in the text. And the elementary school children may not literally recite their rule about confronting new words but may simply use it. Teachers, for their part, may not always think to suggest such strategies to students who need them, and instead may leave them to devise such strategies for themselves. In many cases, some students do succeed in finding the strategies they need. But in other cases they do not, and teachers are responsible for helping those students—the ones who need help with *how* to learn.

Verbal Learning

Gagné distinguishes three other forms of learning in addition to intellectual skills and cognitive strategies: verbal learning, motor skill learning, and attitude learning. Each of these depends to some extent on a fund of cognitive knowledge, but each also contains its own qualities that teachers must keep in mind when planning for instruction.

Verbal learning is acquiring names and labels, facts, and larger units of language or discourse. By definition, verbal learning must be capable of being put into words, but perhaps more important, it must also be meaningful in some sense to the learner. Learning that the French word for "eat" is *manger* is learning a label; learning that the capital of Canada is Ottawa is learning a fact; and learning the main themes underlying the Bill of Rights is learning a connected discourse.

learning labels, facts, and connected discourses

Verbal learning, especially of facts and discourse, should not be confused with other types of learning. It does not necessarily mean memorizing words verbatim or by rote: doing so would constitute only such verbal conditioning as the behaviorists describe. But it also does not mean acquiring only the kernel ideas from verbal material, devoid of their expression in words. In principle, acquiring essential ideas requires intellectual skills, not verbal learning. In practice, though, intellectual and verbal skills are learned and used together. You may sense, for example, that one of your students knows more than she can say, but in practice she can usually say what she thinks, at least to some extent. As stated earlier in Chapter 3, language and thought cannot be easily separated.

Verbal learning provides many of the building blocks that intellectual skills require. Consider those students who are just beginning to learn the somewhat abstract concept of democracy. Forming a clear concept of this term requires using many discriminations, concepts, and rules, all the intellectual skills described earlier. But to use these skills, students must also be able to state in words many terms, facts, and ideas. To define democracy, they must make (or think to themselves) a statement like "Democracy is majority rule with checks and balances," or something along those lines. To understand the terms and relationships in this definition, they must in turn make statements like "Majority means more than half, and 'to rule' in democracy means to lead in response to others, not to dictate." Even these more specific verbal statements may need still further verbal explanations. A full understanding of the concept of democracy, then, will draw on a host of verbal knowledge, and the students must acquire it all.

Motor Skill Learning

Motor skill learning refers to the acquisition of action-oriented skills, as opposed to thinking-oriented ones. But this distinction can create some confusion at times, since most of what we do also requires some thought (Posner & Keele, 1972). Driving a manual-shift car, for example, requires both knowing what you are supposed to do and actual practice in operating a clutch pedal. Most sports demonstrate this same mixture of knowledge and practice, as do all of the supposedly motor activities that occur in schools: studying musical instruments, learning to print letters, practicing for the school play, or whatever. All consist of procedures assembled from specific physical skills by some sort of organizing process, commonly called "thinking." Helping students acquire such skills, then, requires that teachers attend to thinking as well as doing.

integration of motor and intellectual skills

The intellectual skills of motor learning call for the same analysis already outlined above. Learning to play basketball, for example, means learning certain rules of the game, when to dribble and when not, how the scoring works, and so on. These in turn assume that the students understand the concepts that the rules refer to, what a dribble is or what shooting a basket means. Each of these concepts, in turn, assumes that the students can correctly distinguish true examples from false ones; they must know a dribble when they see one and not confuse it with similar seeming behaviors. Besides all of these intellectual skills, they must learn strategies for evaluating plays, not only when dribbling is permissible, for example, but also when it is desirable.

importance of practice

But these theory skills are complete only if the students also acquire the physical skills needed for the game, the actual acts of dribbling, passing, shooting, running, and so forth. Unlike the intellectual skills, these seem to depend much more on sheer practice than on insight. In the case of basketball, the students must stand at the free-throw line shooting ball after ball, and they must practice dribbling over and over again. After some practice they can attempt many (amateur-looking) games that help them assemble their partial skills into their proper places. At that point, though, any thinking skills they have in regard to the nature of the game will begin to guide their actions as well.

helping students understand skills

Educational Implications   How can teachers help this whole process? As already implied above, part of their job is to help students understand the skill intellectually, its rules and concepts and general strategies. Their teaching must, of course, be adjusted to the learners' existing intellectual skills: concepts alien to them have to be explained in terms of other concepts they already know or to be related to simpler component knowledge that they already possess. If students in a sewing class do not know what a "flat-felled seam" is, then their teacher must either relate that concept to others they already know ("A seam folded double and hemmed along each border") or else show them ("It looks like this and not that"). The latter technique is essentially discriminative learning.

Motor skills are learned best by combining practice sessions with occasional demonstrations and feedback on how the students are doing. Practice time, however, is often scarce in school settings, since by its nature it uses up large chunks of the school day. As a result, students often receive practice in their homework: learning a new selection on the clarinet, filling out extra work sheets of printed letters, or learning to make a hook shot for the basketball team. In theory, students can work on these skills largely on their own, and therefore after school. In reality, they may have even more trouble finding practice time at home than at school, in which case they will greet their teachers with little more skill than they had when they left school the day before.

Students and teachers often wonder whether practice is more effective when *distributed* through many small sessions over a long period of time or *massed* together into longer sessions spanning a relatively short overall period. Research comparing the two patterns has produced conflicting results, possibly because the best method seems to depend on the nature of the task. When motor skills are involved, large bunches of practice often depress performance by causing physical fatigue (Whitely, 1970). Children practicing penmanship, for example, can get cramped hands and fingers relatively rapidly. The improvement in performance after a period of rest suggests that distributing practice may work best for such skills. Complex motor skills may eventually need to be practiced in their entirety, however, if they are to be perfected fully.

distributed versus massed practice

When intellectual skills are involved, the best pattern of practice depends on the type of material being learned. Facts or ideas are usually retained better if learned in separate contexts or situations, apparently because each bit of learning becomes associated with distinct cues (D' Agostino & DeRemer, 1973; Elmes et al., 1972). This advantage of distributed practice is sometimes called the **lag effect** because of the gap in time between learning sessions. The dates of the French Revolution (1789) and the American Revolution (1776), for example, may be easily confused if learned together. But they may seem very distinct if learned several months apart. Learned apart, each fact has its own reminders working for it: 1789 may be learned in a context of facts about European history, but 1776 may be surrounded by facts about the American Constitution and history. Some associations may even be irrelevant to the content itself: 1789 may remind the student of snow, therefore of the winter semester, and therefore of the European history course taken that semester.

lag effect

Some intellectual or verbal content, however, is learned more effectively in single, massed sessions. In particular, ideas that make sense only in conjunction with other ideas may have to be learned together. An essay may be comprehended more effectively by reading it in one sitting rather than in many; distributing this task may chop up its essentials beyond recognition. Or watching a film in many small sittings may completely obscure its message. Or reading a paragraph quickly may actually lead to better comprehension than reading it slowly would—in this case by helping the reader relate the paragraph's ideas more successfully.

Whether teaching motor skills or intellectual skills, teachers must decide how and when practice should be divided. In principle, they can follow two guidelines in deciding about any given content:

guidelines for massed and distributed practice

1. The amount of previous, related learning the students have acquired. If they have learned all of the prerequisites to a concept or rule, then they may benefit from learning the concept or rule as a whole. If not, the students may need to practice the components separately.
2. The intrinsic connections in the specific content to be learned. A concept or rule that intrinsically forms a whole may have to be learned as a whole. The definition of a verb, for example, depends intrinsically on the meanings of the other parts of speech; perhaps, therefore, they all should be learned together.

Attitude Learning

Attitude learning refers to a disposition to behave in a certain way, rather than to any actual behavior itself. If you "like ice cream," for example, it means that you tend to eat ice cream, but it does not imply that you have an ice-cream cone in your hand on every possible occasion. This indirect relationship to behavior makes it difficult to know when attitude learning occurs. If I do not see you eating ice cream on a certain occasion, does that mean that you have changed your attitude toward that food or just that I happened not to see you at the right time? I can settle this question only by observing you repeatedly and comparing how often I see you eating ice cream with how often I do not. This procedure, of course, can be a lot of work.

Teachers face the problem of assessing attitudes, along with other kinds of learning. In one form or another, they wonder about their students' attitudes: their feelings about school, a particular course, or even a particular assignment. In doing so, teachers wonder what students *think* ("What would they say about thus-and-so?"), as well as how they *feel* ("Will they like the course?"). Perhaps most important from a practical standpoint, however, teachers may wonder what students will do ("Will they be likely to recommend me to their friends?"). All three aspects—thoughts, feelings, and behavioral tendencies—make up the notion of attitudes. In this way they resemble values (see Chapter 3), except that they are not so strongly held or so resistant to change.

elements of attitude learning

As a milder form of values education, therefore, attitude learning provokes some of the same ethical controversies mentioned earlier: is it right to try to change students' attitudes? Do teachers have any business playing with students' feelings? And so on. Some attitudes, however, seem beyond these controversies. Nearly everyone, for example, would favor students' developing positive attitudes toward school, a respect for others, or a love of learning. These attitudes, in fact, form the core of most teachers' concerns about developing attitudes among their students. They are on safe ground ethically but may not know how to proceed.

Educational Implications   Gagné suggests several conditions that improve the learning of attitudes. Students must, first of all, *know* something about whatever they are expected to have an attitude. They cannot form an attitude toward the two-party system, for example, or ecology, until they have mastered the concepts and relationships that constitute knowledge of these areas. Such learning presumably can be helped by the suggestions for intellectual skills made earlier in this chapter and to be continued in the next chapter.

integration of attitudes with cognitive skills

At the same time, the emotional and behavioral aspects of attitudes may need more than mere knowledge if they are to be conveyed effectively. For these, Gagné recommends combining observational role modeling and reinforcement procedures, essentially the social learning theory described in the last chapter. Teachers can, for example, demonstrate good habits of courtesy, careful thinking, or any other attitude they deem important. As a supplement to setting a good example, they can ask students to *role-play* situations that express valuable attitudes, which may help students understand the attitudes and how they are expressed.

modeling of attitudes

At the same time, of course, naturally occurring expressions of good attitudes can and should be reinforced whenever possible. Courtesy should be recognized whenever it occurs, as should behavior that shows a respect for individuals or indicates good work habits. Given the nature of our society, these predispositions can only help the students who express them, and teachers therefore have an obligation to reinforce them.

reinforcement of attitudes

Instructional Applications of Gagné's Theory

As my grandmother used to say, "Sometimes one thing happens, and sometimes another." Gagné's theory is based on a variation of this idea, that learning comes in many different forms and therefore needs many different explanations. It is *eclectic,* meaning that it draws on diverse sources of information and psychological theories. It makes room for behavioristic forms of learning; yet it allows for intellectual skills to be treated on their own terms, much as information-processing theory does. And it finds a place for observational learning. By drawing on various theories, Gagné recognizes the complexity of learning with which teachers must reckon.

eclectic view of learning

In the process, his theory loses some of the systematic quality and consistency of the other theories. But this may be a small price to pay if it reflects the nature of learning more accurately. If learning really is complex, then perhaps a practical theory of it must be complex as well.

To use Gagné's theory, then, one must know when to apply the other theories of learning contained within it. A teacher must in effect perform a **task analysis** on the material to be learned, in order to find out what sort of processes are involved and to sequence them appropriately. If you expect students to learn the principle of gravity, for example, then you must first determine what concepts make up this principle—concepts, perhaps, of up-down, heavy-light, and slow-fast. If you wish to improve your students' attitudes toward science, then you must first distinguish between what they must know about the subject and how you might affect their behavior and feelings about it through modeling. If you hope to improve a student's motor skills at lab work, then you must provide enough time and incentive to practice, as well as appropriate demonstrations and theoretical guidance. Each of these goals requires you to look carefully at the behaviors you expect from your students and to tailor your methods accordingly.

task analysis

Often, of course, classroom learning is a confusing blend of intellectual, motor, and attitude changes. What if the instructional goals are to make the students into good musicians? A careful examination of this goal will indicate that it contains an array of possible skills: comparing musical works (intellectual), learning to play the piano (motor), liking music and buying more records (attitudinal), and many more. A closer examination suggests that individual activities for implementing the general goal may serve all the areas of learning at once: learning to perform on the piano may also increase the students' knowledge of music, as well as help them like music more. Given these kinds of overlaps and the ambiguities of some teaching goals, an analysis of tasks and goals becomes both more needed and more difficult. Gagné's theory of learning is intended to help with such analysis, as are the systems described in the next section.

OTHER CLASSIFICATIONS OF LEARNING

In addition to Gagné, other psychologists have made classifications of learning outcomes.

Bloom's Cognitive Taxonomy

One well-known system was originated quite a few years ago by Benjamin Bloom and his associates (1956) and has proved useful ever since for both research and teaching (Furst, 1981). Bloom's **taxonomy**—or classification system—pertains to the cognitive objectives of instruction and divides them into several types. These range from goals referring to relatively concrete intellectual skills to ones referring to very abstract thought. Bloom classifies learning into the following categories.

focus on cognitive goals

1. *Knowledge*—the ability, on request, to remember, recall, or recognize facts or ideas. Remembering the atomic weights of all the metallic elements is an example of this type of learning, as is recognizing all the capitals of the American states from a list that the teacher provides.
2. *Comprehension*—the ability to use knowledge that is remembered more or less as it is originally presented and intended to be used. Explaining the causes of inflation, for example, qualifies as comprehension as long as the student does not merely recite the teacher's statements on the subject.
3. *Application*—the ability to use general ideas or principles in particular situations. Finding a certain book in the library, for example, constitutes application if the student has previously learned only the general ways by which the library organizes books.
4. *Analysis*—the ability to separate the elements of an idea or passage and to examine each one individually. Writing a critique of a film, for example, requires analysis if the student must respond separately to several aspects of it—its plot, photography, theme, and the like. It would not involve analysis, though, if the student simply expressed general feelings about the film—"I loved it" or "I hated it."
5. *Synthesis*—the ability to combine elements into greater structures or wholes. Writing an essay about several films, for example, uses synthesis if the student has to find and describe aspects that all the films have in common. It does not involve synthesis, though, if the student's essay merely paraphrases synthesizing ideas found elsewhere, such as in a film review magazine.
6. *Evaluation*—the ability to judge how well ideas and materials satisfy certain criteria. An essay or oral commentary on the merits of a particular historical theory is an example that requires evaluation if, and only if, the criteria for judging the theory are clear and explicit to the student.

Krathwohl's Affective Taxonomy

Because Bloom's categories analyze only cognitive learning, other psychologists have created a separate taxonomy for classifying feeling-oriented or **affective goals** (Krathwohl et al., 1964). All of these categories indicate the ways that learners become aware of and adopt the values and attitudes that guide human conduct. The categories themselves range from those that imply very little involvement or commitment, to those that imply quite a bit of it.

focus on affective goals

1. *Receiving*—the willingness to be sensitive and to attend to various kinds of stimuli. Noticing the different uses of color and perspective in two paintings, for example, requires this willingness.
2. *Responding*—the desire to do something about stimuli or ideas besides merely notice them. Discussing the differences between two paintings, for example, shows responding ability in this sense, regardless of what the learner actually says about them.
3. *Valuing*—the feeling and belief that some object, ideas, or group of ideas has worth. In essence the learner adopts an attitude that already exists somewhere else—perhaps in the teacher, peers, or family. Deciding that knowing about masterpieces of painting is worthwhile, for example, shows valuing—as long as the decision is sincere.
4. *Organization*—the relationship of specific values to one another in order to form a system, as well as deciding these values' priority in one's life. One may, for example, decide that knowledge in general is desirable, and thus a knowledge of art masterpieces would be only one part of this general commitment.
5. *Characterization by a value or value complex*—the organization of values into systems, as well as the integration of the systems themselves with one another. One, therefore, reconciles one's conduct with one's beliefs as much as possible, as well as one's values across widely different realms of activity. This may include expressing one's general valuing of knowledge by actually obtaining further education or by finding both work and leisure activities that consistently express this value.

Educational Implications

As with Gagné's classification of learning, the taxonomies by Bloom and Krathwohl can help teachers analyze their goals for instruction. A close look at them also shows two difficulties: first, writing and implementing specific educational goals at the highest levels on each of these taxonomies and, second, specifying the prerequisite, simpler skills needed to reach higher-level goals (Bergan, 1980). These difficulties may partly explain why, for example, one study found that virtually all the questions, exercises, and activities suggested by history textbooks concentrated on only the simplest of Bloom's cognitive categories—knowledge goals. In general, these books asked students only to remember, recall, and recognize information, but rarely to do anything more with it (Tractenberg, 1974).

Krathwohl's affect-oriented classification presents the same problem of clarity at the higher levels, as well as another one. How, in particular, do teachers know whether they are legitimately implementing affective goals or whether they are merely imposing values on students? When are students "organizing values" about, say, the importance of making money and when are they distorting their ideas to please that powerful person, their teacher? This sort of problem was studied in Chapter 4, under moral behavior and development. The other problem, achieving clarity in setting instructional goals, will be taken up in the next chapter.

CREATIVE THINKING

Although they touch upon the topic, none of the cognitive theories described so far focus explicitly on **creativity**: the production of new ideas, activities, or objects. Considering that creativity is to some degree a thinking process, this omission may seem surprising. In part, the omission may be attributed to the number and variety of the term's definitions. One definition of creativity, for example, emphasizes its rational, problem-solving quality (Guilford, 1977); another treats creativity as an expression of good mental health or self-actualization (Maslow, 1954); still another regards creativity as a result of disguised or partially unconscious needs and thoughts (Jung, 1971). These definitions do not so much conflict with one another as emphasize different aspects of the same underlying process. The first of these definitions—the cognitively oriented one—has proved the most useful to educators, and certain psychologists and educators have elaborated on and clarified it.

variety of definitions

The Nature of Creative Thinking

One common viewpoint explains creativity as **divergent thinking** (Guilford, 1977; Mansfield & Busse, 1981), the ability to produce a wide variety of solutions to a problem, however unusual or unconventional these may be. Divergent thinking is often contrasted with **convergent thinking**, the ability to produce one relatively well-defined solution to a problem. Some situations and problems lend themselves more to convergent thinking; and others, to divergent thinking. Some individuals, however, seem predisposed to provide convergent solutions—and others, to provide divergent ones—no matter what the problem is. Because quite a bit of instruction rewards convergent problem solving (see Chapter 13 on the evaluation of learning), the talents of creatively disposed students may often go unrecognized.

Divergent thinking has four important features. The first of these is **fluency**, the ability to produce, without interruption, numerous responses to a stimulus or problem. A second feature is **flexibility**, the ability to approach a problem from a variety of angles without getting fixed on any one in particular. A third is **originality**, the ability to make an unusual or out-of-the-ordinary response. The fourth is **elaboration**, the ability to add richness or detail to a response.

qualities of divergent thinking

Psychologists have designed tests to measure some of these aspects of creativity (Yamamoto, 1964; Torrance, 1974). One such test presents individuals with a common object—perhaps a cup or a stocking or a brick—and asks them to think of as many uses as possible for that object. For a brick, a person might suggest the following uses: wall material, house material, a doorstop, a paperweight, a weapon, a gift to a friend, a footstool, a type of dumbbell—and perhaps others as well.

The number of uses a person thinks of for such objects reflects his or her fluency. In the example above, for instance, the individual produced eight responses. In addition, the person produced four response types—an indicator of flexibility. Doorstop, paperweight, and dumbbell refer to a brick's weight; weapon and gift refer to personal interactions; house material and wall material refer to building activity; and footstool is perhaps in a category by itself. Whether these amounts of fluency and flexibility are comparatively good or bad depends on their context: how well others respond to this particular test item, how well this person responds to other items and (for some educational purposes) how well the individual responded previously to this item and to others like it.

The amount of originality in the above responses depends on how unique or uncommon they are. Of the uses for a brick that the individual named, perhaps the most uncommon are the weapon and the gift for a friend—though we cannot assume this without first testing large numbers of people. Some tests of creativity (or of divergent thinking) attempt to provide the norms or information needed for making such comparisons with large, representative groups (see Chapter 14 on standardized testing).

Measuring originality poses special obstacles to psychologists and educators, in part because originality as defined on psychological tests refers only to how commonly an idea occurs among large numbers of people. In doing so, it excludes another definition of the term, personal originality. **Personal originality** refers to how uncommon or new an idea is for a particular individual, whether or not it is new for society at large. A child's first drawing of a flower may be considered "original" for that child, even though thousands of other children have already drawn countless other flowers. Furthermore, by simply producing many such drawings fluently, the child can improve his or her chances of making one drawing so unusual that everyone—even the most hardened cynic—would consider it truly original. For this reason, among others, some tests of originality may amount largely to tests of fluency. Some research, in fact, supports this relationship (Hocevar, 1979): fluent individuals, by dint of fluency, tend also to have more numerous original ideas.

Encouraging Creativity in Students

Teachers can encourage creative behavior and thinking in a number of ways. First and perhaps most obviously, they can reward or reinforce orig-

unusual uses test

problems in
measuring and
defining originality

inal ideas and activities whenever they occur. Doing so may be easier at some times than at others. It may be easier, for example, during an art activity or creative writing class, when students are supposed to be creative anyway. But it may be harder during a focused discussion in which the teacher is trying to convey certain points to the students; then, divergent comments may seem more like interruptions than creativity. With practice, though, teachers can learn to recognize and encourage creative contributions consistently, even when they are not expecting them.

rewarding creative contributions

Another way to encourage divergent thinking is brainstorming (Osborn, 1963). **Brainstorming** consists of listing or naming all the relevant ideas or solutions to a topic or problem without evaluating them. Consciously separating the production of ideas from their evaluation helps make the production more fluent—and as pointed out above, fluency of thinking is apt to lead to some fairly original ideas. When brainstorming occurs in a group setting, it also helps make individuals more confident about proposing ideas in front of others. Ordinarily, in a group discussion, evaluative comments tend to discourage the production of ideas, and the group may end up debating the value of just one suggestion. The same problem can occur, too, within the mind of a single individual who is trying to generate ideas or solutions to a problem. The person may persist in pondering the pros and cons of one idea instead of searching for many ideas.

deferring judgment

Deferring judgment and reinforcing originality may happen more easily if teachers provide diverse materials and activities for students. Studies of creative persons seem to reveal such diversity in their personal backgrounds (Goertzel et al., 1978; Mansfield & Busse, 1981). Throughout their childhood and youth, they were provided with ample opportunities to explore ideas, activities, and materials. Such experiences convey a message: that fluent, flexible, original, and elaborated thinking and behavior are both possible and valuable. To the extent that teachers can provide diverse experiences and choices for all students, teachers should succeed in encouraging the creativity that exists in everyone, and not only in a few potentially eminent individuals.

providing diverse experiences

A number of commercially published programs exist to encourage diversity in teaching and the creative learning associated with it. Most of these are meant to supplement, not replace, the teacher's own efforts to encourage creativity in the classroom. One program consists of a series of booklets for elementary school children that provide instruction in problem-solving skills (Covington et al., 1974). Some of these skills, though not all, promote divergent thinking. Another program comprises audiotapes and printed exercises for children designed to emphasize and stimulate creative thinking (Feldhusen et al., 1975). Still other materials are books for teachers (for example, Shallcross, 1981; Feldhusen & Treffinger, 1977) intended to help them select among and use various creativity exercises and programs. Reviews of materials and programs like these suggest that they may not have the power to make students exceptionally creative in the long run, but they do help foster the conditions needed for

using commercially published programs

creative behavior in the short run (Mansfield et al., 1978). Few students will earn the Nobel Prize because of instruction in creativity, but many may learn to write more creative essays or to express more creative ideas.

Key Points

1. Compared with the behavioral theories of learning, cognitive learning theories focus more on the internal, unobservable processes of thinking that lead to and result from behavior.
2. Information-processing theory models human learning on the operation of a high-speed computer.
3. The information-processing model has several elements: sensory detectors, a sensory synthesizer, short-term memory, long-term memory, and a response generator.
4. Each element of the information-processing model has implications for improving instruction.
5. Information-processing theory has been criticized for oversimplifying thinking and for merely renaming well-known cognitive processes.
6. Jerome Bruner has written extensively about learning as a cognitive process.
7. Bruner identifies three processes of thinking (acquisition, transformation, and testing) and three modes of learning (enactive, iconic, and symbolic).
8. Bruner discusses several elements of an effective theory of instruction: understanding students' purposes and motives, organizing and sequencing knowledge to aid learning, and using reinforcement as information for the learner.

9. Robert Gagné distinguishes several types of learning outcomes: intellectual skills, cognitive strategies, verbal learning, motor skill learning, and attitude learning.
10. In the category of intellectual skills, Gagné distinguishes discrimination learning, concept learning, rule learning, and problem solving.
11. Each type of learning calls for its own methods of instruction if it is to be acquired successfully.
12. Benjamin Bloom has devised a taxonomy of cognitive learning types, and David Krathwohl has devised a taxonomy of affective learning types.
13. All classifications of learning help teachers plan instruction systematically and clearly.
14. Creativity is the production of new ideas, activities, or objects, and it is often expressed through divergent thinking.
15. Tests of creativity or divergent thinking often measure fluency, flexibility, orginality, and elaboration.
16. Teachers can encourage creativity in students by recognizing creativity whenever it occurs, by explicit techniques such as brainstorming, and by using commercially available programs that foster creativity.

Case Study

How Well Do You Process Information?

Here is a problem that most adults solve *incorrectly*. It requires no special knowledge. See how you do at it:

> The two beakers shown here contain different liquids. Beaker A contains pure water, and beaker B contains pure juice. A teaspoon of the liquid from beaker A (water) is poured into beaker B (juice) and stirred thoroughly. A teaspoon of the mixture in beaker B is then poured back into beaker A. The result is that both beakers now contain some impurity.

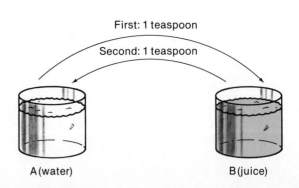

First: 1 teaspoon

Second: 1 teaspoon

A (water)   B (juice)

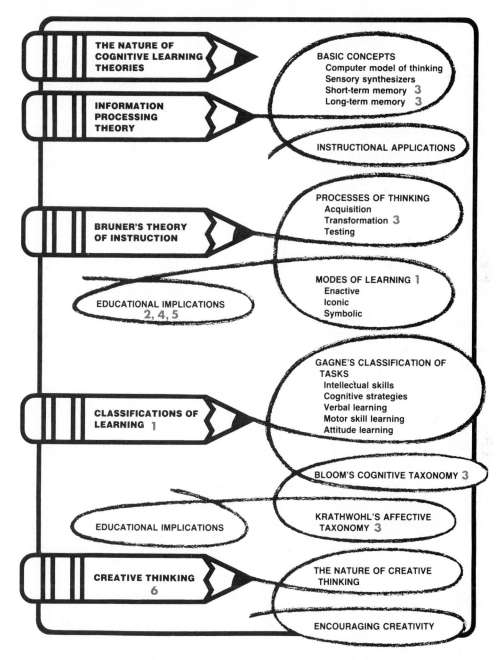

THE NATURE OF
COGNITIVE LEARNING
THEORIES

BASIC CONCEPTS
  Computer model of thinking
  Sensory synthesizers
  Short-term memory 3
  Long-term memory 3

INFORMATION
PROCESSING
THEORY

INSTRUCTIONAL APPLICATIONS

BRUNER'S THEORY
OF INSTRUCTION

PROCESSES OF THINKING
  Acquisition
  Transformation 3
  Testing

MODES OF LEARNING 1
  Enactive
  Iconic
  Symbolic

EDUCATIONAL IMPLICATIONS
2, 4, 5

CLASSIFICATIONS OF
LEARNING 1

GAGNE'S CLASSIFICATION OF
TASKS
  Intellectual skills
  Cognitive strategies
  Verbal learning
  Motor skill learning
  Attitude learning

BLOOM'S COGNITIVE TAXONOMY 3

EDUCATIONAL IMPLICATIONS

KRATHWOHL'S AFFECTIVE
TAXONOMY 3

CREATIVE THINKING
6

THE NATURE OF CREATIVE
THINKING

ENCOURAGING CREATIVITY

1 Piaget's theory of cognitive growth
   (Chapter 2)

2 Learning as behavior change (Chapter 6)

3 Making instruction more effective
   (Chapter 8)

4 The motivation to learn (Chapter 11)

5 Humanistic perspectives in education
   (Chapter 12)

6 Reporting on learning (Chapter 14)

Assuming that fruit juice does not dissolve in water, is there more impurity in beaker A or in beaker B, or are these amounts the same?

If you are like most adults, you probably concluded—wrongly—that more water went into the juice, than juice into the water. If you did so, consider the following hints to the correct solution before discussing the questions below:

Hint 1: You were not asked how much impurity went *into* each beaker but how much *remained* at the end.

Hint 2: The transfers can be diagrammed like this:

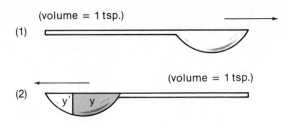

Hint 3: Why does the volume of water transferred $= 1$ tsp. $- y'$? Why does the volume of juice transferred $= 1$ tsp. $- y'$?

Do you still believe that one beaker has more impurity than the other does? If you do, try reading the discussion of this problem in either Case, 1975, or DeBono, 1967.

Questions for Discussion

1. This problem apparently exceeds the short-term memory capacity of most adults. Explain exactly what is forgotten in coming to the wrong conclusion.

2. How do the hints compensate for the limitations of your short-term memory?

3. If a teacher wants to teach her students the "principles of diluting liquids," what simple rules, concepts, or discriminations will she need to teach to make sure that her students reach this general goal?

4. Suppose that this teacher wants her students to discover by themselves the "principles of diluting liquids." How can she do so in a way that both makes success likely and promotes independent learning?

Suggested Readings

Estes, William, ed. *Human Information Processing.* Hillsdale, N.J.: Lawrence Erlbaum Associates, 1978.

Lindsay, P., and D. Norman. *Human Information Processing.* 2nd ed. New York: Academic Press, 1977.

These two books explain in some detail the information-processing theory and its relationships to other psychological and educational viewpoints. The first is a collection of essays by various experts in this field, and the second is one of the most popular textbooks based on the information-processing approach.

Furst, E. J. "Bloom's Taxonomy of Educational Objectives for the Cognitive Domain: Philosophical and Educational Issues." *Review of Educational Research,* 51 (1981), 441–453.

Seddon, G. M. "The Properties of Bloom's Taxonomy of Educational Objectives for the Cognitive Domain." *Review of Educational Research,* 48 (1978), 303–323.

These are two thoughtful reviews of Bloom's widely used taxonomy. The first one focuses on philosophical and educational issues, and the second one discusses somewhat more statistical questions about the taxonomy. Neither writer believes that Bloom's taxonomy is perfect. Both articles make hard reading in places, but they have the advantage of being fair minded.

Gagné, Robert. *The Conditions of Learning.* 3rd ed. New York: Holt, Rinehart & Winston, 1977.

Gagné, Robert, and Leslie Briggs. *Principles of Instructional Design.* New York: Holt, Rinehart & Winston, 1979.

The first of these books is a thorough and fairly readable discussion of Gagné's classifications of types of learning. The second one shows how teachers can plan instruction using, among other things, Gagné's classifications of learning.

Goertzel, T., M. Goertzel, and V. Goertzel. *Three Hundred Eminent Personalities*. San Francisco: Jossey-Bass, 1978.

This book describes the personalities and life experiences of a wide variety of creative and talented people. So does an earlier work by the same authors, *Cradles of Eminence* (Boston: Little, Brown, 1962). For works that help in teaching creativity, see the "Suggested Readings" list at the end of Chapter 12.

Chapter 8

MAKING INSTRUCTION

MORE EFFECTIVE

George Lunston, air force captain: I train new pilots—or actually, I introduce the new trainees to the program when they arrive. We pride ourselves on teaching them well and on not graduating any bad pilots. You can't afford to take any chances with pilots: people's lives are at stake whenever a plane flies, and did you know that a lot of our pilots go on to flying commercial passenger planes?

One thing that helps is making all the trainees spend hours up in the air—just flying airplanes. Dozens of hours before they are allowed to go out alone and dozens more afterwards. Some of the trainees get pretty frustrated with all that flying. They feel as though they already know how to fly a plane, after just a few times up. I suppose they're right in a way: they *can* fly that soon—as long as the weather is beautiful, the plane is in perfect shape, and they're completely rested and alert. The trouble is, in real flying you can't count on always having those wonderful conditions. That's why all the extra practice: it immunizes them, you might say, against the unexpected. It makes them ready for anything.

Something else we're proud of is our flight simulator, a room that looks like a real cockpit and that presents new pilots with seemingly real flight experiences. They actually *see* the "runway" coming at them, and the dials actually read the way they would in real life. The pilots try to "fly" the simulator as they would an actual plane. It's a good way to get experience before going up in the real thing. The simulator looks so much like a real plane that the skills it teaches just have to carry over; I'm convinced of it. Anyway, it's sure better than using someone like me to just *tell* them how to fly!

Still, I think, there are some things that they learn better if somebody tells them. Like how the different mechanical systems of the plane work. They get a chance to inspect the "insides" of real planes, of course, but they use their time better if one of the instructors organizes their time, tells them what to look for. We're not training airplane mechanics here, just people who know how to diagnose troubles when they occur. They spend only a little time puttering around with the workings of the plane itself.

That shortage of time is always bothering me. I find I have to know exactly what I want to teach the trainees and exactly how I want them to use their time, before I even see them. If I don't, then we just don't have enough time to finish the program. Ironic, don't you think? The new pilots spend hours and hours flying planes, but there's still only barely enough time to train them.

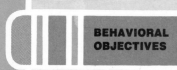

BEHAVIORAL OBJECTIVES

ADVANTAGES

ELEMENTS OF SUCCESSFUL
OBJECTIVES
   Observable behaviors
   Minimum acceptable standards
   Conditions of performance

CRITICISMS

THEORIES OF TRANSFER
   Formal discipline
   Identical elements
   Generalized principles

**TRANSFER OF
LEARNING**

INSTRUCTIONAL APPLICATIONS
   Similarity of elements
   Overlearning
   Organization of material
   Advance organizers

THEORIES OF FORGETTING
   Forgetting as a motive
   Forgetting as interference
   Forgetting as changes in
      perception

**RETENTION OF
LEARNING**

METHODS FOR AIDING RETENTION
   OF LEARNING
   Overlearning and transfer
   Recitation
   Activity
   Mnemonics and imagery

TEACHERS face two, sometimes conflicting, challenges: by doing something specific, they must create some sort of general result. No matter how the students may feel about it, they usually spend less time receiving instruction than living the rest of their lives. Since classroom time is thus a relatively scarce commodity, teachers must make the best possible use of whatever time they and their students have. One way of doing so is to encourage **transfer**—making classroom learning as applicable as possible to new situations and ideas. Another way is to promote retention (or minimize forgetting) of whatever students learn. Still another way is to specify learning goals as clearly and precisely as possible: learning may be worth remembering and applying only if it has been clearly selected and presented. This chapter will consider all three of these strategies, beginning with the last one.

INSTRUCTIONAL PLANNING WITH BEHAVIORAL OBJECTIVES

Advantages of Behavioral Objectives

How can teachers know exactly what they intend to teach? Possibly, some educators say, by using behavioral objectives. As shown in the previous chapter, the taxonomies of Gagné, Bloom, and Krathwohl can help clarify educational goals by classifying them according to type or complexity. Translating these types of goals into actual instructional plans, however, may also require stating them as specific behaviors that students perform, called **behavioral objectives**. Advocates of behavioral objectives say that because of their ambiguity, general goals inhibit the planning and success of instruction (Mager & Pipe, 1970).

behavioral
objectives

Consider this general goal: "By the end of this course, the students shall appreciate English literature." The students could achieve this goal in numerous ways: by reading lots of literature, writing reports on selected works, or writing a short story in the style of an older work. Although all of these are worthwhile classroom activities, the general goal itself does not allow teachers to choose among them and therefore begin preparation for teaching. Only the specifics contained in the generalization suggest a plan of action. Compare the following, more behaviorally oriented objective with the original, more general goal above: "By the end of this course, the students shall read ten literary works, write a report on two of them, and write a short story in the same style as one of the works." The emphasis in this objective has shifted from the students' qualities or states (their appreciation, understanding) to the tasks they must perform. Implicitly, the emphasis also shifts to what the teacher must do, away from what the teacher merely wishes would happen.

plan of action

Using behavioral objectives, then, is a strategy for making instruction effective. Its advantage lies in avoiding confusion and ambiguity and in promoting purposefulness and clarity in teaching and learning. Behavioral objectives focus the attention of everyone—both teachers and students—on what the students actually do when they are learning, rather than on what the teachers themselves do when they are teaching. Such objectives require no commitment to any particular psychological theory, save a commitment to the careful and precise analysis of goals. The next section will offer some guidelines for making such an analysis.

greater purposefulness and clarity

Elements of Successful Behavioral Objectives

Good behavioral objectives try to eliminate as many hidden assumptions about learning and instruction as possible. Usually, therefore, they must state not only what is expected from the student but also something about the situation in which the behavior is to be displayed. Mager (1962) described these three criteria for judging the objectives' effectiveness:

1. *Behavioral objectives should specify what the students must do or say in order to achieve the objectives*. Usually the behavioral objectives emphasize action words: *list, describe, execute, write,* and the like. By the same token, they should avoid states or qualities as their objectives: *knowing, appreciating, understanding,* and the like. The latter words may make good general goals, but not good behavioral objectives, because they cannot be observed directly. Compare the following examples:

greater purposefulness and clarity

stating goals as behaviors

General goal: "The student shall understand fusion power."
Behavioral objective: "The student shall list the reasons for developing fusion power."
General goal: "The student shall know how to make architectural drawings of a house."
Behavioral objective: "The student shall make an architectural drawing of a house."

The first example in each pair can refer to a variety of behaviors on the part of the students. They may show their understanding of fusion power, for example, by finding references to the topic in a textbook, rather than by listing in writing the reasons for its development. And they may demonstrate their understanding of architectural drawings by explaining how to make one, rather than by actually doing so. Some psychologists argue that when such ambiguities become widespread in classroom instruction, they interfere with student learning and make instructional planning difficult (Popham, 1973).

2. *Behavioral objectives should state minimal levels of expected performance*. Behavioral objectives should state, "List *all* the reasons for fusion power," or "List *four* reasons for it." Adding such a quantification clarifies the objective. In the other examples given above, how accurate should the

By following clearly specified goals, this student can wire a computer circuit—a result she might not achieve otherwise. (© Eileen Christelow/Jeroboam, Inc.)

specifying minimum expected performance

architectural drawing be? One hundred percent? Two errors? Five? Critics of behavioral objectives have complained that some learning goals cannot easily be quantified and that stated levels of performance may be quite arbitrary, but advocates of the approach urge setting levels for as many behavioral goals as possible.

3. *Behavioral objectives should state the conditions in which the behavior should be performed.* For the above examples, should the learner perform the behaviors with any particular equipment or information (a textbook or specifications for the house)? Should the objective be performed at a particular time or place (a take-home test versus one in class)? Establishing conditions like these help make clear when and where to expect the behavior and avoid any misunderstandings about these factors that the students may have.

specifying conditions of performance

Criticisms of Behavioral Objectives

Overdetailed Statements   Stating objectives precisely can be carried too far, of course. Do teachers need to state completely the conditions of achieving a particular objective? If so, then they may need an extremely long list of conditions: "During the current year, the student should do X during class, sitting at a table, using no books, writing with a pencil or pen, on paper lined or unlined. . . ." And so on. The list becomes ridiculous because it includes many conditions of performance that are implicitly understood by both teachers and students. Most teachers and students assume, for example, that school learning should be displayed during school and that writing should occur on paper and not on stone tablets. To state such assumptions explicitly may interfere with stating the important information in an objective—information that cannot be assumed.

One issue regarding behavioral objectives, then, centers on how much information about their learning goals that teachers can safely leave unstated. Advocates of the behavioral objectives approach argue that teachers tend to assume too much and that writing out behavioral objectives helps counteract this problem (Airasian et al., 1979). Consider a goal like this: "The student shall describe the causes of the American Revolution." If teachers assume that this statement refers to an in-class test using no books or notes, they may have a rude awakening. Some students may interpret the goal differently: that it specifies an oral report, for example, or an open-book test. In this case, more explicitness may help—unless, ironically, it proves to be unnecessary! Moderation, then, may be the best strategy in specifying learning conditions for behavioral objectives, although the meaning of moderation may vary with the particular classroom, teacher, and students.

Rigid Goals   The same can be said for the other qualities of behavioral objectives. Stating levels of acceptable performance, for example, helps avoid ambiguities only up to a point, after which it becomes nit-picking rather than precision. Teachers may legitimately care whether their students understand much, most, or all of a particular topic. But do they really care whether they understand, say, 79 percent of it as opposed to 80 percent? In general, specifying standards also carries with it a responsibility to be reasonable.

Trivial Goals   The use of explicit precision in setting goals has been criticized for other reasons as well (see Duchastel & Merrill, 1973). Some have argued that only trivial goals can be stated precisely—theories that are already precise even without the help of the behavioral reformulation. The most important goals are often vague—"To develop an understanding of English literature," for instance. Can these really be translated into precise behavioral terms? The advocates of this approach say that they can, though only after their general content is analyzed into its specific parts. The analysis is helped by using some sort of general taxonomy of learning goals, such as the three described in Chapter 7. Figure 8–1 shows how "understanding English literature" can be analyzed into behavioral terms and how the analysis then implies specific behavioral objectives. Critics argue that such an analysis gives a false sense of precision and that educators should recognize and incorporate the inherent fuzziness of many educational goals into their instructional planning (Horvath et al., 1980).

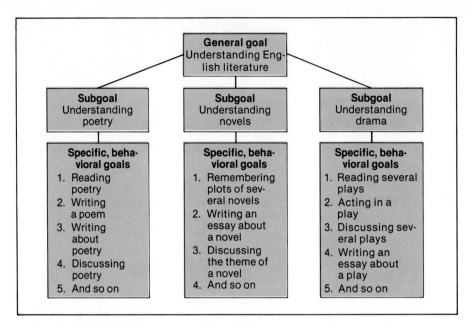

Figure 8–1 Stating a Goal in Behavioral Terms
Stating goals in specific, behavioral terms may often help in planning daily instruction.

Critics also assert that relying on a group of specific goals tends to make teachers forget their more important purposes, most of which cannot be stated in specific behavioral terms. Instead of seeking to make students "understand mathematics," for example, teachers concentrate too much on their list of specific tasks: doing long division, listing geometric theorems, making Venn diagrams, or whatever. Even though these have the advantage of focusing on the students' behavior rather than the teachers', they take the heart out of teaching by being so specific. But advocates of the behavioral objective approach reply that general goals consist of many specific goals anyway, and so teachers would do well to work directly from the specifics.

Loss of Flexibility and Spontaneity   By the same token, critics of behavioral objectives say that a certain vagueness about teaching allows teachers to remain flexible and spontaneous in their work with children and to capitalize on unexpected "teachable moments." Working from a list of specific goals often prevents such flexibility by focusing the teachers' attentions too closely on their plans. Advocates of behavioral objectives reply that using specific goals need not preclude unexpected incidents of learning from happening. In and of itself, planning does not—or should not—exclude spontaneity. If some teachers have had that experience, they say, then they have misunderstood the nature and purposes of behavioral objectives: probably they have overextended their use.

Despite these disagreements, virtually all educators consider clear educational goals essential to the good management of instruction. The debate is over how much planning to do and how much detail to seek from it. Though too much detail may indeed sometimes limit flexibility and spontaneity, too little can lead to class sessions that seem pointless, haphazard, or even chaotic. Perhaps for this reason, many educators urge new teachers to overplan rather than underplan if they are wondering how much to do. Overplanning may take more work, but it also helps ensure well-managed encounters with students (Kohut & Range, 1979).

TRANSFER OF LEARNING

Since school learning usually occurs away from the time and place at which it is supposed to be used, teachers face the problems of *transfer* of learning: how can students be helped to use their knowledge in other studies or in the real world? If they learn about the operation of an electric motor in science class, for example, can they later use their knowledge at home when the vacuum cleaner breaks down? If they learn ways to compose ideas for English compositions, can they use the same techniques in writing an application for a job? For most students, such a transfer must occur in order to make their schooling worthwhile in the long run. Very few people plan to write essays for their entire lives, nor do most expect to fix only the kinds of motors they see in school.

Theories of Transfer

Historically, theories of transfer centered on two points of view, each with its own implications for teaching.

Theory of Formal Discipline   The older of these viewpoints was the doctrine of **formal discipline**. In this view, the human mind consisted of several general abilities, or "faculties," which could be trained by learning certain subject matters. Foreign languages and mathematics, in particular, were thought to build the student's general ability to think and reason in a wide variety of situations. Studying Latin, for example, supposedly built intellectual strength, just as physical exercise built physical strength. This belief conveniently supported the existing curricula of the times, which usually emphasized the formal subjects of mathematics and classical languages. Even the sciences were able to edge their way into schools around the turn of the century by claiming to train the mind as well as the older subjects did, or even better.

transfer as
training of general
thinking skills

    This theory of transfer was seriously challenged after 1900 by the psychologist Edward L. Thorndike. In a series of studies (1913, 1932), he tested the idea of formal discipline by comparing gains in IQ scores in the traditionally formal subjects, such as Latin and math, with those in more vocational subjects, such as bookkeeping or the sciences. If studying a formal subject really developed the mind, then students who took such a subject should improve in general intelligence more than students who took other subjects. Instead, Thorndike found little, if any, gain in IQ traceable to *any* school subject. Students who took certain subjects, notably science, did get better marks in other subjects later on, but they also showed a higher ability for *all* subjects in the first place. In essence, the smart kids elected to take the hard subjects, but the discipline itself influenced their school performance very little, or not at all.

tests of theory of formal discipline

Theory of Identical Elements   This finding led to a much more restricted theory of transfer, that of **identical elements** (Thorndike, 1913, 1932). In this view, transfer occurs only to the extent that aspects, or "elements," of the learning situation duplicate those to which the learning is to be applied. Thorndike found that learning to add three-digit numbers, for example, happens faster if the student has previously learned to add two-digit numbers. Presumably both the stimulus and the student's responses share certain elements in this transfer situation—the arrangement of digits in columns, the need to carry a number to the next column, and so on. But such a specific transfer is a far cry from the sweeping transfer claimed by the theory of formal discipline.

transfer as duplication

Both viewpoints on transfer, incidentally, are still alive and well among teachers and the general public. Certain present-day school subjects—usually the older, more established ones—are often regarded as generally helping students to think. Depending on who is doing the nominating, the basics, or core subjects, may include science, mathematics, English, and history in high school, and reading, language arts, and mathematics in elementary school. Since these are thought to help students with other subjects more than the other way around, they amount to formal training, though that term may not be used. Thus Thorndike's theory of identical elements persists in a modified form to justify much of practical education. In providing on-the-job training, for example, a business implies that school learning does not transfer very well to job situations, presumably because the two are so different. And critics of teacher education sometimes rely on a similar idea when they maintain that "you only learn to teach by teaching": in other words, previous training does not transfer to the real thing.

Theory of Generalized Principles   An alternative to these extremes is what might be called a **generalization** theory of transfer (Ausubel, 1978a; Stokes & Baer, 1977), in which students extract the underlying general principles of what they learn and apply them to new problems or situations. According to this viewpoint, transfer does not occur either by training general thinking skills as such or by duplicating life problems or life situations that the students will later encounter. Instead, transfer

transfer as generalization

offers a number of relevant generalizations that may apply to certain new tasks at a later time. Writing compositions for English class, for example, may give students various useful—but general—principles to guide future nonschool writing tasks like making a job application or constructing a memo for office circulation. English compositions probably do not, however, either exactly duplicate later writing needs or train students to solve all sorts of problems unrelated to writing. The same can be argued for most other examples of school learning: fixing a car in auto mechanics class transfers to fixing a gasoline lawn mower by showing the student the principles involved in gasoline engines. It does not transfer by duplicating the layout of the lawn mower (they differ considerably) or by making the student more intelligent overall.

At its best, the generalization of underlying principles essentially resembles the process of problem solving that Gagné includes at the top of his hierarchy of intellectual skills (Gagné, 1977). In problem-solving activity, the learner brings many general rules to bear on a new and similar task. A new jigsaw puzzle, for example, cannot be solved by fitting the pieces together exactly as one would do on previous puzzles. Doing so would assume that the old and the new puzzles have completely identical elements, which in this case would lead to almost certain failure on the new one. A more successful strategy would rely on the general principles of puzzle solving: what types of pieces usually go together and the color patterns that tend to occur in jigsaw puzzles generally. This kind of transfer is neither completely general nor completely specific. It requires both previous experience with jigsaw puzzles and a readiness to use the principles involved in all of them. Bruner's method of discovery learning may therefore prove ideal for improving puzzle solving ability, since it encourages and motivates students to accumulate experience in their own way and to apply the ideas and skills that emerge from their experience.

transfer as discovery

Sometimes, however, such transfer does not happen automatically, and teachers may need to guide students to look for principles and apply them. In calculating a grocery budget for an imaginary family of four, for example, the teacher may need to call attention to the budget's essential features and distinguish them from its superficial ones. It is not that potatoes cost $2.00 per week (or $4.00 or whatever) that matters but, rather, the process of arriving at this figure and its general implications for family management (can they afford the price?). Without help from their teacher, these underlying principles may be lost on some students.

guided transfer

Presumably, of course, every person has limits on how well he or she can learn such principles, even in the best of times. Some limits may be set by the students' developmental level: young children may learn the simple principles of counting change, but not the more abstract principles of a money economy that make counting change necessary. They may not even learn the simpler principles without help from their teachers or other interested adults. And so the next section will suggest ways for giving such help in classroom settings.

Instructional Applications of Transfer

Similarity of Elements   As much as possible, teachers should try to make the teaching situation similar to the future situation to which the learning presumably will be applied. This will be easier, of course, for some content than for others. At one extreme, you may want students to transfer a specific skill—say, the translation of foreign words and phrases—only as far as a test you will give at the end of the semester. In this situation, you have complete control over the similarity of the learning and application situations, and you should use it: the words and phrases given in lessons should resemble the ones given on the test and should even be given under similar circumstances. At the other extreme, however, the conditions of application can only be approximated. Such may be the case in the early stages of learning to drive a car. Students can be told about driving, can be shown movies about it, and can even by allowed to sit behind a dashboard. But in the earliest stages of acquiring this skill, they cannot safely be given the real experience—the unaccompanied driving of an actual car in traffic. Despite this obstacle, the principle remains the same: driver training is helped by making the training as similar as possible to the final goal, independent driving. For this reason, most driver education courses include behind-the-wheel instruction.

positive transfer

Keeping the teaching situation as similar as possible to the application situation helps ensure **positive transfer**, the correct performance of previously learned behaviors in new situations. To ensure the most possible positive transfer, both the stimulus and response should be as similar as possible. In discussing a story of the Old West, for example, these two questions seem much alike (the stimuli) and require essentially the same answer (the response):

"Did the hero love the girl or the horse?"
"Did the hero love the horse or the girl?"

Most students will probably transfer their answer from one question to the other without change.

Sometimes, however, very similar stimuli call for rather different responses. Compare the two sentences above with this one, which resembles the others quite closely:

"Did the hero love the girl, or did the horse?"

Or, consider again the problem of driver training. If students learn on an automatic transmission car but must eventually drive a manual transmission car, the stimulus of pedal arrangements will look very similar for both. But one will require a very different response from that required by the other: the left-most pedal on an automatic will brake the car, but the left-most pedal on a manual shift will merely disengage the clutch! In this case the literal transfer of the braking response could actually cause an accident.

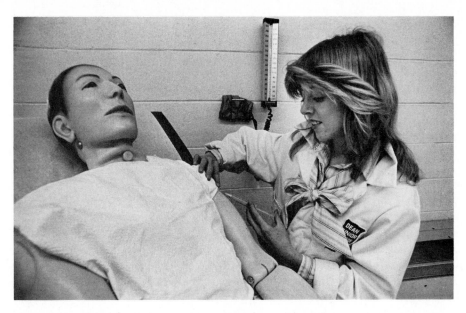

Transfer is more likely if the learning situation resembles the performance situation as closely as possible. (Ellis Herwig/Stock, Boston)

Psychologists often call such examples **negative transfer**, the inappropriate generalization of responses. Negative transfer is most likely to occur when the learning problem or situation seems similar to the application situation but nevertheless requires rather different solutions for subtle or unknown reasons. The following equations illustrate the problem in yet another context:

negative transfer

$$6 + 2 =$$
$$6 \times 2 =$$

The two problems look very much alike to some elementary school children, but they call for very different responses. In cases like these, in which negative transfer is likely to occur, teachers must highlight the key elements that differentiate the two problems; then, perhaps, the differences between them will no longer seem so subtle to the students. Some ways of setting stimuli apart from their surroundings were discussed in the previous chapter, as part of information-processing theory.

Overlearning A skill is overlearned when further practice on it causes no immediate improvement in its performance. As a rule, overlearned skills seem to transfer more, and more accurately, to new situations than do other skills. Typing, for example, transfers better to the noisy conditions of an office if it has been learned extremely well—so well, in fact, that further practice brings no significant improvement in speed or accuracy. A piano sonata will be performed better in front of a live audience if it has first been overpracticed without the stress or distraction of real listeners. Because overlearning, by definition, produces no immediately visible improvements, teachers may unfortunately have difficulty persuading their students to engage in it. The benefits come in the long run, and the long run may seem hundreds of years away to many students. Some of them may think they know how to do long division, but their teacher may suspect that their knowledge will not hold up to the stress of a test or to even slight complications in the presentation of long-division problems.

Providing ample practice, then, may be one way to encourage the eventual transfer of learning. To be effective, such practice must include a variety of problems related to the skill or concepts being learned. Practice in writing, for example, should include practice with several kinds of writing—stories, essays, reports, and the like. Practicing only the same sort of writing (for example, book reports) limits students in two ways: by leading to boredom and by depriving them of the chance to distinguish the principles of writing in general from the principles of writing only book reports.

practice as a means of overlearning

Organization of Material

Learning will transfer more successfully if the information that students must learn is presented in an organized way. Learning the bones of the human skeleton, for example, can help in learning the skeletal structure of other animals, but it will help more if the original information has been taught—and learned—in some sort of structured way. Bones that occur together physically or that serve the same function should be grouped for purposes of teaching, and by doing so, the same groupings in other animals will be more easily recognized and remembered in spite of their differences from those in humans. At the same time, parts that might cause negative transfer should be labeled carefully to avoid confusion between the original and the transferred learning.

organizing content

The value of organizing material applies to all levels of schooling. Young children learning to read, for example, may often confuse certain letters that look very similar: *b* and *d, p* and *q*, or *u* and *n*. The confusion is really another case of inappropriate, negative transfer. The children apply their knowledge of how one letter looks (for instance, *b*) to a wrong instance, with the result that "big" may be read as "dig" and "dig" read as "big." The teacher can minimize such confusion, however, by carefully labeling the letters and providing numerous examples in an organized fashion: *b* words can be compared with *d* words as a systematic learning activity.

The principle of organizing material can be used with a variety of teaching methods. The bones described two paragraphs above can be taught as a laboratory exercise, with students following work sheets and examining real bones, or they can be taught in a lecture. In either case, the information must be presented in a logical, rather than random, way. For the

Without this periodic table of the elements to organize the information, learning chemistry would be far more difficult. (Mimi Forsyth/Monkmeyer Press Photo Service)

first method, this may mean carefully grouping and labeling bones in drawings on the work sheet and perhaps also labeling your own spoken comments, using real bone specimens to illustrate whenever appropriate.

Advance Organizers A good technique for encouraging transfer is the use of **advance organizers** (Ausubel, 1978b): very general comments that put particular content into its overall context. Advance organizers are more general than typical summaries or overviews, which usually just restate the essential points of the content that follows. Advance organizers can help introduce new material and clarify the relationship between previously learned and new material. In the second case, the advance organizer points out explicitly both the similarities and the differences between the old and new content. In one demonstration of this use of advance organizers, Ausubel showed that college students studying Buddhism tended to confuse this knowledge with their preexisting, and much more familiar, knowledge of the Judeo-Christian tradition (1963). This problem was largely avoided, however, when the information about Buddhism was preceded by an organizing passage that compared the two religions in general terms.

Advance organizers usually take the form of written prose passages preceding the actual learning material. In principle, though, they can take

organizers to help orient students

other forms as well: graphic diagrams or maps, introductory questions, or spoken comments from the teacher. The graphic flow charts at the beginning of each chapter in this textbook are a type of advance organizer. All of these help put new information into its proper perspective.

The use of advance organizers implies, of course, that the content to be learned does in fact fit into some superordinate structure of knowledge, that the teacher understands how it does, and that the students can understand the very general terms that advance organizers normally use. Although most teachers and other educators might agree that the first of these three conditions is usually true, they might not agree about the other two. In particular, some educators have questioned whether advance organizers can actually be constructed in a way that differentiates them reliably from ordinary overviews and summaries; after all, organizers are, by definition, abstract and therefore cannot be specified. Likewise, some students may lack the verbal and intellectual skills needed to benefit from such abstract material, no matter how helpful it may be in principle. Research studies of advance organizers provide some support for these criticisms (Hartley & Davies, 1976), though the issue is far from settled yet (Ausubel, 1978b, 1980; Spiro & Anderson, 1981). The notion that prior orientation should help learning seems difficult to criticize in principle.

Whatever their differences, advance organizers, overviews, and summaries have certain qualities in common. They all may work at least partly by helping students construct a sort of mental filing system for what they learn. In this way these learning devices may operate differently from **stimulus predifferentiation** overlearning, which depends more on the strengthening of particular responses and associations. Organizing strategies may also prevent negative transfer, by carefully labeling crucial information that students might otherwise confuse. Sometimes psychologists call this last process **stimulus predifferentiation**, meaning the ability to see small or subtle differences in the stimulus that actually require significantly different responses.

RETENTION OF LEARNING

Why do students (or teachers or anyone) forget? Not just because of the simple discarding of memories, since most people periodically have the experience of "lost" memories coming back. Most adults may forget the names of their early teachers, for example, but under the right conditions **mixture of memory and forgetting** the visual memories of these people may return. Most of us forget the exact books or articles we read just a few weeks or months ago, but faced with a page from one of them, we often remember it in detail once again. If you used to knit or skate or play bridge, you may think you have forgotten how, but only a little practice will usually be enough to bring back the skill to nearly its original level. If memory traces in the brain had simply frittered away into nothingness, then these experiences could not take place. All theories of psychology and learning must account for the mixture of memory and forgetting that characterizes most individuals. On the one hand, forgetting occurs inevitably, but on the other, specific memories need not be forgotten, and forgotten information sometimes comes back uninvited.

Theories of Forgetting

Forgetting as a Motive Psychodynamic theories (for example, Erikson, 1963) point out that we seem to forget certain things on purpose, though we may not be conscious of doing so. One student may forget the name of his teacher, for example, because he had a bad experience with her, or another may forget her part in the school play because she is afraid of performing in public. At a conscious level, however, they are not "trying" to forget. The students may sincerely try to remember the teacher's name or the lines in the play and yet still fail. Much psychotherapy, in fact, pertains to this gap between behavior and intentions and assumes that in such cases there exists a deeper, unconscious motive that has been repressed.

unconscious motives

For teachers, however, searching for unconscious motives may provide little more than interesting speculation. Teachers deal primarily with their students' conscious intentions—what they think about a subject, what they choose to learn, and what they choose *not* to learn. Usually time does not allow teachers to become too concerned with their students' hidden motives, even if their training did qualify them to do so. At most, therefore, theories of unconscious forgetting serve to remind teachers that students are human, too, and bring experiences to school that rarely show themselves in actual classroom behavior. As a practical matter, teachers must look to other theories of forgetting for more useful explanations.

A milder version of the psychodynamic theory, in particular, may describe motivated forgetting in more the way that teachers recognize it. In this milder form, students may forget information because they do not expect ever to use it—the names of all the capitals of the world, for example, or the atomic weights of all the elements. Or they may forget information they dislike learning by failing to study it as carefully as they should, in essence, by not learning it as well in the first place rather than forgetting it afterward. These actually are problems in motivating students, rather than in thinking as such. They are cured by persuading students of the relevance of what they learn or of its desirability. For suggestions on how to do so, see Chapter 11.

conscious forgetting

Forgetting as Interference According to a widely held viewpoint, forgetting results from the interference between newer memories and older ones, rather than from the disappearance of the older ones. A teacher may have trouble, for example, in remembering the name of a particular student because of competing memories of other students from the same class or even from other classes in other years. The memory is not gone so much as it is simply muddled with other similar ones. Like the psychodynamic viewpoint, then, this theory sees forgetting as a problem of retrieval rather than preservation. The basic problem becomes putting memories into forms that will allow recall. And for teachers: presenting new information to students so as to ensure recall. Unlike the other viewpoint, though, the interference theory sees the answer as depending on the efficient management of information: the conscious mental effort to separate accurate information from inaccurate information. Forgetting happens because the mind is more like a badly kept library than a locked vault containing hidden material. Teachers, in this analogy, must help students keep their libraries in order.

confusion of old and new information

Some support for this viewpoint comes from memory experiments in which individuals are asked to learn lists of nonsense words or syllables, like the ones shown in Figure 8–2. Learning these shows a so-called **serial position effect**, in which the first and last parts of the list are remembered more accurately than the middle parts. The middle items are supposedly forgotten because the memory of them becomes rather cluttered with the memories of neighboring items. Because of their serial positions, however, the ends of the list do not suffer as much from such interference. In classrooms, too, analogous phenomena can often be found. Children beginning to learn the alphabet will remember the first and last parts of it better than the middle; the first and last lines of the national anthem may be recalled more accurately than the middle ones are; and the beginning and ending of a story may stand out more than many (though not all) of its middle parts. Despite the equal opportunity to commit the entire batch of content to memory, the middle often proves harder to retrieve, presumably because of competing memories.

serial position effect

To the extent that forgetting consists of interference, then, teachers should help students sort out what they have been learning. Hence there is a need to organize content for students, a need stated repeatedly in this book and in the teaching profession generally. Hence, too, there is a need to "predifferentiate" the stimuli that teachers give to students, by carefully labeling and defining parts or using advance organizers. These techniques assume, of course, that the students possess a conscious willingness to learn. But if such willingness is missing, then some version of the psychodynamic viewpoint—that forgetting may reflect a lack of motivation—should be combined with strictly cognitive efforts to clarify the subject matter. Probably, most real, live students need a bit of both.

Forgetting as Changes in Perception Some psychologists who stress the organizing properties of human thinking also emphasize these

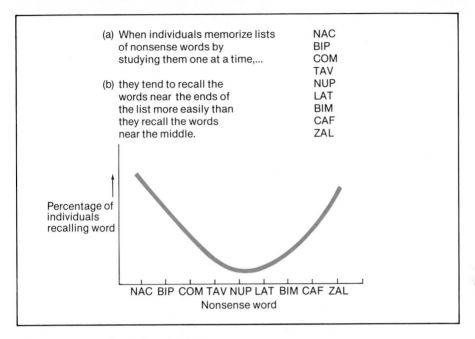

(a) When individuals memorize lists
of nonsense words by
studying them one at a time,...

NAC
BIP
COM
TAV

(b) they tend to recall the
words near the ends of
the list more easily than
they recall the words
near the middle.

NUP
LAT
BIM
CAF
ZAL

Percentage of
individuals
recalling word

NAC BIP COM TAV NUP LAT BIM CAF ZAL
Nonsense word

Figure 8–2 The Serial Position Effect

features in human memory (see Riley, 1963). According to this view, memory
is analogous to perception, rather than to verbal associations as suggested
by interference theory. In the same way that certain visual patterns seem
to belong together, certain memories or ideas also may form coherent
wholes—and can be recalled more easily when they do. The lines in Figure
8–3 illustrate the belonging process for visual perception. The dotted lines
seem to pair off naturally, even though all the lines are evenly spaced. In
this case the lines form perceptual wholes on the basis of similarity and
are remembered as such. In the same way, it is argued, ideas are learned
and remembered as wholes, rather than as associations of parts. An example is memory for language. Even if you have been carefully reading
this chapter, for instance, you probably will not remember its individual
words or sentences, but you may remember its underlying ideas—the perceptual wholes of language.

As with interference theory, some support for the perception analogy
has been found in studies of certain simple memory processes (Asch, 1969).
One study compared the recall of visual patterns when presented in parts
to students with their recall of it when presented as a unit. Figure 8–3
shows some examples of the perceptual items used in each of these ways.
When the subjects were later tested for how well they remembered the
visual displays, it was found that they remembered the unified ones far

*changes in
perception*

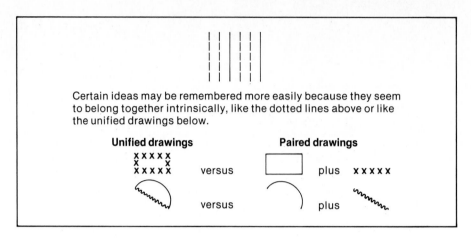

Figure 8–3 Memory as Perceptual Unity

better than the paired ones, even though both contained the same visual information. Why? Because, it was argued, the unified displays form perceptual units that can be directly stored as wholes, whereas the paired displays have to be combined mentally to be remembered.

Probably for the same reason, grammatical sentences can be recalled better than random strings of words can, which can in turn be recalled better than equally long lists of nonsense syllables can (Tarpy & Mayer, 1977, chap. 11). The sentences can presumably be stored as units—as "ideas"—without remembering their words individually. A random list of words probably must be stored as a collection of miniunits, one word at a time, but without attention to their individual letters. Nonsense syllables present the most difficult storage problem of all, since even their individual letters must be attended to one at a time.

For teachers, this view of memory suggests that teaching ideas as whole units may often be more effective than teaching them as parts. This belief underlies the use of advance organizers discussed earlier, for example. By using advance organizers, the teacher can convey a broad sweep of information in a relatively short and concise way, thereby allowing the lesson itself to become part of a larger context.

remembering
unified ideas

Methods for Aiding Retention of Learning

By now it should be clear that human learning, transfer, and memory are closely related processes—some might even argue that they are really the same process viewed from different angles. One psychologist (Rothkopf,

1970, 1971) coined the term *mathamagenic activity* to refer to the behaviors underlying them all. The term has Greek roots meaning to "give birth to learning"; **mathamagenic activities** are the specific actions of students that actually cause them to learn. Obviously, quite a few specific behaviors may have this effect, some of which have already been discussed earlier in this and previous chapters. How, in addition to these, can students improve their memory in particular?

mathamagenic activities

Learning and Transfer   Because theories of learning, transfer, and memory are closely interwoven, the first suggestion for helping students remember better may sound evasive: encourage retention by encouraging learning and transfer in every way possible. Content that is not learned well cannot be retained, and content that transfers successfully will be more likely to be remembered. In addition, however, several more suggestions can be made to help the retention of learning.

Recitation   A number of studies suggest that reciting material, that is, saying it out loud, helps in remembering it (for a review, see Berelson & Steiner, 1964). The benefits of recitation have been shown for learning nonsense syllables, the vocabulary of a second language, and the facts and rules of arithmetic and spelling. These benefits also have been demonstrated for both choral speaking (the whole class together) and individual speaking.

The value of recitation, however, may be strongest for learning relatively arbitrary associations, such as a foreign vocabulary or new technical terms. Meaningful materials, such as sentences and prose, respond less to overt recitation, possibly because individuals prefer to remember the meaning of such material rather than its particular expression in words. A study by Sachs (1967) compared adults' abilities to identify sentences that they had earlier memorized but that were changed slightly for the test. Some of the changes retained the sense of the original, but others—equally slight—made a significant difference. In linguistic terms, the first kind amounted only to *paraphrasing,* whereas the second kind changed the *deep structure* (see page 59 in Chapter 3). Here is an example:

limited uses of recitation

Original sentence learned: "There, he met Howard, who urged him to join the search."
Paraphrase: "There, he met Howard, who urged that he join the search."
Meaning change: "There, he met Howard and urged him to join the search."

The result? Sentences that paraphrased the original meaning were mistaken for the original much more often than were sentences that had made equally slight, but meaningful, changes. Apparently the adults were retaining the sense of the sentences better than their actual words.

For learning meaningful prose in class, then, teachers may do better to invite students to express ideas in their own words and not to concern themselves with exactly how the ideas are phrased. The principle makes good common sense, though it sometimes may be easily forgotten. Discussing the rights of citizenship, for example, can be done just as well in casual, everyday terms as in the more formal language of books or legal documents. Of course, if the instructional goal is to learn certain formal terms or statements regarding a topic, then using such words and phrasings may be crucial. This might be the case in learning the Pythagorean theorem in geometry: "The sum of the squares of the lengths of the sides of a right triangle is equal to the square of the length of the hypotenuse." Since paraphrasing this idea may be difficult to do without getting it wrong, exactly learning and reciting the statement may actually help students recall it more easily. This suggestion should be used sparingly, however, since it can quickly lead to rote memorization if it is overdone— knowing lots of sentences, but not their meanings.

Activity   Sometimes memory is improved by acting out the words or thoughts being learned. To learn a procedure in a science lab, for example, students can literally describe the procedure to themselves as they do it. Indeed, any action-oriented activity has an instructional advantage because it can be remembered more easily—cooking a meal, for example, or building a cabinet. Some parts of a foreign language can also be connected with actions, most notably commands and descriptions of actions. Several activities for young children rely on action and manipulation of materials, from making hand gestures while singing songs to pouring quantities of water into containers. Such activity is valued in part because it helps children think and, it might be added, to remember what they have learned. Among older students, the opportunities for action-oriented learning are less frequent, possibly because they may seem undignified. But the need for them does not disappear.

practical
experience

Both recitation and activity ensure that the learners concentrate on the content they are supposed to learn. Stating the causes of the French Revolution, for example, usually means that the students are thinking about the causes as well. Merely hearing their teacher state the same ideas does not carry the same guarantee nor does looking at a page in a book that expresses them in print. Likewise, activity during learning helps focus attention: raising a hand while saying *Je lève la main* helps a student to notice the meaning of that phrase and experience it in context. At the same time, both recitation and activity may help students process or sort out what they are learning. Extraneous ideas about the French Revolution, in the first example, or wrong guesses about the meaning of the foreign phrase, in the second, can be compared with the right ideas and meanings. Such thinking happens covertly but may aid the learning and retention of other, related content.

focusing attention

No matter what their ages, students often learn more effectively if they can get involved actively. (Marion Bernstein)

Mnemonics and Imagery   **Mnemonics** are any relatively simple devices for aiding memory; in a broad sense, then, many of the suggestions in these chapters might be considered mnemonics. In common usage, however, mnemonics often refer to a motley assortment of tricks for remembering specific facts or associations (Bellazza, 1981). One such technique uses acronyms, abbreviations based on the first letters of a set of terms. The lines on a musical staff are the notes E G B D F, which are easy to remember if you decide that they stand for "Every Good Boy Does Fine." The spaces, furthermore, spell the word F A C E, which does not even need a sentence to aid recall. A mnemonic for the Pythagorean theorem, mentioned earlier, consists of fracturing the prose in it: "The squaw of the hippopotamus is equal to the sum of the squaws of the two adjacent sides." The examples go on indefinitely; you may remember some from your own school experience.

simple memory aids

Some mnemonics rely on visual images, in addition to verbal ones. The names of the spaces on the musical staff, for example, may be easier for some students to remember if they imagine a face on a staff, and the dates for historical events can be remembered by imagining what the events *looked* like.

Mnemonics and imagery are more than just interesting tricks for performing feats of memory, as a magician at a circus does. There is accumulating evidence that adults use such methods habitually, and often without consciously thinking of them. More important for teachers, perhaps, is the possibility that children use such strategies far *less* often than adults do. Several psychologists have proposed this idea to explain the differences in results of certain memory experiments (Case, 1978; Flavell & Wellman, 1976). The visual recall of abstract paintings, for example, has been shown to be the same for children of all ages, whereas the recall of visual patterns improves with age (Flavell, 1970).

Why the difference in the two tasks? Possibly because recognizing abstract paintings cannot benefit from the memory strategies suggested in this book, whereas recognizing visual patterns can. Unlike a purely irregular design, a pattern contains parts that can be labeled, numbered, and even measured mentally. It contains triangles, squares, and so on; there are usually two of them or four or whatever, and they look twice as big, half as big, or some other amount. It appears that older children use such information without being explicitly told to do so. The younger ones may often have just as much perceptual ability but do not organize their new learning to help them recall it better later on (Flavell et al., 1981). If Flavell's hypothesis is correct, then teachers need to help children—especially younger children—learn organizing and mediating techniques for storing information and recalling it at the right times. They must also help children practice the techniques until they occur naturally and spontaneously.

Key Points

1. Making instruction more effective requires planning with behavioral objectives and attending to the problems of transfer and retention of learning.

2. Behavioral objectives help in setting realistic and clear goals for instruction.

3. Good behavioral objectives are stated in terms of observable behaviors, and they include information about the minimum acceptable standards of performance and the conditions of performing the objectives.

4. Behavioral objectives have been criticized for being too detailed, rigid, and trivial.

5. Transfer of learning refers to the use of learning in other appropriate instructional situations or in the real world.

6. Three theories of transfer are the theory of formal discipline, the theory of identical elements, and the theory of generalized principles.

7. Teachers can promote better transfer of learning by striving for a similarity of elements between the learning and transfer situations, by encouraging overlearning, and by organizing the learning material.

8. Retention of learning enables the appropriate transfer.

9. Forgetting may be caused by unconscious or conscious motives, interference from other remembered content, or changes over time in the perception of remembered content.

10. Teachers can promote better retention in several ways: by encouraging thorough learning, using recitation and other active modes of learning, and encouraging mnemonics and imagery as memory aids.

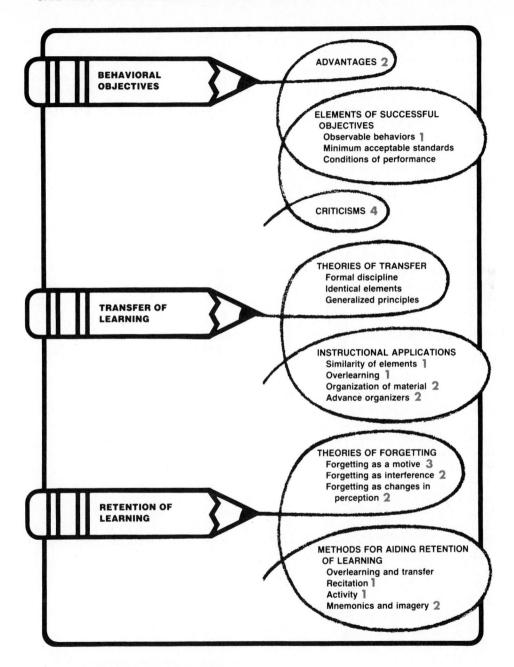

BEHAVIORAL OBJECTIVES

ADVANTAGES **2**

ELEMENTS OF SUCCESSFUL OBJECTIVES
Observable behaviors **1**
Minimum acceptable standards
Conditions of performance

CRITICISMS **4**

TRANSFER OF LEARNING

THEORIES OF TRANSFER
Formal discipline
Identical elements
Generalized principles

INSTRUCTIONAL APPLICATIONS
Similarity of elements **1**
Overlearning **1**
Organization of material **2**
Advance organizers **2**

RETENTION OF LEARNING

THEORIES OF FORGETTING
Forgetting as a motive **3**
Forgetting as interference **2**
Forgetting as changes in perception **2**

METHODS FOR AIDING RETENTION OF LEARNING
Overlearning and transfer
Recitation **1**
Activity **1**
Mnemonics and imagery **2**

1 Learning as behavior change (Chapter 6)

2 Learning to structure knowledge (Chapter 7)

3 The motivation to learn (Chapter 11)

4 Humanistic perspectives in education (Chapter 12)

Case Study

Improving Learning About Dinosaurs

Jack Davidson took his sixth-grade class on a field trip to a museum of natural history in a nearby city. The museum guide took them to the part of the museum showing reconstructed skeletons of dinosaurs and other prehistoric animals. As they looked at each, the guide said a few words. At one especially large skeleton, she said, "Here we have one of the few carnivorous dinosaurs, *Tyrannosaurus Rex*. It used to eat small mammals. If you look at its teeth, you can see why it was well suited to preying."

The next day, Jack asked his students to write about the trip, and he was both puzzled and amused by what some of them seemed to have learned. Here, for instance, is what Jason wrote:

"We took a long bus ride. When we got there, we saw a lot of bones, especially dinosaurs. The person talked a long time. One of them Tyronsorus wrecks animals, but he looked like he had big teeth. She said the dinosaur believed in God, and how can a dinosaur do that?"

A few days later, Jack asked his students for another assignment, comparing the animals at the museum with ones they knew about from their own world. To this, Jason responded, in part:

"Lions eat animals and so does Tyranosus. They both have teeth, but only the dinosaur has a skeleton. No one talks about lions in the same way they talk about dinosaurs."

Questions for Discussion

1. **a.** Judging by the information given here, what seems to be the learning goal for Jack and the museum guide? State this goal in behavioral terms, specifying, if possible, the performance itself, the minimum standards of acceptable performance, and the conditions under which the performance occurred.
   b. Suppose that Jack could plan the trip and its follow-up again. What revisions, if any, in his behavioral goals and methods for these experiences would you suggest to him?
2. **a.** Why do you think Jason's responses contain inaccuracies? Consider the effect, if any, of each of these factors:
   1. Negative transfer
   2. Lack of general principles to guide transfer

   3. Motivation to forget
   b. For any of the factors above that contributed to imperfect learning, suggest some ways that Jack could minimize their effect and thereby improve Jason's learning.
3. What prior skills or knowledge does Jason need to reach the goals you stated in your answer to question 1? Consider each of the following prerequisites to the extent that they are relevant:
   a. Concepts, rules, or principles regarding the natural history of dinosaurs
   b. Knowledge, comprehension, and applications regarding the natural history of dinosaurs
   c. Affective responses and values regarding the natural history of dinosaurs

Suggested Readings

Day, D., C. Edlund, and A. Graham. *LTR, Learning to Remember: Procedures for Teaching Recall.* San Rafael, Calif.: Academic Therapy Publications, 1978.

Kail, R. V. *The Development of Memory in Children.* San Francisco: W. H. Freeman, 1979.
Both of these books describe the processes involved in memory and therefore also involved in appropriate transfer. The first book offers more practical advice, and the second one outlines some of the research findings on how children gradually become better at remembering information.

Eisner, E., ed. *Reading, the Arts, and the Creation of Meaning.* Reston, Va.: National Art Education Association, 1978.

Layton, J. R. *The Psychology of Learning to Read.* New York: Academic Press, 1979.

McKim, R. H. *Thinking Visually: A Strategy Manual for Problem Solving.* Belmont, Calif.: Lifetime Learning Publications, 1980.
There are many books about the teaching of reading. The one by Layton, listed above, emphasizes the cognitive processes in reading: it is not really an "idea" book for teachers. The books by Eisner and McKim both describe alternatives to the relatively linear (one-thought-at-a-time) thinking sometimes considered important in reading. Eisner explores the relationships between learning to read and learning about art, and McKim's book is helpful to anyone who must think visually, for example, architects.

Kapfer, M. B., ed. *Behavioral Objectives: The Position of the Pendulum.* Englewood Cliffs, N.J.: Educational Technology Publications, 1978.
The original enthusiasm for behavioral objectives held by some educators in the 1960s and 1970s has given way to more balanced and more thoughtful positions. This book is just one example of this process; it contains essays that speak to the variety of issues surrounding the use of behavioral objectives.

Chapter 9

INSTRUCTIONAL

MANAGEMENT

Elizabeth Wong, Grade 3 teacher: Without a doubt, the worst problem I had during my first year of teaching was managing my class. I was convinced I would be "friends" with my students, not boss them around as I remembered a couple of my teachers doing to me. So in the fall I asked them, "What do you want to do today?" They just looked at me and giggled. After I tried the question several days in a row, in fact, somebody answered me by *belching!*

I think that's when I first really started losing control that year, because after that, whenever somebody did something funny or embarrassing, someone else was bound to belch in "reply." Our room was perfect for it: a high ceiling and a hardwood floor, so anything sounded loud in there. Very reinforcing to the kids, I suppose. I did eventually stop them from doing it, but they still pantomimed a belching gesture—hand on the mouth, puffed cheeks. By Christmas, it had gotten to be our class trademark.

Eventually they were driving me up the wall with it. They would have little "conversations" around the room, consisting of pantomimed belches intermingled with giggles—and occasional real belches, too. I appealed to their better judgment: "I *know* that *you* know what you should be doing now," and that sort of thing. Meaning, they should work instead of goof off; but instead they just kept up their teasing. I tried reminding them of classroom rules about being quiet at certain times—also no luck. Another teacher suggested praising the students for behaving quietly—but unfortunately the ones who needed to change their ways were never quiet enough to deserve any praise!

That all was several years ago, and now, thank goodness, that sort of thing doesn't happen to me nearly so much anymore. I suppose the kids at this school may have changed over the years—more well behaved now. But I think, more likely, that I handle things better: I sense potential problems before they become big and real. And I know better now how much responsibility Grade 3 students really can handle. One thing they can't do, I'm now convinced, is plan on their own their entire academic curriculum for the year. That's sort of what I asked them to do way back then. I have to be clear about what I expect them to learn, as well as how I expect them to behave. I can do both those things better now than at first, but I do wish someone had shown me sooner how to do them.

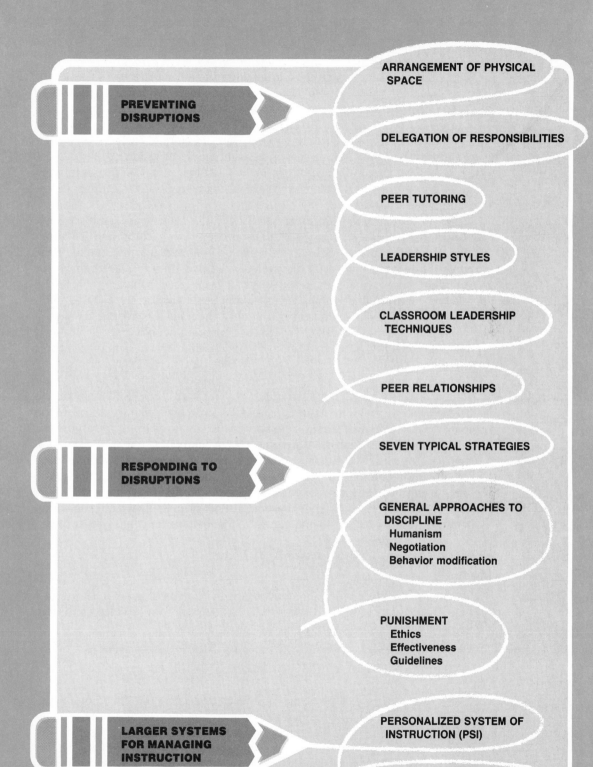

PREVENTING
DISRUPTIONS

ARRANGEMENT OF PHYSICAL
SPACE

DELEGATION OF RESPONSIBILITIES

PEER TUTORING

LEADERSHIP STYLES

CLASSROOM LEADERSHIP
TECHNIQUES

PEER RELATIONSHIPS

RESPONDING TO
DISRUPTIONS

SEVEN TYPICAL STRATEGIES

GENERAL APPROACHES TO
DISCIPLINE
  Humanism
  Negotiation
  Behavior modification

PUNISHMENT
  Ethics
  Effectiveness
  Guidelines

LARGER SYSTEMS
FOR MANAGING
INSTRUCTION

PERSONALIZED SYSTEM OF
INSTRUCTION (PSI)

INDIVIDUALLY PRESCRIBED
INSTRUCTION (IPI)

THE events of teaching and learning do not necessarily happen in a logical order, at an even pace, or in a single sequence. Instead they present a kaleidoscope of interactions and decisions—and disruptions, too. The latter may be either social in nature (mischief) or learning related (confusion or discouragement), and, of course, one type may contribute to the other. Whatever happens during instruction, teachers must keep track of the multifaceted picture that this instruction presents; they must try to prevent problems in it from surfacing; and they must correct them when they do.

No matter how well-organized and skillful a teacher is, some students will probably behave in ways that interfere with teaching and learning. One child daydreams when he should be reading; another makes wise cracks that interrupt group discussions. A third child hits and pinches to get what she wants but instantly returns to good behavior before the teacher can see what happened; a fourth child constantly asks for help with learning tasks, even though she does them easily once the teacher is looking over her shoulder. If several of these behaviors occur at once or if even just one happens too often, even very patient teachers may lose their poise.

When teaching goes well, of course, the behaviors that are socially and educationally helpful far outnumber the difficult ones. But even in the best of times, problem behaviors remain problems, if only because the teacher has to prevent them from recurring. **Instructional management** refers to the coordination of activities and behaviors so as to accomplish teachers' and students' goals efficiently and effectively. It includes both preventing problems and correcting them, and it requires attention by the teacher both to the class and as a group and to the individuals within it. This chapter looks at each of these aspects of management and some suggestions that psychologists and educators have made for dealing with them.

coordination of teaching activities

PREVENTING DISRUPTIONS

To some extent, good management means preventing problems before they happen in the first place. Preventive strategies are quite varied and may be used either before actual instruction or during it.

Arrangement of Physical Space

Many of a classroom's physical conditions affect the likelihood of disruptions (Zimring, 1981). Cold (or hot) room temperatures and poor ventilation, for example, may be hardly noticeable to the busiest person in the class—the teacher—but they can seriously reduce many students' ability to concentrate on educational content. Areas for quiet activities will more likely remain quiet if they are laid out differently from other areas: book-reading corners, for example, may need to be separated from the rest of

effects of physical comfort

the room, with cushions to invite sitting and staying, rather than standing and moving. Sometimes furniture and materials can be arranged to suggest particular numbers of students for a center: only so many chairs, for example, or only so many headphones at a listening station. Certain supplies that students use frequently—crayons, for example, or a dictionary—can be placed where students can get them easily and without disturbing the teacher or other students. Although teachers cannot control all the physical conditions in their rooms (the amount of space, for instance), they can influence many of them, and instruction will flow more smoothly if they do.

effects of room arrangement

Delegation of Responsibilities

Teachers can also prevent certain disruptions by delegating specific responsibilities to students. Certain individuals can be assigned to clean the chalkboard every day, to pass out supplies, or to close the windows in case of a fire drill. Such jobs can take teachers extraordinary amounts of time if they try to do them alone. Delegating tasks, therefore, not only saves teachers time and reduces interruptions but also gives students a sense of responsibility for their own welfare. Teachers can rotate the responsibilities as the year goes on so that all students get a chance to serve.

Peer Tutoring

In many cases, students can help one another with particular educational tasks. One can drill another with vocabulary cards, or two can complete a science experiment together. Often teachers need not formally designate these educational helpers, although they can sometimes ask one student to help another if they discover an especially helpful combination of individuals. Some teachers and psychologists have organized and studied systematic programs of peer tutoring (Good & Brophy, 1978). In these arrangements, one student may teach a subject to another for designated periods of time. The students need not be the same age or have the same ability in the subject. Such programs have generally produced good results for both the tutor and the tutored. Both seem to learn the material better than without tutoring, no matter what their relative ages or abilities. In the bargain, of course, the teacher gains a more individualized program of instruction and more time to devote to other teaching needs.

individualized teaching

Leadership Styles and Group Climate

By promoting certain kinds of relationships among students and between teachers and students, teachers can significantly influence the atmosphere of their classes and the likelihood of disruptions. A classic study by Lewin,

How do this classroom's furnishings and arrangement contribute to a smoothly running educational program? (B. Griffith)

Lippitt, and White (1939) dramatically illustrates this idea. Lewin trained adults to lead after-school clubs for boys according to one of three styles of leadership, which he called democratic, authoritarian, and laissez-faire. The *democratic* leaders invited opinions from the boys about how the group should use its time, though the leaders retained the right to make the final decisions. The *authoritarian* leaders continually bossed their children: they told the boys exactly what to do and when to do it. The *laissez-faire* leaders purposely refrained from initiating ideas or activities; they responded to questions about information but did very little else.

After a number of weeks the groups showed definite differences, both in how productive they were and in how positive they felt about their experiences. The boys in the democratic group showed the most positive feelings about their group. When their leader was present, they did not work quite as fast as did the boys in the authoritarian group when theirs was present. This difference was compensated, though, when the leaders temporarily left the group: then the democratic group kept working relatively steadily, but the authoritarian one quickly halted and waited for its leader to return. The laissez-faire group failed at both morale and production: the boys could not get themselves organized and ended up bickering and arguing more than the others did about various matters, both large and small.

democratic

authoritarian

laissez-faire

democratic groups

Although this study has since been criticized on various grounds, its essential features have been supported by more recent research. A major study of styles of child rearing, for example, identified three groups of parents, which the study called authoritative, authoritarian, and laissez faire (Baumrind, 1971, 1973). Parents in the second and third groups behaved in much the same ways as did Lewin's authoritarian and laissez-faire group leaders, respectively. Parents in the first group—the *author-itative* parents—resembled Lewin's democratic group leaders: they invited opinions and comments from their children but retained the final authority for decisions. They acted on the assumption that they in fact deserved to exercise authority by virtue of their greater experience and maturity. Baumrind found that authoritative parents raised children who seemed more independent and self-confident that the children from other kinds of families. Their children resembled the boys in Lewin's democratic clubs, who liked their group more than average and produced more for it on their own initiative.

authoritative parents

Actually, neither the authoritative parents nor the democratic leaders were ever fully democratic in the sense of giving equal influence to all members of the group (or family) or in the sense of making decisions by majority vote. Instead, they worked for group consensus whenever possible and based the consensus on what the leader (or parent) considered the best ideas and information, wherever these happened to come from.

Classroom Leadership Techniques

Teaching, of course, differs from both child rearing and club leadership. Unlike child rearing, teaching brings together a group of comparative strangers who must then get along for educational purposes, and unlike club leadership, it brings together individuals for comparatively serious and long-lasting purposes. Unlike both other activities, teaching usually entails relatively large groups—too many individuals, usually, to interact as a whole all the time. How do these complications affect teachers' ability to manage instruction, and especially to prevent disruptions from occurring?

Jacob Kounin (1970) found several answers to this question. Teachers who successfully avoided disruptions generally were unusually *well prepared* for their class sessions. Since they had a clear idea of what they wanted to accomplish, they had an easier time maintaining a lively pace of activity and discussion. The lively pace and clear goals in turn helped students attend to learning rather than mischief.

being well prepared

Successful teachers also managed to keep track of more than one activity or event at a time. Kounin called this skill **"withitness."** The teacher might, for example, focus actively on one particular child or group, yet remain aware of other groups or individuals elsewhere in the room. This skill allowed the teacher to respond to difficulties as soon as they occurred,

being aware of several groups

rather than a few minutes later when they might have mushroomed out of proportion. Dividing attention probably came more easily to "withit" teachers because they had also prepared well and therefore did not have to concentrate as hard on remembering what they wanted to do from one minute to the next.

Dividing attention also helped successful teachers implement *overlapping* activities. While one group was still finishing its lesson, for example, another might have already begun a new one; or while most of the class gathered for a film, a few individuals finished up earlier work. In such a class, no one point in time ever seemed like an ending or a beginning for the entire group—except, perhaps, the major breaks at the beginning and end of the day. Instead, activities seemed to flow smoothly into one another. The teachers in such classes had a knack for sensing when and how to control this flow; in Kounin's terms, their management had *smoothness*.

overlapping activities smoothly

Peer Relationships

Cooperation, Competition, and Individualism Differences in styles of parenting, leadership, and teaching all work partly by influencing *peer relationships,* that is, by offering students particular opportunities for cooperating among themselves, competing, or working independently of one another. Recent research has compared the effects of these different opportunities in a variety of school and school-like settings (Johnson et al., 1981). The results consistently favor cooperative learning, those situations in which success depends on the mutual success of a group. Not only do students learn more when they cooperate, but they also feel more positive about themselves, what they learn, and their fellow students. Unfortunately, schooling all too often provides competitive opportunities or individualistic ones. Typically, one student's gain is another's loss, or one student's gain has nothing to do with anyone else.

benefits of cooperation

Probably school leans toward competition and individualism because North American society highly values these motives. They belong to the American dream: through hard, individual effort, every person supposedly can succeed, even if it sometimes happens at the expense of other people. Although the dream makes sense only for persons in economically favorable circumstances, all parts of society nonetheless often subscribe to it. The schools, and the students in them, cannot really be faulted therefore for reflecting attitudes of competition and individual effort; after all, the students will need them after they finish their schooling.

difficulties of promoting cooperation

For practicing teachers, then, the issue may not be as simple as Johnson's research first makes it seem. Despite Johnson's findings, competition and individual incentives admittedly do cause some students to work harder in certain cases. Furthermore, studies of cooperative tasks sometimes show what teachers already know from experience: that individuals often "re-

Cooperative learning projects can make instruction go more smoothly—and sometimes also counteract prejudices held by students about race, sex roles, and handicaps. (David S. Strickler/The Picture Cube)

vert" to competition even on tasks for which they know that cooperation would help them both mutually and individually (Ames & McKelvie, 1982).

Suggestions for Combining Cooperation and Competition

Teachers may therefore do better if they foster a mixture of motives, based on what the students want and what the teacher thinks they need. Educators have suggested a number of ways of doing so. The *jigsaw classroom*, for example, models learning after a puzzle that must be solved by a group. Each member of the class receives part of the total information that he or she needs to solve a problem, and that person must work with the other members of the group or class to piece together the complete solution (Aronso et al., 1978). Each person may receive just one sentence from a paragraph, for example, and the group must assemble the whole passage; or each person may receive just one clue to defining a new concept, and

jigsaw classroom

the group must construct a complete and correct definition. In this technique, individuals can compete in offering suggestions for the final solution, but they must also cooperate if they ever expect to find it.

Another way of combining cooperative and competitive motives is to set up *learning teams* (Slavin, 1978). In this approach, teams rather than individuals compete with one another for overall marks or credit. To succeed, however, individuals must cooperate with their teammates to maximize their group's overall credit—perhaps through the peer tutoring already mentioned or other, related self-help behavior. The system therefore encourages mutual help and the division of labor in learning, just as in a team sport. But whereas the approach may be routine in athletics, it is hardly so for academic learning in North America. Certain societies outside North America, however, have relied on group competition much more than we have (Dembo & Gurney, 1982).

learning teams

RESPONDING TO DISRUPTIONS

Despite your best efforts to prevent classroom disruptions, some usually happen anyway. Imagine this scene. During a lively class discussion, one student—and only one—is doodling on his desk top. A minute later he pokes his neighbor to show off his masterpiece, even though the neighbor had been participating in the discussion up to that point. Neighbor 1 looks over and giggles, which distracts neighbor 2 sitting nearby, who then whispers to neighbor 3 to look at the drawing. Neighbor 3 is inspired to make a drawing of her own, although up to that point she had been listening attentively to the discussion. Neighbor 3's drawing, however, includes a four-letter obscenity that causes neighbor 4 sitting nearby to guffaw in spite of himself. Out of an originally attentive group, then, the teacher has now lost five individuals—four neighbors plus the original—and the end of the distractions has not yet come. Less than two minutes have elapsed since the incident began.

**disruptions
inevitable**

Seven Typical Strategies

How can teachers respond to such disruptions? Wolfgang (1980) has identified seven ways that teachers can do so, though no one of them, of course, works in all circumstances or would be equally desirable even if it did. These responses range in order from strategies that exercise very little direct power over students to ones that call for the explicit use of it:

1. *Visually looking on.* Sometimes the teacher simply looks hard, if briefly, at the disruptive student. This may be a way of telling the student to solve the problem himself or herself, a way of showing disapproval, or a way of getting an accurate picture of the disruption. Or the teacher

looking on

may intend a combination of these. In the example above, the teacher may simply glance at the doodles and at the related series of events without necessarily interrupting the main flow of discussion.

2. *Nondirective statements.* Sometimes teachers simply state in words what they see happening; in the example above, the teacher might say, "I hear you whispering." The purpose of this response, again, varies with the circumstances: the teacher may seek to clarify what is happening, to imply disapproval of it, or to convey "withitness" in Kounin's sense.

verbally showing
awareness

3. *Questions.* After a disruption, teachers may seek more information. In the incident above, the teacher may ask, "Why do you doodle instead of participate?" Such questions, of course, qualify as questions only if the teacher sincerely seeks information from them. "What do you think you're doing?" may sound like a question, but every student knows it really serves as a direction or a punishment, such as described below.

questioning

4. *Directive statements.* Often teachers will correct misbehavior by telling the misbehaving student how to act: "Stop doodling," the teacher might say in the incident above, or "Start listening instead of drawing." In essence the teacher commands proper behavior, even though phrasing the actual utterance as a request.

directing

5. *Modeling of correct behavior.* Instead of speaking, teachers may respond to disruptions by physically moving a student through the desired behaviors. The teacher may take the pencil and drawing paper out of the student's hand, put them in his or her desk, and perhaps even physically sit the student up straight to encourage more active participation in the discussion. Or the teacher may seek the same result by pointing out another student who already is behaving correctly.

modeling

6. *Praising and ignoring.* Instead of directly responding to the disruptive behavior, teachers may try ignoring it, while at the same time praising and otherwise rewarding correct behaviors. This strategy forms the essence of *behavior modification,* discussed in more detail later in this chapter. If the combination of praising and ignoring does not work, the teacher may also respond with punishments: reprimands, the removal of privileges, or the like.

judicious
reinforcement

7. *Physical intervention and isolation.* Sometimes teachers will intervene by sending a child out of the room or to an isolated part of the room. If their frustration is great enough, they may grab, shake, or even paddle a student, though all of these responses are rather rare and may also be forbidden in some schools.

physical
responses

The fact that teachers do use these responses to disruptions naturally does not make them equally effective in all cases, or even ethical. Which strategy to use depends on the circumstances of the disruption: the nature of the students involved, the expectations of the school and community regarding discipline, the seriousness of the disruption and its frequency, and last but not least, how the teacher views his or her role as a professional.

Teachers typically respond to disruptions in a variety of ways, no one of which is foolproof. (Nancy Hays/Monkmeyer Press Photo Service)

General Approaches to Discipline

Educators typically propose combinations of techniques, with the emphasis reflecting their philosophical beliefs about what the students are like and what schools should be for. At the risk of oversimplifying these beliefs, this next section will describe three general positions in regard to corrective discipline and some typical suggestions that each one makes to teachers.

Humanism   One position might be called the *humanist* approach to discipline, and it is based on the same attitude toward education as that described in Chapter 11. It emphasizes faith in children's reasonableness and their willingness to correct their own behavior and solve their own problems without hurting others. Thomas Gordon's *Teacher Effectiveness Training* (1974), described in Chapter 12, illustrates this approach well. Gordon's most visible strategies for correcting misbehavior are ones that exert very little direct power over the students. Gordon urges teachers to listen carefully to the students' problems, to mirror their feelings back to them, and to state explicitly their (the teachers') own feelings about misconduct. Power and influence are present, but only obliquely: rearranging

humanist
responses to
disruption

indirect influence

daily classroom procedures, for example, may make desirable behaviors more likely to happen and will reinforce them if they do. Gordon's approach does not deny the existence of influence or its necessity for managing students, but in keeping with humanist principles, it relies on students to influence and correct themselves as much as possible. The teacher simply provides the emotional support for students to do so. This faith in the students as people has much to recommend it, though as pointed out in Chapter 12, it also has met with certain criticisms.

providing support

Negotiation   Another position might be called the *negotiation* approach to discipline. Although this approach expects students to take some responsibility for their misconduct and for correcting it, it also expects the teachers to modify and direct their efforts in certain specific ways. William Glasser, for example, has described a system of discipline based on these assumptions (1969, 1978). In part he urges teachers to ask so-called what questions of misbehaving students: "What are you doing?" or "What is the rule about this?" or the like. Since these questions focus on the facts of the misbehavior, they encourage the students to think through the precise consequences of their actions, both for themselves and for others. In so doing, teachers show faith in the students' ability to solve their problems themselves.

discussing misbehavior

But Glasser also urges teachers to direct students explicitly to correct misbehavior: "Stop doodling, you should be listening now" or "You hit her, which is against the rules." Such comments imply that students will not necessarily recognize or accept the consequences of their own wrongdoings without help from the teacher. The same attitude—that students need help in becoming responsible—pervades other aspects of Glasser's suggestions as well. Teachers should, for example, press students to plan how they will avoid further misbehavior in the future and to agree on suitable consequences for further infractions. The teacher does so by a combination of questioning ("How can you learn to stop hitting?") and direction ("You have to plan how to stop hitting, and I will help you.").

urging correct behavior

Although much of this questioning and directing can be done on a one-to-one basis, Glasser also encourages teachers to use group meetings to accomplish it. In these, the class as a whole discusses some general sort of problem behavior or even a misbehavior committed by one particular student. They might, for example, discuss "What shall we do about all the name calling that is going on lately?" or "What can Rachel do about her insisting on standing first in line?" The teacher should guide such discussions to unravel the actual, objective nature of the problem behavior, its consequences for individuals and the classroom group, and how the members of the group can alter those consequences. Such meetings are probably the most widely known and tried of Glasser's suggestions for instructional management, though many educators have criticized using them to discuss individual students. Individuals, some argue, should not have their

group meetings

misbehaviors exposed in detail to their peers, who may have far less skill than their teachers do at handling them tactfully.

using natural
consequences The teacher's direct influence stops with confrontation and planning. He or she does not, in particular, directly reinforce or punish students for good or bad behavior but instead tries to let the natural consequences of their behavior do so. If, for example, hitting other children leads to social isolation, but smiling at them leads to social acceptance, then the teacher relies on these consequences to encourage the desirable alternatives.

Teachers should intervene directly, according to Glasser, only if their efforts to negotiate or encourage class discussions with a student have failed. Then, and preferably only then, they should physically isolate the student, with instructions to formulate a plan for changing the misbehavior. Depending on the age of the children and the layout of the classroom, the isolation may be in a far corner of the room itself, out in the hall, or in some specially designated "isolation room." In most cases, however, teachers do not need such drastic measures. Usually, suggests Glasser, they can successfully follow a middle road in exercising control: by expecting—indeed, insisting—that students take personal responsibility for their behavior, they can usually get them to do so.

Behavior Modification   A third approach to classroom discipline is **behavior modification**, the application of behaviorist principles described in Chapter 6. This approach emphasizes the importance of the positive and negative consequences in controlling behavior. Teachers, in this view, should judge all discipline strategies by their reinforcing effect—or lack thereof. Several educators and psychologists have described systems of instructional management based on this assumption (for example, Axelrod, 1977, or Walker & Shea, 1980). Behavior modification has been used successfully in nonschool settings, and most notably in psychotherapy (Wolpe, 1981). Whatever the setting, the technique uses several different strategies for influencing behavior:

1. *Observe* and count the problem behavior. This strategy helps the teacher determine precisely what the problem behavior is. In keeping with behaviorist principles, observations should focus as specifically as possible on the behavior itself, and they should, whenever possible, be quantifiable.

gathering accurate
observations of
misbehavior If, for example, a student disrupts a class by getting angry, exactly how does she do so? By frowning, hitting others, or speaking in obscenities? If the latter, does she use obscene words, say, twenty times a day, or only three? Although such focusing discourages attention to the underlying meaning of misbehavior, it does try to prevent uncalled-for speculation about the student's motives and personality. It also helps the teacher set clear goals for modifying the misbehavior. If, for example, the teacher knows only that a student uses obscenities "too much," she may not really know when she has reduced the behavior "enough." But if she knows that

As a last resort, some educators recommend "time out" or isolation for a student who disrupts a class significantly and continually. (Victoria Arlak)

the student uses them twenty times a day, then she can always compare the student's progress with this base line.

2. *Reinforce* the behaviors you want to occur. As pointed out in Chapter 6, attractions and rewards vary in nature with the child and the situation. Sometimes a glance or quick smile can reinforce very effectively, at other times, a verbal exchange, and at still other times, tokens to exchange for desirable things and activities. And, as pointed out before, reinforcement can be given directly to the student involved or indirectly through a model. Sometimes praising another student who is behaving correctly influences a misbehaving one to change. But the reverse does not necessarily occur. Reprimanding one misbehaving student may actually lead to further misbehavior by others, instead of inspiring others to correct themselves, as social learning theory might predict. Some call such spreading of mischief the "ripple effect" (Kounin, 1970).

using positive reinforcement

3. *Extinguish* the behavior you want to stop. Given the pervasiveness of reinforcers, this may prove harder than it first seems. If even a quick glance reinforces certain students for disrupting class, for example, then the teacher may need outstanding self-control to extinguish that behavior effectively. Teachers can, however, learn to do so.

ignoring misbehavior

In using extinction, the teacher and class must be able to tolerate the unwanted behavior while it is extinguishing. Since some behaviors may not be tolerable, some advocates of behavior modification suggest the limited use of punishment, in ways described more fully below. If a student frowns whenever the teacher asks him to work, for example, the teacher can probably afford simply to ignore the behavior; but if the student shouts obscenities or literally spits at other students, ignoring him may not work.

4. Establish *contingency contracts* with students. **Contingency contracts** are agreements to reward students in some specific way if they perform some specific work or behave in some specified, desirable way.

bargaining

For example: "If you work quietly for fifteen minutes, then you can listen to records for the rest of the hour" or "Do five problems correctly, and then you can do whatever you like." Contingency contracts can be written or oral and can cover short bits of work or long units of it. In one study, students on a school bus were allowed to listen to music on the bus *only* if they maintained less than a certain level of noise (Greene et al., 1981).

5. *Accept approximations* of desired behavior. This is a restatement of Skinner's notion of shaping (see pages 155–156): if teachers insist on perfect behavior before beginning to reinforce it, they may never obtain the

shaping correct behavior

behavior they want. A noisy student may not read quietly for thirty minutes at first, for example, but she may do so for three minutes and work up to longer intervals if rewarded for her approximations.

6. *Time out* can sometimes help by interrupting the usual cycles of reinforcement that sustain some undesirable behaviors. The procedure consists of temporarily isolating the student until the problem behavior has stopped. A classroom clown, for example, may continue his antics

isolating

indefinitely because his classmates cannot keep from laughing at him. "Time out" for him may help break the pattern of laughter and clowning and allow everyone a fresh start. Occasionally, isolation inadvertently reinforces students by making them seem very special in the eyes of the teacher. More often, though, students would rather participate correctly than do nothing, and so returning to class becomes positively reinforcing.

Punishment

Like it or not, teachers often use punishment in managing difficult behaviors. Most teachers almost daily reprimand students for at least small offenses, and most can remember using more severe punishments like isolating students or shouting at them. And although many teachers may not want to publicize the fact, a surprising number have grabbed or shaken students in anger or frustration, even if they have not actually hit them. All of these strategies constitute **punishment**: they follow an unwanted behavior with adverse, negative consequences.

Ethics of Punishment   Despite how much they use it, however, educators usually do not recommend punishment, at least in its extreme forms, as a way of managing misbehavior. Their reasons are both ethical and practical. Teachers, like other human beings, usually dislike punishing children, no matter what they have done to deserve it and no matter what form the punishment takes: it just does not feel right or humane. If it is possible, most teachers prefer to use positive, or at least indirect, ways of controlling behavior. Discussing the students' misdeeds with them feels better than removing their privileges, and praising them for correct behavior feels the best of all.

But in certain circumstances, other ways of managing misbehavior are often too slow or ineffective. A student who frequently has violent temper tantrums, for example, poses real problems for himself and the group. A teacher cannot really afford to let him express himself openly in class, as the humanists might urge, nor can she hope to discuss his anger rationally, as the negotiators would suggest. Nor can she ignore the tantrum, as the behaviorists might suggest, in the hopes that it will extinguish. Even if these methods did work in the long run, they might not do so fast enough to save the class from a lot of grief and disruption. To produce results immediately, then, the teacher may turn to punishment. In the case of a tantrum, for example, she may scold the student severely, physically sit him down, or send him out of the room.

ineffectiveness of other methods

Effectiveness of Punishment   How well does punishment work? Common experience shows that it can produce dramatic results in the short run, but psychologists and teachers fear several undesirable side effects in the long run. They point out, first, that punishment may overgeneralize, inhibiting behaviors unrelated to the one originally punished. If, for example, a teacher criticizes a student's homework too strongly, he risks making homework generally unpleasant for that student and therefore also risks inhibiting her from efforts to improve. The inhibition could even spread to school in general, if the student often received very harsh criticism. To the extent that these problems result from punishment, teachers lose their ability to reward and encourage students.

inhibition of desired behaviors

A second undesirable side effect of punishment is its modeling power. If teachers rely too heavily on criticism, aggression, and other aversive behaviors, then they inadvertently model these behaviors to their students. They should not feel surprised to see their students use their own punishing responses with one another. As the most important member of the class, teachers may serve as models to their students more than they realize (Bandura, 1965; and see Chapter 6 of this book).

modeling negative behavior

In any case, punishment loses its impact the more it is repeated. Studies of animals who have been punished by electric shock consistently show that they react in less and less "emotional" ways as they receive shocks on more and more learning occasions (Walters & Grusec, 1977). The few exceptions to this trend were punishment procedures that were far more severe than usual. For ethical reasons, children cannot usually receive punishment nearly as often or as severely as did the animals in these studies, but information from observation suggests that the same process occurs with them also. After several occasions of criticism (or scoldings or spankings), children begin to show immunity: they seem less upset by the punishment than at first and may not suppress the misbehavior as much.

Guidelines for Punishment   Nevertheless, both research and teaching experience suggest that punishment may sometimes help in managing certain problem behaviors. To minimize the undesirable side effects, teachers need to keep several guidelines in mind (O'Leary & O'Leary, 1977):

1. *Use punishment sparingly.* As already pointed out, punishment decreases in effectiveness as it increases in frequency, and in any case it may not always be ethical.
2. *Explain why you are punishing.* Without a rationale, students may come to the wrong conclusions about the situation. They may, for example, decide that they, rather than their behavior, are bad.
3. *Provide an alternative way for earning positive reinforcement.* Since positive reinforcement may have fewer bad side effects, students should always have this option open to them. For suggestions about making positive reinforcement work, see the first part of this chapter, as well as pages 151–158 in Chapter 6.
4. *If possible, reinforce behaviors incompatible with the misbehavior.* If a child is running around the room, for example, find a constructive alternative that precludes this behavior (like reading quietly), rather than one that can combine with it (like passing out textbooks).
5. *Avoid physical punishment if possible.* Since a teacher may punish only sparingly at most, the severest forms of punishment should almost never be used. This presumably includes physical punishment.
6. *Avoid punishing when angry or upset.* Since at these times you focus your attention on your own needs and away from the students', you risk reacting too severely.
7. *Punish the initiation of a behavior rather than its completion.* In general, studies of both animals and children show that punishment works more effectively at the beginning of a misbehavior than later on (Solomon, 1964; Walter & Grusec, 1977). If a student begins eating candy in class, for example, you will stop future eating more effectively by reprimanding her when she first takes out the food than at any time after she has already started eating it. Being "withit" in Kounin's sense, of course, helps catch such actions at their beginning.

These guidelines suggest, but do not explain, how to apply punishment in any given teaching situation. Does Sarah's whispering deserve a reprimand or merely a scowling look? Should Billy Joe lose his free time for having talked back at the teacher during the day, or should he stay after school for a Glasser-style discussion about behaving responsibly? Or should he just be ignored? The answers to such questions depend partly on circumstances that only the teacher in those situations can know. But responding to disruptions also depends partly on two general considerations discussed in this chapter. First, what is ethically right for the students and their classmates? And second, what is effective for them?

judgment needed in specific cases

LARGER SYSTEMS FOR MANAGING INSTRUCTION

The suggestions for managing instruction made so far assume that the teacher and students function as a relatively small and self-contained unit. Usually this assumption is accurate: teachers must single-handedly create a learning environment and must themselves correct any problems that arise. Some educators, however, have created very successful systems of instruction by coordinating the effects of many teachers or their assistants and by combining the techniques of task analysis described in Chapters 7 and 8 and reinforcement described in Chapter 6. Here are two examples of such systems.

Personalized System of Instruction (PSI)

The Personalized System of Instruction (PSI) is also called the Keller plan, after the psychologist who originated it for teaching large introductory courses in colleges and universities (Keller, 1974; Ryan, 1974). The **Keller plan** relies on dividing the course into many units, each of which the students study and on which they are given a short test. Students proceed through the units and tests at their own pace, though for administrative convenience, extremely slow paced students may need a bit of pushing. Since the tests themselves are graded according to an absolute standard rather than a competitive one (see Chapter 13), the students are encouraged to concentrate on learning the content rather than to compare themselves with their classmates. Failure to achieve an acceptable standard of performance does not penalize the students, since they are allowed to test themselves on the unit again after some restudy and special tutorial help.

Keller plan

self-pacing

The Keller plan uses advanced students to help new ones with problems and questions and to review the tests. These peer tutors also encourage learning, both directly through positive reinforcement and indirectly by providing a model for the newer students to imitate. The plan does allow for the traditional methods of college instruction, such as lectures, films, and demonstrations, but they are used relatively rarely. In fact, the plan

peer tutoring

tries to use them as rewards or incentives for completing specified amounts of study, rather than as a major dispenser of information.

In various forms, this system has been used widely to coordinate and individualize instruction whenever large numbers of students must take courses. Generally it has produced both higher achievement and higher motivation among students than have conventional ways of teaching very large courses (Block & Burns, 1977). Students report that they particularly enjoy the self-pacing feature, as well as the personal contact with a peer tutor, which is not usually available in very large courses. Although some students do have trouble pacing themselves under this system, there are various techniques that can alleviate this problem. Target dates for completing particular units of study seem to help, as do letters or even phone calls to remind students who procrastinate too long.

positive results

All in all, the Personalized System of Instruction succeeds only by the combined efforts of many individuals. The analysis of course content, for example, is an enormous job if a single teacher must do it alone and even more so if he or she must also construct multiple versions of tests for each of, say, twenty units of study. Since the tutors account for much of the success of the course, they must be prepared in advance for their jobs and supported and helped in their work as they go along. Facing such organizational needs, the head instructor or teacher must coordinate both people and content, rather than functioning without help from others.

Individually Prescribed Instruction (IPI)

Individually Prescribed Instruction (IPI) is sometimes also called **adaptive education** (Glaser, 1977; Resnick, 1975). Like Keller's PSI, it depends on analyzing a curriculum into specific units or instructional goals. These are stated as much as possible in behavioral terms so as to allow easier implementations and a clearer evaluation of the students' success. Compared with PSI, IPI spells out its units and goals in more detail, in recognition of the younger students for which it is intended. Teachers using IPI prescribe activities for students according to their current learning needs. Individual students therefore do not necessarily follow some traditional allocation of topics, such as found in many curricula. Like PSI, IPI uses tests evaluated by absolute criteria rather than competitive ones. A grade of *A* may depend on getting, say, 90 percent of a problem set correct rather than on getting more problems correct than most of the other students do.

schoolwide reorganization

similarities to PSI

entire school staff needed

To help these techniques work effectively, IPI applies them to an entire school at the same time. This fact allows fast-learning students to move ahead of the content conventionally assigned to their grade level, and it allows slow-learning students to take longer with it. It also, of course, requires an enormous amount of instructional planning to make it work—

so much so, in fact, that planning usually has to be done by curriculum consultants and other specialists. Under this system, therefore, classroom teachers become relatively less responsible for determining particular instructional goals and relatively more responsible for implementing the overall program. Generally they devote considerable time to diagnosing the learning needs of individual students and to prescribing tasks for them based on the diagnoses. This task usually requires quite a bit of record keeping, and so recent versions of IPI use computers to help.

Adaptive education and its variants have not produced as much research to evaluate its effects as Keller's PSI has, but what research has been done is promising (for example, Cooley & Leinhardt, 1975). In general, the system seems to produce higher achievement and more motivation to learn than does the conventional organization of instruction. Even so, some educators have questioned the method on a number of grounds (Scriven, 1975):

1. For example, can all curriculum areas be analyzed into specific, easily tested units of instruction? This question came up in Chapter 8, as a possible criticism of behavioral objectives in general. Some educators claim that instructional analysis such as done in IPI only works in fields that emphasize large amounts of technical knowledge, such as science or mathematics (Jaynes, 1975).

criticisms of IPI

2. Even if the curriculum can be analyzed, can teachers as a group live with and support the results of the analysis? It may be unrealistic, some say, to expect some teachers to give up their traditional prerogative to decide what goals to pursue with particular students. Some teachers may conceive of individualized instruction as a form of close personal contact with their students, rather than as carefully laid-out content.

3. Even if all the teachers in a school did support a particular IPI scheme, would it give the students everything they need from their education? Under IPI, would they, for example, get enough social contact with their peers or with highly trained experts in the field? If these instructional systems do have hidden costs like these, then the costs might be reduced by mixing the systems with other, more conventional methods of instructional organization. Most versions of IPI, in fact, do just that: students work on planned, sequenced units for only part of each day and spend the rest of their time on various other, more usual activities.

THE RELATIONSHIP OF INSTRUCTIONAL MANAGEMENT TO LEARNING

Instructional management itself is not part of learning, but it makes learning possible by preventing disruptions to learning and by minimizing the impact of disruptions when they do occur. It accomplishes these goals by smoothly coordinating the many specific behaviors of the students and the instructor. At least it does so in the ideal. Since real classrooms are probably never managed perfectly, most teachers learn to live with occasional awkward moments: lessons that should go well but do not, or students who seem involved but then disrupt anyway. Students learn from these incidents, of course, but probably learn more about life in schools than about whatever instructional goals the teacher has in mind.

The differences between management and learning are important to remember—and easy to forget. A smoothly running classroom is not, in and of itself, a classroom in which learning is occurring. It is only a place in which learning *could* be occurring. Or, stated differently, good instructional management is necessary for learning, but not sufficient for it. To ensure that real learning is actually taking place, teachers must attend to the many other facets of education described elsewhere in this book. The first two parts examined two of these: the development of learners and the precise nature of learning. The remaining two parts will turn to two others: motivation and evaluation.

Key Points

1. Instructional management is the coordination of teaching and learning tasks so as to make instruction effective and efficient.
2. Instructional management is both preventing disruptions and responding constructively to them once they do occur.
3. Teachers can prevent some disruptions by attending to the physical conditions and arrangement of the classroom, by delegating tasks, and by using peer tutoring.
4. Teachers can improve a group's productiveness and attitudes by using a democratic leadership style.
5. Fostering cooperation among students can benefit student learning and attitudes, but teachers should be aware that many students also wish, or feel driven, to compete.

6. Teachers typically use a variety of strategies to respond to disruptions, though none works all of the time.
7. In general, programs for responding to disruptions can be grouped into three categories: humanistic approaches, negotiation approaches, and behavior modification.
8. Punishment is less desirable for influencing students than are positive methods of management, and in some ways it is also less effective.
9. If teachers must use punishment, then they should follow certain guidelines for doing so.
10. Instructional management may also mean coordinating the work of many teachers, instructors, or their assistants.

Case Study

Mary, the Student Teacher

The day began well enough. The ninth-grade class worked diligently and quietly at the work sheets the regular teacher had left for them while Mary, the student teacher, took over for a while. Mary quietly walked around the room, answering questions and offering suggestions to individuals.

After about ten minutes of this, Ralph burped loudly, causing a ripple of giggles around him.

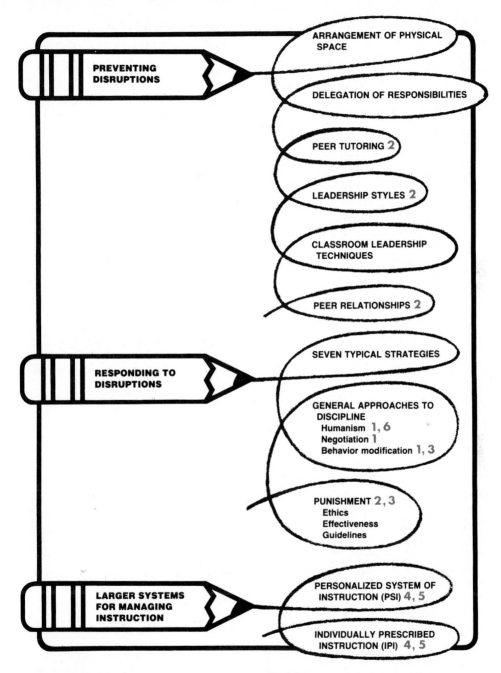

PREVENTING DISRUPTIONS

ARRANGEMENT OF PHYSICAL SPACE

DELEGATION OF RESPONSIBILITIES

PEER TUTORING 2

LEADERSHIP STYLES 2

CLASSROOM LEADERSHIP TECHNIQUES

PEER RELATIONSHIPS 2

RESPONDING TO DISRUPTIONS

SEVEN TYPICAL STRATEGIES

GENERAL APPROACHES TO DISCIPLINE
Humanism 1, 6
Negotiation 1
Behavior modification 1, 3

PUNISHMENT 2, 3
Ethics
Effectiveness
Guidelines

LARGER SYSTEMS FOR MANAGING INSTRUCTION

PERSONALIZED SYSTEM OF INSTRUCTION (PSI) 4, 5

INDIVIDUALLY PRESCRIBED INSTRUCTION (IPI) 4, 5

1 Moral behavior and development (Chapter 4)

2 The social context of learning (Chapter 5)

3 Learning as behavior change (Chapter 6)

4 Learning to structure knowledge (Chapter 7)

5 Making instruction more effective (Chapter 8)

6 Humanistic perspectives in education (Chapter 12)

Mary was embarrassed inwardly, but she decided to ignore the behavior in the hopes that it would not recur. Unfortunately, it did: this time by George, Ralph's best friend, who sat across the room. A new ripple of giggles and smiles followed. Some students looked obviously distracted, and a few looked irritated. One finally said, "Be quiet, you guys! She's only a student teacher, you know." Mary did not know the name of the student who said this.

After another minute or so, Fred began to sing to himself—an old Beatles song, as it happened. George and Ralph looked at each other and smirked. "Can't you sing anything newer than that?" asked Ralph. Fred stopped, but his face showed frustration. "Shut up!" he said.

Mary was getting more and more uncomfort-able with all of these events. "If you people cannot work quietly, I'll have to keep you after class—all of you," she said in as stern a voice as she could muster. Then a mocking imitation of her own voice piped up: "Work quietly! All of you!" It was the "nameless" student who had spoken a moment before. She produced a general peel of laughter.

Mary was furious. "What's your name?" she shouted. "Don't you dare speak to me like that!" The student just stared at her blankly. For a moment the class was absolutely silent. Then three students began whispering together—ones who had not spoken before. Mary couldn't hear what they were saying, because at that moment the regular teacher walked in again. "How did it go?" he asked pleasantly.

Questions for Discussion

1. How much do you believe that Mary contributed to these behavior problems in the first place? What, if anything, could she or the regular teacher have done to prevent them?

2. a. How should Mary respond to the regular teacher's question at the end of this incident? Explain.

b. Should Mary discuss this incident with the regular teacher after class? If so, suggest how she might begin.

3. Even though this chapter cautions against punishing students out of anger, Mary seemed to do it in this incident. How do you think her display of anger might affect her ability to manage this class, both in the long run and the short run? Consider the positive effects of her anger as well as the negative ones.

Suggested Readings

Glaser, Robert. *Adaptive Education: Individual Diversity and Learning*. New York: Holt, Rinehart & Winston, 1977.

This book presents the principal reasons for schoolwide individualization of instruction and offers some general guidelines for implementing it. It does not, however, give a step-by-step plan for actually doing so.

Herman, T. M. *Creating Learning Environments: The Behaviorist Approach to Education*. Boston: Allyn & Bacon, 1977.

Pine, G. J., and A. V. Boy. *Learner Centered Teaching: A Humanistic View*. Denver: Love Publishing, 1977.

Both of these books take a prevention-oriented view of management problems. As the names imply, the first book relies on behaviorist techniques, and the second one relies on more humanistic ones.

House, E. R. *Survival in the Classroom: Negotiating with Kids, Colleagues, and Bosses*. Boston: Allyn & Bacon, 1978.

This book deals with instructional management outside the classroom as well as inside. It points out that the other professionals in a teacher's life can be challenging to deal with, and it makes some suggestions for doing so.

Kohut, S. *Classroom Discipline: Case Studies and Viewpoints*. Washington, D.C.: National Education Association, 1979.

Maggs, M. *The Classroom Survival Book: A Practical Manual for Teachers*. New York: New Viewpoints Press, 1980.

Weiner, E. H., ed. *Discipline in the Classroom*. 2nd ed. Washington, D.C.: National Education Association, 1980.

These are three very practical discussions of management problems from a teacher's viewpoint. They are not committed to any particular philosophical position.

Lovitt, T. C. *Managing Inappropriate Behavior in the Classroom: What Research and Experience Say to the Teacher of Exceptional Children*. Reston, Va.: Council for Exceptional Children, 1978. This booklet is only forty-four pages long, but it contains some good suggestions for one specialized, but important management problem: dealing with the behavior problems of exceptional children.

Chapter 10

TEACHING CHILDREN

WITH SPECIAL NEEDS

Roger Branburg, Grade 4 teacher: When I first heard that I was getting a retarded student in my class, I thought, "No way! This will never work." I had a hard enough time as it was, keeping up with my supposedly normal kids and giving them some semblance of individual attention. It's nice to be democratic and include handicapped children and all that, but I really didn't think it was practical, at least for me.

But Jenny managed to change my mind. She was slow, all right, but it didn't stop her from enjoying class as much as anyone else did and from learning in it. She turned out to be less helpless than I had expected. For instance, she could take herself to the bathroom and back very reliably—that had been one of my fears. And anyway, she wasn't actually *in* my room for more than about half the day. The rest of the time she spent getting special help from others, mostly the resource teacher but also a couple of parent volunteers and the phys-ed teacher.

It took me a while to learn how much to expect of her. Jenny was supposed to be reading and writing at an early Grade 1 level, but she always took so long even just to write her own name that I didn't believe at first she could do it. The resource teacher finally convinced me that she could read a little when she came to my room one day to read with Jenny during one of our individual work times. She gave me a couple of tips about Jenny that helped, too, like making sure to praise her *explicitly* for her achievements.

A couple of my other students, I thought, were too helpful at first with Jenny, always holding her coat for her or showing her how to do things instead of letting her try for herself. They still are, I think—too helpful, I mean. But I'm working on it, telling them to let Jenny do more for herself. Most of the others seem to be getting along fine with her. Or at least they accept and tolerate her—I'm not sure that she actually has close friends in this class. That bothers me, but I'm not sure right now what to do about it.

I'll say one thing for having a slow learner like Jenny in my class: it really makes me rethink carefully what my educational goals are! With Jenny around, I can't afford to take my usual plans for granted—they just may not work. I've had to plan carefully and specially for Jenny, and it's made me take a second look at some of my ideas for everyone else, too.

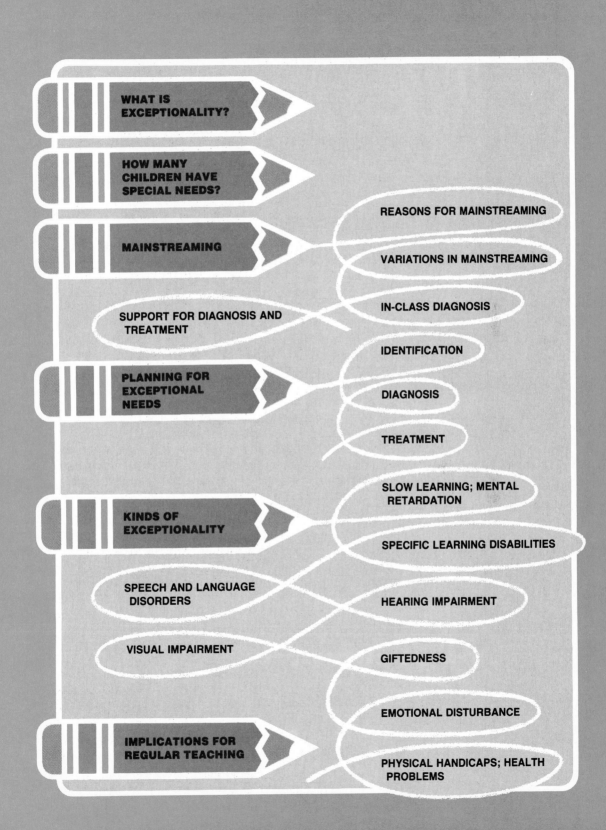

THE history of schooling contains two contradictory themes. One of these is the belief that school is a privilege rather than a right. Children who could meet its rigors were admitted and promoted, and the others either quit of their own accord or were dropped from the system because of the combined effects of low grades and advice from the school authorities. Public school became a major sorting institution for society, identifying the fit and casting off the misfit. Usually the misfits came disproportionately from low-income families, out-of-favor ethnic groups, and the handicapped.

But schooling has also been considered a great social equalizer. By getting an education, children from all walks of life were supposed to have a fair chance to make the most of their individual qualities and talents. This view assumed that schooling was a right rather than a privilege and that it belonged equally to everyone, including any "misfits." Schools, in this view, have no business classifying children and should confine themselves to helping children realize their personal potential.

In recent years the view that schooling is a right has become dominant and has resulted in the creation of various programs to help children in unusual circumstances, whether disadvantaged economically or somehow different physically or mentally. This chapter will consider one large group of such children, those known as "exceptional" or "special needs" children. Although most of these children have handicaps or limitations of some sort, not all do; some are exceptionally gifted rather than exceptionally handicapped. This chapter will keep this distinction in mind and refer to special needs and exceptionality as including unusual gifts as well as unusual problems.

As we shall see, even knowing what to call such children has proved to be a bit of a problem for educators and the general public. Recent legislation in both the United States (PL 94–142) and Canada has required improvements in the educational services provided for such children. In general the improvements call for exceptional children to participate in regular classrooms more than before and for regular classroom teachers to understand and provide for the needs of such children better than they used to. At the same time, the teachers and their children can expect more help than before in meeting these goals.

WHAT IS EXCEPTIONALITY?

Usually **exceptionality** refers to significant deviations from normal characteristics. This chapter examines the following such deviations:

1. Slow learning and mental retardation
2. Specific learning disabilities
3. Speech and language disorders
4. Hearing impairment

5. Visual impairment
6. Giftedness
7. Emotional disturbance
8. Physical handicaps and health problems

Sometimes, of course, these deviations come in combinations, so-called *multiple handicaps*. As a statement about attributes, however, this definition suffers from the same problems that other attribute theories do, such as those discussed in Chapter 5: the qualities that are being named just do not remain constant long enough to make the label meaningful.

This is particularly true for handicaps that refer to behaviors rather than physical qualities. Children with a tendency toward, say, hyperactivity may actually appear quite normal on many occasions, depending on their mood and on the situation in which they find themselves. To call them "hyperactive" implies a much wider range of negative behaviors than may actually occur. And even a physical or sensory handicap may surprise us with its variability. Consider partially deaf children: their physical hearing impairment may be relatively constant as measured by an audiometer, but their typical hearing behavior may vary considerably. They may, in effect, seem to hear better or worse at any one moment, depending on their motivation to hear, for example, on the distractions that happen to occur, or on whether they can see the person speaking to them. When these factors all act in their favor, their hearing may seem quite normal indeed.

> difficulties of using fixed categories for variable behavior

Despite these ambiguities, some sort of definition of exceptional children seems necessary to guide general planning for their needs. Legislation to finance special needs programs must determine, however crudely, for whom the program is intended. Likewise, parents or teachers seeking information on various handicaps must know what they are looking for, even if they know that no real child—normal *or* exceptional—ever fits any simple category description. Although labeling children's conditions certainly does not explain them, it can at least suggest to parents and teachers how a particular child may resemble or differ from certain other children in need. The labels provide a general orientation, if not detailed or accurate information about individuals.

HOW MANY CHILDREN HAVE SPECIAL NEEDS?

There are a variety of statistics regarding how many children have special needs. If being exceptional means receiving year-long special services from the schools, then the estimates may run as low as 5 percent of the total school population. If it means receiving some sort of special help at least occasionally during a school year, then the estimate may be closer to 10 or 20 percent of the total. But if exceptionality includes needing some sort of special services sometime during a child's entire schooling, then esti-

> incidence versus prevalence

mates run as high as 40 percent of the population, or even more (Reynolds & Birch, 1977). These differences depend on the distinction between incidence and prevalence. **Incidence** refers to how many children have special problems at one time or another, but **prevalence** refers to how many have a problem at a particular time.

The estimates also assume that the numbers of children receiving special services reflect the numbers who actually have needs. In reality, however, the percentage varies considerably with the type of need: over 80 percent of speech-impaired and retarded children receive help, but less than 20 percent of learning-disabled, emotionally disturbed, or hearing-impaired children receive assistance. These differences in part reflect the history of special educational services: learning disabilities, for example, are a relatively new concept, and the services for such children have had less time to become established. In part, too, the differing estimates reflect the comparative ease or difficulty of identifying certain problems and arranging for help. Complete deafness may show itself rather early in life, for example, but a slight hearing loss may be present for a long time without being noticed.

fewer helped than in need

In looking at Table 10–1 and Figure 10–1, note too that most exceptional children have their needs defined or diagnosed primarily by the differences in their behavior: communication disorders, learning disabilities, mental retardation, emotional disturbance. These conditions all describe things that children *do* rather than conditions that they *have*. This fact helps explain the unease that many educators feel about such categories. Most exceptional children are defined by what they typically do or fail to do, and yet what they do varies from one situation to another—as it does for everyone else. This ambiguity exists, even though some behavior-based exceptional ties may also be defined by physical qualities. Some retarded children, for example, may look "odd" by usual standards, and

Table 10–1 Prevalence of Major Forms of Special Needs

Type of need	Number	Percentage of children enrolled in school
Speech impaired	1.2 million	2.6
Learning disabled	1.1 million	2.4
Slow learners and retarded	920 thousand	2.0
Emotionally disturbed	300 thousand	0.6
Deaf and hard of hearing	86 thousand	0.2
Vision impaired	33 thousand	0.1
Crippled and other health impaired	178 thousand	0.4
Total special needs	3.9 million	8.4

Source: *U.S. Statistical Abstract, 1980.*

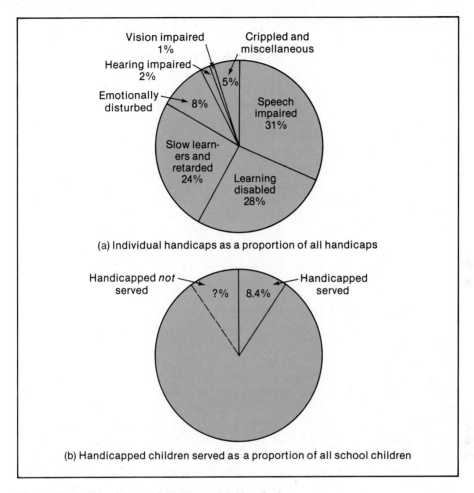

Figure 10–1 Proportions of Children with Handicaps
(Source: *U.S. Statistical Abstract, 1980,* Table 575, p. 351.)

some crippled children may not perform well in school indirectly because of their handicap. The fact remains, however, that behavior—not physique—accounts for most of what teachers mean by exceptionality.

MAINSTREAMING

Recent trends in special education have favored keeping children with special needs in regular classrooms as much as possible—so-called **mainstreaming**. Special, segregated classes have become less common, though they certainly have not disappeared.

Reasons for Mainstreaming

Several reasons account for the shift toward mainstreaming. One is that research studies have failed to show any consistent educational advantage to children placed in special classes (Boylan, 1976; Guerin & Szatlocky, 1974). Apparently, on the whole, teachers in segregated classes either do not, or cannot, tailor their programs in ways that lead to higher overall achievement for exceptional students. At the same time, the segregation of such classes has been criticized repeatedly for preventing both exceptional and normal students from getting acquainted with one another. Presumably the learning environment of the handicapped students is enriched by the presence of normal children and their activities, and presumably also the normal students learn more tolerance for exceptionality if they have direct contact with the handicapped. Recent research suggests that these benefits may in fact occur often, though not automatically (Gresham, 1981; Guralnick, 1981).

Variations in Mainstreaming

The extent to which children are incorporated into regular schooling depends on the extent and nature of their handicaps. Most mild physical problems—visual or hearing loss, for example—do not really interfere with children's ability to function. The same can be said for various health problems—epilepsy, for example, or diabetes—at least as long as the conditions are only moderate. Somewhat more severe problems can often be handled in regular classrooms if modifications are made in the normal content and methodology and if such modifications are supplemented by help from appropriate consultants or other helpers. Children with learning disabilities in reading, for example, may function quite normally in most areas of classroom life, including most academic areas. Only their reading performance may need special help. And even there, they may not always need a special, remedial class for help if their teachers can provide them with essentially the same materials as in the regular program. Doing so, of course, means taking seriously the principle of "individualizing instruction," and it may also mean getting suggestions for how to individualize from other school personnel.

integration according to individual needs

Children with still more severe problems may need more help, including, in a few cases, special activities or programs that can take place only outside a regular classroom. A hearing-impaired child, for example, may profit from periodic visits with a speech therapist, away from the noisy distractions of the classroom. And a few very severe handicaps, of course, may need more special help than can reasonably be expected from even the most individualized classroom. A profoundly retarded child, for ex-

completely separate education needed by few

Mainstreaming can help all children become more sensitive to the needs of exceptional children. (© Mitchell Payne/Jeroboam, Inc.)

ample, or one with extreme limitations in language ability, may require placement in a special class or school.

Advocates of mainstreaming point out that the number of children who require special placement is small compared with the number who can be incorporated in various ways into normal schooling. They argue that the need for special places for exceptional children may not be nearly as great as the need for special activities and provisions for them in regular places, that is, normal classrooms. Hearing-impaired children, for example, may be helped as much by redesigning the acoustics in their classrooms so that they can hear better as by having them visit a speech therapist. By accommodating their classrooms to them, hearing-impaired children can experience language in its classroom context—and make more friends in the process. In the long run, these are more important experiences than learning language in one-to-one tutorial sessions that may differ in style and content from classroom teaching.

In-class Diagnosis

In addition to teaching exceptional children in regular classrooms, mainstreaming also includes diagnosing special problems as much as possible in the situation in which the children spend most of their educational time—the classroom (Haring & Batemen, 1977, chap. 4). As much as possible, furthermore, the initial diagnostic observations should be done by the people who actually implement the children's individualized programs, usually their regular teachers. Although many problems definitely should be referred to specialists, referral without observations by the classroom *classroom* teacher can be harmful to the children in question. First, an uninvolved *observations* teacher may feel less committed to whatever suggestions for treatment the specialist makes. In addition, diagnosing by referral can imply that the problems exist only in the children themselves, rather than in a mismatch between the children's needs and certain aspects of their environment. Speech-impaired children, for example, may communicate well as long as they do not have to talk at great length, and so a lesson or activity that requires extended language may in a sense "cause" their handicap to appear. In the same way, other mismatches can occur as part of regular, unmodified instruction: hearing-impaired children "acquire" their handicap when they must sit too far away to hear easily. Learning-disabled children are disabled only when asked to use whatever skill they do not possess. Emotionally disturbed children may have a problem only when put under too much stress. And so on. These environmental effects are obscured or even forgotten completely if children are diagnosed and treated away from their environment, which for school-aged children means a regular classroom.

To make mainstreaming work, then, teachers must become careful observers of their children. Knowing just the general labels for exceptional children is not enough; they must also know some of the details about the children's behavior and their responses to classroom life. Knowing, for example, that a child is "reading disabled," for example, says very little *need for precise* that helps a teacher provide the child with constructive reading instruc- *observations* tion. More to the point are the answers to a host of specific questions: Does the child consistently reverse his or her letters? Which ones? Does the child skip certain words on a page when reading? Does he or she read some materials better than others? Answers to questions like these constitute an informal diagnosis of the child's learning disability. The chances are that the teacher will discover some reading behaviors that do not seem so disabled after all—despite the label given to the child.

Support for Diagnosis and Treatment

The drive toward mainstreaming has been accompanied by various strategies to help regular classroom teachers diagnose and plan for their children. Most of these pertain to consultation from a mixture of specialists and consulting or **resource teachers**. A school nurse may screen children for health problems and hearing and vision impairments. A speech therapist may visit periodically to detect children with language and communication problems. A physical education teacher may provide special programming for children with poor coordination. In principle, these people are supposed to advise and support teachers in dealing with unusual learning and behavior problems in their classes. In practice, of course, schools with only modest budgets may not have all these staff members, or if they do, they may have to cover so many schools that any one child may see them very seldom indeed.

supporting staff

Sometimes, in addition, a special resource room or center may be set up for such staff for talking with teachers, helping individual children, and storing useful materials for the rest of the staff. In principle, these activities are intended to keep exceptional children functioning in regular classes as much as possible, rather than to remove them from regular classes. Special help for special students is supposed to maximize normal school experience, not minimize it (Meisgeier, 1976).

resource room

PLANNING FOR EXCEPTIONAL NEEDS

Before mainstreaming can occur, teachers must discover which children have special needs and precisely what their problems are. This process often begins with the regular classroom teacher, though it quickly expands to include other professional staff, as well as the parents of exceptional children. The details of the process vary among communities and schools, but the general outline usually includes the steps below.

Identification

Children whose behavior differs significantly from the usual for the group must first be identified. When there is no obvious physical problem, then the classroom teachers are often the first to notice subtle problems, since they see the children far more than any other school personnel do. Their position as identifier remains important even though some school districts have now set up screening programs using specialists as well as classroom teachers. Whoever is involved, however, their purpose at this point is only to find the children who differ from the usual, not to specify the nature of those differences. The identified children have only one quality in common:

teacher often first to see problems

they deserve further, more careful observation in order to diagnose their individual problems, or indeed to verify whether they really have any problem at all. Identification, then, is a relatively short, though important, step in the overall process of special education. Classroom teachers, for example, may rely simply on incidental observations of their children, combined with examples of the children's work that they have assigned in the normal course of their teaching. Some teachers may also refer to school records of the children's past performance, though others may avoid this source for fear of biasing their own observations. At this point, few or no special tests or observations are collected. Even if there is a special, schoolwide screening program, it will use only the simplest tests: a young child may be asked to draw a stick figure of a person or to answer a few thinking questions. These will be used only to answer the basic question of identification: does this child require further observation?

Diagnosis

Having identified those children whose behavior differs significantly from the average, the teacher and other professionals then need to *diagnose* the children's specific needs, which means that they must gather as much information as possible about the exact nature of the children's behavior. Who makes the diagnosis and how it is made depend on the children's

referral for more careful observation

general kinds of problems. Children who show signs of hearing loss or vision loss, for example, may be referred to a school nurse or doctor to test for these possibilities. Children with learning disabilities may receive more careful observation from their classroom teachers or from a resource teacher, and both teachers may look for more detailed information about the children's academic skills. Quite commonly the children will be seen by several people, since many special problems affect several areas of their school life at once. Children whose speech is impaired may also have academic problems and therefore give the impression of having learning disabilities as well.

In addition to any formal testing by special teachers, the regular classroom teachers can gather information by constructing their own informal tests or inventories of content that they normally teach in class: samples of reading material, for example, or groups of math problems or simple

use of informal classroom tests

writing assignments. These can be given to the children either during or after class time and have the advantage of representing the achievements normally expected of children in that particular class more precisely than standardized tests may. Adding these informal results to those from more specialized or formal observations gives a more complete picture of the children's ability to participate in the class. For more suggestions about informally assessing children, see Moran (1978).

Treatment

After diagnosis, presumably, comes "treatment" or "special help." Unfortunately, this phase of work with exceptional children is the most easily neglected, since by definition it may require sustained effort by a group of busy professional people. If the treatment must last for long periods, its original purposes may be forgotten ("Why is Johnny getting speech therapy, anyway?"), and the staff giving the help may even change substantially (at the least, Johnny will have a new classroom teacher every year).

To respond to this problem, treatment plans in North America now often use some sort of contract, often called an **individualized educational plan**, or IEP, to specify the help that an exceptional child is to receive and the reasons for receiving it. A recent U.S. law (PL 94–142), in fact, now requires that such a plan be drawn up once a year for every special-needs child in the country (see Reynolds, 1978, for an analysis). The plan is negotiated jointly by the parents of the child, by his or her various teachers, and by a representative—other than his or her teachers—of his or her school district. Typically it contains information about the following:

IEP

1. The child's current educational status
2. The goals and instructional objectives planned
3. Any special services required to meet the goals
4. The extent to which the child is to be mainstreamed
5. The responsibilities of the parents, teachers, and special staff for individual parts of the plan
6. The methods and dates for evaluating the child's progress and revising the plan

By spelling out these features in a written document, the individualized educational plan helps ensure that the child actually receives the help he or she has been diagnosed to need and that the various people involved will work for his or her common good. It forms a kind of contract between and among the relevant people, one that has some permanence even during the pressures of daily teaching.

KINDS OF EXCEPTIONALITY AND INSTRUCTIONAL STRATEGIES

How can regular classroom teachers identify exceptionality, and how should they respond to it? The most accurate answer may be the least helpful: it depends on the individual child. Some general suggestions can also be made, however, as long as they are taken as flexible guidelines rather than specific dictates to be used unmodified with each child. Real children usually present a more confusing picture than our comments below suggest.

Slow Learning and Mental Retardation

Characteristics   Slow learners and mentally retarded children have low general learning performance, often combined with some difficulties in getting along with others. Usually their low performance is reflected in a low score on a standardized IQ test. If their performance is low enough, they are called **mentally retarded**. Educators sometimes group retarded children into several categories according to how much general cognitive disadvantage they have. In practice, they define these groups by their scores on intelligence tests or on other tests of general abilities. Table 10–2 shows one common breakdown of degrees of retardation (for an explanation of the meanings of the IQ scores, see Chapter 14). Note that the categories may have more than one name and that the IQ ranges are defined differently by different educators; these two facts probably reflect the inherent ambiguity of such categories, discussed earlier in this chapter.

Table 10–2 Degrees of Mental Retardation

Degree of retardation	IQ range	Abilities by adolescence
Slow learners	70–85	Elementary school academic skills and some basic high school academic skills; vocational and personal independence usually possible.
Educably mentally retarded (EMR): mildly retarded	50–75	Elementary school academic skills; vocation possible, though sometimes with guidance.
Trainable mentally retarded (TMR): moderately retarded	35–60	Early elementary school skills (for example, literacy); unskilled vocation possible under supervision.
Custodial mentally retarded (CMR): severely or profoundly retarded	Less than 35	Basic language and cognitive functions, if any; basic physical skills (for example, walking); sometimes capable of simple chores under supervision.

The retarded children that teachers encounter in their classrooms may belong to any of these groups, but most commonly to the least disadvantaged two groups: the slow learners and the educably mentally retarded (EMR). In the preschool years, such children may not seem very handicapped, but by the time they are in elementary school, their rate of learning will seem definitely slower than that of most of their classmates. By the time they finish school, they may be able to perform the basic academic skills of a late elementary school child (Grade 5 or 6), especially if given special help in learning. In adulthood they should be able, to a large extent, to manage their own life and vocation, at least if they do not have to cope with unusually difficult stresses or problems.

low overall cognitive performance

Teaching Strategies   In general, teachers and schools have adapted to the needs of slow learners and EMR children by a combination of slowing down, simplifying, and stretching out the regular curriculum. If reading normally begins in Grade 1, for example, it may be delayed until some later grade for the very slow learners, when they seem more ready for it. The reading instruction may also be simplified—for example, by leaving out some enrichment material—and by extending it over a relatively long period of time. Since making these adjustments can take considerable effort for a teacher, various curricula for slow learners have also been developed commercially (see, for example, Cegelka, 1976; Turnbull, 1979). Some of these, though far from all, have relied on behaviorist principles such as those discussed in Chapter 6 (see, for example, Gardner, 1974). The fact that we lack a specialized body of methods for these children reflects their great diversity and their comparatively good ability to learn compared with that of more profoundly retarded children. Mainstreaming has probably helped continue the use of ordinary, but slower, teaching for slow learners and EMR children (Lilly, 1979).

slower and simpler pacing

Teaching such children can be successful or not, depending partly on whether the teachers focus on the children's achievements or failures. Describing a mildly retarded child's long-term prospects as "a limited ability to learn the school curriculum" tends to discourage that child's efforts to learn, as well as the teacher's efforts to teach. But describing the child's prospects as "an ability to master the essentials of the curriculum" tends to challenge teachers to identify those curricular essentials, an effort that should incidentally benefit all learners.

What, then, are the essentials that slow learners and EMR children should master? One educator has suggested that they can be summarized in two terms: teaching children to *think critically* and teaching them to *act independently* (Goldstein, 1974). Any activities or methods that contribute to these goals should have an important place in a program for slow learners or mildly retarded children. The best teaching methods for achieving these goals depend, of course, on the students' individual

teaching critical thinking and independence

qualities, but most educators of slow or retarded learners favor the use of somewhat structured techniques. Consider the following list of suggestions:

1. Begin where the learner needs to begin, not where the curriculum says he should begin;
2. Utilize ample repetition and review, though varied to hold interest;
3. Divide content into small, but meaningful bits of learning;
4. Keep the learning setting free of distractions as much as possible;
5. Check the learner frequently for how well he is paying attention.

(Reynolds & Birch, 1977, p. 303)

To an extent, these suggestions make good advice for teaching some normal children, as well as exceptional ones. But they do not leave as much room for self-guided learning as some educators prefer for normal students. Methods of discovery learning such as those advocated by Bruner (see Chapter 8) may not work well with exceptionally slow learners. If they do work, then they must be carried out in such a way that the teacher or other adults can keep accurate track of what the learners are doing and respond helpfully to it.

structured,
planned teaching

Moderately and severely retarded children usually require very structured instruction, teaching that implements and reinforces precisely defined goals. Typically a specialist of some sort (psychologist, resource teacher) carefully assesses what skills such a child already can use and therefore what skills can reasonably be taught. Both the assessment and the teaching may be done largely by the classroom teacher, but he or she probably will not work as independently as with the more normal children. Moderately and severely retarded children, furthermore, typically spend less time in a regular classroom than less retarded children do and on that account may present more specific instructional demands to the teacher.

teaching the very
retarded

During the time such children do participate in the class, however, the teacher should expect to implement whatever particular goals the special teacher and other staff have agreed on. Sometimes, for example, a moderately retarded child may be asked to work with a normal child on a simple academic task, with the normal child acting as tutor. Or the teacher may work on teaching the child some table game that the child can later play with classmates. Both the game and the tutoring can help the retarded child to belong to or participate socially in the classroom more effectively—which is a common goal of mainstreaming.

Specific Learning Disabilities

Characteristics   Despite being one of the most prevalent categories of exceptionality, **specific learning disabilities** have one of the most ambiguous definitions. They refer to children whose achievement falls well

definition

below their ability but who show no obvious cause for their underachievement. One widely accepted definition is in federal legislation PL 94–142, requiring educational services for handicapped children:

> "Specific learning disability" means a disorder in one or more of the basic psychological processes involved in understanding or in using language spoken or written, which may manifest itself in an imperfect ability to listen, think, speak, read, write, spell, or to do mathematical calculations. The term includes such conditions as perceptual handicaps, brain injury, minimal brain dysfunction, dyslexia, developmental aphasia. The term does not include children who have learning problems which are primarily the result of visual, hearing, or motor handicaps, or mental retardation, of emotional disturbance, or of environmental, cultural, or economic disadvantage. (USOE, 1977, p. 65082)

The regulations that follow this legislation explain how specific learning disabilities can be identified in practice. Educators have identified such a disability if:

1. The child does not achieve commensurate with his or her age and ability levels in one or more of seven specific areas when provided with learning experiences appropriate for the child's age and ability levels.
2. The team finds that a child has a severe discrepancy between achievement and intellectual ability in one or more of the following areas:
   a. Oral expression
   b. Listening comprehension
   c. Written expression
   d. Basic reading skill
   e. Reading comprehension
   f. Mathematics calculation
   g. Mathematics reasoning

(USOE, 1977, p. 65083)

Typically, the disability is confined to one or a few academic skills, including, most commonly, reading and language arts. Sometimes, too, a learning-disabled child shows signs of distractability, physical awkwardness, or poor perception of sights and sounds. There can be so many combinations of specific disabilities that no simple list of skill-deficits is fully reliable. The general category of specific learning disabilities, though, does exclude the general learning disability of mental retardation discussed earlier, as well as any other conditions (like visual, hearing, or motor handicaps; emotional disturbances; or social cultural, or economic disadvantages) that more obviously cause learning problems. Because a learning disability is a problem without any obvious cause, its status as a category of exceptionality has been disputed by some educators and psychologists (for example, Cruickshank & Hallahan, 1975, p. 310).

relatively isolated academic problems

Notice that defining learning disabilities depends on distinguishing between ability and achievement. Somehow, teachers must have reason to believe that learning-disabled children *can* do more than they *do* do in some area of academic functioning: they can read better, work math problems better, or whatever—even though they usually do not. The gap exists, furthermore, even though they give every evidence of trying to perform well. In practice, the discrepancy may not really have to be measured on a formal test of ability or intelligence, although it can be in some cases. More likely in actual practice, the discrepancies that matter are between and among informal expectations for the children—expectations by the teacher, the parents, or the students themselves. Any or all of these people may judge that such students can do better if the conditions are right: they may point to high grades in nondisabled subjects, to good performance at home and away from school pressures, or to ups and downs in achievement over time. They may also point to the students' comparative inability to focus attention on tasks involving their learning disability. A standardized ability test may contribute to this picture but make up only part of it. Altogether, the information must suggest that actual achievement does not reflect potential ability—and by quite a bit.

Teaching Strategies   The great diversity of specific learning disabilities and their lack of any simple causes have inspired many suggestions for alleviating them (for a review, see Neff & Pilch, 1978). Some psychologists and educators explain learning disabilities in terms of information-processing theory, such as discussed in Chapter 7 (Farnham-Diggory, 1978). Some children who cannot read well, for example, fail because they do not

learning disabilities as failures of information processing

recognize printed letters quickly or accurately. In these cases, their "feature detectors" or "synthesizers" may not work normally, even though their other mental processes have no impairment. If so, then the teachers of such children should not present visual information too quickly; flash cards should be slowed down, even though oral instructions need not be. For the same reasons, the teacher might also encourage the children *not* to scan a line of print as fast as they see their classmates doing. If they go too fast, their short-term memory will receive garbled information, impossible to process.

This kind of interpretation, however, ignores the emotional problems that often accompany learning disabilities and that sometimes even seem to cause the disability itself. Children who constantly fail at a particular academic skill (say, reading) may soon become self-conscious about even

learning disabilities as emotional blocks

trying to acquire it and may eventually feel badly about themselves because of their failure. Their discouragement may in turn aggravate the disability itself, putting them farther and farther behind in their efforts to learn. Eventually, then, their teachers may have trouble determining which problems deserve more help: the children's poor attitudes toward themselves and toward learning or the specific learning disability itself. This dilemma has led some educators to propose counseling for many students with learning disabilities (Morse, 1976). Variations of counseling strategies have been adapted for use by teachers, two of which are examined in Chapter 9 as methods for managing classroom disruptions—William Glasser's "reality therapy" and Thomas Gordon's "Teacher Effectiveness Training."

Speech and Language Disorders

Characteristics   Classroom teachers can encounter speech and language problems in several forms. The first of these, *language delay,* is commonly associated with mental retardation, as discussed above: children with a generally slow rate of cognitive development may show a slow rate of language development as well.

language delay

Another form of speech impairment, *stuttering,* seems to involve speech production specifically and overall thinking ability relatively little. The causes of stuttering are still obscure, though it does seem to be aggravated by stress and excitement. But this does not mean that teachers should avoid at all costs arousing children who stutter, only that they should expect fluctuations in the severity of the problem depending on circumstances.

stuttering

A third form of impairment, *articulation disorders,* is the most common form of speech impairment among school children. Such children may mix up, omit, or substitute certain sounds of language, giving their speech a "babyish" quality: "a vewy fuwwy beaw," they may say, instead of "a very furry bear." Although such errors occur most commonly among younger children, they can persist well into adolescence for a few.

articulation disorders

Teaching Strategies   Help for speech and language disorders depends, of course, on the nature of each particular disorder. Language-delayed children may need help that goes beyond language skills as such, to include special instruction in a variety of learning and thinking skills. As in teaching normal children, speech for the language delayed is treated as a tool to aid thinking and learning, rather than as a communication device in need of special repair in an otherwise normal child.

Teachers can help children who stutter by treating them in as normal a way as possible. Usually this means calling on the stutterers in class neither more nor less often than on the other children. Avoiding talking with them to save them the embarrassment of stuttering in public may actually single out their problem as much as would explicitly labeling them stutterers in front of their classmates.

Most children with articulation problems benefit from practice in producing the correct sounds (Pflaum, 1974). Often schools have speech therapists available who can either give such children tutoring in articulation practice or guide teachers and volunteers in doing so. Before beginning such tutoring, though, teachers should make sure that such children do in fact *hear* the difference between their erroneous sound and the conventional one. If they cannot detect the difference, then they may have a physical hearing impairment, such as those discussed below, which may require more than simple practice to help.

Hearing Impairment

Characteristics   If a hearing impairment occurs early in life, it can be much more serious for a child than stuttering or articulation defects are. Why? Because hearing gives very young children access to language learning, which in turn affects a host of educational skills learned later in their lives: their ability to hold conversations, for example, their ability to learn to read, and perhaps even their ability to think (see Chapter 3, on language and communication). Older children who lose some or all of their hearing have already formed these skills to a large extent and therefore may be damaged only in the most obvious way, in their ability to hear speech. This age difference holds true whether the loss is a partial one—a *hearing impairment*—or a complete one—*deafness*.

Most of the time, classroom teachers encounter children with only a partial hearing loss and who have at least some of the language arts skills needed to function in ordinary classrooms. Such hearing-impaired children may, therefore, actually confuse their teachers with their inconsistent behavior. At times they may seem unable to follow directions or pay attention, be reluctant to speak in class, and rely on fellow students for help with assignments. Yet at other times their language ability may seem quite normal: when speaking in a one-to-one conversation in a quiet room, for example. Such contradictions in behavior may sometimes happen more often for a case of mild hearing loss than for a more severe one, in which the deficit may show itself more obviously.

signs of hearing loss

Teaching Strategies   In any case, hearing loss can usually be accommodated in regular classrooms by a number of techniques. For example, the teacher should stand close enough to the child, and in good enough light, for the child to use whatever lip-reading skills he or she may have. Distracting, "covering" noises (for example, an air-conditioning fan) should be minimized as much as possible, because these usually interfere with comprehension more for a hearing-impaired child than for others. Such children should be encouraged to use any hearing-aid device they may have, and the teacher should know how it works in case they need help with it. Perhaps most important of all, their teachers should try to give them as natural a stream of language to respond to as possible. Although it is probably good to supplement spoken instructions with written ones, it is probably neither necessary nor helpful to by-pass whatever hearing ability the children do have by "not bothering" to tell them what the written instructions contain.

Visual Impairment

Characteristics As with hearing, visual impairment occurs in different degrees. *Partially sighted* children have no better than 20/70 vision in their best eye, even after correction with glasses. With this quality of vision, they can read letters about one and one-quarter inches high at a distance of twenty feet. In the United States, if their vision is no better than 20/200 after correction, they are considered *legally blind*. With this amount of impairment, they qualify for various state and federal aid programs for blind persons. Notice, though, that they need not be *totally blind* to do so; someone with 20/200 vision can still read letters about two and one-half inches high at a distance of twenty feet.

In the classroom, children may show signs of visual impairment in both their appearance and their behavior. If their eyes look unwell day after day, they should probably be checked by a school nurse or doctor: they may look swollen, watery, or red colored. One eye may not converge properly on close objects ("wander"), or the eyes may cross when they are not supposed to. Commonly, too, such children's behavior will show problems even if their eyes do not. They may blink constantly, squint, stumble over objects, lose their place even in easy reading, or tilt their head as if to see better. Normally sighted children also do these things, of course, but if children do them continually or in exaggerated forms, they may suggest problems in seeing. For a more complete description of classroom symptoms of visual impairment, see Hanninen (1975).

signs of visual impairment

Teaching Strategies In and of itself, visual impairment does not require major changes in most instructional programs. Obviously children with limited vision should be seated where they can make the best use of whatever vision they do have, usually close to the front and in good light. In many cases, visually impaired children will need special visual aids, such as large-print books, a Braille typewriter, or a slate and stylus for printing in Braille by hand. Since these tools usually take more time to use than do ordinary typing and handwriting, teachers must allow for extra time whenever it is needed. Partially sighted children may also need persons to read to them from curricular materials and books; these can often be fellow students, as well as community volunteers. In general, any activity or lesson requiring much visual activity will need to be modified, but again, fellow students can often prove surprisingly helpful in making

special visual aids

the necessary changes. A film, for example, may need a "running commentary" to be fully understood, spoken quietly enough not to disturb others, or a map may need to be felt rather than seen, in the form of cardboard cutouts of the important geographic areas.

A more challenging problem with partially sighted children is in their physical education and other active learning. Many of the conventional physical education games have rough-and-tumble qualities that can make them unsafe for students with visual impairment. Such children probably could not play ordinary basketball, for example, without immediately having collisions with other players. But solutions have been found even to this problem by changing certain rules for team sports and by incorporating more individual activity (for example, "mime" and gymnastics) into the physical education program. For suggestions, see Loescke (1977).

physical activities for the visually impaired

Giftedness

Characteristics   Gifted children show unusually high abilities in the various skills taught in school, most notably in their oral and written language, mathematics, or the performing arts. They seem to develop unusually quickly and to promise unusual success in the future. They may score above some very high level of standardized ability tests, though the proposed cutoffs vary (IQ over 140? over 125?). More important for teachers, however, is that the needs of the gifted cannot be accommodated easily in the ordinary school curriculum without explicit efforts to individualize instruction. Such students may cover in a matter of weeks what most children need months to learn: if so, should they then wait patiently for the class to catch up? Since gifted children also often direct their own learning better than average children do, it would seem that the extra time could be used for various kinds of independent study, combined with the continued acceleration of the basic curriculum whenever possible. Supervising such study for even one gifted student therefore can challenge even the most dedicated teacher!

fast and able learners

Teaching Strategies   One method of helping such students—**double promotion**, or "skipping a grade"—has been studied carefully by educators concerned with the gifted. In general, long-run follow-ups of students who have skipped a grade have found no harmful effects to the individual student (Gallagher, 1975; Keating, 1976). On the contrary, in fact, among equally bright students, the ones who skipped a grade during their schooling became more successful later on in life, both vocationally and socially, than the ones who did not (Stanley, 1977). The practice of double promotion, however, seems to meet continued resistance from teachers and school administrators. Many fear that the practice will cause gaps in the chil-

double promotion

Among other characteristics, gifted children show an unusual ability to learn independently. (Paul Conklin)

dren's learning or that being placed with older children will put the gifted children at a social disadvantage.

Whatever its effects on individual students, double promotion does have limitations as a way of helping the gifted. Promoted children may actually finish their higher-grade curriculum almost as quickly as they can finish the lower-grade curriculum of their age-mates. In that case they pose the same challenge to their teachers as before promotion: how to use the rest of the school year constructively? And double promotion may not be socially healthy for such children if used repeatedly: what if they graduate from school five or six years earlier than their age-mates do, instead of just one or two? Such child prodigies do occur. They make the news, but it is not clear that their lives have been improved by the experience.

These issues highlight the ambiguity of double promotion with regard to the philosophy of mainstreaming. Does skipping a grade deprive children of a normal social and educational setting, or does it offer them a new and better one? If it mainly deprives them, then double promotion contradicts the intent of mainstreaming—to integrate exceptional children with normal ones. If it gives them a new, normal environment, then the policy should be pursued more vigorously, despite its elitist overtones.

As an alternative to double promotion, schools sometimes create special **enrichment** programs for gifted students. These offer more in-depth experiences along with conventional curriculum topics, without accelerating the students beyond their peers. While the regular class studies one particular tribe of Indians, for example, the gifted students may study several. At the end of the unit they are still at the same general place in the overall school curriculum that most of their classmates are, thereby avoiding the isolation that can result from too much acceleration.

Enrichment programs have much potential, though they have also had to cope with two practical problems. First, keeping gifted students "in step" with their classmates has proved difficult and probably is not even desirable ethically. Second, enrichment programs are time consuming to construct, given the rather small number of students that use them. These two problems may contribute to the tendency of some enrichment programs to become fragmented experiences rather than in-depth ones. Instead of thoroughly pursuing one topic, gifted students may sometimes touch lightly on many. One week, perhaps, they visit a hospital surgery room; the next week, they may study ballistic missiles; and the next, they do something else again.

Emotional Disturbance

Characteristics   Emotionally disturbed individuals seem to feel unhappy or uncomfortable, without any obvious or immediate reasons. They show their disturbance in many ways (Hewett & Blake, 1973):

1. Physical discomfort, such as fatigue or aches and pains, that is unrelated to any discernible physical cause
2. Tense or anxious behavior that seems unremitting or continuous
3. Specific bizarre or unacceptable behaviors, for example, lack of bladder control
4. Fears or phobias that seem to have no basis in reality
5. Delusions or hallucinations
6. Extreme inefficiency or lack of responsibility for behavior

All people show these signs at least occasionally; once in a while, even a vivid daydream may verge on being a delusion. Truly emotionally disturbed individuals, however, show these signs more often and more independently of their immediate circumstances. No matter how supportive and warm their teachers and classmates may be, they may still be anxious or may still burst into an angry rage for no apparent reason.

enrichment

signs of disturbance

Emotional disturbances derive from a combination of influences, most of which are beyond the control of individual teachers. Families, for various reasons, may sometimes form relationships that put unbearable pressures on a particular member for very long periods of time. Larger social circumstances can do the same; poverty, for example, can make life difficult, at least for individuals who aspire to conventional middle-class lifestyles. Even bodily constitution may contribute to disturbances—for example, by influencing hormone levels that in turn affect a person's happiness or depression. The nature of such physical contributions remains ambiguous, however, and in any case understanding them may not offer much help to teachers confronted with actual disturbed students.

Because everyone behaves unaccountably at times, it is important for teachers to find out whether such behavior in a student reflects a serious, long-lasting problem, or only some relatively temporary, but stressful event. Young children entering school for the first time, for example, may show an extreme phobia (or dislike) regarding school. They may kick and scream or hide in a corner for hours. Most such children overcome their fears of school and of leaving home and soon function quite normally. Genuinely disturbed children, however, may not adjust, and at some point their teachers will have to decide whether their phobia deserves further, special help.

emotional disturbance versus temporary stress

Teaching Strategies What can teachers do for emotionally disturbed students? As with other handicaps, the answer depends partly on the nature and severity of the problem. Minor stress or other discomfort may simply call for ordinary consideration and support of the student as a person—neither more nor less. Somewhat more severe signs of disturbance may require modifying learning goals for that student—usually in the direction of expecting less work to be done in a given period of time. At the same time, the teacher and class may have to learn to tolerate unusual behavior from the student. How hard this may be will depend on the nature of the behavior. On the whole, a student that turns his or her disturbance inward can be tolerated in a group setting more easily than one who turns the disturbance outward. Anxiety, for example, can be tolerated more easily than temper tantrums can. The former may arouse concern within the class, but the latter can also bring its normal activities to a standstill.

In any case, emotional disturbance often calls for special therapy which teachers have neither the training nor the time to conduct. Some very disturbed individuals may be referred to psychologists or others who can establish and maintain the rapport needed for intensive and intimate discussion of their problems. Others may join a small group led by a therapist. Group therapy encourages individuals to share their concerns and in this way to act as "therapists" for one another. One special, but important, form of group therapy involves families, seen by the therapist either all together or in some sort of turn-taking arrangement. A relatively recent

support staff for disturbed students

form of therapy uses principles of behavior modification: rather than delve into the causes of emotional disturbance, it uses reinforcement and extinction procedures to change specific, disturbing behaviors. This technique has proved to be useful and effective, for example, in curing bedwetting and bladder control problems. In the bargain, it often alleviates the chronic tensions of those who suffer from these problems.

Physical Handicaps and Health Problems

Characteristics   Children with physical handicaps or health problems have a tremendous variety of special needs, but they all require extraordinary medical attention or (sometimes) hospitalization. They all also have conditions that are **chronic**; that is, they persist over long periods of time. Table 10–3 lists several physical handicaps and health problems and their major characteristics. They all are serious enough to affect such children's lifestyles significantly. As with other kinds of special needs, a few children may have to cope with more than one physical or health problem.

long-term medical attention

Such children have much more profound encounters with disease and its medical treatment than do most children. They may sometimes lack social experience with peers because their illnesses or treatments require

Table 10–3 Partial List of Physical Handicaps and Health Problems

Condition	Definition and characteristics
Cerebral palsy	Acquired damage to the nervous system that causes poor motor coordination; may interfere with thinking, but not necessarily.
Cystic fibrosis	Inborn tendency to produce mucus in the lungs, which in turn makes the child vulnerable to severe infections, such as pneumonia.
Spina bifida	An inborn defect of the spinal column that leads to paralysis in the lower limbs and to other physical or neural disabilities.
Leukemia	A type of cancer in which white blood cells increase excessively, thereby leading to anemia and various infections and disabilities.
Diabetes	An inability to store sugar in the blood, leading to weight loss, thirstiness, frequent urination, and (at the extreme) unconsciousness.
Limb deficiencies	One or more limbs missing, because of accidents, diseases, or birth defects.

various forms of isolation. Their education may not have the continuity of a normal school year, because of repeated setbacks of their condition or repeated interruptions for medical treatments. Such experiences, needless to say, may sometimes undermine self-confidence and the acquisition of educational and social skills helpful in managing life independently (Hart, 1979).

Teaching Strategies   Children with physical handicaps and health problems need instruction that takes account of these facts. Curriculum, when it is used at all, has to be constructed in units small enough to allow frequent interruptions and an easy return to where the child left off in the work. For some children, teachers may need to encourage independent behavior more than usual. In the hospital or at home, they may have many more personal needs taken care of than is possible or desirable at school. Even an eight-year-old may be helped to dress herself to go outdoors, despite not really needing the help. At school, she may need help in learning how to do this chore—and in learning that she *must* do it once she has learned how.

allowing for interruptions

independence training

Given their frequent absences, such children may find the social life of the classroom hard to cope with when they return. Here, too, the teacher may be able to help them reenter the group as smoothly as possible, for example, by assigning them to a work group in which they are likely to be accepted easily. The teacher should keep in mind that such children's hospital experience has probably been much more intense than usual. Comments that trivialize illness, therefore, may not be appreciated ("Oh, kids never get *really* sick!"), but neither will efforts to hide the truly more benign nature of most classmates' illnesses.

special social needs

IMPLICATIONS OF SPECIAL EDUCATION FOR REGULAR TEACHING

Some of the methods of special education, though not all, can benefit the education of all children, normal or exceptional. As special educators have sometimes said, "What may be good for special children, may be especially good for all children." Several themes in this chapter have illustrated this idea, though a careful look at them also shows the obvious differences between the two types of teaching.

Individualized Learning Goals

To make education work for exceptional children, teachers must strive to individualize instruction for them. How else could a very slow learner, for example, hope to survive in a regular class? Presumably if teachers use the principle of individualizing for all of their pupils, the results can only be better learning and teaching for everyone. Why? Because even "average" children, as any teacher will affirm, are never really average. They may learn relatively well in math, for example, but not as well in language arts; they may have a special liking for airplanes, but a special dislike for spelling. All in all, they are unique, just as exceptional children are. If a teacher can meet the unique needs of all kinds of children, everyone should benefit.

For new teachers, the problem is learning how to meet these needs. A combination of skills seems to be needed, none of which is learned overnight. Letting children set their own pace of learning should help, as long as they set *some* pace instead of choosing to stand still. Within reasonable limits, assignments can usually be completed sooner or later without interfering with the overall organization of the teaching program: does a certain story *really* have to be read by day X?

Teachers can even encourage students to choose their learning goals to some extent. Is it really necessary for every student to read the same short stories in English class, to type the same writing samples in typing class, or to build the same furniture in woodworking class?

Beyond a certain point, however, such individualization may be less important for normal students than for exceptional ones. Why? First, most educational programs, whether in school or out, exist to accomplish certain goals. Although these goals may sometimes allow considerable leeway for individual differences among students, an extreme emphasis on such differences may undermine the original purposes of the program. Suppose that society decided that all young people should learn world history. How much should teachers, in the name of individualizing instruction, allow students to choose *not* to learn it rapidly? How much should they allow individuals to choose not to learn it at all? These questions go to the core of humanism in education, which we will take up again in Chapter 12.

Even if some teachers believe that individualization is ethical, they may encounter practical problems in implementing this philosophy with more than just a few students. High school teachers may see almost two hundred students per day, and most for scarcely one hour. Under those conditions, they may have trouble providing appropriate and truly individual experiences for everyone. No matter how valuable individualized programming may be in principle, teachers may need to save it for the students who need it the most, often the exceptional ones.

possible limits to individualizing with normal students

Diagnosis Before Teaching

As pointed out earlier in this chapter, exceptional children cannot be helped before their special needs have been identified and diagnosed. No sensible

With handicapped students—as with all students—effective instruction usually requires careful and individual diagnosis of the skills and knowledge they already have. (George Bellerose/Stock, Boston)

teacher would knowingly begin teaching blind children, for example, before first determining the extent of their blindness, their present academic levels, and any special arrangements that they may need in order to learn. For normally sighted children, the same principle often holds, as well. Instead of diagnosing first, the teacher may instruct first, with diagnosis, if any, following along later in the form of testing and evaluation.

What does diagnosis consist of for normal children? One part of it seems to include **observation**, the collecting of tentative information about students for making inferences about their learning needs. At the beginning of the year, for example, teachers can lead a discussion for the purpose of getting to know their students, rather than evaluating their ability to participate or their knowledge of subject matter. In fact, any contact with students, whether a casual conversation or a "trial test," can be used for diagnostic observation as long as it is not also used for the final evaluation of their achievement and as long as the students are convinced of this fact. The results of such observations can allow teachers to begin where the students are, rather than at some arbitrary point designated by the curriculum they happen to be teaching.

need for observation

Such diagnosis can overlap both the learning and the evaluation processes. While a teacher sizes up his or her students through a class discussion, for example, the students may be learning from it, and the teacher in turn may be evaluating how well they have learned the topic thus far in the course. In this way the diagnosis of normal students differs from the diagnosis of exceptional ones; the latter, by definition, have been "identified" somewhere in the past through a process like the one described earlier in this chapter. Later, of course, after this experience, they may also receive a lot of combination diagnosis-learning evaluation. But for normal students, such a blended diagnosis may be the norm.

diagnosing special versus normal needs

Schooling as More Than Academic Learning

Teaching exceptional students forces the recognition that children's lives are affected by much more than the subjects they learn in school. A daily encounter with a handicap can remind us that children are not "learning machines"; that they need love and support as well as instruction; and that even if some fail to learn as much as the others do, they all still deserve the best that schools have to offer. Even though normal children deserve the best just as much as exceptionals do, normal needs can be overlooked more easily sometimes, since they can cope with the consequences of such neglect more successfully, or at least less visibly. Teachers usually know in principle that every child is special to someone—or should be—but the presence of children with special needs in the classroom can make this point more graphic and real. School achievement is not everything, their presence says, even though it may sometimes seem that way to teachers busy with their work.

Even so, many parents and teachers would not want to change significantly the goals of schooling for normal students, even if they attend school with handicapped ones. For such parents and teachers, schooling serves a particular social purpose, namely, to educate children and young people to know more, think more clearly, and use more skills. In this view, schooling should not dilute these functions in order to recognize students' other, noncognitive needs, unless it needs to do so for certain individuals.

These implications of mainstreaming for teaching are not meant to imply that having special needs is better than having none or that exceptionality is somehow good, fun, or enviable. With the possible exception of being gifted, most exceptional students would assure their teachers that they would trade any of the supposed benefits of their condition for being normal. At the same time, exceptionality is not a curse, like leprosy in the Bible, requiring children with special needs to remain permanently isolated from general society. It is simply a problem, and one that regular classroom teachers can cope with to a very large extent, especially if supported for doing so.

Key Points

1. Exceptionality refers to unusual physical, emotional, or mental conditions or to unusual specific behaviors or gifts that affect learning.

2. Although most forms of exceptionality are considered problems or handicaps, one (giftedness) is often considered an advantage.

3. The number of children with special needs constitutes a significant proportion of all children, though the estimates vary.

4. Mainstreaming is the educational practice of placing exceptional children in the least restrictive learning environment.

5. How much an exceptional child should be mainstreamed depends on the nature of his or her condition.

6. Teachers should participate as much as possible in the diagnosis and treatment of exceptional children.

7. Planning for the needs of an exceptional child usually has three stages: identifying the problem,
accurately diagnosing its nature, and carrying out an instructional plan of treatment.

8. Traditionally, exceptionalities have been classified into several general categories: slow learning and mental retardation, specific learning disabilities, speech and language disorders, hearing impairment, visual impairment, giftedness, emotional disturbance, and physical handicaps and health problems.

9. Because some of these categories are extremely general, many educators and parents object to using them as a basis for planning instruction for exceptional children.

10. Although special education does differ from regular education, it also has influenced regular education in certain ways: by fostering individualized instruction, encouraging diagnosis before teaching, and broadening the traditionally academic focus of some regular teaching.

Case Study

Dealing with Special Needs

You are a teacher of a fifth-grade class. You have thirty children, of which about half are girls. The children range in age from nine years old to twelve years old, but most are about ten or eleven years old. Their reading abilities vary from a first-grade equivalent to about a seventh-grade equivalent.

Several children in your group have special needs:

1. A nine-year-old boy who learns extremely quickly and well.

2. An eleven-year-old boy who is very active, both physically and verbally, and who often gets into fights with other children.

3. A twelve-year-old girl with an intelligence test score that is "low," though you do not know how low.

4. A ten-year-old boy who seems perfectly bright and happy but who cannot read very well.

5. A partially sighted girl who is working at about the average level for the class.

Questions for Discussion

1. For each of these students, how can you, as the regular teacher, be most effective? Be specific and consider each of the following:

    a. Techniques for ensuring good attention and motivation.

    b. An analysis of appropriate instructional goals.

    c. Ways of ensuring that each student in the class makes and keeps friends.

2. In addition to all the strategies you have named above, what special help would benefit these students? Consider how outside teachers, consultants, and aides might each help each child. Try to think of roles for these people that would keep

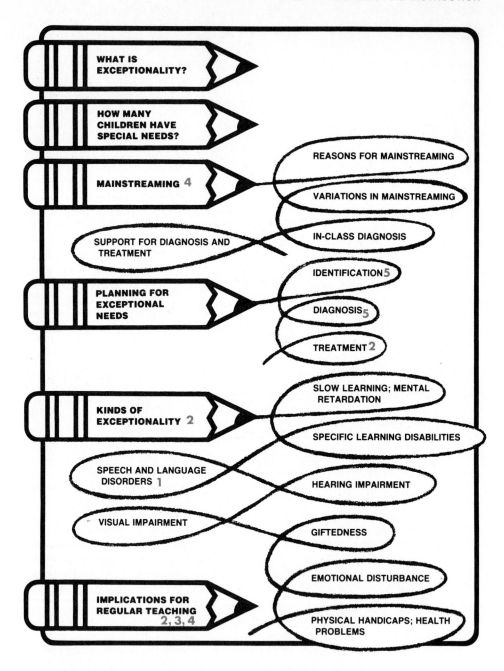

WHAT IS EXCEPTIONALITY?

HOW MANY CHILDREN HAVE SPECIAL NEEDS?

MAINSTREAMING 4

REASONS FOR MAINSTREAMING

VARIATIONS IN MAINSTREAMING

SUPPORT FOR DIAGNOSIS AND TREATMENT

IN-CLASS DIAGNOSIS

PLANNING FOR EXCEPTIONAL NEEDS

IDENTIFICATION 5

DIAGNOSIS 5

TREATMENT 2

KINDS OF EXCEPTIONALITY 2

SLOW LEARNING; MENTAL RETARDATION

SPECIFIC LEARNING DISABILITIES

SPEECH AND LANGUAGE DISORDERS 1

HEARING IMPAIRMENT

VISUAL IMPAIRMENT

GIFTEDNESS

EMOTIONAL DISTURBANCE

IMPLICATIONS FOR REGULAR TEACHING 2, 3, 4

PHYSICAL HANDICAPS; HEALTH PROBLEMS

1 Language and communication (Chapter 3)

2 Making instruction more effective (Chapter 8)

3 The motivation to learn (Chapter 11)

4 Humanistic perspectives in education (Chapter 12)

5 Evaluation (Part IV)

each child functioning in the regular classroom as much as possible.

3. Which techniques and help from the two ques-

tions above might also benefit the rest of the students in the class? Which seem irrelevant or inappropriate?

Suggested Readings

Cruikshank, William. *Concepts in Learning Disabilities: Selected Writings.* Vol. 2. Syracuse, N.Y.: Syracuse University Press, 1981.

Not everyone has wholeheartedly supported the idea of mainstreaming. William Cruikshank is one of its more outspoken and knowledgeable critics, and this book includes some of his most prominent criticisms of mainstreaming.

Farnham-Diggory, Sylvia. *Learning Disabilities.* Cambridge, Mass.: Harvard University Press, 1978.

Gallagher, J. *Teaching the Gifted Child.* Boston: Allyn & Bacon, 1975.

Gottlieb, Jay, ed. *Educating Mentally Retarded Persons in the Mainstream.* Baltimore: University Park Press, 1980.

Hewett, F. M., and F. D. Taylor. *The Emotionally Disturbed Child in the Classroom.* Boston: Allyn & Bacon, 1980.

Many books about special education focus on one particular category of exceptionality, even though, quite often, they object to using traditional categories to label individual children. These are four such books, each about a different type of exceptionality.

Turnbull, Ann P., and J. B. Schulz. *Mainstreaming Handicapped Students: A Guide for the Classroom Teacher.* Boston: Allyn & Bacon, 1979.

This book provides some relatively specific suggestions for classroom teachers, along with good explanations of the suggestions. Among other things, it has chapters on several different curricular content areas and how teachers can implement them with special needs students.

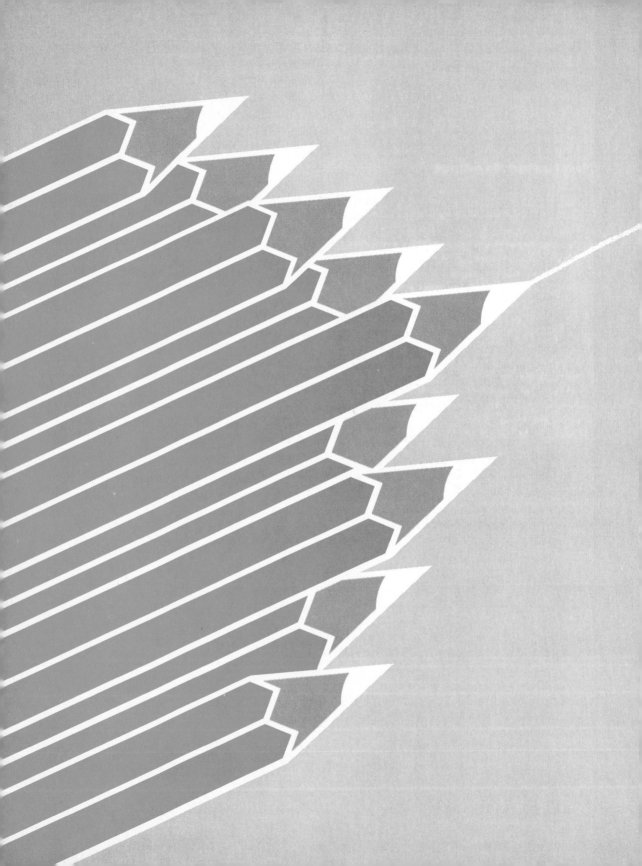

Part III
MOTIVATION

Even the most carefully designed instruction will not work without motivated students. Motivation is the link between teaching and learning: teaching can provide an opportunity to learn, but motivation ensures that the opportunity will be used. The variety of human motives requires many explanations and many teaching strategies.

Chapter 11 discusses several of these explanations of human motivation. The explanations differ widely in their terms: some are based on behaviorist theories of learning; others follow cognitive theories; and some are more complete than others. The differences, however, do not necessarily show conflict among the theories so much as differing emphasis or focus.

Overall, explanations of motivation all seek to help teachers answer the question: "How can I get students to *want* to do what they *should* do?" To this question, one approach to motivation—humanism—has a strikingly simple answer: decide that what students want to do is *by definition* what they should do. This humanistic point of view is the topic of Chapter 12. As we shall see, it has much to recommend it, though it also has certain limitations.

Chapter 11

THE MOTIVATION TO LEARN

Janice Cranston, Grade 11 physical education teacher: When I began teaching, I completely underestimated how much the motivations of my students would challenge me—and tax my patience. I expected that everyone would *want* to play at sports, and want to get better at them. I guess that was naive of me. My own enthusiasm for being active made me overestimate everyone else's. Enthusiasm is better than too much pessimism, but still, I had some learning to do about why real, live students ever bother to play softball or do gymnastics. They all *had* to take physical education—that is what took me so long to realize. So I couldn't make any assumptions about how they felt about my classes.

Sure, there were some students who were real achievers. I remember Betty, for instance, from two years ago: when we were doing track events, she was so busy practicing or exercising that she almost never talked to anyone. She wanted to run the mile in less than six minutes, she said. Not really very fast, but fast for her. She finally did, too.

But a lot of others didn't really seem to care much about improving themselves. While Betty was busy practicing, some would stand around talking, and "forget" to take their turns until I came around and reminded them. Apparently they liked the social life more than the running. Maybe that's why a couple of them told me they preferred the team sports—like softball and soccer—over the individual ones. The teams gave them legitimate reasons to be together and help each other out. Everybody could at least belong to a team, even if not everyone could be a star on one.

The toughest ones are the few students who seem not to care about sports in any way, shape, or form. Like Brenda this year. In the fall she was "sick" more times than anyone else in my 9:00 class, until I suspected that she just didn't enjoy changing clothes or being active. I praised her when she did participate and that seemed to help. But it also made me feel defeated: why couldn't she get going on her own steam? Especially when most of the others managed, at least to some extent?

When I was gone for two weeks in December, the substitute told me Brenda just didn't cooperate at all—missed classes a lot and didn't play with the others even when she came. When I got back, she was better again, even if not perfect. It was as if she were performing for me, and sports had nothing to do with it. I still don't know what to do to make her more enthusiastic. Surely she has motives lurking around inside her, like every other human being; but so far I haven't found out what they are—at least not clearly enough to get her moving in my class.

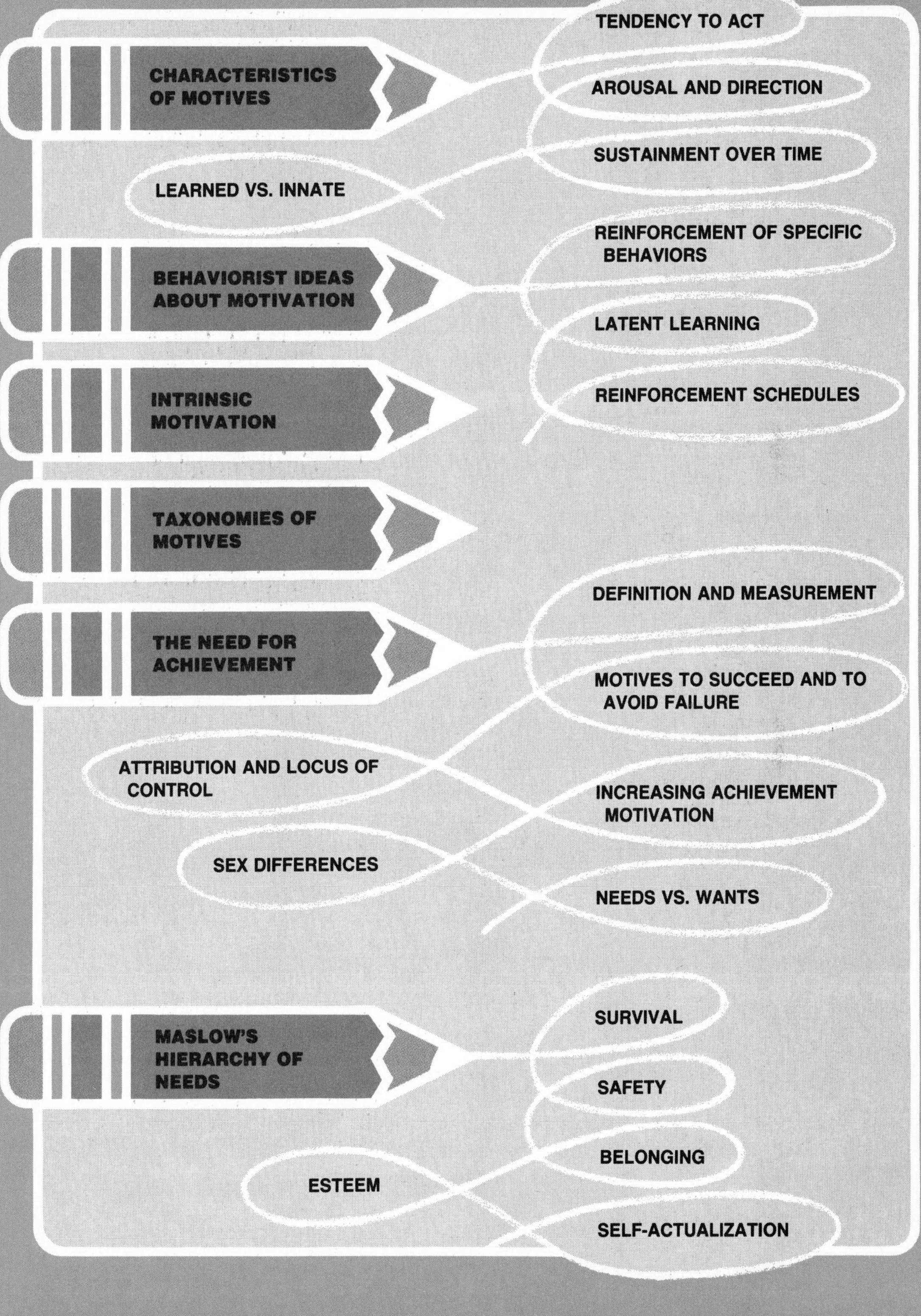

CHARACTERISTICS OF MOTIVES

TENDENCY TO ACT

AROUSAL AND DIRECTION

SUSTAINMENT OVER TIME

LEARNED VS. INNATE

BEHAVIORIST IDEAS ABOUT MOTIVATION

REINFORCEMENT OF SPECIFIC BEHAVIORS

LATENT LEARNING

INTRINSIC MOTIVATION

REINFORCEMENT SCHEDULES

TAXONOMIES OF MOTIVES

THE NEED FOR ACHIEVEMENT

DEFINITION AND MEASUREMENT

MOTIVES TO SUCCEED AND TO AVOID FAILURE

ATTRIBUTION AND LOCUS OF CONTROL

INCREASING ACHIEVEMENT MOTIVATION

SEX DIFFERENCES

NEEDS VS. WANTS

MASLOW'S HIERARCHY OF NEEDS

SURVIVAL

SAFETY

BELONGING

ESTEEM

SELF-ACTUALIZATION

MOTIVATING students means persuading them to do—and to *want* to do—whatever leads to learning. It means persuading them to read the assigned chapters in a text, to do the required problems in math, or to ask good questions during a class discussion. It means inspiring them to do these things of their own accord, and not just because the teacher has coerced them with grades or course requirements. Ideally, it may even mean inspiring students to enjoy the work of learning. Ideal students, if they exist, complete all of their assignments on time, ask their teachers insightful questions with a sparkle in their eyes, contribute to discussions during class, and maybe even ask for extra work. And why? All because they want to: because they know it is worthwhile for the future or because they enjoy the subject itself, or both.

THE PROBLEM OF MOTIVATION

Such students, of course, are rare at best. More often, real students only approximate motivated behaviors to a greater or lesser extent—and perhaps too often to a lesser extent. Whether in classrooms or in other teaching situations, teachers find motivation a major problem, often *the* major problem. The fact that a lot of education is compulsory may have something to do with it. Because the law makes children come to school, their

compulsory schooling presence in a class does not in and of itself prove that they are interested in learning. Even supposedly voluntary teaching and learning contain elements of compulsion. Businesses and the military, for example, may make their personnel attend training programs, like it or not, and even supposedly voluntary university education may coerce individuals indirectly with promises of better jobs and salaries later in life. As a result of such forces, the interests, curiosities, and attitudes of students are often unknown factors to teachers, at least at the beginning of an instructional program.

The general arrangements for instruction often aggravate this problem. First, teachers must deal with large numbers of students, as, for example, in secondary schools. They must therefore keep track of a multitude of motivational information without getting confused: "Did Roosevelt say he

large numbers of students liked this assignment, or did Jim?" Or "Someone asked a good question last week about this, but who was it?" Or "Did I remember Michelle saying she had watched *War and Peace* on television?" The answers reveal something about the interests and attitudes of particular students, but a teacher must sometimes be a memory expert to sort out all of them.

The sheer magnitude of information to monitor contributes to another common problem in managing students' motivation: the overuse of the

overuse of motive concept idea of *motive* to explain behavior. When we lack much solid information about a particular child or when we know only a few isolated facts about him, it is tempting to attribute the facts prematurely to motivation. "Manny won't learn computer programming because he's afraid of it," a teacher may say, when in fact the only evidence of his fear is his nonperformance on one particular occasion. Or "Rachel is bored by reading—she hasn't done her assignment," when the only reason for inferring boredom is the incomplete assignment itself. The reasoning is circular: a general cause seems to explain a specific event but is in fact defined only by the event itself.

In practice such explanations may actually serve as hypotheses or thoughtful guesses about what the student will do next time, in a similar situation. "Manny is afraid of computers" may really mean "I had better notice whether Manny shows signs of fearfulness the next time he works at the computer terminal." It may *not* really mean "I have concluded, on the basis of ample observation, that Manny will always and forever be fearful of math." If the original statement really functions in this way, however, it probably can do so more effectively if it is phrased as a hypothesis rather than a conclusion.

Even when teachers do accurately discern their students' motives, they may discover that many students have values alien to education or training. They may discover, for example, that Joan would rather visit her friends in the evening than do her homework or that Frank would rather work on his car or at a part-time job. These students may not lack motivation in general so much as academic motivation in particular. Possibly their interest in education is hidden—waiting for a skilled teacher to awaken it. But even if it is, such students simply present a conflict of values to their teachers: is it better to study a lot or to do other various things? Reconciling this sort of gap is a serious problem for teachers whenever students must be educated. Because so much education is compulsory, unmotivated students cannot simply be turned away. Differences in values must be faced and dealt with, and for some suggestions for doing so, see Chapter 4, on moral development and values education.

influence of value differences on motives

CHARACTERISTICS OF MOTIVES

A **motive** is a tendency or disposition to act, rather than an action itself. It arouses or energizes the individual, directs him or her toward some sort of goal, and sustains the movement toward that goal over a period of time. A motive may be either learned or innate or both. None of these aspects of a motive can be seen directly but must be inferred from other, more specific actions or behaviors. As a result, many psychologists and some teachers find the concept overly ambiguous. Let us look at these sources of ambiguity and why the notion of motive persists as a useful way of explaining much of human behavior.

The Tendency to Act

We cannot "see" a tendency, but only the actions that add up to that tendency. We cannot see, for example, a motive to achieve, but only the various achievements that result from this motive. It is, as psychologists say, a **hypothetical construct**: a variable or factor presumed to exist in order to explain a variety of observations, yet is unobservable itself. For example, if a student continually makes friendly conversation with his teacher and classmates, his teacher may say that he has a motive to affiliate or to make friends. In fact, though, the motive itself remains invisible. The teacher observes only the conversations and infers that they signify a motive.

ambiguity of motives

Since the actions resulting from a motive can often be construed in more than one way, inferring its presence can pose real problems for teachers. A student may earn a *B* in a math course, but her performance could show either hard work or "coasting." Or a student may ask the teacher many questions about a topic but do so either from curiosity or from a desire to impress the teacher. Such ambiguities are an occupational hazard for teachers, who often have only limited time for any one student.

inferring motives from observation

The solution may depend on observing each student's behavior over the longest possible periods of time and in situations as varied as possible. A *B* in one math course, for example, can be interpreted more easily if the teacher knows that student's marks in other math courses as well. A *B* in the middle of a pattern of high grades may suggest a relatively low motivation to achieve in that particular course, but in the middle of a pattern of relatively low grades, it may suggest the opposite. It does not, of course, prove these possibilities—it just makes them more reasonable and likely. Students may get lower than usual grades for several reasons: they may dislike a particular teacher, or they may have been sick during the course and missed several weeks of it. And they may get higher grades for many reasons: the teacher may grade higher than the others do, or the students may greatly like the subject. These further ambiguities can sometimes be resolved by gathering more information about the students—informal conversations with them, for example, or careful perusals of their assignments. In the end, their teachers may still wish they had more information, but they can probably make wiser inferences about their students' motives than when they began. Throughout the process, the principle remains the same: judging motivation requires making inferences. Teachers can choose only whether to judge on more information or less.

Arousal and Direction

The above example also illustrates another property of motives, namely, their energy and direction. Motives, by definition, seem to be going some-

For some politicians, friendliness may be a permanent quality of their personality. (Arthur Grace/Stock, Boston)

where and to reflect some sort of drive or effort to do so. Consider two motives to achieve: one to earn all *A* grades and the other to play the piano perfectly. The motives here refer to the efforts to improve performance rather than to the final outcomes of these efforts. In the first case, then, it might refer to all the work done to get the high grades, and not to the final grades themselves; and in the second, it might refer to the practicing leading to musical perfection, and not to whatever piano pieces finally are learned. Other motives have the same quality of striving. A motive to gain power, for example, consists of a drive or effort to gain influence over others, not of the absolute level of influence that a person has at any one moment. A motive to make friends refers to the effort to do so, not the number of friends a person has at any one moment.

Sustainment over Time

Although all motives, by definition, extend over a period of time, some exist only as a relatively temporary *state,* triggered by special circumstances; whereas others may persist so long that they constitute a virtually permanent *quality* of the individual. An example of a temporary motive is hunger: most of the time, it has little influence on the behavior of a

motives as states

well-fed person. Periodically, though, it can compete with nearly any other motive in importance: for confirmation, watch students carefully during the last half-hour before lunch. Another temporary motive is the anxiety of many students about taking a test: a desire to perform well mixed with a fear of doing badly. As with hunger, this motive may not even exist most of the time. Not, that is, until the day of a test, when that familiar "sinking feeling" returns.

On the other hand, some motives are more usefully considered permanent qualities rather than passing states. Many young elementary students, for example, show a continual need to "check out" or explore situations and people. Any moderately new situation will clearly show this motive—the start of a new school year, for example, or an unusual field trip later on in the year. The motive to explore even applies to ideas if they are *motives as qualities* perceived as somewhat new—hence the suggestions made earlier in this book to strive for variety in methods of teaching (see Chapter 8). As with other personal traits, children and students vary in how much their behavior expresses particular permanent motives, and indeed how permanent each motive seems in the first place. Some will be more curious than others, or more achievement minded, or more friendship minded; and for each of these motives, some will seem more generally and consistently motivated than others. Part of teaching is accurately understanding these differences.

Learned Versus Innate Motives

In addition to being either permanent or temporary, motives vary in how much they seem to be learned or innate (that is, inborn or instinctive). Consider the motives mentioned above. Hunger probably does not need to be learned, but test anxiety may have to be. Curiosity and exploration are so widespread in the behavior of young children that they seem to be innate, whereas there is evidence that the motive to achieve can be, and is, trained in some individuals more than in others. No matter what their original causes, though, they all qualify as motives—they all have energy and direction and refer to trends in behavior.

For practical teaching the distinctions between learned and innate motives, and between temporary and permanent ones, are difficult to make. A student may learn to worry about test taking, for example, but also be *learned elements as motives* born with an emotional temperament that predisposes him to worry. Another student may show little innate curiosity, but she may learn to show more of it if given the right encouragement. A third student may become achievement motivated if, and only if, given instructions to "care" about his performance on an assignment. And a fourth student may act hungry all the time, and not only before lunch!

Despite their ambiguities, however, all of these behavior patterns can be identified as motives: they all seem to lead somewhere or to be carried out for some purpose. And they all draw energy from some source, whether the source is in the student or the environment or both. Most important of all, these behavior patterns all contain at least some elements that teachers can influence either directly or indirectly. Even a motive as seemingly basic as hunger can be dealt with and guided: important teaching, for example, can be rescheduled away from lunch time, and students can be shown ways to live with their expectation of lunch without disrupting the end of class. For other motives, teachers' methods may not be this concrete, but they are nonetheless important to their success in teaching. The rest of this chapter will examine some of these methods in more detail, and will speak to this question: What motives seem to guide student behavior, and how can teachers use them to help learning occur?

BEHAVIORIST THEORIES OF MOTIVATION

Nearly every general theory, including behaviorism, accounts for motivation. Only the most radical behaviorists find the ambiguities of the concept too difficult to tackle. Skinner, for example, rejects the notion of motivation: consistent with his focus on specific behaviors and reinforcements, he feels that motives have no reality that can be understood scientifically. In essence, to Skinner, motives are simply histories of relationships between learned behaviors and their reinforcements.

Reinforcement of Specific Behaviors

What does this idea imply for teaching practice? It suggests that teachers need not concern themselves with motivating students in the ordinary sense of the term, but only with arranging effective—and specific—reinforcers for desirable behavior. If students pick up a book, complete an assignment, or ask a good question, then praise them or otherwise reinforce them. Do not devote time to wondering why they may or may not have behaved well; influencing their specific behaviors, the Skinnerians say, is all that motivating students amounts to, anyway.

reinforcement as a motivator

This focus on specifics has much to recommend it, but as discussed in Chapter 6, identifying and applying reinforcers often pose serious practical problems for teachers. In addition, the patterns of behavior or tendencies to act that constitute motivation do not disappear just because teachers shift their attention from the patterns to the individual elements of the pattern.

Latent Learning

Many behaviorists have shown that even the simplest learning situations are influenced by underlying tendencies that seem like motives. More than forty years ago, the psychologist Edward Tolman illustrated this idea by training two groups of rats to run through a maze (Tolman & Honzik, 1930). One group received a food reward at the end of the maze, and as reinforcement theory would predict, its performance improved steadily with each trial. The other group received no reward for its first ten trials, and as reinforcement would again predict, its performance improved very little during this time. But when Tolman began rewarding the second group on the eleventh trial, the second group's performance improved suddenly and dramatically. Apparently they had "learned" the maze during their bumbling, error-ridden trials. The reward affected performance rather than learning, or, stated another way, it provided an incentive or motivation to perform.

Tolman called this phenomenon **latent learning**, since it occurs without obvious reward or the "intention" of the rat. Implicit in the concept is a distinction between learning and performance, with reinforcement acting directly only to motivate performance. The practical experience of teachers offers ample confirmation of the distinction. Sometimes, for example, a student may produce very good work, but only for a reward, such as a grade. Reinforcement affects his performance, apparently, but not necessarily the learning that went into the performance. The learning itself may have happened well before he undertook the work, and it may or may not have been explicitly reinforced.

learning versus performance

Reinforcement Schedules

Behaviorists have extensively studied how variation in reinforcement patterns may affect performance. As pointed out in Chapter 6, they have generally found that partial reinforcement takes longer to build up a behavior, but it also causes the behavior to persist longer after the reinforcement is removed. In addition to this general finding, they have also found that different patterns, or **schedules**, of partial reinforcement produce predictable patterns of responses. All of the following examples hold true in experiments with animals and help explain certain patterns of motivation in students as well (Rachlin, 1980).

Fixed Ratio Reinforcement　　Suppose that an animal is reinforced regularly after a fixed number of responses, what behaviorists call a **fixed ratio** schedule of reinforcement. Under this condition, the animal tends to stop responding soon after each response but then finally resumes again with a rapid burst of responding. It is as if the animal "knows" that it must work a certain amount before it can receive its next reward and finally buckles down to doing so.

rapid bursts of responding

Students often show a similar pattern of behavior whenever grades or other reinforcements are given only after predictable amounts of work.

Consider the typical grading practice for a series of short written essays: the mark is given only after finishing each essay, and not for the intermediate steps within each essay. In this situation students often procrastinate before beginning to write: but once they do begin, they may work furiously until they finish the essay. Then they procrastinate again. This work pattern may occur even without any timed deadlines for turning in each essay.

Fixed Interval Reinforcement   Suppose that an animal is reinforced regularly after a fixed amount of time passes, rather than after a fixed number of responses. This is what behaviorists call a **fixed interval** schedule of reinforcement. In this case, the pattern of responding resembles the fixed ratio schedule above, though not quite. Instead of periods of rapid responding interspersed with periods of no responding, the animal is more likely to respond with a gradually accelerating pattern as it approaches the time of its next reinforcement. Just before the actual reinforcement, the animal's rate of responding increases dramatically—only to fall off again after it occurs.

gradually accelerating responding

Here, too, under similar conditions, students often show this pattern of behavior. Consider a student completing a work sheet during class while his teacher slowly circles the room. He is, in essence, performing according to a fixed interval schedule of reinforcement: every couple of minutes, no matter how much he has done, the teacher will pass by and offer a reinforcing comment or smile. Under these conditions the student is most apt to procrastinate just after she leaves him, gradually pick up his speed of working while she is away, and show a sudden burst of energy just before she arrives again.

Variable Schedules of Reinforcement   Suppose that an animal is reinforced after a variable number of responses—a so-called **variable ratio** schedule. Instead of being reinforced after every fifth response, for example, suppose the animal is reinforced after only three responses on one occasion, but after seven on the next, and after some other number on the one after that. Such a schedule produces a very even rate of responding in between reinforcements, almost as if the animal did not "know" when its next reinforcement would occur and therefore had no reason either to procrastinate or to speed up. Even more evenness of responding results from reinforcing the animal after a variable amount of time—a so-called **variable interval** schedule. Both variable schedules, in addition, lead to strong resistance to extinction; after the reinforcement is removed, the animal persists in responding for an especially long time (see Figure 11–1).

relatively even rate of responding

Variable schedules of reinforcement characterize quite a few interactions between teachers and students. For instance, in class discussions, a teacher may praise or support any particular student at irregular times

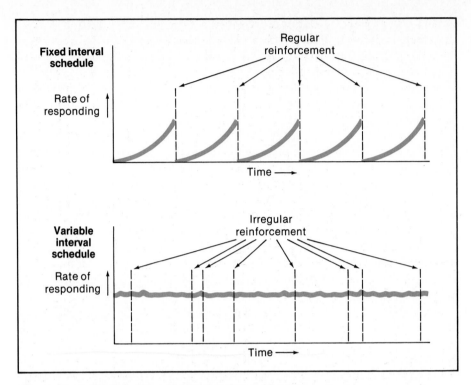

Figure 11–1 Effects of Two Partial Schedules of Reinforcement

or after irregular amounts of effort by the student. As long as the teacher's praise does not come too seldom for a particular student, that student is likely to continue participating in the discussion to a reasonable extent. Or consider the common teaching practice of writing comments throughout a student's essay. Assuming that these are reinforcing more often than not, they resemble a variable ratio schedule of reinforcement: the student must write an unpredictable amount in order to earn any particular comment. The variability contributes, in part, to the student's relatively constant effort throughout the essay. Since he or she never knows exactly on what the teacher will comment, the student puts out his or her best efforts throughout.

Partial Reinforcement Effect   Not only does partial reinforcement create a stronger resistance to extinction than full reinforcement does, but also less frequent (but partial) reinforcement creates even stronger resistance than does more frequent reinforcement. This *partial reinforcement effect* has important implications for motivating students. As pointed out in Chapter 6, it means that teachers need not reinforce students continuously in order to influence their behavior; but perhaps even more importantly, it suggests that teachers may not even need to reinforce very often—

strong resistance to extinction

Since a teacher cannot call on every student on every occasion, students inevitably receive this form of reinforcement only part of the time. (Paul Fortin/Stock, Boston)

at least in order to maintain already existing behaviors. During the acquisition of new behaviors, however, generous reinforcement usually acts faster and more strongly than does "stingy" reinforcement.

For this reason, behaviorists often recommend that teachers begin a phase of instruction using ample reinforcement but gradually reduce its frequency as the desired behaviors become established. The first several times a usually quiet student contributes to a class discussion, for example, the teacher should be ready to praise him immediately and clearly. Later, though, she may be able to move toward reinforcing him only once in a while. It is fortunate that teachers can maintain many such behaviors with only occasional reinforcement; during normal instruction, they often are too busy to reinforce every desirable thing that every student does!

Notice that the partial reinforcement effect is difficult to explain in strictly behavioral terms. Since a partial schedule provides less reinforcement—if reinforcement does indeed influence motivation—then a student given partial reinforcement should have less incentive to perform than should a student given continuous reinforcement. This seems to hold true during the acquisition of a behavior, but not during its extinction, when the student's persistence suggests more motivation, not less. Behavioral psychologists offer various explanations of this apparent paradox. One is that under partial reinforcement, the student has a harder time noticing when extinction actually begins. Because the few reinforcements are given only occasionally during learning, their removal is not missed as quickly or as much as they would be with continuous reinforcement.

As plausible as this explanation may sound, it does have a problem in regard to behaviorism: it admits that mental activity somehow affects learning and motivation. Many psychologists and educators have accepted this idea more readily than the behaviorists have, however, and have used it to construct further theories of motivation, like the ones described in the next sections.

explanations of partial reinforcement effect [margin note]

INTRINSIC MOTIVATION

Some activities seem to be undertaken just for the sake of doing them: they are their own reward. If so, we say that they are **intrinsically motivated**. A young child may, for example, play in a sandbox for long times, for no other apparent reason than the chance to experiment with the sand. Or an adult may read all the short stories she can find, for no other apparent reason than her interest in reading them. Both the child and the adult may receive other, extrinsic rewards as well, of course. The child may be praised for the castles he builds, and the woman may discover that her reading makes her a more interesting dinner guest. But if the activities are primarily motivated intrinsically, these other rewards will not really matter very much.

When an activity itself is reinforcing, a person may work at it long and carefully without needing external rewards or recognition from others. (Frank Siteman/ Stock, Boston)

Explanations of Intrinsic Motivation

Psychologists have proposed several ways to account for intrinsic motivation. Some consider it an inherent human drive toward competence or mastery (White, 1979). Others call it by the slightly less awesome sounding name of curiosity (Hutt, 1976). Still others point out that intrinsically motivated activities help the individual escape from both boredom and too much uncertainty (McReynolds, 1971). Intrinsic motivation is really a drive toward optimal stimulation, an idea that resembles Piaget's concept of equilibration (see Chapter 2), which refers to the tendency of human beings to strive for harmony and consistency with their environments. These various definitions have much in common when applied to specific examples of intrinsically motivated activity. All such activities seem to lead individuals toward greater mastery of some sort, while in the process drawing on their curiosity and making them feel more competent and "stable."

reasons for intrinsic motivation

Use of Intrinsic Motivation in Teaching

Students, no less than others, engage in many intrinsically motivated activities, but these do not always relate to their teachers' educational goals. One student may enjoy stamp collecting, and another may enjoy fiddling with pocket calculators. A third may enjoy reading, but only stories that have to do with space travel. Whether any of these motives actually advances their education depends on the instructional goals that the students are given and their teacher's cleverness at bridging the gaps between his or her goals and their motives. For example, a motive to play with pocket calculators may be fairly easy to use in a mathematics course. It may be harder to use in a social studies course, though not impossible—perhaps the student could write a paper about the history and current status of pocket calculators. Stamp collecting, on the other hand, may contribute fairly easily to a lesson on political geography by aiding comparisons among countries, but it may not contribute so directly to the study of science. Here again, though, connections may be found. There is probably scientific knowledge needed, for example, in the engraving and printing of stamps.

intrinsic motivation and teaching

Effect of Extrinsic Reinforcement on Intrinsic Motivation

Teachers try to awaken new motives in their students, of course, as well as capitalize on preexisting ones. Doing so is one of the major challenges of teaching. How can a student who never chooses to read, for example, be coaxed into reading? Or one who hates mathematics be coaxed into doing math? In these situations, teachers must use a mixture of external incentives (grades, praise) and threats (fear of failure) to get their students started. Once launched into the new activity, one hopes that the student will discover its intrinsic attractions and need little or no further external motivation. We described in the previous section one technique for making this shift: the teacher can reduce the reinforcements from continuous to partial levels as the student's behavior becomes established. Although this does not completely eliminate external motivators, it at least makes them relatively less visible.

In practice, however, the transition from external to internal motivation sometimes does not occur, or even worse, the original use of external incentives may actively interfere with the shift. Several research studies show this process quite clearly. In one series of studies, college students were asked to solve several three-dimensional block puzzles (Deci, 1972). Some of the students were told in advance that they would be paid for working on the puzzles; some were never offered any money; and some were offered money, but only unexpectedly and after they had finished working. After the main session of problem solving, all of the students had a chance to work further on the puzzles if they wanted to. How much they did presumably measured their intrinsic motivation for the task.

extrinsic reinforcement and performance

Under these conditions, the students who were never paid or who did not expect to be paid worked at the puzzles afterward much longer than did the students who expected to be paid. Why? One explanation hinges on how the different groups defined their reasons for doing the task. The group expecting money may have rationalized to itself that it was not working because of its interest in puzzles, but for money. But the other two groups may have reasoned that they worked from intrinsic interest; after all, why else would they work for nothing? Even the unexpected-money group may have thought this way, and so their payment did not really have a reinforcing effect on them.

rationalizing overt behavior

Essentially similar results were found in a study of children's behavior in drawing (Lepper & Greene, 1976). These psychologists asked school-children to make drawings with felt-tip pens. Some drew their pictures for a reward that they expected; others, for a reward that they did not expect; and still others, for no reward at all. When Lepper and Greene observed these children a week or two later, they found differences among the groups in how much they chose to use felt pens during free-play periods. The expected-reward children chose this activity less often during these periods than did the other two groups. The unexpected-reward children chose the pens about as much as did the no-reward children. Apparently they attributed their motives to themselves rather than to the external reward, as the first group seemed to.

Although these findings show that external rewards can undermine intrinsic motivation, they do not show that they always do so. This interference may not apply to all possible activities or behaviors, and in particular it may not apply to very unusual behaviors. A student who never reads, for example, may react differently to rewards for reading than one who does. He may, in particular, find that the external reward does in fact awaken his intrinsic interest in reading by forcing him to experience the rewards of what is, for him, an unusual activity. But a student who is already an avid reader may simply find external rewards distracting and therefore also find reading for reward less motivating than reading for its own sake. In the real world of actual instruction, teachers must judge whether factors like these may be operating.

TAXONOMIES OF MOTIVES

psychoanalytic explanation of motives

Some psychologists assume that motives occur in more than one form and that these are not reducible to each other. Classical psychoanalysis, for example, proposes two basic energizers of human behavior, **eros** and **thanatos**, which correspond roughly to a drive toward love and a drive toward destruction, respectively. More modern versions of psychoanalysis, including Erikson's theory, as described in Chapter 5, have added ego-enhancing motives to these—the motives for self-esteem, competency, self-realization, and the like. These ideas in turn have been divided further by various psychologists and psychotherapists interested in particular aspects of human behavior, producing, in some cases, very long lists of motives.

Murray's psychogenic needs

One very long and systematic list of such aspects was constructed by Henry Murray (1938), who included fully twenty-eight different psychological needs, not counting various other social and physiological needs. Each need in Murray's taxonomy functions as a motive: a predisposition to act in a certain way. The list shows that many kinds of human behavior can be explained by a comprehensive theory of motivation, and in doing so, it also corresponds well to common-sense intuitions about why people behave as they do.

criticisms of assuming large number of motives

The length of the list, however, makes it difficult to use as a theory for predicting human behavior. To do so, a relatively small number of motives must explain a relatively large number of behaviors. As the number of alleged motives increases, however, the number of human behaviors that each one explains becomes smaller, and the job of explaining particular examples of behaviors becomes more and more cumbersome. Murray's list has been criticized on these grounds. By using such a large number of motives to explain behavior, it tends to function more as a description of human behavior than as a true theory. Rather than suggesting statements like "Most behavior is caused by X, Y, and Z," it instead suggests statements like "Sometimes people do X, and sometimes Y, and sometimes Z."

Teachers and other people already know this; what they want to know instead is why?

On the other hand, the parsimony of a theory of motivation cannot be bought at the price of its accuracy in describing real, live children and students. Piaget's idea of equilibration, for example, is an economical explanation of why children acquire new concepts; it is a sort of minitheory of motivation. Yet it may not explain important behaviors and motivations of children in actual teaching practice: that some children, for example, may not choose to learn even when the content *is* carefully adjusted to their levels of development. In this case, is Piaget's theory of equilibration wrong or just incomplete? Should teachers look for other sources of motivation in their students besides the intrinsic cognitive difficulty of the material? Common sense says that they do, but it also suggests that they should not have to pay attention to twenty-eight different psychological motives, as Murray suggests. Somewhere between these extremes there must be a practical compromise between parsimony and comprehensiveness. The sections that follow suggest three candidates for such a compromise: need achievement, attribution theory, and Maslow's hierarchy of human needs.

theories of motivation versus descriptions

THE NEED FOR ACHIEVEMENT

Definition and Measurement of nAch

One of the needs in Murray's system, the so-called need for achievement, has special relevance for teachers and has been extensively studied by psychologists. The **need to achieve** (abbreviated nAch) refers to the general motive to work toward some standard of excellence. The motive is planning and striving for a goal, no matter how prestigious or humble the goal itself may be: a person can show nAch as a bank teller or a college professor, or as a baseball player or a student. What matters is the approach to the task rather than the results themselves. A bank teller high in this motive tries to do his job as well as possible, regardless of whether it makes him famous, rich, well liked, or politically powerful. In real life, of course, he may strive for these other results as well, but to the extent that he does so, his behavior is guided by other motives in addition to his need for achievement.

working toward a standard of excellence

Typically, nAch has been measured by a **projective technique**, so called because the test takers are asked to impose or "project" their ideas or feelings onto the test materials. In the case of nAch, the child or adult makes up stories about a particular series of pictures (McClelland et al., 1953). For each picture, the individual is asked such questions as: What is happening? Who is (or are) the person (or people)? What led up to the situation? What will happen? And so on. The stories are then scored in

projective technique

To the extent that these students aspire to a high standard of musical excellence, they are motivated by a need for achievement. (Marion Bernstein)

TAT

various ways, but most notably for a theme related to nAch and for particular comments that contribute to such a theme. Since the pictures themselves are ambiguous, the fabricated stories presumably reflect people's need to achieve. One hopes that these stories do so more accurately than by simply asking people to talk about their motives. The use of fabricated stories has been made into a moderately, though not fully, reliable procedure called the **Thematic Apperception Test** (TAT for short).

As you might expect, individuals vary in how much nAch they show on the TAT and in how consistently they show it across various tasks and situations. People who score consistently high in the motive, however, differ from consistently low-scoring people in a number of ways relevant to teaching. The "highs," for example, tend to do all of the following more often than the "lows" do:

qualities of high achievers

1. They choose working partners according to their skills rather than their friendliness.
2. They persist longer at tasks and are more likely to resume a task after interruption.

3. They perform equally well at a school task whether or not the teacher is supervising their work.
4. They choose tasks of medium difficulty rather than very easy or very difficult ones.
5. They choose larger rewards in the future in preference to smaller ones in the present.

For a review of these differences and others along the same lines, see the article by Vidler (1977). Altogether, these differences present a picture of someone who might be a hard-working student, though not necessarily a popular one.

Relationship Between Motives to Succeed and to Avoid Failure

Some of the findings listed can be explained more convincingly by assuming that everyone has a motive to succeed (abbreviated M_s) and a motive to avoid failure (M_{af}) and that the need for achievement results from the combination of these two motives (Weiner, 1972). Persons high in nAch have a stronger motive to succeed than to avoid failure ($M_s > M_{af}$), and those low in nAch have the opposite relationship ($M_s < M_{af}$). This assumption explains why high achievers, compared with low achievers, choose tasks of medium difficulty. An extremely difficult task offers little hope of success, and thus there is little incentive to try it; but an extremely easy one offers little challenge, and thus there is a vague or no standard of excellence against which to compete. The middling task offers the best compromise for high achievers: reasonable value and reasonable likelihood. Since it also carries a threat of shame from failure, it is the most strongly avoided by the failure avoiders. They choose extreme levels of difficulty because they are safe, from the standpoint of success: one extreme carries no chance of failure, and the other carries so much certainty of failure that they need not feel responsible for it.

fear of failure versus motive to succeed

This analysis has been supported by a number of studies. One found that college students high in nAch tended comparatively often to choose major fields of intermediate difficulty rather than very easy or very hard fields (Isaacson, 1964). Another study found that success-oriented children tended to choose arithmetic problems of middling difficulty but that failure-avoiding children chose problems that were extremely easy or extremely hard (DeCharms & Carpenter, 1968). A third study found that high achievers generally had more realistic vocational goals than did low achievers; for most, greater realism presumably meant more middling career aspirations rather than either prestigious or humble ones (Mahone, 1960). All of these findings support the idea that high achievers prefer just enough difficulty to give them pride of achievement, but not so much as to deny them the likelihood of achievement. This idea sounds very much like the advice commonly circulated by both textbooks and practicing teachers: give your students work that challenges them, but not so much that they cannot succeed at it. In Piagetian terms, the advice might be phrased differently: call on thinking processes more advanced than the ones students currently use, but not so advanced that they cannot accommodate their thinking to the new processes. Education, it seems, favors students high in the motivation to succeed, rather than those high in the motivation to avoid failure.

Some research, however, suggests that both kinds of students may become especially well motivated, but under different circumstances. Students high in M_{af}, in particular, may be spurred to greater effort by success experiences, whereas those high in M_s may be spurred more by failure (Weiner, 1970). The latter finding seems at first to contradict common sense. But it does not if it is assumed that M_s students are comparatively strong believers in effort as a source of success: in that case failure signals to them that they must put forth more effort. The tasks in question are based on moderately easy tasks given in experimental situations. Since, in contrast, tasks in the classroom can come in all levels of difficulty, presumably even the most success-oriented students will risk becoming discouraged if they fail badly enough and often enough.

Attribution Theory and Locus of Control

These ideas and findings also suggest that cognition has to be included in nAch theory if it is to explain human motivation accurately. A number of psychologists (for example, Weiner et al., 1972) have pointed out that achievement behavior may be influenced not only by a task's objective qualities but also by how individuals attribute responsibility for success on the task: this is **attribution theory**. If they attribute success to their own efforts or abilities, they will more likely show achievement behavior, but if they attribute it to luck or the task's inherent difficulty, they will not. This difference in attribution is sometimes called *locus of control*. Some individuals are consistently "internals" (effort and ability people), and others are "externals" (luck and difficulty people). Though locus of control relates to nAch, they are different concepts: nAch refers to a pattern of behavior, and **locus of control** is the place where an individual believes that the control of his or her behavior lies (Fanelli, 1977).

attributions of success and failure

locus of control

Including the cognitive side of achievement behavior makes a lot of practical sense for teachers. In daily work with students, teachers must interpret what students say about their work as much as the work itself. For every assignment that teachers give and evaluate, they also receive a host of comments about it (usually oral). Some reflect an internal locus of control, and others reflect an external one, as in the following examples:

Internal: "If I try, I can do the problems correctly."
"I failed that test because I didn't study enough."
External: "Getting an *A* on this test is just a matter of luck."
"I can't do problems as hard as those."

As a rule, the internal comments make teachers feel better than the external ones do, but they must accept both.

Teachers can use several general strategies to promote an internal locus of control among their students. They should first examine carefully their methods of teaching and evaluation to see how easily their students can in fact attribute their success to their own abilities and efforts. If, for example, the teachers' grading depends heavily on biases and chances (heaven forbid), then the students may be right in adopting an external perceptive. (Incidentally, for help with reducing biases in grading, see Chapter 14.) This chapter and most of the others in this book contain suggestions intended to foster a relatively internal sense of responsibility. Several explicit suggestions are also given in the next section.

Training Programs for Increasing Achievement Motivation

Various special programs, for both adults and children, have attempted to increase achievement motivation. In some of these, the participants learn to score the achievement content in short stories, newspaper stories, fairy tales, or even ordinary conversations. In other programs, the participants learn games that reward achievement behavior, or they engage in discussions about the concept of need for achievement in general. The concept may be related to their personal lives by, for example, asking each participant to imagine himself or herself doing a task exceptionally well and to share this vision with the others. Or the participants may be taught the difference between striving for success and success itself, by being rewarded only for the striving: in a ring-toss game, for example, they may get points for correctly guessing their performance rather than for successful tosses as such.

Such training methods have been tried with students as well as with adults. One program gave training to low-income black students (De-Charms, 1976). The program was carried out during the regular school year and emphasized developing an internal attribution of responsibility, as opposed to practicing achievement behaviors as such. At the end of the year, the students were reported to have, on the average, higher achievement motivations, as well as more internalized loci of control.

But such programs do not always work (Alschuler, 1973). Some psychologists question whether nAch has much meaning to older persons (Maehr & Kleiber, 1981), since they often have fewer incentives to compete for social or economic success. Training programs for school-age persons, in addition, do not always lead to improved grades (Fyan, 1980). Although this conclusion may mean that the training procedures are not really improving nAch as they claim to do, it just as easily suggests several other possibilities. First, schools' grading policies may not always recognize achievement motivation as much as they are intended to, especially if school assignments are marked very subjectively or if the teachers have preconceptions of their students' abilities that ignore their real performance. Second, some school assignments may be so ambiguous, difficult, or easy that they do not stimulate achievement motivation among students. Third, some students—perhaps even many—may regard school not as a normal place to achieve but as a place to express other motives such as making friends. Such students may regard programs to train achievement motivation as irrelevant to their schooling, no matter how the programs are constructed. This last possibility is closely related to an important limitation of nAch theory discussed in the next section: its difficulty in explaining achievement in women.

grades and nAch (margin)

An Important Proviso: Sex Differences in nAch

The theory of achievement motivation applies much more consistently to men than to women. On the whole, men show more achievement imagery in their TAT stories than do women, especially when the instructions for the test appeal to their abilities and leadership. The difference seems to reflect sex-role expectations: men, more than women, are expected to achieve and accomplish a multitude of work-oriented tasks. As a result, they may "see" an achievement theme in even ambiguous pictures, like the ones on the TAT. On the other hand, women, more than men, are conditioned to prepare themselves for marriage and family rather than the world of work. French and Lesser (1964) tested this possibility by administering the TAT to women with instructions that applied to female sex-role expectations: they were led to believe that the test reflected their social skills and marital success. Given this prior orientation, the women showed more achievement imagery than under more usual conditions.

women's responses to the TAT (margin)

This study and reviews of achievement in women (for example, Hoffman, 1974), suggest that women are motivated more than men are by the need for affiliation, the desire to form and maintain friendly relations with people. Cultural and social expectations lead women to care much more than men do about their roles as spouse, parent, and family manager. To the extent that achievement motivation figures at all in their thinking, it is likely to be tied to these social and family needs, as indeed was found by French and Lesser. For these women, success means family success or interpersonal success rather than job achievement. Even though these sex differences may be becoming less and less apparent, they still may be

need to affiliate versus nAch (margin)

enough in evidence to influence studies of achievement motivation in women. In effect, achievement motivation theory as described in the preceeding sections of this chapter explains male behavior better than it does female behavior.

But the need for affiliation is definitely not confined to women, a fact that was shown in a study of first-year college students taking an introductory psychology course (McKeachie, 1975). Students who showed a strong need for affiliation achieved better in the course if their instructor was warm and friendly, presumably qualities associated with affiliation. But high-achieving students did better with an instructor who was relatively more oriented to the subject matter being taught, a quality more in line with their own achievement orientation. Both types of students included men and women.

Some psychologists have proposed too that women not only are more affiliation minded but they also actively fear success, including academic success (Horner, 1972). This fear leads to those patterns of behavior described earlier that characterize low achievers rather than high ones, and persons with an external locus of control rather than an internal one. Other research, however, suggests that the fear of success occurs in men about as often as in women and that it is affected by a variety of factors that have nothing to do with gender: for example, age, social class, national culture, and personal beliefs about sex roles (O'Leary & Hammack, 1975). It seems, therefore, that teachers should search for their students' individual needs rather than assume that their students' social categories determine their needs or motives in any simple way.

fear of success

MASLOW'S HIERARCHY OF NEEDS

One of the most comprehensive theories of human motivation evolved from the writings of Abraham Maslow (1962, 1970). He proposed a hierarchy of needs in which lower-level motives must be largely satisfied before higher-level ones can begin to operate. In its original form, the hierarchy contained five steps (see Figure 11–2).

Survival Needs

At the lowest level of motivation, people are concerned about their basic physical needs, that is, adequate food, water, sleep, or other physiological comforts. These needs may be found in the classroom more often than teachers realize. Certain students may skip breakfast, for example, fail to get enough sleep, or have to use the bathroom during class. If these needs are very strong, they will preempt all other motives: concentrating on learning can be difficult in the best of times, but on an empty stomach it can be nearly impossible. Some survival needs may be caused by the school

level 1: basic physical comforts

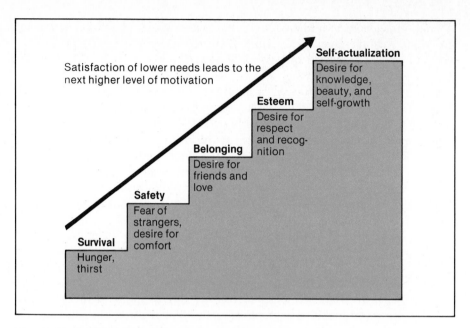

Figure 11–2 Maslow's Theory of Human Motivation

staff itself rather than the students: the room may be too hot or too cold or too full of distracting noises. One need that teachers may overlook is the need for moderate sensory stimulation—a reasonable amount of variety in what students see or hear (Wlodkowski, 1978, chap. 4). Whatever the cause of physiological needs, teachers should try to satisfy them as much as possible, even if they cannot do so completely. Without comfortable students, learning cannot occur.

Safety Needs

Once survival needs are met, people's attention shifts to a concern for regularity and predictability in their environment and for freedom from fear and anxiety. In extreme cases students may express safety needs fairly obviously: a student may visibly tremble before giving an oral report or may incessantly ask for even more clarification of an assignment or grading procedure. Often, though, students' worries remain hidden, since most learn fairly early in school to behave with proper classroom decorum in front of teachers. A student's dignity can fool the teacher into thinking that the student worries less about his or her safety than is actually the case.

level 2: safety and
security

How can teachers meet safety needs in the classroom? One way is to organize their teaching programs as completely and clearly as possible.

Before the needs for belonging, esteem, and self-actualization can become important to a student, the needs for physical comfort and security must first be met. (Marcia Weinstein)

The use of specific behavioral objectives and clear evaluation methods may be steps in this direction (see Chapter 8). In addition, students who seem especially fearful or anxious probably should not be forced into activities or situations that accentuate these feelings—forced "volunteering" during discussions, for example. Doing so can backfire just as easily as help.

Belonging Needs

After both survival and safety needs are met, people begin wanting to belong to a group and to give to and to receive affection from its members. This motive resembles the need for affiliation mentioned earlier in this chapter. As pointed out there, some students seem especially interested in forming and maintaining warm relationships with other students and may learn well only if their teacher shows a similarly warm temperament. They have a need to belong.

level 3: belonging and affection

Assuming that most teachers genuinely like their students, at least to a reasonable extent, then being warm with them should pose no real problem. Sometimes, however, a particular teacher may not have the time or personality to build a relationship as warm or as close as a particular student seems to need—or as professional ethics allows. In these cases teachers can, for example, arrange group projects that encourage social interchange among students as well as content learning, and teachers can generally support students for their own efforts to be friendly and supportive with one another. In the long run, of course, students will have to rely on their peers rather than their teachers to meet their belonging needs—schooling does not last forever.

Esteem Needs

Having satisfied all the preceding needs, people now are motivated by the desire for self-respect and recognition from both others and themselves for their particular talents and qualities. Note that people may desire either acclaim from others or self-respect and inner strength. In its other-directed form, this desire amounts to a distorted need for belonging: a drive to be loved and admired, though without the corresponding willingness to give affection in return. In its inner-directed form, this desire resembles the internal locus of control discussed earlier, though with self-evaluation added: persons needing self-esteem are in essence establishing their confidence in their abilities and competencies and are convincing themselves of their usefulness. At its best, education of all kinds tries to meet this need. At its worst, it can prevent students from reaching this level of motivation by failing to give them clear feedback about their achievements or even by failing to teach useful skills.

level 4: esteem and self-respect

Teachers can make sure that they meet their students' needs for self-esteem by assigning learning activities that reflect their students' current abilities and interests, yet challenge them to stretch themselves beyond their current capacities. This idea, you may notice, is very close to the advice given earlier for fostering a student's need for achievement. Furthermore, new content should be organized so as to encourage independent learning in so far as it is practical. For more about this, see Chapter 12 on discovery learning and its limits or read Berry (1979). And students should be recognized for their genuine achievements, which can be done by comments on papers, special letters home, or public displays of work. Note, though, that the more that such recognition becomes public, the more it can become confused with the other-directed need for fame and status and the less it may therefore help students become truly independent.

fostering self-esteem

Self-actualization Needs

If life is kind to people, they may satisfy the four aforementioned needs well enough to become concerned with self-actualization, the highest need.

Self-actualization is the motive to become all that a person is able to be. Its expression depends on the prevailing circumstances: it can be a desire for new knowledge and understanding, for example, for the appreciation of beauty, or for a generally balanced growth in all areas of living. In one way or another, self-actualization requires personal growth, whereas the lower levels of motivation require remedying deficiencies in personal circumstances.

level 5: self-actualization

This difference between growth orientation and deficiency orientation has important implications for how individuals behave and how teachers may relate to them as students. Growth-motivated persons find self-actualizing activities pleasurable and therefore seek more of them, whereas deficiency-motivated persons mainly try to eliminate their particular motives. Deficiency needs are inherently unpleasant and lead people to shift their attention away from them as soon as possible. For example, once students feel truly accepted by their peers (belonging need), they do not seek still more peer acceptance but instead turn toward satisfying another need, such as establishing their self-esteem.

growth needs versus deficiency needs

Teachers must foresee this kind of shifting and even encourage it. They must understand that deficiency-motivated students whose motives climb up the hierarchy of needs are not necessarily behaving inconsistently or showing ingratitude for their teachers' help in satisfying earlier needs. If teachers successfully help students to feel secure, for example, they may discover that the students then show much more concern for belonging socially. The change may not mean they did not need or appreciate their teachers' efforts but simply that they now feel secure enough to concern themselves with belonging.

Since individuals seek growth-motivated activities, self-actualization operates more autonomously than earlier, lower-level needs do. Self-actualizing persons seemingly cannot get enough new knowledge or wisdom, or enjoy beauty enough, or find enough new ways to grow personally. By definition, their needs do not require other people to satisfy them, as is true for individuals motivated by lower-level, deficiency needs. Self-actualizers are therefore teachers' ideal students: those who seem to be intrinsically motivated by learning and who need no prodding with grades, special reassurance with attention, or arbitrary rules to help them work.

As Maslow would point out, however, these good behaviors do not happen unless *all* the preceding needs have been met, at least in large part. Some motives that seem self-actualizing at first may really be lower-level motives in disguise: "seeking new knowledge," for example, may really only amount to "passing the exam" (safety) or "pleasing my parents" (belonging). Usually students' environments, both at home and at school, must support them very well before self-actualization can become a significant motive for them. They must live and work in a physically comfortable and safe place, feel loved by their families and liked by their

difficulty of reaching self-actualization

friends, and have ample self-esteem for their abilities. These supports furthermore must be reliable and last for a long enough period that they can turn their attention toward realizing their full potential in all areas of life and work. Though some students may meet these preconditions, certainly not all of them do so.

To foster self-actualization, teachers can emphasize self-directed learning and encourage their students to branch out into new areas of learning and skill development. The official curriculum, in particular, may fade in importance, since the drive for knowledge and understanding among such students helps guarantee that they will eventually learn it anyway, although not necessarily during the current academic year. The approach, in fact, has much in common with the advice given for gifted students in Chapter 10 (pages 282–284), although Maslow in no way meant to imply that self-actualizing persons are necessarily gifted.

Since life circumstances do not usually combine to foster self-actualization, most students (and their teachers) are preoccupied with lower-level, but more potent, personal motives. Some, particularly those in low-income communities, may worry about where their next meal will come from or where they will sleep from one week to the next. Others will find themselves somewhere in the middle of the hierarchy or vary in where they seem to belong in it (Conger, 1981). From Maslow's perspective, then, the teacher's job consists partly of identifying the students' current needs and meeting them as well as possible. Only by doing so will the students be freed to operate at the next higher level of motivation. Implicit in this idea is a value judgment, that the higher levels of motivation really are "better." Also implicit is an empirical judgment, that the levels of motivation really must occur in the order that Maslow describes. In the end, practicing teachers must test both of these judgments for themselves. Does self-esteem, for example, really require first satisfying the need for belonging, and even if it does, is this motive really better than the motive to belong?

Maslow's theory of motivation has much in common with the humanistic philosophy of education, described in the next chapter. The self-actualizing person describes the sort of student that humanistic educators expect to have: someone who works well both alone and in groups and who is quite capable of wisely choosing his or her own learning activities. Maslow differs from some humanists, though, in proposing that many students need help to become self-actualizers, in particular those who have various deficiency-oriented needs. Some humanists, in contrast, believe that all students have the potential for personal growth, no matter what their life circumstances may be. They propose techniques for directly fostering such growth, without first diagnosing and remedying lower-level needs. The next chapter describes some of these techniques and the rationales behind them.

Key Points

1. All teachers face the problem of motivation, of persuading students to want to learn.
2. Motives have several characteristics, including a tendency to act in particular ways, arousal and direction, sustainment over time, and various learned features.
3. Behavioristic theories emphasize the importance of reinforcement schedules to motivated behavior.
4. In addition, some behavior seems to be acquired by latent learning, that is, without explicit reinforcement.
5. Some behavior appears to be motivated intrinsically; that is, its reinforcement comes from the behavior itself.
6. Extrinsic reinforcement can sometimes interfere with intrinsic motivation.

7. The need for achievement refers to a motive to measure up to some standard of excellence.
8. Individuals vary in the relative strengths of their motives to succeed and to avoid failure and in how they attribute the causes of success and failure.
9. Training programs often increase the need for achievement or increase achievement-related behavior.
10. Sometimes the research on the need for achievement seems to explain motivation in men more accurately than motivation in women.
11. Abraham Maslow has evolved a theory of motivation based on a hierarchy of needs.
12. Maslow's hierarchy of needs includes survival needs, safety needs, belonging needs, esteem needs, and self-actualization needs.

Case Study

Motivating Mr. Garcia's Students

Mr. Garcia prided himself on praising students whenever they did good work. "I am determined not to be as inconsistent about giving praise as some teachers I know," he said, "or as inconsistent as I used to be." He started off the year with high hopes that using ample praise would boost morale. Whenever a student made a useful comment during a discussion, for example, Mr. Garcia would acknowledge it and elaborate on it, or as soon as a student finished a section of problems, Mr. Garcia invariably was alert to this fact and praised him or her immediately.

But as the year went by, Mr. Garcia noticed that his consistent praise did not lead to consistent results. All went well with Harry: he worked diligently at assignments and contributed well to discussions, and he seemed to appreciate Mr. Garcia's praise.

Fran, however, typically chose extremely easy problem sets and easy reading materials, even though, in Mr. Garcia's opinion, she was capable of much harder work. Naturally she performed very well on the work that she did choose and

therefore "earned" considerable praise from Mr. Garcia. When he sometimes suggested that she try more challenging activities, she just shrugged her shoulders or seemed not to listen.

Lou, on the other hand, often ignored Mr. Garcia's willingness to praise students. He was well liked by the others and rather capable, but his actual academic achievement was consistently low. He could have earned ample praise, given Mr. Garcia's resolve to use it, but he often chose instead to make wisecracks or off-color remarks. These drew criticisms from Mr. Garcia but giggles and smirks from his classmates; they apparently envied his courage to make them. "Why bother doing school work?" he once asked. "Whether or not you succeed at it doesn't depend on *you* but on Mr. Garcia. He always praises everybody no matter what they do—just look at Fran."

This comment so irritated Mr. Garcia that he finally gave up his resolve to praise students consistently. Fran and Lou both noticed almost immediately the change in him, but neither was

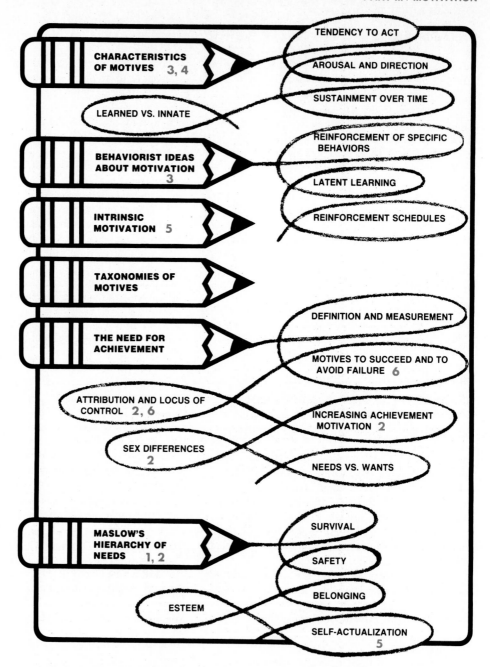

1 Other stage theories (Chapters 2, 4, and 5)
2 The social context of learning (Chapter 5)
3 Learning as behavior change (Chapter 6)
4 Learning to structure knowledge (Chapter 7)

5 Humanistic perspectives in education (Chapter 12)
6 Evaluation (Part IV)

sure at first how to react. Harry, however, started becoming more lazy and indifferent to his work. Mr. Garcia pondered all of these facts. He still had not found the key to motivating his students, and he wondered why.

Questions for Discussion

1. Consider the ideas from this chapter about schedules of reinforcement, intrinsic motivation, the need for achievement, and Maslow's hierarchy of needs. How would each of these theories explain the responses of these three students to Mr. Garcia's use of praise?

2. If Mr. Garcia could turn back the clock to before he began his experiment with praise, what suggestions could you make to him to motivate each of these students more effectively? How do your suggestions use the ideas about motivation discussed in this chapter?

3. If Mr. Garcia instead had to pick up from where the description above leaves off, how would your suggestions to him differ from the ones you made in your answer to question 2?

Suggested Readings

Gilbert, T. F. *Human Competence: Engineering Worthy Performance*. New York: McGraw-Hill, 1978.

White, Burton, B. T. Kaban, and J. S. Attanucci. *The Origins of Human Competence: Final Report of the Harvard Preschool Project*. Lexington, Mass.: Lexington Books, 1979.

These two books offer ways of improving human achievement, both directly by motivating individuals and indirectly by improving their skills and abilities. The first book is aimed at business settings as well as school learning. The second one concerns competence in young children and is aimed at parents and professionals who work closely with parents.

Kolesnik, W. B. *Motivation: Understanding and Influencing Human Behavior*. Boston: Allyn & Bacon, 1978.

This book gives a more thorough treatment of the general topic of motivation than is possible in this chapter. It makes a good starting point for further reading on the subject.

Lasch, Christopher. *The Culture of Narcissism*. New York: W. W. Norton & Co., Inc., 1979.

Yankelovich, Daniel. *New Rules: Searching for Self-fulfillment in a World Turned Upside Down*. New York: Random House, 1981.

There are many books that explore the limits of Maslow's idea of self-actualization, and these are two of them. The first one is somewhat more pessimistic about the prospects for self-fulfillment than is the second.

Ouchi, William. *Theory Z: How American Business Can Meet the Japanese Challenge*. New York: A & W Publishers, 1981.

This book provides an interesting perspective on the concepts of nAch, attribution, and locus of control by showing that many successful Japanese businesses do not rely on these motivations nearly as much as North American companies do, and yet they succeed economically.

Wlodkowski, R. J. *Motivation and Teaching: A Practical Guide*. Washington, D. C.: National Education Association, 1978.

This book is aimed especially at classroom teachers, as the title implies. It puts more emphasis on practical implications and examples than on underlying theory.

Chapter 12

HUMANISTIC PERSPECTIVES IN EDUCATION

Kevin Sunderton, camp counselor: I teach junior high mathematics during the winter, but I've been a summer camp counselor now for several years. It's a sleep-away camp—the kids come for various lengths of time, but none for less than two weeks and quite a few for as long as eight weeks.

I like teaching math, but there's no doubt that I feel closer, personally closer, to youngsters at summer camp. The contact there is so intense that I suppose we just *have* to like each other to survive. And we just have to respect each other's personalities and interests. I supervise the nature program, which fortunately is the sort of thing that the kids can actually manage for themselves to a large extent. I can suggest, for example, that we go walking in the woods, but they do the actual observing and collecting of objects. And they, not I, often have the best ideas for displaying their collections afterwards and for telling others about what they find. One fellow collected a huge number of pine cones, for instance, and decided to make them into a facsimile of a pine tree. It was a big hit around camp—and with his parents. My idea had been only to mount and label the cones on a board. A good thing, that time, that he didn't do what I suggested!

But it's not just a matter of learning science. The kids seem like more complete people than in school because I see them so much: from before breakfast to campfires at night. That breadth makes me realize how complicated everyone is. Joey was good at nature studies, for instance, but not so good at swimming; he got homesick repeatedly at camp but only showed it to me and to one good friend of his. He wrote more letters home in two weeks than some kids do in two months. He read them all to me, somewhat to my surprise. Not one letter talked about being homesick, or even about his good times exploring in the woods. Teaching at school, of course, I know that students have lots of sides to them. But at camp I see that first-hand.

That closeness works the other direction, too. The kids see me a lot more than at school, and for some it's a real revelation. I remember one blurting out at a campfire one night, "Mr. Sunderton likes to sing!" Maybe he thought only music teachers did that. Camp forces me to be myself. I just cannot afford to put on any airs with the kids. At camp I have to say what I really *feel* about everything, or I don't get along with the group more than a minute. I try to be sincere at school, of course; but there, I always find myself keeping just a bit distant from my students. Maybe it's because at school, I always have grading and evaluations hanging over my head—and theirs. At camp the only "report card" is whether the kids say they enjoyed themselves.

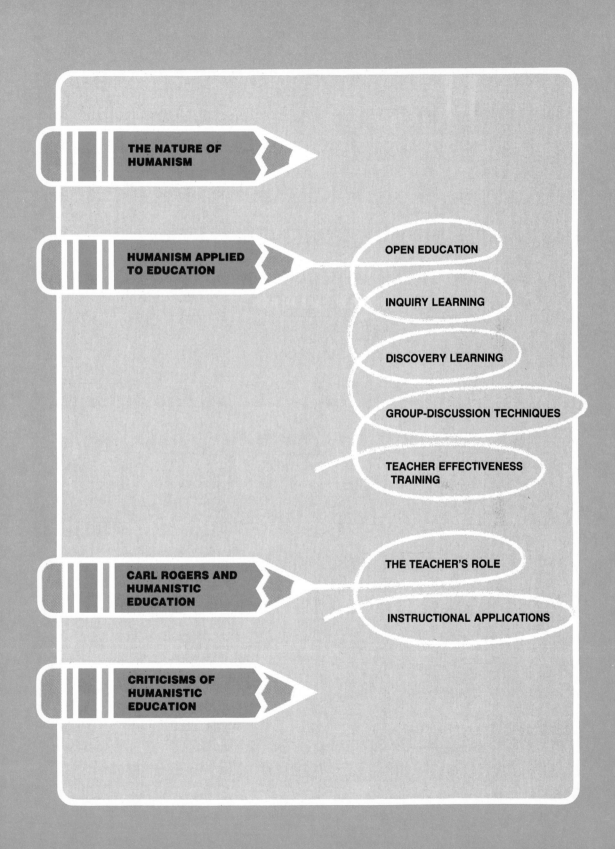

THE NATURE OF HUMANISM

HUMANISM APPLIED TO EDUCATION

OPEN EDUCATION

INQUIRY LEARNING

DISCOVERY LEARNING

GROUP-DISCUSSION TECHNIQUES

TEACHER EFFECTIVENESS TRAINING

CARL ROGERS AND HUMANISTIC EDUCATION

THE TEACHER'S ROLE

INSTRUCTIONAL APPLICATIONS

CRITICISMS OF HUMANISTIC EDUCATION

HUMANISM, a philosophy that places the highest importance on individual experience and growth, has found a place in many aspects of teaching and learning. Teachers of all kinds have helped this happen because the philosophy expresses a lot of what they believe about students, or would like to believe. To an extent, humanism is really a restatement of the democratic ideal: that the individual takes precedence over the groups or institutions to which he or she belongs. Even though this belief is difficult to live up to at times, it remains ethically desirable in societies like ours. Many teachers therefore never give up searching for new and better ways to individualize and humanize their teaching, even though their experience shows them that the circumstances of instruction in many ways can interfere with the search.

THE NATURE OF HUMANISM

Humanism is not so much a field of knowledge as a way of studying knowledge, a way that emphasizes the importance of the individual and his or her conscious experience of life. It differs from cognitive theories (for example, Piaget's) by including feelings and thinking among its concerns, and it differs from psychoanalytic approaches (for example, Erikson's) by showing relatively less concern with unconscious processes. It differs from behaviorist psychology in its focus on freedom in human behavior. Although both humanism and behaviorism study the individual, behaviorism explains his or her behavior mostly in terms of specific environmental effects—reinforcement contingencies, stimulus cues, and the like—in which the self plays a relatively limited role at best. In contrast, humanism puts concepts like *choice, responsibility,* and *intention* at the top of its priorities: it is very much a theory about how people can and should <u>control</u> their own destinies.

Humanism has a strong following in education; to a greater or lesser extent, most teachers and educators have a noticeable humanistic streak in them. It seems to belong with the profession: the best teaching fosters the abilities of individual students to cope with their own lives, both in the short run and the long run. It does so by speaking primarily to their conscious experiences and thoughts, unlike, for example, some forms of psychotherapy. In practice, of course, teaching may not always live up to these humanistic goals, but the goals remain prominent as ideals.

emphasis on the individual

Humanism's emphasis on individual conscious experience accounts for several of its other qualities (Shaffer, 1978). This approach shows a marked tendency, for example, to emphasize the *present* in its attention to human behavior. Humanists, whether they work in education or psychotherapy, seem more interested in an individual's current feelings and thoughts than in constructing the history that led up to them or in making educated guesses about where a person's current experiences will lead him or her

emphasis on the present

in the long run. Humanism therefore differs from the large standardized testing movement in psychology (see Chapter 14), whose major purpose is to show how a current sample of behavior can account for past behaviors or predict future ones. A humanistic teacher wonders more, for example, about how a certain student has reacted to a particular class session than about why his attitude is what it is or where it may lead him in the future.

Consistent with its belief in the self, the humanistic approach emphasizes that individuals (including students) are essentially "whole" or complete people and should be treated as such. People are *complex patterns of thoughts, feelings, and actions*. They are not just outgoing or shy, just achievement minded, just interested in science, or just athletically inclined: they are all of these and more, combined in a particular way. The theory of achievement motivation discussed in the previous chapter violates this belief by comparing individuals almost entirely along a single dimension, the need for achievement. Such a simplification, according to the humanists, helps one understand the concept of achievement, but it does not help one understand individuals. For example, two students may score the same on measures of need for achievement, yet present very different impressions as persons. Knowing their nAch scores does not help their teachers to know them in their entirety.

view of person as a complex whole

Carried to its logical extreme, the belief in individual complexity leads to the conclusion that *human nature can never be fully understood*. From the humanistic perspective, individuals are defined by what they do, think, and feel, rather than by any general statements about what people are like in the abstract. In principle, people's actions, thoughts, and feelings can never be known completely, not even by themselves, since even they remain ignorant of much of their own future. Individuals will always be something of a mystery, most especially to others, who presumably know them even less well than they know themselves. Nevertheless, the individual remains the primary focus of attention and concern among humanistic psychologists and educators.

unpredictable aspects of human nature

Since humanists believe that individuals can never be fully predictable, they also believe that human nature is essentially *free and autonomous*. In a way, of course, this idea cannot be completely true, since everyone obviously is confined by a variety of worldly constraints. In North America, to take a simple example, none of us has the option of driving on the left-hand side of the road, and to take a more profound example, none of us is "free" to remain healthy indefinitely or to live forever. Humanists, however, are not so interested in such constraints as in the choices we make regarding them: even someone who suffers from a troubling illness can choose among a variety of attitudes toward the experience. And even students who are forced to learn a certain subject are free to choose whether or not to like doing so. Often they are even free to choose not to learn at all and to suffer the consequences of low grades and disapproval. Recognizing such freedom, of course, does not relieve the humanistic teacher

freedom and autonomy of individual

from responsibility for helping the students learn and like learning. Humanists would just remind the teacher that every student is ultimately his or her own "boss" and that teachers therefore facilitate learning rather than cause it to occur. According to this viewpoint, teachers invite and provide opportunities for learning; only students can actually make learning occur, through their own efforts.

X   These beliefs all lead humanistic psychology to take *conscious experiences at face value,* rather than reduce them to theoretical concepts. A student who behaves in a friendly way is considered—perhaps naively—as simply friendly. Her behavior is not interpreted as a hidden expression of psychological drives (whether sex, anxiety, or Erikson's crisis of intimacy) or as the indirect result of reinforcement schedules. By the same token, negative feelings are taken at face value: anger is anger, for example, and fear is fear. These feelings, and the behaviors that go along with them, are not thought to hide any deeper feelings or motives or to express hidden defense mechanisms. The approach to understanding human behavior is *ad hoc* and accounts for why humanistic psychology is often not considered a theory so much as an attitude toward understanding people. Unlike most psychological theories, humanism contains no basic and relatively few theoretical constructs that are meant to explain a large body of human behavior.

conscious experience taken at face value

HUMANISM APPLIED TO EDUCATION

Several teaching styles and methods have grown out of the humanistic philosophy outlined above. They vary in their details according to the age of the children being served and the predispositions of the psychologists or educators originating them. All, however, base their practices on one fundamental assumption, that individual students should receive very high priority in the time and attention of their teachers. They should, in fact, receive higher priority than does the class as a group, the school as an institution, or the curriculum as a body of knowledge. We now shall consider a few applications of this principle to education.

principle of humanistic education

Open Education

Although sometimes applied to older students, **open education** usually refers to a very informal way of organizing a classroom for preschool and elementary school children (Marshall, 1981). Typically, children in an open classroom choose from a variety of materials or activities made available to them in centers around the room, and they work at the centers for as long as they wish. The choices vary over the long run but often include arts or crafts projects, blocks or other building materials, sensory mate-

By offering many centers to choose from, this open classroom respects students' abilities to guide their own learning. (Bohdan Hrynewych)

rials such as sand and water, dramatic play areas for playing house, and an area for reading or other quiet games. "Quiet," however, is relative only to the other activities, since an open classroom by definition invites considerable hustle and bustle—and talk—among the children. The method owes much of its inspiration to the infant schools for young children in Great Britain (Plowden, 1967); there, the mild weather encourages teachers and children even to work outdoors for a larger part of the school year than is possible in much of North America. On this continent, the approach has received its strongest support in early childhood education (for example, Read, 1979) and from teachers of young school-age children (Marshall, 1972; Silberman, 1973).

British influences

The teachers in such a program mainly help the children with the activities that they have chosen for themselves and try to extend their learning beyond what they might accomplish on their own. The teachers also choose and prepare toys and other materials for the children. These are selected and presented so as to build as much as possible on the abilities and interests of individual children—and on the changes in their interests that inevitably occur over time. The teachers in an open classroom must therefore observe and understand their children as individuals. They should have more commitment to their children as people than to curricular goals in the usual sense of the term. Though open classroom teachers are not likely to think of their work in philosophical terms, they behave very much as humanistic educators would: as facilitators of individual potential rather than conveyors of thinking knowledge only.

Inquiry Learning

For children who are able and willing to interact verbally for extended periods, some humanistic educators suggest the method of inquiry (see Postman & Weingartner, 1969). **Inquiry learning** requires teachers to ask "penetrating" questions during a group discussion of a topic. Students are encouraged to look deeply into questions and ideas of all sorts and not to remain satisfied with easy or glib answers to them. For example, why do dogs chase cats? If this question came up in class, the inquiry-oriented teacher might follow it up with a host of further questions: Do dogs chase cats because of instinct or because of learning? What do we mean by "instinct" and "learning"? Do dogs always chase cats, or just sometimes? How can we find out? Would ethical principles allow us to experiment with dogs and cats chasing one another? And so on. Since the exact questions depend on the replies and comments made to preceding questions, the outcome of such a discussion cannot be predicted. The resulting uncertainty is, in fact, intentional: through an inquiry session, students are shown that there are no fixed or simple right answers, that the truth is found in active thought rather than the passive reception of information, and that understanding new ideas requires modifying preexisting concepts. In essence, the inquiry method highlights the student's individual importance in learning and therefore also his or her own responsibility for growing as a person.

method of discussion

Unlike the open education described previously, inquiry teaching, by definition, relies exclusively on verbal exchange. The students must be skilled enough with the give and take of discussions to consider such activity worthwhile and to tolerate the teacher's prompting them to carry the discussion as far as possible. Teachers using the inquiry method must be especially nimble as discussion leaders. They must ask telling questions—neither foolishly easy nor confusingly hard. And they must ask them at the right moments and to the right people in the group, all in order to draw out the students and to lay bare their hidden assumptions. Feelings about the topic being considered inevitably enter such discussions, though compared with other so-called humanistic approaches to education, the inquiry method focuses somewhat more on clarity of thinking and somewhat less on the expression of feelings as such.

Discovery learning encourages students to formulate ideas by their own activities and efforts as much as possible. (Christopher Brown/Stock, Boston)

Discovery Learning

The discovery-learning approach to education grows primarily out of the cognitive theory of learning originated by Jerome Bruner, discussed in Chapter 7. **Discovery learning** is not so much a specific way of conducting a class as an attitude toward learning held by both teachers and students, an attitude that makes certain inquiry-oriented behaviors more likely to occur. According to Bruner (1966), this attitude contains six important elements:

the discovery attitude

1. The belief that learning means discovering relationships, not just accumulating facts.
2. The willingness to make new learning "one's own" by relating it to one's existing knowledge and beliefs.
3. The confidence that this sort of learning is inherently rewarding.
4. The knowledge of different ways of using information for discovery—for making and testing hypotheses.

5. The skills for articulating one's existing knowledge, whether or not one is aware of it.
6. The wisdom of managing new information as it comes along so that such information, too, can be included in the act of discovery.

To Bruner, discovery learning constitutes a sort of general skill in actively handling information and experiences so as to go "beyond the information given"; he even published a book by that title (1973).

Bruner and discovery learning Discovery learning, as defined above, leads to insights whenever it is applied. These insights create what Bruner labeled the "eureka experience"—the feeling that "I have found it!" Since this feeling is inherently satisfying, students learning by discovery can often quite successfully direct their own activities for long periods. Bruner assumes that students already have skill in discovery learning to some extent without any training but that encouragement from teachers can improve their abilities still further. At both the starting and ending points of discovery learning, then, must be a free, curious, and intellectually active young person, though he or she is assumed to have these qualities more fully after the learning than before.

In discovery learning, Bruner makes no particular commitment to the relative value of learning by doing versus learning by talking, though his writings and examples imply that most students need a variety of modes in order to learn successfully. Bruner also does not propose discovery as the only way that the students can or should learn. Much of the knowledge of the students' cultural heritage—its history, conventions, and the like—cannot be discovered by each student individually but must be told or shown to him or her. In this respect, discovery learning coincides with inquiry learning, which also is *not* meant to occupy a student's education entirely, but it differs from open education for young children, which in its fullest expression can indeed constitute an entire school program.

Group-Discussion Techniques

Useful styles of handling small-group discussions have been developed by humanistic psychologists. These discussions usually contain elements of group psychotherapy, though they can be used with educational content and with student participants instead of patients. One such method is the use of class meetings originated by William Glasser and described in Chapter 9. These meetings provide opportunities for students to express their concerns in a way that respects each individual as much as possible. As pointed out in Chapter 9, however, Glasser's reasons for having such meetings are not entirely humanistic: often the meetings are part of a system of group management for limiting socially undesirable behaviors. Glasser is more willing to exert social pressure on individuals than are the more thoroughly humanistic psychologists and educators described later in this chapter.

Another such group technique, that suggested by Robert Cohn (1972), uses **theme-centered discussions**, in which the teacher encourages group members to discuss a topic (say, a short story in an English class), but with several special ground rules added:

1. Students are encouraged to bring up any frustrations they may feel about the discussion, however unrelated they may seem to be to the comments currently being made.

2. Students are encouraged to speak in personal rather than abstract terms. They should say, "I feel . . . " or "I think . . . " instead of "One feels . . . " or "Everyone knows. . . . "

3. Students are continually reminded that they have a personal responsibility for learning in the discussion, that no one else, not even the teacher, can learn for them. Each student must therefore remember to talk (or to remain silent) in ways that optimize his or her own learning.

theme-centered
discussions

These rules help make *feelings* as important as thoughts during the discussion. They give priority to interpersonal disturbances whenever they occur (such as "I feel that you are dominating the discussion too much"), though not so much priority that disturbing feelings must be resolved completely before discussion of content can resume. This method therefore assumes that personal feelings about the discussion will be minor enough that they can be handled by the group and that they can be left partially unresolved if necessary. Otherwise, the method would turn the discussion into a psychotherapy session, which most teachers are presumably neither equipped nor motivated to handle. The teachers in such sessions should balance their attentions among all the needs of the students, in this case including both educational and emotional needs in equal parts. Teachers are less imparters of cognitive knowledge and more facilitators of learning and group processes.

By their nature, theme-centered discussions respect students as complete individuals and avoid creating exclusively academic roles for them. The ensuing well-rounded relationships should ensure that the students want to learn and that the teachers accurately and sympathetically understand their students' learning needs and desires. In the long run, humanists argue, the students should learn just as much as they would in classrooms focused more traditionally on academics. Although the evidence does not consistently support this last idea (Horwitz, 1979; Marshall, 1981), there is no doubt that humanistic styles of teaching do work well with some students and teachers. But such methods must be partly justified or criticized on ethical grounds, and not only in terms of their academic efficiency.

advantages of
theme-centered
discussions

Teacher Effectiveness Training (TET)

Teacher effectiveness training (TET), devised by Thomas Gordon, draws on humanistic principles to help teachers establish and maintain better relationships with their students (Gordon, 1974). Compared with the other applications of humanism examined in this chapter, TET puts more emphasis on interpersonal relationships as such and less on facilitating learning in the usual sense, though it clearly implies that teachers who establish good relationships with their students can expect more and better learning to occur as well.

Teacher effectiveness training urges teachers to distinguish among problems that are "owned" by the students, those "owned" by the teachers, and those shared by both. Problems that are owned by students might be high anxiety or poor self-esteem; for such problems, Gordon recommends simply listening carefully to the students' concerns or problems, inviting them to talk about them, and listening "actively." The last process includes responding to what the students say as well as attending to it and responding in ways that convey the teachers' concern for their students. Teacher-owned problems occur whenever the students behave in a way that irritates or frustrates the teacher. These problems usually can be resolved by a combination of the teacher's actively listening and sharing his or her feelings as openly and honestly as possible.

problem
"ownership"

Gordon named such honest sharing "I" messages. Ideally, these messages include a specification of the behavior that is bothering the teacher, its exact effect, and how the teacher feels afterward. The teacher may say, "When you talk during class (bothersome behavior), I am distracted from what I am saying (effect), and I feel hurt that you don't care (feelings)." Such a message creates intimacy between the teacher and the students without forcing it; it resembles, in fact, Carl Rogers's advice to be genuine with students (discussed in the next section). Nonhumanistic alternatives to "I" messages interfere with this process by focusing on the bad points of students' behavior and concealing the teacher's reaction to them.

"I" messages

If a problem is owned by both the teacher and the student, then there will be more complicated conflicts. A student may have poor self-concept (his problem), but this may lead him to do things that frustrate his teacher (the teacher's problem). But Gordon still believes that these problems can be solved by the teacher's active listening and clearly stated "I" messages. In these conflicts, it is important for teachers to adopt a "no lose" policy: a solution must satisfy all parties involved and must not be at the expense of any one of them. This policy may be challenging for teachers, since they have specially designated powers over students that they can always resort to using. If they do so, however, Gordon believes that they will lose their chance to establish genuine and effective relationships with their students.

CARL ROGERS AND HUMANISTIC EDUCATION

One prominent psychologist, Carl Rogers, applied a number of principles of humanism to teaching, which are, as he put it, "a view of what education might become" rather than what it currently is (1969).

The Teacher's Role

According to Rogers, significant learning can occur only if teachers fulfill three conditions. As with Cohn's approach discussed above, these conditions make teachers more psychotherapists than instructors.

1. *Being real.* Like many other humanistic educators, Rogers assumes that students have many feelings about their learning, which must be aired if schooling is to be effective. Teachers can help this process, Rogers believes, by sharing their feelings with their students as openly and honestly as possible. The feeling need not—and in fact should not—be only frustrations and complaints but may also include feelings of warmth, caring, and liking for the students. If teachers do not possess such feelings, Rogers questions whether they then should even be teaching. In addition, "being real" means admitting to one's personal limitations—of knowledge, patience with students, or energy—and giving up any illusions of omnipotence that teaching may encourage. Again, the attitude must come naturally if it is to work: being real may be more of a description of good teaching than a prescription of something teachers can intentionally do to become better.

the teacher and humanistic education

2. *Valuing students as people.* Teachers need not, of course, value everything that every student does, but they must find some qualitites or abilities that they do sincerely respect and prize, and they must convey their appreciation of them to the students. They can do so by saying so to them, but to be convincing they must show their admiration in more than just words. They can, for example, listen carefully to the student—probably more carefully than is usual in traditional teaching—and respond to the student thoughtfully and as objectively as possible. To work well, these behaviors must be based on faith in the students as individuals and learners, as well as knowledge of their specific abilities and interests. Blind sentimental commitment to loving humanity or loving students will not do.

3. *Empathizing.* Teachers must put themselves in the place of the students to the extent that they are able. In doing so, they may be able to understand both their cognitive mistakes and their emotional obstacles to learning: the teachers will, in effect, "know" the students in the broadest sense of the term. Empathy sets the stage for leading students to new ideas and new learning goals; valuing students and discussing real feel-

"Being real" with students means responding to them as complete human beings, and not only in their roles as students. (Victoria Arlak)

ings with them completes the process. In all, Rogers calls for a genuine, positive, and personal relationship between the teacher and the students, but one that somehow deals with learning. The distinction between learning and personal growth is not always clear in Rogers's writings, but it supposedly is the difference between humanistic teaching and humanistic psychotherapy.

Instructional Applications

Teaching conditions can be improved in a variety of ways, some of which have also been suggested by other humanistic psychologists and educators. Rogers makes the following general suggestions for humanistic teachers:

1. *Build on problems that students perceive as real.* The most important curriculum from the students' point of view is the problems that they personally experience: getting along with a friend or relative, for example, or finding work that honestly challenges them. New ideas and attitudes can be related relatively easily to such problems, since they involve the

students' whole selves and do not force them to deny their personal needs. The problems that a particular student considers real will, of course, depend on his or her age, life situation, and previous experiences. A young child whose parents read often themselves may consider learning to read a very "real" problem, whereas one whose parents read rather little may not. If the teacher nonetheless considers reading a crucial skill for the second child, she or he will have to begin teaching it by relating it to whatever personal interests and needs the child already has. This may be a challenge, but it can be done. The teacher can, for example, provide reading material focused on the child's concerns (cars? dinosaurs? divorced parents?) and thereby build a link from that to the "alien" skill of reading.

suggestions for teaching humanistically

2. *Provide resources.* Rather than planning what they will do from one day to the next, teachers should spend time finding materials for the students to select: books, films, tools, or special equipment—even human resources in the form of special visitors. These materials should be made easily available to the students. They should *not* be assigned as required work, since students' needs and interests can be expected to differ and since allowing choice helps build students' responsibility for their own learning.

3. *Use contracts.* Particularly in large classes, teachers can make agreements with each student about the amount and kind of work that he or she will do. If the agreement can be written down as an informal contract between the two parties, then it essentially is the technique of contingency contracting described in Chapter 8. Unlike many other educators, however, Rogers does not insist that contracts be stated in behavioral terms.

A contract helps give students some control over their own learning, at least as long as it is truly negotiated rather than simply imposed on them by the power of the teacher. A contract also promotes the students' responsibility for learning throughout the course, long after a merely verbal agreement at the first class may have been forgotten. In especially large classes, a contract helps preserve the personal tie between the teacher and each student.

4. *Vary the use of class time.* According to Rogers, it is neither necessary nor desirable to use every minute of scheduled class time for official teaching functions such as lecturing and discussion. Doing so, in fact, often makes using up time a more important goal than real learning. Instead, Rogers urges teachers to vary their use of scheduled time as much as possible and in particular to give students more responsibility for their use of time. For example, class members who wish may sign up for class time to make a presentation on a particular topic, or they may arrange for the teacher to do the same at their request. On many days, teachers need not be physically present in the classroom for time to be used well: they can simply make themselves available to students in their offices or available to a group of students interested in discussing a particular problem or doing a particular activity.

Such suggestions may impress many teachers as more appropriate for college or university teaching than for the public schools or other instructional settings, in which bureaucratic constraints often require the physical presence of teachers in their classrooms. With slight modifications, however, Rogers's suggestions may work in public schools as well. Wherever they do work teachers need not be in charge of their students every minute. They may take certain segments of time to work with individual students or small groups in a relatively secluded part of the room while others pursue activities that they have more or less chosen for themselves. Many teachers already use such practices, of course; Rogers urges more teachers to use them and to use them more often.

practical constraints on time

5. *Use varied teaching methods.* Given the many differences among students, teachers should strive to make their teaching repertoires as varied as possible. Inquiry learning, such as described earlier in this chapter, can and should be used to stimulate more incisive thinking whenever appropriate, though like any other technique, it can lose its effectiveness if it is overused or used without conviction. Group-centered techniques, in which students explore one another's feelings, can free students to form more effective working relationships, ones that allow more and better learning to occur. This method resembles Cohn's theme-centered discussions discussed earlier, as well as Glasser's class meeting idea discussed in Chapter 9. Simulations, in which students act out family, school, or political situations, can give them a better feel for their learning than can the more detached analysis of discussion or lecture. Programmed instruction, in which students learn from a computer or other specially organized materials, can often teach specific skills more efficiently than a live teacher can. Although programmed instruction is also claimed by the behaviorists as an application of behavioral conditioning (see Chapter 6), it is not really inconsistent with humanistic intentions if used as Rogers suggests—namely, as a way of varying and individualizing selected aspects of education. Used this way, programmed learning frees teachers to do what humanists believe that they do best, which is to foster human, educationally oriented relationships with their students.

programmed learning as humanistic

Using such a variety of methods demands many skills from teachers, who may not feel capable of them all, even though they may believe that they do benefit their students. Rogers does not speak directly to this problem, though presumably he does not consider it impossible to solve. For instance, teachers could call on the talents of specific students to conduct certain activities that the teachers feel unsure of conducting themselves, or they could invite visitors to do the same. Eventually, perhaps, teachers will learn in their university and in-service training the many different skills for which Rogers calls. Nonetheless, Rogers would probably remind us that no specific skill matters as much as *who* teachers are as persons. If teachers can be real with their students, if they sincerely value them as people, and if they try to understand them, then they will teach effectively, that is, humanely.

By providing both emotional and academic support, teachers can teach and motivate their students more effectively over the long run. (Marion Bernstein)

CRITICISMS OF HUMANISTIC EDUCATION

Despite the many good ideas for teaching proposed by humanistic education, this movement has also encountered a variety of obstacles and criticisms, and almost every one of its basic tenets has been challenged as well as supported.

Reliance on Personal Testimony

Many of the evaluations of humanistic education have been based on self-reports—"I found that the approach worked (or did not work) for me"—rather than on objective research. One study interviewed former graduates of a well-known humanistically oriented school, Summerhill, and found mixed reports from its graduates when they looked back on their experience (Bernstein, 1968). In general the students appreciated the school's help in teaching them to get along with others, but they were not impressed with its academic preparation. For that reason, in fact, most were not enthusiastic about having their own children attend the school. On the other hand, there are quite a few highly supportive, albeit personal, evaluations of humanistic programs (see Smith, 1975; Waterman, 1981). Although such evaluations may reflect humanism's emphasis on individual experience, they remain personal and individual rather than objectively scientific.

Ambiguous Research Support

There are a few objective reviews of humanistic education, and they provide ambiguous support for humanistically oriented programs. As a rule, children in such programs perform academically as well as or slightly less well than do children in more traditional, teacher-centered programs, but their attitudes toward learning often seem to be more positive (Gage, 1978; Peterson, 1979). These findings can be construed as either support or criticism of humanistic education, depending on the relative values that teachers place on achievement and attitudes. The findings suggest that students pay a small price in achievement for the benefits of more positive attitudes; therefore their teachers, it would seem, should value positive attitudes *more* than achievement in order to make humanistic methods worthwhile. On the other hand, some teachers may define positive attitudes as themselves a type of achievement, in which case humanistic methods do not entail for them any sacrifice of learning as a whole—just a different, and more humane, pattern of learning.

support or criticism

Depending on Students to Manage Their Own Learning

Evaluating humanistic education, then, still depends largely on resolving basic questions of values. Can students, for example, really be trusted to manage their own learning if, as Rogers suggests, teachers simply make materials available to them? Although most teachers would like to agree that they can, many would also hedge on this question. They may cite incidents that seemingly refute humanistic values and assumptions: the child who stole all the magnets from the science center one day or the student who talked too much or too foolishly during inquiry discussions and always chose the easiest center to work at. Even in the time span of a school year, some students may never freely choose to do what most teachers would judge to be essential learning tasks—reading a book, for instance, or experimenting with topics or materials of which they are currently unaware. Humanistic teachers may guide such students to new experiences some of the time, but can they do it all of the time? Probably not, but then neither can teachers always guide learning successfully with more directive methods. So the question remains open. In the minds of

ascertaining students' judgment

some teachers, a humanistic belief in individual worth and dignity leads to these questions:

1. Can all or only some students be trusted to learn?
2. Can all students be trusted to learn on all occasions, or only on some?
3. Can all students be trusted to learn all possible educational content, or only selected content?

Humanists urge educators to carry their trust of students as far as possible, but for various practical and philosophical reasons, many teachers stop short of going all the way.

Overemphasis on Expression of Feelings

Another value question concerns students' feelings: how much can, and should, teachers delve into the feelings that students have about one another and about what they learn? In our society, feelings usually are considered a private matter, something displayed in public only with care, or even not at all. Yet humanistic educators would have teachers violate this convention to some extent by inviting students to share their feelings in a semipublic situation, the classroom. Can teachers reasonably expect students to do so, and even if they can, *should* they expect students to do so? Humane teachers need not force students to say more in front of others than they want to say. But by setting up a climate of self-expression, they may indirectly pressure even shy students to disclose more about themselves than they may otherwise choose to do.

discussing
feelings

But not discussing feelings may prevent certain students from sharing certain concerns with their fellows or teachers that they are in fact eager to share: it may, as the humanists claim, foster feelings of alienation from learning and from school. There is no perfect policy as long as teachers must steer a road between hurting students with too much self-expression and alienating them with not enough. Despite the humanists' claims, elevating the importance of affect and interpersonal relationships in the classroom does not guarantee either higher-achieving students or happier ones.

Difficulties in Evaluating Learning Gains

Even if such questions of value can be resolved, evaluating humanistic education is complicated by its concern with what students *do* do in addition to what students *can* do, or in a psychological sense, its concern with both performance and competence. In conventional education, students' learning is judged largely by asking them to display new skills or knowledge on demand. They are "tested" in the broadest sense of the term:

by writing essays, taking exams, doing experiments, or answering questions that the teacher asks. Even though these behaviors may show the students' competence—what they *can* do—they do not prove that students *do* use their skills in other, nontesting situations. Because ultimately such transfer of learning justifies the existence of education, teachers often go to some lengths to promote it (see Chapter 8). Usually, teachers cannot observe transfer situations nearly as well as they can observe learning on demand.

By emphasizing choice and playing down the "demand" quality of schooling, humanistic education incurs a much more difficult problem in evaluating its own success. By definition, students in a choice-oriented program succeed if they learn in ways that are personally relevant and that are geared to their own interests as they see them. In a sense, then, such a program cannot fail: reading comic books and reading Shakespeare both are proofs of success if they have been chosen rather than imposed.

In another sense, however, the program does not succeed unless the students actually gain new knowledge or skills from their choices: some, for example, might actually learn more by choosing to read comic books rather than Shakespeare. Yet testing such cognitive gains often cannot be done in a humanistic program without putting "demands" on students to show what they have learned. A teacher cannot assess, for example, whether reading comic books really leads to learning for a particular student without finding out what the student knew beforehand, as well as what additional knowledge the student acquired afterward from experience. Sometimes a teacher may be able to assess this change informally through the good, personal relationship teachers are supposed to have with their students. But this may not happen as often as a teacher wishes. Testing a student more formally, on the other hand, can compromise a teacher's humanistic principles: too many conventional tests may spoil the atmosphere of the program's self-directed learning.

What, then, is the teacher to do? Many humanists suggest that students evaluate themselves using whatever standards they consider appropriate and fair. In principle, then, different individuals may judge themselves in different ways—one by reading achievement, for example, another by classroom participation, and a third by "effort" regardless of performance achieved. Under this system, the same final grade may thus represent very different outcomes. Humanists argue that allowing such individualization shows respect for the individuality of each student, that it encourages intrinsically motivated learning, and that in any case the students often have more information about their work than does their teacher, who can at best only observe samples of it. Critics of self-evaluation argue that such a system cannot really be fair, since students inevitably choose standards of evaluation that emphasize their most positive qualities. These may not correspond, critics argue, to the qualities most needed or valued in school or society. Only teachers have the detachment needed to apply these larger standards to all students equally.

Margin notes:

wide range of possible standards

self-evaluation

Multiple and Complex Goals

Part of the problem in both implementing and evaluating humanistic education stems from its goals' ambiguities: the movement seeks to accomplish many different educational purposes, and often these overlap and vary from the very specific to the very general. The humanists are not the only educators to have this problem, but they may experience more of it because of their intention to help students grow as people, rather than just to instruct. One educator (Wittrock, 1966) pointed out several confusions that may arise with regard to discovery learning, though his concerns also are relevant to other applications of humanist philosophy to education:

1. *Is humanistic education an end in itself or a means to learn other subject matter?* Teachers hope that ultimately the students' self-direction, such as in discovery learning, will transfer to all of life's problems after the students graduate from school. At a more practical level, though, teachers face pressures from parents, the school curriculum, and their professional colleagues to accomplish something with their students by the end of specified periods of time, usually the current school year. One way to reconcile these pressures with their humanistic principles is to use discovery methods to achieve particular curricular goals. By making available certain scientific equipment and materials, for example, and by giving a minimum of instructions, teachers can hope that their students will acquire not only knowledge of certain scientific principles as such but also skills in—and a commitment to—discovering them. But whether such a combined approach really works for all students in all circumstances remains a major unsettled question about humanistic education.

achieving curriculum goals humanistically

2. *How much can actually be learned through discovery learning and other humanistic methods?* In choice-oriented programs, do students acquire specific facts, general rules, or methods of solving problems? Probably "all of the above," as they say on multiple-choice tests. But humanistic methods may not serve all kinds of goals equally effectively: how, for example, could a student most efficiently learn the vocabulary and grammar of a second language? By discovery? By inquiry-oriented discussion?

To the extent that such methods work at all for such a goal, they may do so only by allowing students to set up relatively structured learning experiences. They may "discover," for example, that they can grill their teachers for information about the foreign language, or they may discover that foreign-language teaching materials have been made available in their classroom. As mentioned earlier, Rogers recognizes this sort of learning when he recommends the use of programmed materials along with other teaching methods. Some teachers, however, may feel that it stretches the term to call such learning "discovery" oriented or "humanistic."

3. *How should the teacher sequence and pace the learning of new materials?* Methods of choice-oriented, humane teaching tend to assume that the best rate of learning is the one that the students choose for themselves.

The approach essentially has faith that students will not dawdle over content that is too easy for them or overreach themselves with material that is too hard. Although this faith makes a lot of sense for many students and learning situations, successful pacing probably also depends on the teachers' efforts to guide their students away from overly difficult goals and to make available materials and choices that truly challenge them. Open, choice-oriented methods therefore do not really let the teachers off the hook in pacing their students' learning. Even if it sounds "un-humanistic," the teachers must still take some responsibility for the students' choices (Bennett, 1976).

teachers' planning for self-guided learning

And what about sequencing? Discovery learning and other humanistic methods often give the impression that learning occurs best when it proceeds from specifics to generalities or from concrete experiences to verbal ones. This bias seems to underlie both the open classroom of early childhood education and Carl Rogers's advice to make materials available to students rather than to lecture about them. In both cases students are given specifics and are expected to learn regularities and generalizations from them. But some psychologists point out that this sequencing may really be a form of discovery, an inductive form. Some students, they argue, may more easily discover deductively, by being given generalizations from which they must discover specific applications and examples. There is little research evidence to assume that one sequence is inherently more challenging than the other, but there is much evidence to suggest that students differ in the sequence that they personally find the most challenging (Bergan, 1980). To succeed in using the self-direction of learning, teachers must ensure that their students can sequence their learning so as to favor their personal styles. The teachers may have to give relatively specific materials and information to some, but relatively general ones to others.

sequencing

As a philosophy of education, humanism has found quite a lot of support among teachers, for two reasons. First, it states what many, or even most, teachers believe about human nature and its effects on learners. Even teachers who do not have the humanistic faith in the individual still say they would like to have such faith. Second, humanism has led to many useful suggestions for teaching practice, some of which were given in this chapter. These need not be used only in public school teaching; in fact, they often assume or even urge quite varied arrangements for learning, such as might occur in non–school-based training and education. This quality of humanistic education may partly reflect the professional origins of some of its principal advocates, many of whom came to education from other fields, most notably psychological counseling.

The critics of the philosophy and practice of humanistic education have focused on several issues. One of these, the lack of clarity of humanistic goals, was discussed in this chapter. As it turns out, this problem also affects humanism's ability (or lack thereof) to evaluate students. The next two chapters consider why this may be so for both humanistic education and teaching generally. We also shall discuss why some educators believe that successful evaluation depends on a more thorough analysis of teaching and learning than some humanists are willing to make.

Key Points

1. Humanistic education is a philosophy that puts the highest value on the individual, that views the person as a complex and autonomous whole, and that accepts conscious experiences at face value.
2. Humanistic education has found many applications, including open education, inquiry learning, discovery learning, group-discussion techniques, and teacher effectiveness training.
3. One of the foremost proponents of humanism in education is Carl Rogers.
4. According to Rogers, a humanistic teacher needs to be "real" with students, to value them as people, and to empathize with them.

5. To fulfill this humanistic role, the teacher should build on problems that the students perceive as real, give resources to the students, use contracts when appropriate, and vary the use of class time and teaching methods.
6. Humanistic education has been criticized on a number of grounds: for relying on personal testimony, for lacking clear research support, for depending too much on students to manage their own learning, for overemphasizing the expression of feelings, and for setting goals that are so complex and ambiguous as to make their evaluation difficult.

Case Study

Making Humanism Work for You

Herb Kohl is an educator and advocate of humanistic methods in education. He suggested that teachers wanting a more "open" classroom style begin with just ten minutes a day devoted to this goal.

> Some specific hints on the use of the ten minutes:
> In English class it is possible to read, write (set 3 or 4 themes and leave it open for students to develop other themes), talk, act.
> In mathematics the students can set problems, solve problems, build computers, compute, design buildings (or other structures or things), talk about money, set problems for each other and the teacher.
> In social studies it is possible to talk about history; about newspapers, events, people; write about them; compose or listen to poems, play songs about them; talk or invite people in to talk about what's happening.

> In all classes students can do nothing, gossip, write, start a newspaper, a newsletter, listen to music, dance, talk about or play games, bring in things that may interest the teacher or other students and talk about them, write about them. . . .

> Think about what is happening during those ten minutes and learn to be led by the students. If certain things are particularly interesting to one group, find out about those things, learn as much as you can, and, seeing their interest, present them with ways of getting more deeply into what they care about. If, for example, a group of students is interested in animals and their relationship to people, you can refer them to fables, to Konrad Lorenz, to experimental psychology, to whatever you can discover yourself. . . . Then—and this is crucial—step out of the way again. (Kohl, 1969, pp. 70–71)

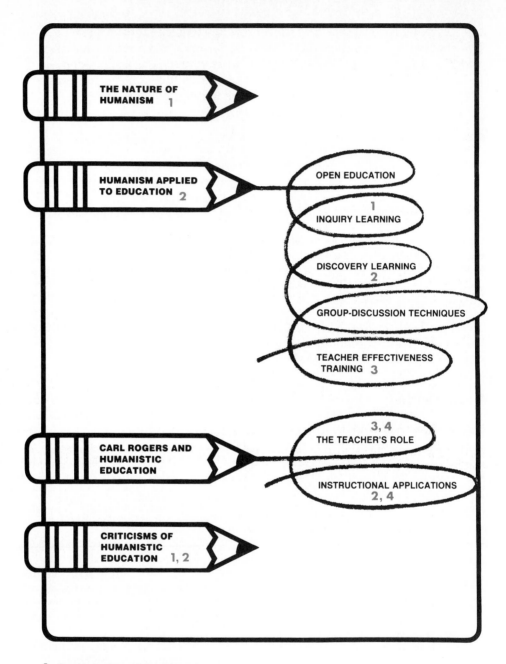

THE NATURE OF
HUMANISM   1

HUMANISM APPLIED
TO EDUCATION   2

OPEN EDUCATION

1
INQUIRY LEARNING

DISCOVERY LEARNING
2

GROUP-DISCUSSION TECHNIQUES

TEACHER EFFECTIVENESS
TRAINING   3

3, 4
THE TEACHER'S ROLE

CARL ROGERS AND
HUMANISTIC
EDUCATION

INSTRUCTIONAL APPLICATIONS
2, 4

CRITICISMS OF
HUMANISTIC
EDUCATION   1, 2

1 Moral behavior and development
   (Chapter 4)

2 Learning to structure knowledge (Chapter 7)

3 Instructional management (Chapter 9)

4 The motivation to learn (Chapter 11)

Questions for Discussion

1. Do you think that Kohl's suggestions are desirable and useful for all sorts of children and all sorts of teaching situations? Or only for certain sorts? Explain.

2. Suppose you wanted to increase your "humanistic" period of the day from ten minutes to three hours. What complications do you foresee with Kohl's suggestions as they are stated above? Using one of the imaginary classes he describes, extend or modify his suggestions so as to take into account the longer period of time.

3. How would you explain this ten minutes to a skeptical parent? Precisely what would you say? How would your explanation differ if you had to explain three hours of "openness" instead of just ten minutes?

Suggested Readings

Biondi, A. M., and S. J. Parnes. *Assessing Creative Growth.* 2 vols. New York: Creative Synergetic Associates, 1976.

These two volumes have a lot to offer on the subject of creativity. They are collections of essays from the *Journal of Creative Behavior,* an important professional journal in this field.

Kirschenbaum, H. *On Becoming Carl Rogers.* New York: Delacorte, 1979.

This book is a biography of Carl Rogers as a person and a professional. It shows the tremendously wide range of his interests over the years, and it helps make understandable the similarity of his suggestions to teachers and to psychotherapists.

Maslow, A. H. *The Farther Reaches of Human Nature.* New York: Viking, 1972.

In addition to the books by Maslow already cited in the text, this is one that beautifully conveys the author's essential faith in people.

Meier, J. *Facilitating Children's Development: A Systematic Guide for Open Learning.* Baltimore: University Park Press, 1979.

Here are some practical suggestions for creating an open classroom. The book is written with the younger grades (down to nursery school) in mind, as are many books on this topic.

Milgram, S. *Obedience to Authority: An Experimental View.* New York: Harper & Row, 1974.

The author describes some slightly disturbing experiments in which persons who were usually very humane and considerate were persuaded, as part of a "learning" experiment, to punish severely other individuals.

Shallcross, D. J. *Teaching Creative Behavior: How to Teach Creativity to Children of All Ages.* Englewood Cliffs, N.J.: Prentice-Hall, 1981.

One result of the humanistic approach to education is the fostering of creative behavior in students. This is one book on the subject—a relatively practical one.

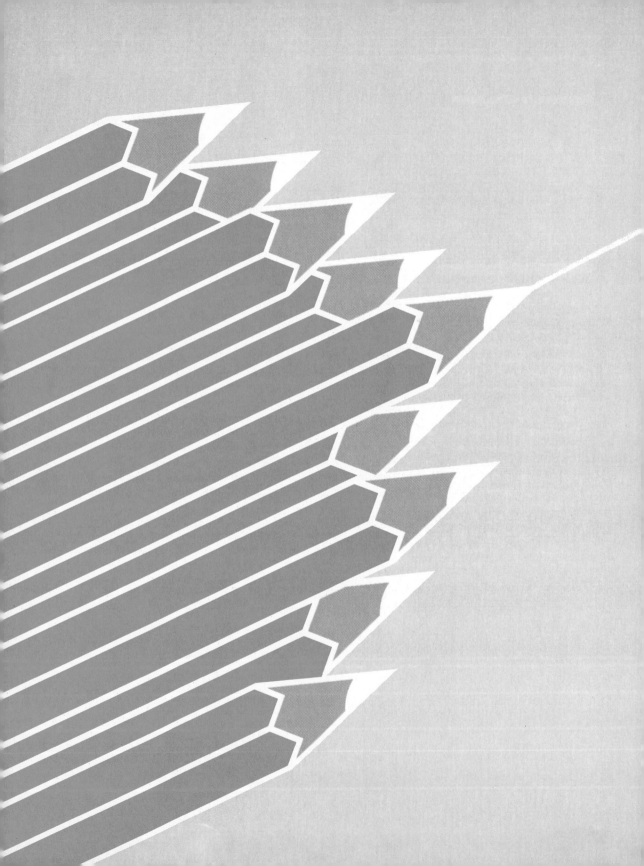

Part IV
EVALUATION

For a number of reasons, teachers need information about how well their students are learning. Such information can help, for example, in planning the next phases of instruction. It can also help in selecting which students have been best prepared for jobs or other activities related to their learning. Such planning and selection usually requires teachers to judge their students' learning according to certain standards, either implicitly or explicitly. Altogether, the planning, selection, and judging covered in Chapter 13 constitute the *evaluation* of learning and lead to the ways of reporting on learning discussed in Chapter 14.

Although evaluation of and reporting on learning are closely related, in teaching practice they tend to occur separately. To gather information about students, teachers must evaluate learning, but reporting occurs only when the evaluations are shared with other relevant people. This distinction has guided the selection of content for Chapters 13 and 14. In general, Chapter 13 examines the ways that teachers can gather information and interpret its meaning to themselves, usually through informal observations and teacher-made tests. Chapter 14 discusses grading, parent conferences, and standardized tests. The last topic is included in Chapter 14 because this book assumes that classroom teachers most often use the results of standardized tests to report on learning and that they generally do not construct them.

Teachers often find evaluating and reporting to be difficult, usually because of the value judgments they require and sometimes also because clear-cut information about students' learning can be hard to find. Nevertheless, because evaluating and reporting contribute to better teaching and learning, they indirectly contribute to all other phases of teaching, from understanding student development to improving actual instruction to motivating students. To the extent that teachers can perform evaluation well, they can improve all areas of their work.

Chapter 13

MAKING EVALUATIONS OF LEARNING

Barry Hendrick, Grade 5 teacher: Being fair in my evaluations of students is hard, especially the first few times I teach new material. It would be easy if I just wanted them to remember facts; then I could just ask them to write them all down on a test. But I want more than that: I want them to understand concepts and principles, and use them. I want them to like learning, too. Those are honorable goals, I think, but they give me a lot of work. How do I evaluate goals that are complex and so varied?

That unit on weather—a new one for me—is a good example. It's easy enough to make my students memorize names and facts about weather: all the different kinds of clouds, say, or all the common weather instruments. I suppose I could even make them memorize a few principles while they're at it, like "warm air rises" or "cooling makes moisture condense." But why leave it at that? I want them to know those terms and ideas and use them—not just state them in words.

I think that means I need "fruit salad" evaluations—a little bit of everything. Some questions on a test may call for definitions of weather terms, such as cloud names. That's all right, but it's not enough. I try to supplement the identifications with true-false statements about weather patterns or with multiple-choice questions. I like the multiple-choice questions best, but they take longer to write, so I can't rely on them completely. Sometimes, too, I ask students to write briefly about some aspect of weather: "Compare the major types of clouds and the weather associated with them." Recently I've used slides during the test, to identify clouds, for instance. The pictures seem more realistic and get away from a lot of verbiage. In real life, after all, people *see* clouds and weather, no matter how much they also talk about them!

My "fruit salads" give the students some variety but not really enough. Some of my students dislike tests, and a few dislike them passionately. They get anxious about them, don't study for them—even, I think, blame me for using them at all. It hurts to see that, because I happen to know that some of my test-anxious students actually do understand what I've been teaching. They talk about it during discussions; ask good questions every now and then; point out cloud types out the window. They do know the material, but they do not like being put on the spot by an official test.

To be fair to those students, I sometimes feel that I should keep a record of such incidents—the ones where they show they've learned. I've been doing some recording recently, but I'm still not satisfied with my notes. They take so much time to keep that I've only done them for a couple of extreme test-avoiders. But that's not fair, either; I should find a way to keep observations on *all* my students. Don't you think so?

THE NATURE OF EVALUATION
- KEY ELEMENTS
- EVALUATION VS. MEASUREMENT
- BASIC TYPES OF EVALUATION

QUALITIES OF GOOD EVALUATIONS
- RELIABILITY
- VALIDITY
- USABILITY

TEACHER-MADE OBSERVATIONS
- INFORMAL WRITTEN OBSERVATIONS
- CHECKLISTS
- RATINGS
- INVENTORIES OF INTERESTS

TEACHER-MADE TESTS
- NORM- VS. CRITERION-REFERENCED TESTS
- TABLE OF SPECIFICATIONS

KINDS OF TEST QUESTIONS
- TRUE-FALSE
- MULTIPLE-CHOICE
- COMPLETION
- ESSAY

LIKE it or not, teachers inevitably evaluate students: our only choices consist of how to do it and for what purposes. If you talk informally with your students on the first day of school, you are evaluating them. Why? Because even in such a conversation, you learn what the students already know and the sophistication or detail of what they know. At the same time, through subtle cues in your responses, the students learn something of the adequacy of their knowledge of the subject—whether you think they know a lot or a little or what parts of their previous knowledge you consider especially important. Presumably these first-day exchanges help both you and the students with your respective jobs: even on the first day, you all begin to discover what each of you must do to reach the goals of the course and what your prospects for success may be. Such "sizing up" may be still a bit vague and haphazard on the first day of the year, but it is a form of evaluation nevertheless.

THE NATURE OF EVALUATION

Two Key Elements

For a teacher, evaluation consists of two elements: (1) information about students collected to help make decisions about instruction and (2) some sort of standards against which to measure this information. The opening-day conversation has both these features: it collects information—even though some teachers might feel that it does so only haphazardly—and compares it with a standard, in this case the teacher's preconceptions of what students ought to learn in the course. The comparisons allow the teacher to decide what to teach.

information and
standards

From a student's point of view, evaluation usually means self-appraisal, but otherwise it contains the same elements of decision making and standards that it has for teachers. The first-day conversation, for example, helps students gather information both about what they know and what they should know. This knowledge helps them indirectly decide how much they can and wish to meet these expectations, how much, in other words, to be motivated to learn.

Implied in the entire process of collecting information are a host of value judgments: teachers have ideas about what their students should learn, and students have ideas about what teachers should reasonably expect

value judgments

from them. These values are a crucial part of education and are discussed in detail in other parts of this book. But they are only one part of evaluation itself. To "evaluate" means literally to "come out of values" or to be derived from them; evaluation therefore refers to what teachers do as a result of what they want to do.

Evaluation Versus Measurement

Evaluation should not be confused with **measurement**: the process of quantifying or attaching numbers to observations so as to assist their analysis and comparison. Measurement occurs whenever teachers assess student performance through classroom tests, whenever teachers assign grades on the basis of these tests, or whenever students demonstrate their ability or achievement through standardized tests. Strictly speaking, these measurements do not set values on the various performances of students; rather, the teachers, parents, and students do so. Since the precision of a measurement affects its ability to provide clear evaluations, all educators can benefit from knowing how to make educational measurements as reliably and validly as possible. This problem is so important, in fact, that much of Chapter 14 discusses it.

Types of Evaluation

In evaluating students, teachers draw their observations and measurements from a variety of sources. Most of the time, they rely on **teacher-made tests**, those that they themselves construct, based on content that they know their students have covered. An alternative to these are **standardized tests**, those that have been constructed by experts and are intended to compare particular students or groups with large, even nationwide, samples of students. Standardized tests are discussed in detail in Chapter 14. This chapter will examine teacher-made tests and other, relatively informal teacher-made observations. In practice, these activities are important to evaluating learning, both in classrooms and in other, classroomlike situations.

teacher-made versus standardized tests

QUALITIES OF GOOD EVALUATION

Whether teacher-made evaluation is made informally or through written tests, it must satisfy certain criteria. The first criterion is **reliability**: the evaluation must provide consistent results each time it is made. The second criterion is **validity**: the evaluation must predict or relate to instructional decisions in the ways that it is supposed to. And the third criterion is **usability**: the evaluation must do these jobs relatively easily or conveniently for teachers.

Reliability

Reliability is illustrated more easily with formal tests than with informal methods of evaluation. A test is reliable to the extent that it ranks each student who takes it about the same on each application. On a reliable test, high-scoring individuals tend to score high again if given a second chance to take the test, and low-scoring persons tend to score low again. Their scores need not be exactly the same—and in fact they seldom are—but they should be nearly the same, and their relative placement in the group should also be about the same as before. Since the results of any two test takings seldom agree completely, reliability is a matter of degree: a test is more or less reliable, but seldom completely so.

Tests of Reliability   The reliability of tests can be measured in several different ways, all of which require students to provide two measures of their performance, though not necessarily to take the test twice. The first method is **test-retest reliability**, which, as the name implies, means taking the same test on two occasions. The scores on the two testings can be compared: a relatively close match shows high reliability. Psychologists have worked out statistical procedures for estimating the amount of match, or correlation, as they usually call it, and the procedures are described in many books on educational and psychological statistics. For information on computing correlation, try the book by Stanley and Hopkins (1972).

test-retest reliability

This type of reliability assumes that an individual's score on the second testing will be affected in known ways by the practice he or she gains from having taken it before. If some students "learn" the test better than others do, then the method does not really give information about the test's reliability. Such learning seems especially likely if the retesting is given too soon after the first testing. But if the retesting is given too long after, some students may learn information from their general life experiences that gives them a special advantage the second time: in the interim, they may have matured, read a few more books, taken another course in math, or whatever else may improve their scores.

To try to avoid these problems, psychologists sometimes use the method of equivalent forms to test reliability. In the **equivalent forms** method, a group takes a test twice, but each time the test uses a different version of the same general content. Presumably, this method minimizes individuals' remembering the precise answers to the original test, though it may not prevent some general transfer from occurring. Since by definition both forms of the test share many elements, some persons may learn the underlying principles involved in the test, even though they may not learn its specific answers. From a practical standpoint, the method of equivalent forms presents an even more serious challenge: how to construct two tests that are indeed equivalent. Most classroom teachers, in particular, probably have their hands full in making up just one good version of any test that they give.

equivalent forms

This problem leads to the third way of testing reliability, the so-called **split-half reliability** method. In this method, the group takes the test

In spite of the anguish and tension that it causes in many students—and teachers—evaluation remains an important part of learning and instruction. (Victoria Arlak)

only once, but for scoring purposes the test itself is split into two equivalent subtests. Odd-numbered questions, for example, are compared with even-numbered questions, just as if they were complete tests in their own right. Since this method requires only one test and one administration of it, it is more convenient than the other two are, but it does have the disadvantage that the two subtests are, by definition, somewhat shorter. **split-half reliability** This fact allows random variation to be more of an issue in the half tests than in the whole test, which makes the test seem less reliable than the other methods do. When reliability is computed statistically, this disadvantage can be partly counterbalanced (Guilford & Fruchter, 1977), but the statistical procedures really only estimate what the other, more accurate methods can actually specify.

Reliability in Informal Observations   The notion of reliability permeates informal evaluations as well as tests, though it cannot be defined as precisely for the informal methods. Whenever teachers talk to students, for example, they hope—or assume—that they are gathering information about them that is consistent and in some sense reliable. Teachers assume that a student's comments during a class discussion, for instance, at least approximate his knowledge of the subject; that in a similar discussion on another occasion, he would make similar comments; and that if another, similar teacher conducted the discussion, he or she would get a similar impression of the student's level of knowledge. Even though in real life these assumptions do not always hold up, students' behaviors do show consistency, and in that way they do have reliability.

Validity

Whether teachers use formal tests or informal observations, their evaluations are valid if they measure what they claim to measure and if they therefore do help teachers reach significant decisions or conclusions about their students. As with reliability, the idea of validity can be illustrated most easily with formal tests. A teacher's history test, for example, is valid to the extent that it indeed measures how much students have learned history and therefore allows the teacher to decide what content he or she should cover next. A test of reading readiness is valid if it indeed distinguishes between children who can successfully begin reading instruction and those who cannot. Viewed from this perspective, no test is ever completely valid, but only more or less so, just as with reliability. Highly valid tests enable teachers to make good guesses, if not firm conclusions, about students' abilities, achievements, and interests.

Kinds of Validity   Also like reliability, validity can be assessed in several ways, each with its own advantages. If, for example, a test seems to measure what it is supposed to measure, it is said to have **face validity**. Most teacher-made tests have this quality: a history test contains questions about history, or a math test contains questions about math. But a test with face validity may not necessarily test the achievements that it is supposed to measure. A biology test may seem valid but contain only questions about the names of animals and plants. It may therefore not test the students' general understanding of the field, but only their abilities to memorize names and to figure out meanings from the many Latin word roots used in biology. A teacher could not in good conscience use such a test alone to judge students' success with biology.

     If a test is based on a more thorough analysis and sampling of an area of skill or knowledge, it is said to have **content validity**. Suppose that complete achievement in biology includes knowledge of certain biological principles and certain experimental techniques as well as knowledge of specific plant and animal names. Suppose, furthermore, that most biology teachers consider knowledge of the principles and experimental tech-

face validity

niques at least twice as important as knowledge of facts. Then a biology test that has content validity will contain items that draw on each of these major areas of the field, and in proportion to their relative importance. In practice, making such an analysis of the field is helped by using some taxonomy of educational objectives—for example, Benjamin Bloom's (1956) (see Chapter 7)—to allocate items, and judging their relative importance is helped by seeking a consensus of experts in the field. In many teaching situations, of course, the major—or even the only available—expert judge is the teacher.

content validity

A third type of validity is **criterion-related validity**, which refers to how well a test predicts some performance outside the test, regardless of the content of the test itself. A test of general vocabulary, for example, may, to a modest extent, predict success in high school biology, even though it may not contain any biological terms in it. If so, the test would lack content validity, but not criterion-related validity. The reasons for the success of such a seemingly irrelevant test make interesting psychological speculation and research, but the reasons themselves are not a necessary part of criterion-related validity.

criterion-related validity

If there are good theoretical reasons for the relationship between tests and final performance, the test is often said to have **construct validity**, meaning that the tests sorts individuals in the same way that the psychological theory on which it is based does. The Thematic Apperception Test for achievement motivation (see pages 314–315), for example, has construct validity. Why? Because the TAT results classify individuals in the same way that achievement theory does: a high scorer on the TAT test behaves as a high achievement–motivated person should behave.

construct validity

Validity in Informal Observations   Informal evaluations of students contain elements of these same kinds of validity. In casual conversations with students, for example, teachers often ask obvious questions to evaluate the students' progress in learning: "Do you know what _____ is?" or "What was the _____ story about?" Such questions have face validity, as discussed above. Even though they ask such questions, however, teachers realize that the answers cannot always be taken at face value—a student's replies may not show that she has learned but only that she can guess well or that she has overheard another student give the correct answer. Therefore teachers often also probe further, asking deeper and more representative questions: "Who were the characters in the story?" "What was its main theme?" And so on. To the extent that teachers cover the material fairly in their questions, the questions can be said to have content validity.

asking relevant questions

Still other questions and observations, however, may have little to do with content but serve only as predictors: for example, "Have you read the chapters?" Strictly speaking, the answer to this question tells nothing about what the student has actually learned but helps predict only what he or she *may* have learned. For this reason, the question has criterion-related validity. Most of the time, of course, the teacher has good reasons for using such questions to predict students' learning. The example given above may be based on the unstated principle that reading leads to learning. To the extent that such a principle constitutes a personal theory of learning, the question derived from it can be said to have construct validity.

In ordinary classroom dialogue, then, validity can occur in the same forms that it does in formal tests. But given the complexity and rapid flow of classroom interaction, identifying the types of validity and estimating their relative strengths are much more difficult than doing so for formal tests, in which the results at least "sit still" long enough to be analyzed. Nevertheless, both formal and informal evaluations share the same feature: if they are valid, they can offer teachers information that really does help them plan instruction and then gauge its success.

Usability

The concept of usability has little to do with psychological theories of measurement, but much to do with practical matters. A test or informal evaluation is *usable* to the extent that it can be given easily and that its results are clearly understandable to teachers, parents, and students. By this criterion, informal evaluation methods may perhaps be more usable than tests. For instance, a series of casual conversations with a student can evaluate him with very little special preparation by the teacher, and it provides common-sense "results" that usually everyone can understand. Unfortunately, casual conversations often fall down in their reliability and validity, so much so, in fact, that most psychologists and many teachers do not recommend them as a replacement for formal tests.

But the most reliable and valid forms of evaluations may not be able to be used by practicing teachers. The Stanford-Binet Intelligence Test (Terman, 1973), for example, has been shown repeatedly to predict success in school unusually reliably and accurately. But since it takes a skilled clinical psychologist to administer it and since it must be given to children individually, it has not been adopted widely in educational practice. Instead, schools generally use tests of ability that can be given in groups and administered by classroom teachers. The Otis-Lennon Mental Abilities Test (1970), for example, takes less than an hour to give to and score for several dozen students. The Quick-Word Test (1964) takes only fifteen minutes and gives an estimate of verbal intelligence, which is a major component of general intelligence. Such tests are much more usable and practical, but their advantage is gained at some loss in their reliability and validity.

(margin notes)

questions as predictors of behavior

ease and convenience

usability versus reliability and validity

The same tradeoffs can occur with teacher-made evaluations of students. The most reliable and valid methods may consist of long conversations with each student in the class, combined with several tests, essays, and other performances. Since such a thorough evaluation is impractical in most schools, teachers often compromise this ideal by giving fewer tests and essays, choosing questions that are scored relatively easily, and spending less time talking with each student. These compromises probably reduce the reliability and validity of evaluation, but they carry a big advantage in practicality. Teachers, after all, must evaluate students with the resources actually at their disposal at a given moment in time; they cannot do this job simply by wishing it could be done better.

TEACHER-MADE OBSERVATIONS

Even though evaluation often means "formal testing" to teachers and students, many educational goals simply cannot be assessed with paper-and-pencil tests. Consider the many motor skills that students often must learn. One student may learn to type in a high school business education course; another, to give injections to patients as part of a nursing course; still another, to operate a piece of earth-moving equipment as part of a company training program. For any of these, a written test can show only that the students know what they should do but not that they can or will actually do it at the appropriate time.

alternatives to formal tests

Or consider the common goal of teachers to influence their students' attitudes. Teachers may hope to generate more interest among their students in a subject, to create friendlier relationships with them, or to motivate them to work harder. Taking a test on such goals makes no sense because affective goals usually refer to what students typically do, rather than to what they can do on demand. Most teachers thus must evaluate at least some learning goals as they occur naturally, and by observing rather than testing them. The section below describes some techniques for doing this.

Informal Written Observations

One way to collect information about children consists of simply writing down what they do and say. If such an observation concerns a single, relatively short incident (say, five minutes or so), it is often called an **anecdote**. It if extends over a longer period of time (say, thirty minutes or more) and covers several incidents, it is more likely to be called a **running record**. To be useful, the anecdote or running record should focus as much as possible on specific, objective facts, rather than on the teacher's interpretation of the facts: it should say, for example, "John spent several

anecdotes and running records

minutes looking through his notes" rather than "John could not remember
what he learned." Space does not allow us to show a running record, but
examples of them can be found in Berk (1976) and Brandt (1972).

By definition, written observations can be made at any time during the
school day. But since they can be time consuming to do, teachers should
probably limit their use to behaviors that they have selected ahead of time
as being especially important or informative. Typically, an anecdote can
be recorded much more accurately if the teacher writes it down as soon as
possible after it occurs—at the end of the class rather than at the end of
the day, or at the end of the day rather than at the end of the week.
Accuracy also improves if the record includes many descriptive words, that
is, adjectives and adverbs, and explicitly mentions negative as well as
positive aspects of the incident. For more suggestions and examples of this
method, see Cohen (1978).

For classroom evaluations, written records probably help the most in
identifying behavioral trends: how often and in what way the child behaves in a certain way. Does she tend to be shy or aggressive or studious?
And if so, what particular circumstances trigger these behaviors? Any one
anecdote, of course, may reveal at the same time more than one of these
identifying trends   qualities, or even contradictory ones. Ignoring these ambiguities, in fact,
in behavior   can lead to some overly simplified impressions of the children. One child
may be labeled "aggressive," for example, because the teacher collects
three written instances of aggression, when in fact these same instances
may be interpreted in other ways as well. To some extent, collecting more
written observations guards against this problem, but since teachers have
only limited time to do so, some risk of jumping to conclusions always
accompanies the use of this method.

Check Lists

A **check list** is a method for measuring the frequency of occurrence of
particular behaviors by noting their occurrence on a prearranged list of
behaviors. This technique provides a simple way to record specific classroom behaviors or outcomes of behaviors. Teachers of young children, for
example, may wish to know which phonic skills that the children have
learned and which they have not: in this case they can use a check list of
all possible phonic skills, marking off the ones that the children seem to
know already. Or a high school teacher of music may wish to know how
a student plays the clarinet: to do so, the teacher can construct a check
list of all the skills relevant to good playing (phrasing, tone quality, memory,
and so on) and credit the student with those that he displays. In either
case, the check list requires very little writing and comparatively simple
judgments by the teacher, but its use is limited to the purposes for which
it is made. Whenever an instructional goal consists of a series of specific,

observable steps, check lists can help evaluate it. Or whenever a goal results in a product that has clearly identifiable parts, check lists can help evaluate the product: a wooden cabinet built in a shop class, for example, or a business letter typed according to a standard format. Check lists probably should be avoided whenever the elements of a task are unclear, variable in content, or changeable over time. They may not work well, for example, in evaluating students' emotional moods or motivations, unless these can be stated in rather specific, behavioral terms.

One way to reduce these sources of bias is to use *time sampling*. With **time sampling** the teacher uses a check list for only specified, appropriate intervals—every thirty minutes, say, for five minutes at a time. Doing so helps make more manageable the observations of frequently or continually occurring behaviors: instead of having to note every occurrence of a social interaction, for example, teachers need note them only when and if they occur at the specified intervals. In between these times, teachers can shift their attention to other aspects of teaching and student behavior. Time sampling also reduces biases in keeping records of relatively uncommon behaviors. Such behaviors, by their nature, stand out unusually clearly from their more common, neighboring behaviors. Teachers are therefore apt to "overnotice" them, and check list records of them may exaggerate their true frequency of occurrence and importance. A student may behave rudely, for example, less often than he shows friendliness, but the teacher may nonetheless notice it more faithfully than she does the friendliness. Time sampling forces the teacher to record the rudeness only if it happens during one of the specified intervals, and in this way it helps keep the behavior in perspective.

time sampling

reducing biases in observations

Ratings

Instead of marking behaviors or qualities as either present or absent, **ratings** measure them by comparing them with different amounts of particular dimensions. How much time, for example, does a young child spend at silent reading? Or how well does an older student speak in front of her class? Usually a rating suggests several choices from which the teacher must choose, and these choices form a scale along a single dimension of behavior—"always-sometimes-never," "good-fair-poor," or whatever is appropriate for the item.

In rating general attitudes, teachers sometimes find it helpful to combine the ratings from several scales into a single, more global rating. "Liking for school," for example, may be estimated by combining ratings of several of its elements: participation in discussions, promptly completing assignments, listening to directions, helping others with their work, and the like. These can be combined by converting each to a so-called *Likert scale,* named after the psychologist who first thoroughly studied and publicized the technique. **Likert scales** assign descriptive adjectives

Likert scale

and numerical values—usually one through five—to each point on a rating scale. If the highest numerical value is always assigned to correspond to the strongest indicator of the attitude, then the individual scales can simply be added together to estimate the strength of the general attitude. In the example above, "liking for school" can be estimated by the teacher's

combining rating
scales

ratings of the student's participation, promptness with assignments, attentiveness to directions, and help given to fellow students with their work.

Ratings have had a long history in educational evaluation, as well as a long history of biases (see Brandt, 1972, chap. 4 for a review of these). A variety of research shows, for example, that individuals who use rating scales are influenced by a **halo effect**, the tendency to respond as though

halo effect

the person being rated were all good or all bad. Raters show various other response preferences as well: some tend to rate at the extremes, but others at the middle. Some rate personal qualities more extremely than they do political and social opinions. Some raters even show a position bias—responding at a certain distance from the left or right end, regardless of its meaning.

But by following certain rules, one can minimize these biases and make ratings a useful technique for classroom evaluations:

1. *The statements or ideas being rated should contain as many observable behaviors as possible, rather than general traits or qualities.* Rating children on how often they read silently, for example, is easier than rating them on how much they like reading in general.
2. *The series of statements to be rated should be balanced so that some refer to positive or desirable behaviors and others refer to negative ones.* If one statement asks for a rating of frequency of occurrence of friendly

guidelines for
reducing biases in
ratings

conversation, for example, the next might ask for a rating of conflicts with peers. Balancing the positive quality of one item with the negative quality of the next will help counteract ratings' halo effect.
3. *The scales used for each rating should be balanced so that the desirable qualities are marked on the left about as often as they are marked on the right.* Suppose that one item asks for a rating of "reads silently," and the next one asks for a rating of "turns in homework on time"; and suppose that the most desirable rating is "always" for both of these items. This desirable extreme should not always be placed on the same end of the rating scale for both items but should be varied: left end for one, right end for the other.
4. *The positions on a rating scale should truly reflect just one dimension of behavior.* Here is an item that violates this rule:

Shows Aggression

☐ Every day ☐ Once a week ☐ Moderately ☐ Once a month ☐ Never

Four out of five positions on the rating scale reflect the dimension of frequency, but the middle one appears to refer instead to intensity of aggression.

With such precautions, ratings can help teachers evaluate many behaviors inaccessible to teachermade, paper-and-pencil tests. For example, they can be used to assess social behavior in children, their motivation to learn, or their attitudes toward work (Pedulla, 1980). Check lists can sometimes serve these purposes, too, but check lists lend themselves better to "all or nothing" categorizing of behavior, rather than to judgments of amount, frequency, or intensity. And written observations can sometimes evaluate such goals, but what written records gain in verbal richness, they may lose in lack of precision and representativeness. Each method has its own strengths and limitations, which are summarized in Table 13–1.

Inventories of Interests

Inventories of interests are structured questionnaires that ask the test takers to describe their interests in a variety of activities, usually vocationally related ones. In one widely used questionnaire of this type, the test takers use a three-point scale to rate over three hundred activities and jobs: carpenter, art teacher, play golf, read poetry, and so on (Strong & Campbell, 1974). For each item, the test takers indicate whether they like doing that activity, are indifferent to doing it, or dislike doing it. The results are compiled into general areas of interest, which can give students

assessing vocational interests

Table 13–1 Comparative Advantages of Different Observation Methods

Method	Advantages	Disadvantages
Informal written records	Provide detail and flexibility of content.	Require much writing, can obscure similarities among incidents because of too much detail.
Check lists	Judge frequency of occurrence of behavior, can apply common standards to many incidents, are easy to use.	Lack detail, may ignore subtle differences among incidents.
Ratings	Compare individuals, judge amount of general qualities and behaviors, are easy to use.	Lack detail, may be biased.

and teachers some ideas about what vocation each student might like. Such an inventory is, strictly, standardized rather than truly teacher-made, as are the other evaluation methods described in this chapter. But they deserve mention here because they help guide students' educational choices—one of the main reasons for evaluating learning. There are many standardized interest inventories, which are geared to a variety of age groups and general types of interests; for a brief summary of some of the principal ones, see Lien (chap. 5, 1980).

TEACHER-MADE TESTS

For a number of reasons, tests remain the most popular form of classroom evaluation. Since they provide standard experiences to which all students must respond, they promise a relatively fair way to judge student learning. And for many objectives, tests yield comparatively large amounts of information, from comparatively large numbers of students and for comparatively small amounts of effort by the teacher. Different kinds of tests, however, combine these advantages in different ways and to different degrees. The right test for any one course, class, and teacher therefore depends on the educational purposes it is supposed to serve. Is it to diagnose the knowledge that students bring into the course, to evaluate instructional progress midway through, or to summarize general student success afterward? As pointed out at the beginning of this chapter, the answer to this question affects how closely the test items will be tied to the specific instructional objectives of the course. But there are two other issues as well: first, is the purpose of the test to compare students according to an absolute standard or with one another? Second, what kinds of content objectives or goals does the teacher have for his or her students? The answers to these questions will determine the best kind of test. Let us look at them one at a time.

Norm-referenced Versus Criterion-referenced Tests

uses of norm-referenced tests

When tests are used to compare one student with another, they are called **norm referenced**. But when they are used to compare each student according to an absolute standard, they are called **criterion referenced** (Nitko, 1980). If we say that on a math test a student scores in the top third of his class, then we are using his score in a norm-referenced way. The individual's score is, as the term implies, "referred to" or compared with what is "normal" or average behavior for the group. Norm referencing tells something about the comparative goodness or badness of the student's performance.

At its best, teacher-made evaluation includes feedback to students that helps them in further learning. (David S. Strickler/The Picture Cube)

Because it emphasizes comparisons, norm referencing finds many uses in identifying diversity among students and aiding their placement in educational programs and the working world. For example, norm-referenced tests help select which students belong to particular ability groups in elementary classrooms, which students take particular courses in high school, and which universities they are qualified to attend. These situations all demand differentiating among individuals, which is the job that norm-referenced tests do best.

Tests used in this way, however, do not indicate the student's absolute level of performance. The student mentioned above might be in the top third of an advanced algebra course or merely in the top third of a remedial mathematics course. Because performance in these two classes is judged according to two very different standards, the norm-referenced information tells little about what a student actually accomplishes in the two situations. That kind of information requires criterion referencing—literally, referring or judging results according to some criterion or standard, rather than comparing them with other students' results. Instead of saying that a student scored in the top third of his math class, for example, criterion-referenced results specify how many math problems he scored

limitations of norm-referenced tests

correctly, what types of problems they are, and whether or not these are sufficient to proceed to the next level or unit of mathematics instruction. Criterion referencing is therefore not as interested in displaying diversity among students as is norm referencing (Popham, 1978).

Because of the kind of information they give, criterion-referenced tests can be especially helpful in planning and revising instructions. They may also reduce competition among students, since such tests evaluate mastery of content rather than performance as compared with that of their classmates. Since everyone can, in principle, achieve the highest possible mark, students have an incentive to help each other learn or at least have no inhibition against doing so. For certain learners and situations, therefore, the method may enhance achievement as well as good feelings in the group.

uses of criterion-referenced tests

Criterion referencing has, however, been criticized for how well it actually achieves its stated goals (Ebel, 1971). Because criterion referencing depends on a very close tie between the test and the instruction that goes with it, the method may be highly influenced by the particular interests or biases of the teacher using it. If a particular history teacher believes that "war" is the key to understanding history and if he wishes to evaluate students of history using criterion-referenced methods, then he is likely to load his tests with questions about war. If, on the other hand, another history teacher believes that the "economics of agriculture" is very important to understanding history, she is more likely to load her tests with questions on this topic. A student who reaches an acceptable standard in one class may thus not reach it in the other. As current and former students, most of us, at one time or another, have probably been on the receiving end of this kind of bias. The problem is aggravated by criterion referencing because of the tendency of those using that method to compare test results with teaching goals.

limitations of criterion-referenced tests

Some teachers also question whether criterion referencing can actually work with all instructional goals. The method seems to work best with goals that can be specified in clear, behavioral terms and that have agreed-on levels of minimum acceptable performance: typing, perhaps, or certain aspects of math learning. The relative clarity of the elements of these skills lend themselves to comparisons with an absolute standard. "Typing well," for example, usually means a group of observable behaviors—accurately striking individual keys, then forming individual words, then copying familiar text, and then typing difficult text. Making progress toward this goal, furthermore, usually means learning each of these skills to some minimum acceptable level before the next one can be attempted. Both of these make criterion-referenced evaluation of typing relatively easy, as well as constructive.

But teachers usually do not restrict their goals to specific or sequential tasks. Typically they also seek to "develop knowledge" of a subject, for example, or to "improve a student's social skills." Can these goals be translated into specific instructional objectives with minimum levels of acceptable performance? Advocates of criterion referencing claim that they can, but for nebulous cases like these they have not convinced as many educators as they have for the more precise ones. According to many educators, some goals may be both legitimate and inherently "fuzzy minded," and these may have to be evaluated in norm-referenced ways.

Despite these problems, criterion-referenced tests do contribute to the evaluation of learning. By avoiding comparisons among students, they may promote motivation in students who feel especially anxious about competition or who especially fear failure. By indicating particular learning behaviors that the student has acquired or failed to acquire, such tests can also suggest how instruction should proceed or be revised, obviously a major concern of teachers. A student's errors and successes on such a test, of course, are not equivalent to the thinking he or she does in taking the test (guessing rather than reasoning), but they do give clues to it.

Table of Specifications

A good classroom test must touch on all the goals of a unit of study and do so in about the same proportions as the unit itself has. A so-called **table of specifications** of the test helps accomplish this task. The table lays out clearly the relationships among the topics taught in a particular unit and the cognitive activities or skills needed for each of them. To make such a table, the teacher needs both a list of the content headings and some sort of taxonomy of educational goals. This book has described three such taxonomies: that by David Krathwohl for affective objectives (pages 203–204) and those by Benjamin Bloom (pages 202–203) and Robert Gagné (pages 193–202) for cognitive objectives. Table 13–2 is a simplified table of specifications for a hypothetical unit in language arts, analyzed according to Gagné's hierarchy of intellectual skills. The table shows the different kinds of cognitive activity required for each topic in the unit.

Table 13–2 Table of Specifications for a Unit of Language Arts

Topic	Knowledge	Discrimination learning	Concept learning	Problem solving	Totals
Poetry	4	2			6
Short stories	4	2	1		7
Novels	2	2			4
Creative writing			2	1	3
Totals	10	6	3	1	20

By making explicit the various thinking skills needed in the unit, such a table helps teachers construct test items that represent the content they have been teaching. According to the information in Table 13–2, about six learning goals out of twenty require discrimination learning, whereas only one out of twenty requires the higher-order skill of problem solving. The table also shows that three learning goals out of the total pertain to creative writing, whereas seven of them refer to short stories. By constructing test items that draw on these topics and thinking skills roughly in the proportions of the table, the test will fairly reflect the content of the unit—it will, in the sense discussed earlier, have content validity.

sampling content fairly

Note that some topics, maybe even most of them, may draw on more than one level of cognitive activity and that identifying the higher levels may prove difficult for many topics. If a student is supposed to "compare and contrast two novels by Charles Dickens," does this goal require problem-solving skills in Gagné's sense, or more conceptual learning? Some psychologists are not sure that such distinctions can be made reliably (for example, Krathwohl & Payne, 1971). In teaching practice, though, they may not have to be. Distinguishing the higher levels in each may not be as important as making sure to include some sort of high-level skills. A table of specifications helps teachers do this by making explicit the relative biases in a unit of instruction. Teachers can then construct individual test items that reflect these emphases, though as will be seen in the next section, they must make some further choices here, too.

including higher-level cognitive skills

KINDS OF TEST QUESTIONS

In composing test items, teachers must choose between *objective questions* and *essays,* though within each of these broad categories are other types of items from which to choose. Since each type has its own advantages and disadvantages, the best choices will depend on the purposes of the test and the unit of study for which it is designed. For many tests, a variety of item types probably most accurately reflects the variety of instructional goals, but teachers should decide this for themselves with each test they write.

objective questions and essays

True-False Items

True-false items are sentences or statements that students must mark as either true or false, right or wrong, correct or incorrect.

Pros and Cons   Because true-false items can be devised and administered relatively quickly, they can cover a relatively wide range of content. Some studies have found that in a given period of time students can answer about 50 percent more true-false items than they can multiple-choice items (Ebel, 1975; Frisbie, 1973). Unfortunately, the statement format of true-false questions lends itself most easily to testing the simplist kind of educational goals, namely, factual knowledge; devising items that test complex cognitive processes is more difficult, though it can be done. One way to do so is to present the students with a short problem or situation that they must analyze in order to answer several true-false items that follow it:

Two men have sixteen jugs of water. The jugs come in three different ◄ sizes—five gallons, one gallon, and one quart. The men must carry four and one-quarter gallons to a car one mile down the road, in order to fill the car's radiator.

T   F   1. The men need five jugs to mix the water.
T   F   2. The men need just two jugs to mix, but three to carry.
T   F   3. If the car were closer, they would need fewer jugs.

Rather than testing recall of facts, these items require analyzing a problem. In this case, the student must analyze ways of mixing water and the difference between carrying it and mixing it.

True-false items are often contaminated by guessing. If students know nothing at all about the content of such questions and if they guess on all of them anyway, they can still expect to score about 50 percent correct just by chance. This chance score can be reduced to zero, however, by applying a correction formula to the results:

correction for guessing

$$\text{True score} = \text{Number right} - \text{Number wrong}$$

But such a formula does not stop "aggressive" guessers from getting a higher score on such a test than do cautious guessers. Why? Because in reality most guessing is not strictly random but is based on at least minimal knowledge, combined with unusual willingness to guess. This gives a special advantage to those students who have relatively little knowledge of a subject. This problem is accentuated because true-false questions test recognition (identification of correct content) rather than recall (memory of content without cues).

Guidelines for Use   Despite this problem, true-false items can contribute to effective evaluations of students, especially when a wide range of content must be tested and when the teacher's effort to score should be simplified as much as possible. Following a few guidelines can help ensure that true-false items are used effectively:

1. *Avoid using extreme terms.* These include words like "all," "none," "always," "never," "the very most," or "the very least." The following items violate this rule:

T   F   The weather in Nova Scotia is always cold.   ◄
T   F   No plant ever grows in the Arctic region.

Since few facts in life are "always" something or "not ever" something else, statements that use these terms can usually be assumed to be false.

Even students with only modest test-taking skills know this fact, though perhaps it is not safe to say that they "always" do!

2. *Avoid using indefinite modifiers.* These have the opposite problem of the extreme terms: they tend to be always true. Consider these items:

▶ T F   The weather in Nova Scotia is sometimes cold (or "often" or "occasionally").

T F   Some plants grow in the Arctic region (or "occasionally" or "a few").

Since most facts are true at least "occasionally," "sometimes," or "often," true-false items that use terms like these are likely to be true, regardless of their content. Since amounts and quantities affect the truth or falsity of these items, they should include specific amounts and quantities as often as possible. The following, therefore, improve on the original examples:

▶ T F   The weather in Nova Scotia is cold for about three months per year.

T F   About one-tenth of 1 percent of the world's plant specimens grow in the Arctic region.

improving true-
false questions

3. *Phrase true-false items as simple declarative sentences.* Any other grammatical construction poses special reading and logical problems, which are not usually the skills that the teacher is testing. Complex sentences, in addition, can confound students by seeming to test more than one idea at a time. For example:

▶ T F   Abraham Lincoln, who was the first president of the United States, helped hold together the Union during the Civil War.

In this example, the main clause ("Abraham Lincoln . . . held together the Union") is true, but the subordinate one is not ("the first president"). How, then, is the student to mark it? Although many true-false items do not contain such obvious factual goofs, they may use complicated grammar irrelevant to the subject being tested. For example:

▶ T F   With no exceptions, the Periodic Table of the Elements does not give unusual information.

The double negatives in this statement translate roughly into the following positive statement:

▶ T F   For ordinary cases, the Periodic Table of the Elements gives typical information.

Given its redundance, this item probably is true, but its original form tests the logical ability to determine the logic of sentences written in English, rather than knowledge of the Periodic Table.

Multiple-Choice Items

Multiple-choice items have two parts: a *stem,* or bit of initial information, and several *options* from which the student selects the best or right one. The stem may be phrased as a question, a statement, or a short paragraph.

Pros and Cons   Despite the recurring criticism of them, multiple-choice items have been used to evaluate numerous cognitive skills, from simply defining terms to comparing subtle and abstract ideas. Table 13–3 lists several different cognitive skills that multiple-choice items can evaluate. Most of these refer to relatively complex skills. In this regard, multiple-choice items have a major advantage over other item types, which tend to work best for a more restricted range of skills.

Such items have some of the same problems with guessing that true-false items have, but to a lesser extent. With four options per stem, for example, a student can expect to get one-quarter or 25 percent of the items correct merely by chance, rather than 50 percent, as with true-false items. This means that multiple-choice items give comparatively less advantage to clever guessers, whether or not a correction formula is used to reduce the guessing score to zero.

Multiple-choice items are not foolproof, however. They require relatively large amounts of careful reading—a skill that not all students have and that not all teachers may want to test. Sometimes small prepositions or conjunctions can entirely transform the meaning of an item, yet be missed by even conscientious and well-prepared students. For example:

Table 13–3 Uses of Multiple-Choice Questions

Use	Sample question stem
Defining terms	What means the same as . . . ?
Purpose	What is the most important reason for . . . ?
Cause	What causes . . . to happen?
Effect	If . . . is done, what will happen?
Association	What behaviors usually accompany the . . . stage?
Recognition of error	Which of the following is *not* correct?
Identification of error	What principle does this . . . violate?
Evaluation	What is the best reason for . . . ?
Difference	How are these . . . different?
Similarity	How are these . . . the same?
Arrangement	Which sequence [e.g., of ideas, procedures] below is correct?
Incomplete arrangement	In the sequence below, which step has been left out?
Common principle	What is the principle relating each of the following?
Controversial subjects	Although people disagree about . . . , those who support it do so because . . . .

Source: Charles Mosier, M. C. Myers, and H. G. Price, "Suggestions for the Construction of Multiple-Choice Items," *Educational and Psychological Measurement*, 5 (1945), 264–267.

▶ Which of the following books was written _____ John F. Kennedy?
1. *Profiles in Courage*   3. *A Tale of Two Cities*
2. *Thousand Days*   4. *The Watergate Scandals*

The answer to this item depends on what word goes in the blank of the stem. If it is "by," then the answer is *Profiles in Courage;* but if it is "about," then the answer is *Thousand Days* (written by Arthur M. Schlesinger, Jr., *about* Kennedy). The student must pay close attention to such details of meaning in multiple-choice items, a feature that has sometimes been criticized (for example, Burns, 1979).

In addition, multiple-choice items test only a student's recognition of correct answers; that is, they test whether he or she can identify correct content from some larger array of content. They do not force recall (remembering content without any cues at all) or reconstruction (assembling correct content from some larger array that includes its elements, but not in their completed form). Recall and reconstruction probably require more thorough learning by the student, but they can be evaluated only by items in which the student must supply the answers himself or herself—short-answer questions and essays. This restriction notwithstanding, multiple-choice items can still challenge students, at least judging by the numbers who make errors in answering some of them.

Guidelines for Use   Teachers can easily construct poor multiple-choice questions, of course. Good questions take comparatively large amounts of effort to compose. For this reason, among others, they will probably never completely replace the other kinds of items used in classroom evaluation, despite their versatility. At the same time, the advantages of multiple-choice questions are real and make them worth at least some of the teacher's time to create. Here are a few guidelines to help in this process:

1. *Use clear, concise language in the stem.* Just as with true-false items, language ability itself should not usually be tested, but rather knowledge of content and particular thinking abilities. Therefore teachers should avoid complex grammatical constructions or unnecessary information when composing multiple-choice questions. Such questions already require more reading and verbal skills than many other item types do, even when well constructed.

2. *Choose reasonable alternatives for options.* Including foolish or unlikely options serves no useful purpose, since no reasonably intelligent student will choose them. Consider this item, which violates this rule:

▶ Who invented the telephone?
1. Thomas Edison   3. Sir Isaac Watt
2. Alexander Graham Bell   4. Mickey Mouse

The first three alternatives all refer to famous inventors and therefore compete for the student's attention. If he knows rather little about the history of the telephone, he may well pick one of the incorrect options (1

(margin notes: problems with multiple-choice items; improving multiple-choice questions)

or 3) rather than the correct one, option 2. But the fourth alternative probably will not receive serious consideration except by a very careless or sarcastic student. For practical purposes, it may as well be left out of the item entirely.

3. *Make options generally similar in form and content.* This idea really extends the recommendation made above to be reasonable in choosing options. Options that have many more words than usual, for example, tend to be chosen more often that others are, regardless of their content (Chase, 1964). On the other hand, options that refer to significantly different domains of knowledge, objects, or activities tend to make the item as a whole easier to answer, whether or not the alien option is the correct one. For example:

Which of the following is a "mammal"?　◀
1. snake　　3. car
2. dog　　　4. robin

Option 3 can be eliminated simply by knowing that a car is a machine and therefore is not any type of animal, including a mammal. Knowing which of the other three options to choose requires more knowledge, since they all belong to the same general group, animals.

To ensure homogeneity in form and content, teachers sometimes use options like "all of these" or "none of these" in multiple-choice items. By definition, these options refer to the same sort of content contained in the other alternatives, but they do not necessarily improve the item as a whole by doing so. Using "all of these" really reduces the thinking needed to answer correctly, because the student needs only to evaluate each of the remaining options in order to decide whether "all of these" is correct. Using "none of these" does not cause this particular problem, but it can create ambiguities about whether the remaining options are really good enough to be "right." Consider this item:

When did the war in Vietnam end?　◀
1. 1968　　3. 1976
2. 1972　　4. none of these

The end of this war can be dated from the final withdrawal of U.S. troops in 1976. But a case can be made that it really ended over a period of time, beginning with the gradual de-escalations of the war around 1968 after President Lyndon B. Johnson's decision not to run for reelection. By including "none of these" as an option, the item gives the impression that it may refer to this process rather than to any conventional, single date.

4. *Make multiple-choice items more difficult by making the options more similar in content, and less difficult by making the options more different in content.* Consider these two versions of the same question:

Easier: Which of the following compounds is produced by photosynthesis?　◀
1. oxygen　　3. citric acid
2. iron　　　4. ice

▶ *Harder:* Which of the following compounds is produced by photosynthesis?
1. oxygen   3. helium
2. nitrogen gas   4. hydrogen

The first version requires that the student know only that photosynthesis produces some sort of gas; since oxygen is the only gas offered as an option, it must be the correct choice. The second version, however, requires knowing not only that photosynthesis produces a gas but also the particular kinds of gas it produces. Because it offers more similar options than the first version does, the second version is more difficult.

Completion Items

Instead of asking students to select the correct response, completion items ask them to supply one. The item can be phrased either as a sentence with a blank for a missing word or phrase or as a question calling for a brief answer.

▶ The southern tip of South America is called _____.
What is the name of the southern tip of South America? _____.

Pros and Cons In either form, such items avoid calling on the recognition of correct responses, on which the other item types rely so heavily, and instead demand the recall and reconstruction of information. In most memory research, these processes have proved to be more difficult than recognition memory: recall requires dredging up information, using relatively few cues. But this does not necessarily make the testing of recall better or more important than the testing of recognition. Which skill should be evaluated probably depends on how the students will typically apply what they have learned. In normal reading behavior, for example, children may more often need to recognize the letters of the alphabet than to recall them, but in addition and subtraction they may more often need to recall the facts. If so, they should be evaluated using test items that reflect this difference. Completion items can help do this by supplementing other, more recognition-dependent items.

By their nature, though, completion items are apt to be ambiguous: despite careful efforts by the teacher, students continually think of unusual, but legitimate words or phrases that he or she has not expected. Consider this completion item:

▶ A car engine burns _____.

Most students would probably answer "gasoline," but some may put down "oil" or "air," and strictly speaking, they would be right. In such cases, the teacher must judge how to credit unexpected answers. Both the room for ambiguity and the teacher's need to make judgments increase as the completion term becomes longer. An item that requires an entire phrase or sentence to complete can usually be answered in more different ways than does one that requires only a single word. For this reason, completion items are better for testing basic, factual knowledge than complex cognitive skills, better, in fact, than other item types are.

Guidelines for Use   Within these constraints, however, completion items can give relatively reliable and valid information about classroom learning. This is especially true if teachers follow a few guidelines:

1. *Answers to completion items should contain as few words as possible.* Consider the two versions of this item:

Worse: To start a car, first _____. ◀
Better: To start a car, first put the key in the _____.

The first version can reasonably be answered in more than one way; the second leaves less room for uncertainty. At its extreme, allowing too many words for the completion response causes the item to lose its content validity. Here is one that has this problem:

Compared with other cities, New York _____. ◀

What answer is called for here? That New York has more people? More crime? More theaters? By allowing so much variability in its response, the item also becomes nearly impossible to score.

2. *The words demanded or omitted by a completion item should be only the crucial ones.* Consider these two versions of one item:

Worse: Most _____ scientists believe that humans evolved from _____. ◀
Better: Most natural scientists believe that humans evolved from _____.

The first version would be acceptable only if it really were important to know what *kind* of scientists have opinions about evolution, as well as *what* their beliefs generally are. Although both of these objectives may indeed be important for some science courses, a majority are probably more concerned with the nature of evolution itself rather than who believes in it. The second version of the item reflects this emphasis better than the first one does.

3. *If a completion item borrows an idea from a textbook, make sure that it is paraphrased significantly.* Otherwise the teacher may simply test the student's rote memory of the text. What makes a paraphrase "significant" may vary with the teacher, the student, and the course. If in doubt, the wording of an idea probably should be changed more rather than less; greater variance with the text can better ensure that students respond to the idea in the item, rather than its surface form.

improving completion questions

Essay Questions

Essay questions ask students to write a composition on a particular topic or theme. Depending on the question, the composition may be relatively short (perhaps only a half-page) or relatively long (entire notebooks).

Because of differences in students' backgrounds, a set of test questions may not be experienced as the "same" by all students. (Peter Menzel/Stock, Boston)

Pros and Cons   Unlike any of the item types described thus far, essay questions call for relatively large amounts of skill in written communication, along with knowledge of the subject. This fact is considered a blessing by some and a curse by others (for a review of both sides, see Chase, 1978, chap. 7). Supporters of essay questions argue that they test complex cognitive skills by making the student organize a potentially large body of information. Like completion items, essay questions require the more

uses of essay questions

difficult memory processes of recall and reconstruction: a good essay answer therefore may reflect more thorough learning than do answers to recognition-oriented item types. And, of course, essay questions can be written relatively quickly, though the teacher pays for this advantage after the test, by working harder at marking them. Presumably during this hard work, the teacher has a relatively good chance to perceive the students' thought processes and to give them lots of partial credit for merely "middling" answers.

   But for some teachers and psychologists, the basic feature of essay questions—their emphasis on writing—is a drawback. Most of the time, the critics argue, teachers do not teach writing skills in their courses, and yet essays hold students responsible anyway for learning them. As important as writing ability may be, it may not be fair to evaluate students' thinking and learning according to this particular skill. This may be so, assert the critics, especially since complex thinking skills can, with some effort, also be tested with objective questions, and most notably with multiple-choice items. These often have higher reliabilities than essay questions do, whose latitude of acceptable responses can make marking difficult and variable. Finally, the critics point out, essay tests usually do not cover as much content as objective tests do, since they take so much time to answer. This fact may undermine their advantage of forcing active recall and organization of information.

Essays are probably not efficient for assessing basic knowledge—objectives that call for "listing," "naming," or "stating," for instance. But given the difficulties of writing good objective questions, essay questions may often make the best practical choice for assessing complex thinking skills. They can help whenever an instructional goal calls for any of these processes:

explaining a process or relationship
solving a problem
evaluating qualities, ideas, or events
organizing pros and cons
comparing ideas or viewpoints

Guidelines for Use   For testing such complex skills, essay questions can be made more reliable and valid by following these guidelines:

1. *Focus each essay question on a specific objective.* Relatively specific questions can be answered more clearly and therefore can also be marked more reliably. Compare these two versions of one essay question:

Worse: Discuss the evolution of humans.   ◀
Better: Explain the roles of tools and bipedalism in the evolution of humans.

The first version can be answered in more ways than the second one can. Although the first one's greater flexibility can help evaluate students' originality of response, most units of study on evolution probably focus
more on the acquisition, organization, and evaluation of existing knowledge about the topic. And the second version tests these kinds of goals more directly than does the first.

improving essay
questions

2. *Indicate all relevant information about the writing style, length of expected answer, and relative importance or weighting of the question.* Given the time that answering essay questions can take, students have a right to know as much as possible about how to tailor their answers to these constraints. Do you want the answer in outline form or fully formed prose? A half-page per question or several pages? Is the question worth 50 percent of the test? If so, it will get more careful attention than if it is worth only 5 percent of it. Unless students know these parameters, they can always claim that they did not know what you wanted in answering a question— and they may be right.

3. Devise a standard scoring formula to help mark essay questions more reliably and validly. Before marking any answers, analyze the question itself to decide what elements it should ideally contain and the relative importance of each. To do so, some teachers find it helpful to write out an ideal answer to each essay question; this usually contains the main elements that the teacher considers important and sometimes also clarifies any assumptions he or she may have.

A scoring formula for the essay on the evolution of humans might look like this:

Relative weightings	*Topics*
1	Knowledge of basic evolutionary mechanisms
1	Knowledge of role of tools
1	Knowledge of role of bipedalism
2	Comparison of the two factors

Total = 5

The weightings are relative, not absolute: if a question counts more than five points or 5 percent on a test, they can be adjusted to reflect this fact. The weightings themselves are somewhat subjective, but using them helps the teacher search for the appropriate elements in each student's answers and give them about equal credit wherever they occur.

4. Mark all answers to the same question before going on to the next question. Doing so helps counteract the halo effect (see page 366), which often can be found in essay exams. If all questions for one student's paper are marked in sequence before going on to the next student's paper, his early essays are likely to set the tone for the marks given on his later essays, even if they do not deserve to do so. Such first impressions created during marking may either help or hinder students' overall grades, but either way they do not necessarily reflect their true performance.

The halo effect is a response to *who* the students are (or who the teacher *thinks* they are) rather than to what they say or can do. The halo effect is especially difficult to combat in marking essay tests because, in truth, such tests allow a relatively large leeway of acceptability of responses and therefore do not constrain the teacher's marking practices as much as do **halo effect** objective item types. All of the suggestions made above are ways of preventing the halo bias by structuring both the students' responses and the teacher's marking of the responses. But the effect of bias is strong nonetheless, and possibly not even under voluntary control. Even an inadvertent glance at the student's name on an essay paper can influence the teacher's opinion, which leads to a final suggestion: try not to see whose paper you are currently marking. Sometimes even covering the name with your hand can help or folding it down or asking students to write their names on the backs of all their exam sheets.

This chapter has looked at how teachers can evaluate student learning, both formally and informally. We have seen that many techniques are available, including some that supplement the most traditional method, namely, teachermade tests. Each method has its own strengths and limitations, and these qualities should ideally be related to the teacher's instructional goals. At its best, classroom evaluation helps both teachers and students to know how well they are meeting these goals and what more they need to do to ensure success with them.

But evaluation serves more than just these purposes. The next chapter will consider two others: first, to inform various people outside the classroom how well the students are achieving and, second, to make long-run predictions of student performance in various areas of activity. These needs are met partly by teachers' grading practices and partly by the proper use and interpretation of standardized tests, and to these topics we now shall turn.

Key Points

1. Evaluation consists of information about student behavior and learning that is judged according to certain standards.

2. Measurement refers to methods of quantifying behavior, often as a basis for evaluation.

3. Good evaluations must be reliable, valid, and usable.

4. Both reliability and validity can be assessed in several different ways.

5. Evaluations may involve teacher-made observations as well as tests.

6. Teacher-made observations can include informal written records, check lists of behaviors, ratings, and inventories of interest.

7. Teacher-made tests can be either norm referenced or criterion referenced.

8. A table of specifications helps in allocating content to test items.

9. Tests can be composed of various kinds of questions: true-false, multiple-choice, completion, and essays.

10. Each type of question has its own particular advantages and disadvantages.

Case Study

Evaluating Learning About Mammals

A teacher wanted to evaluate how well her tenth-grade students had learned a unit about mammals. She used several strategies for doing so, one of which was a rather elaborate test on the topic. The test included several types of items, three of which are presented below:

T F   1. Mammals always live on land.

      51. Compared with most reptiles and fish, mammals tend to give birth at any one time to

    a. fewer young.
    b. about as many young.
    c. more young.
    d. no generalization is accurate.

99. In one page, discuss mammals and how they differ from other sorts of animals.

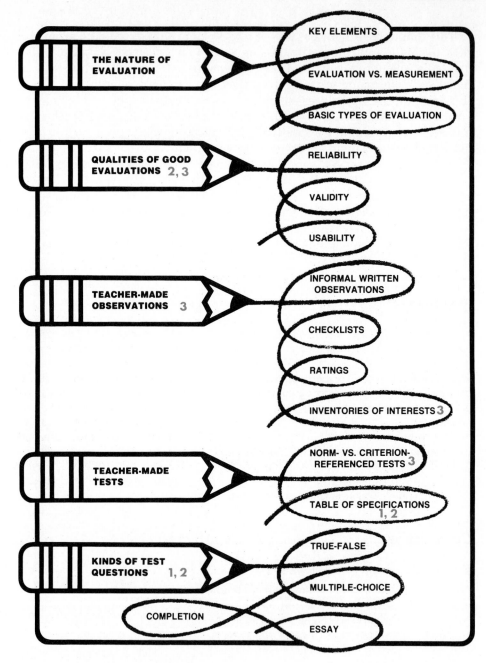

THE NATURE OF EVALUATION
- KEY ELEMENTS
- EVALUATION VS. MEASUREMENT
- BASIC TYPES OF EVALUATION

QUALITIES OF GOOD EVALUATIONS 2, 3
- RELIABILITY
- VALIDITY
- USABILITY

TEACHER-MADE OBSERVATIONS 3
- INFORMAL WRITTEN OBSERVATIONS
- CHECKLISTS
- RATINGS
- INVENTORIES OF INTERESTS 3

TEACHER-MADE TESTS
- NORM- VS. CRITERION-REFERENCED TESTS 3
- TABLE OF SPECIFICATIONS 1, 2

KINDS OF TEST QUESTIONS 1, 2
- TRUE-FALSE
- MULTIPLE-CHOICE
- COMPLETION
- ESSAY

1 Learning to structure knowledge (Chapter 7)

2 Making instruction more effective (Chapter 8)

3 Reporting on learning (Chapter 14)

Questions for Discussion

1. What cognitive skill or skills does each question seem to test? Use the taxonomy of educational goals by Gagné (page 194) or Bloom (page 203) to help you answer this question.

2. Suppose that three students gave the following (oversimplified) patterns of responses to these three questions:

	Student		
Question	1	2	3
1	Wrong	Right	Right
51	Wrong	Wrong	Right
99	Right	Wrong	Part credit

Presumably student 3 learned the unit better than the other two did. How could you test this idea, *other* than by giving another test? Describe how you could use the informal methods of observation discussed in this chapter.

3. a. To what extent can each of the questions above be answered correctly by using just common sense? Explain.

   b. How, if at all, could each of these questions be made more valid or reliable? Rewrite each of them as needed.

Suggested Readings

Almy, M. C., and C. Genishi. *Ways of Studying Children: An Observation Manual for Early Childhood Teachers*. Rev. ed. New York: Teachers' College Press, 1979.

Irwin, D. M., and M. Bushnell. *Observational Strategies for Child Study*. New York: Holt, Rinehart & Winston, 1980.

These are two books that focus on relatively informal (that is, nontesting) methods of evaluating students. The first one examines early childhood education (nursery school through Grade 3), in which informal methods are especially popular.

Green, Joan L., and J. Stone. *Curriculum Evaluation: Theory and Practice, with a Case Study from Nursing Education*. New York: Springer-Verlag, 1977.

To a large extent, evaluating students also means evaluating a curriculum's success. This is a book that illustrates this idea, as applied to nurses' training.

Hopkins, C. D., and R. L. Antes. *Classroom Measurement and Evaluation*. Itasca, Ill.: F. E. Peacock, 1978.

Smith, F. M., and S. Adams. *Educational Measurement for the Classroom Teacher*. 2nd ed. New York: Harper & Row, 1972.

Although many books on measurement and evaluation discuss the construction and use of standardized tests (see Chapter 14), some also consider the needs of classroom teachers. These are two such books, though only about half of the second book is on teachermade evaluations.

Howell, K. W., J. S. Kaplan, and C. Y. O'Connell. *Evaluating Exceptional Children: A Task Analysis Approach*. Columbus, Ohio: Chas. E. Merrill, 1979.

The problems of evaluating children with special needs differ in certain ways from the problems of evaluating other children, and this book discusses how to respond to this fact.

McCormick, E. J. *Job Analysis: Methods and Applications*. New York: American Management Association, 1979.

Public school teachers are not the only ones who must evaluate performance. Business people, among others, must also do so. This is one general text on the problems of evaluation specific to business settings.

Chapter 14

REPORTING

ON LEARNING

Helen Saunders, Grade 3 teacher: I remember trying to get special help for Jason, one of my pupils. Was that ever a job! Jason was basically a good kid, friendly and cooperative in class. But he still could hardly read, even half way through Grade 3. He would stare at a page, then at me (looking for clues), then at the page again. Sometimes he read fairly well, especially books with pictures; I suspected that he was guessing the story from the pictures. But who knows? Sometimes he didn't listen well to instructions—so maybe he couldn't hear. Or maybe he just didn't care.

At first his parents were convinced that nothing was wrong. They pointed to his grades, which were all right, if not the greatest. He almost failed reading in first grade, but got by in second. His parents asked if his teachers had caused his low marks. What could I say to that idea? I knew the teachers and suspected that they had done well, but convincing Jason's parents was another matter.

They did agree to let the school psychologist observe Jason. He came to class and took a lot of notes; then he gave Jason some standardized tests—an IQ one, I think, and a reading test. Sure enough, he did badly on the reading test, but he scored about average on the intelligence test. The psychologist agreed that reading was a problem and suggested inviting the reading consultant to observe Jason.

At this point Jason's parents objected again. Since his IQ was quite satisfactory, they said, what was all the fuss about? Couldn't I just pick up on teaching him reading where the other teachers had left off? Meaning, I guess, that the earlier teachers had fallen down on the job; so I should try to make up for their mistakes.

Things didn't seem that simple to me. I *had* given my best to teach Jason reading already, but without success. I believed that his earlier teachers had also done their best. I agreed completely that Jason was bright, but that did not make up for his troubles in reading. Something was wrong there, even if nowhere else. And I said so.

Finally they agreed to let the reading consultant see Jason. They seemed reassured by my saying I thought his problem was relatively specific. The consultant came and spent time with Jason. And he prescribed some reading-related activities. The principal found a parent volunteer to do some of them with him, and I am doing some others. The consultant will be back next month to see how we are doing.

For now his parents seem content. It took work getting them that way, but I do sympathize with their concerns. I'm a parent myself, and I know I want teachers to be fair and accurate in evaluating my own son and daughter. If my own kids ever need special help, then the teachers had better have good reasons for recommending it.

GRADING

CRITERION- VS. NORM-REFERENCED

ALTERNATIVE METHODS

PASS-FAIL; CREDIT–NO CREDIT

WEIGHTING GRADES

NATURE AND USES
OF STANDARDIZED
TESTS

CENTRAL TENDENCY
Mean
Median
Mode

INTERPRETATION OF
TEST SCORES

VARIABILITY
Range
Standard deviation

NORMS
Standardization sample
Normal curve
z-score

USES

STANDARDIZED
ACHIEVEMENT
TESTS

REPORTING METHODS
Percentile ranks
Stanines
Grade equivalents

CRITICISMS

TYPES

INTELLIGENCE AND
ABILITY TESTS

THE NATURE OF INTELLIGENCE

INTELLIGENCE AND CREATIVITY

USES

SCHOLASTIC APTITUDE AND
INTELLIGENCE TESTS

CRITICISMS

THE previous chapter discussed ways of gathering information about classroom learning. It did not examine in detail how such information can and should be used, other than to point out that a big reason for evaluating learning is to plan instruction: to find out what students know and do not know and therefore what the teacher should teach, either during the remainder of the course or on its next round. In addition, evaluation helps students assess how well they are doing, either in comparison with absolute standards or one another.

But the evaluation of learning is not complete unless it is shared with significant persons outside the classroom, most notably parents, the next year's teachers, college admissions committees, and prospective employers and colleagues. For this purpose teachers need systems for reporting evaluations and relating them to the performance of persons in other times and places. This chapter will consider two major ways of doing so: grading and standardized testing. These activities are far from perfect, but since the need for them remains high, they continue to play a prominent role in education, both in schools and elsewhere.

GRADING

Grades give information about student performance, though only in its crudest, most summarized form. Typically, a **grade** is a single number or letter assigned to represent the overall quality of a student's performance during an entire course. Any one grade can therefore only hint at what a student actually did during the course. Nonetheless, the hints that grades provide are useful. Grades can tell students and others something about the students' progress—whether they are doing well or not so well—and thereby perhaps help them adjust their expectations and plans accordingly. Grades can be used by school officials to promote and guide students into programs or courses in which they seem likely to succeed. And they can indicate to employers whether and how well students are prepared for particular jobs or vocations.

purposes of grades

Naturally, grades provide this information if and only if they are reliable and valid. Ideally, a *B* given by one teacher should reflect the same level of performance that a *B* given by another teacher does, and a *C* in English should mean the same that a *C* in auto mechanics does. As receivers of grades, students are often painfully aware of experiences that fail to live up to these ideals. And their concerns are often well founded: research suggests that teachers vary considerably in how reliably they grade (White, 1975). Furthermore, common sense suggests that a grade in one course may not, or even cannot, mean the same as that in another, since the goals of courses often vary in the extreme.

need for consistency

But despite their individual ambiguities, grades taken as a whole prove to be relatively reliable and valid in important ways. Grade-point averages predict future academic success about as well as, or better than, the other information available, including teachers' judgments and the scores on the best standardized tests (Bejar & Blew, 1981). This fact may be only a small comfort to students who feel that they have received the wrong grades or to teachers who believe that they have given the wrong ones. But it does help account for education's continued reliance on grades. Grades show the "big picture" of students' achievement—their overall performance and their long-run academic prospects.

predictive ability

Criterion-referenced Versus Norm-referenced Grading

To give useful information, grades must be based on either or both of two major sources of information: comparisons with other students and comparisons with specified criteria of achievement. This is the choice between norm referencing and criterion referencing discussed in the preceding chapter with regard to teacher-made tests. Just as with tests, teachers have the opportunity to assign grades by either of these standards of reference or by a mixture of the two. Once again, too, the best choice will depend partly on the goals of the instruction and the philosophy of the teacher.

But the choice will also depend on the kind of information needed by the outside world—chiefly school counselors, administrators, and employers. Compared with classroom teachers, these people face more situations in which a few individuals must be selected from a larger pool of applicants—for a job, perhaps, or a particular training program with limited space. This task is helped by having norm-referenced grades. By definition, such grades emphasize the comparisons and differences among students and thus help identify the most able individuals among them. At the same time, administrators and employers also need assurance that students have the basic competencies needed for particular placements in courses, programs, or jobs. This assurance is given most clearly *not* when grades are norm referenced but when they are criterion referenced: when they reflect what students do, rather than who is better than whom. So the people outside the classroom look for a mixture of criterion and norm referencing.

need for comparisons among students

This need for both kinds of grades can be frustrating to teachers, who usually do not need, or even wish, to make selections among students. Many teachers feel that their need for clearly planning instruction gives them a special reason to use criterion-referenced evaluation almost exclusively. The heavy use of norm referencing, they argue, discriminates against students who compare poorly with their classmates, no matter how good their intrinsic performance may be. In its extreme form, the norm referencing of grades leads to **grading on the curve**: assigning a fixed per-

need to focus on actual achievement

centage of each grade to the class. This practice seems to be based on the (erroneous) assumption that the performance of a relatively small classroom group can be expected to distribute itself in a predictable way around some average or typical score. The policy unfortunately guarantees in advance that some students will receive low marks and that a few will even fail. Generally, teachers should have no reason to expect this result before they have even begun teaching their students; indeed it may become a self-fulfilling prophecy by discouraging some students from trying to work (Musgrave, 1970).

Carried to extremes, the norm referencing of grades can contribute to competition among individuals for the few top grades. Although such competition provides a motivation of sorts, this motivation is not based on interest in the subject matter so much as concern with grades as such. Most teachers probably do not want to encourage such extrinsic motivation among their students, especially if it interfers with their intrinsic enjoyment of learning and if some students are guaranteed to lose because of it. Other school personnel do not want to encourage this, either. But if they are faced with many applicants for only one job, course, or special award, how else are they to decide which one to select?

Pass-Fail and Credit–No Credit Grading

Recently pass-fail and credit–no credit grading have been used by some educators to encourage students to choose courses in which they do not expect to do especially well and for which they thus do not want to risk receiving a low or failing mark. The pass-fail system protects students from low marks, since a "pass" presumably corresponds to any of the conventional letter grades, A through $D,$ but it still threatens them with the possibility of failing the course. The credit–no credit system gives the opposite protection: students can receive any letter grade from A through D but cannot receive an F in the course. Instead, if they fail, the teacher and school simply make no record of their ever having taken the course.

How well have these grading systems worked? There is some evidence that students choose pass-fail courses to explore new areas of study, which was the original purpose (Stallings & Smock, 1971). Both pass-fail and credit–no credit systems seem popular with students, who report that such

reducing the
pressures of
grades

systems do in fact reduce the pressure of earning good grades. On the other hand, students working under such systems may not work as hard as they would under conventional grading systems. Particularly in pass-fail courses, several studies have reported that students often achieve less (see Sgan, 1970) than do comparable students in conventionally graded courses. This fact suggests that the reduced pressure that students report may not translate into a greater willingness to try unusual or new courses, only into doing less work in relatively familiar ones.

The credit–no credit system should combat this tendency, since under

Even when teachers try to make grading confidential, students often choose to compare their achievements anyway—and endure the anxiety that results. (Marcia Weinstein)

it a student's performance must fall all the way to a failing level before he or she can be protected by the system from getting a negative grade. In practice, however, it may not always ensure hard work because the system usually allows students to withdraw from a course at any time without a mark left on their record. Thus if they do not seem to be earning a suitably high grade, they can always drop the course with no penalty.

Weightings for Final Grades

Since most final grades are based on a combination of work, the results of these must be combined in some rational way to arrive at a single, final grade for each student. Unfortunately the marks on assignments or tests cannot usually be added together directly. Some tests may have been given letter grades, others given percentage scores, and those receiving numerical scores may vary widely in their total possible points. These differences have no necessary relationship with their importance in the final evaluation of students.

Some way must thus be found to compare the results of individual assignments or tests so that they can be combined into a final, meaningful grade. Table 14–1 illustrates a simple way to do so for one particular course. Assignments are first given percentage weightings that correspond roughly to their comparative importance, as judged by the teacher. If the grades were originally given as letters, then they must be converted to numerically equivalent scores. One simple way of doing so is to assign a conventional numerical scale to the letter grades: $A = 4.0$ points, $B+ = 3.5$, $B = 3.0$, and so on. The numerical scores must then be multiplied by the relative weighting that has been assigned to that particular assignment. When all of the weighted scores have been calculated, they will reflect the relative importance of each assignment on a single numerical scale and can therefore be combined.

Note, though, that even giving weightings to scores does not really resolve the problem of what letter grade to give a student. To do so, the teacher must still face the issues of norm referencing and criterion referencing debated earlier. Should Barry's final score merit a C, a B, or an A? The answer will depend on several further questions, each of which has been considered in this and the previous chapter:

translating weightings into grades

1. Does Barry's work represent a minimal acceptable achievement for promotion to the next course or unit of study? If so, he merits at least the minimal usual grade given for the promotion. Although this may technically be a D, in practice the minimal acceptable grade is usually higher than this—often a C or a B.

Table 14–1 Assigning Weightings for Final Grades

Example 1: Grades given as letters

Assignment	% Weighting	Letter range	Equivalent numerical range	Weighted numerical range
Term paper	25	A–F	4–0	100–0
Observation project	5	A–F	4–0	20–0
Test: 1	20	A–F	4–0	80–0
2	20	A–F	4–0	80–0
Final exam	30	A–F	4–0	120–0

($A = 4.0$; $B+ = 3.5$; $B = 3.0$; $C+ = 2.5$; $C = 2.0$; $D+ = 1.5$; $D = 1.0$; $F = 0$)

Example 2: Grades given as numbers

Assignment	% Weighting	Numerical range	Weighted numerical range
Term paper	25	50–0	1,250–0
Observation project	5	50–0	250–0
Test: 1	20	50–0	1,000–0
2	20	50–0	1,000–0
Final exam	30	50–0	1,500–0

2. Does Barry's work show better performance than that of most other students? If so, then he should get whatever grade the teacher and the school typically consider comparatively good—often a *B* or an *A*.
3. Does Barry's work show the achievement of previously specified goals, for which a specified grade has already been promised? If so, then obviously he should receive the promised grade, no matter what it is and no matter how many other students may also receive it.

Of course, a teacher may have to resolve all of these questions at once and may wish to treat one of them as more important than another. The resulting, final grade is therefore very much a judgment, a subjective decision that another teacher might make somewhat differently, though perhaps not completely differently. No wonder teachers so often find grading the hardest job in teaching!

Alternative Evaluation Methods

In principle, evaluations need not be confined to a single letter or number summarizing an entire course. Especially in working with younger children, teachers have experimented with various alternatives to conventional grades intended to give fuller information about the performance of each student.

Dual Marking   One of the simplest modifications of the traditional system is **dual marking**: giving one grade for performance and another for effort or improvement. The procedure is intended partly to bolster the morale of those students who may not perform at the top of their class but who may become discouraged from trying if only their performance is evaluated. Dual marking also is intended to share more information with parents and other school people than can be done when only one grade is reported. Unfortunately, though, research indicates that a halo effect (see page 366) prevents teachers from assigning the two grades independently of each other. In general, children graded high on performance tend also to be graded high on improvement or effort, and vice versa (Halliwell & Robitaille, 1963).

improving the richness of grades

Written Evaluations and Letters   Various kinds of *written evaluations* and *letters to parents* also improve the richness of evaluations. These can contain both summaries of important areas of behavior and specific examples of them. At their best, they can explain the meaning of summary grades: what did Jessica *do* to deserve that *B*? Is what she did good enough, either by absolute standards or in comparison with other students? Because different students may receive a particular grade for different reasons, written evaluations allow the teacher to explain the basis for a grade in each particular case, no matter how different they may be from one another.

focus on details of performance

But written evaluations and letters also have drawbacks. Writing about students may take more effort than either talking about them or assigning them grades, and so teachers with large numbers of students—notably high school teachers—may find the practice an impossible burden. In fact, the effort needed for writing may lead teachers to say less about their students than they might orally. At their worst, written evaluations can become merely a list of generalities giving little real information about students and failing to give balanced pictures of them.

Parent-Teacher Conferences   Some of the above problems do not occur if teachers report evaluations through *parent-teacher conferences*. By sidestepping the need to write and by allowing two-way communication, conferences can encourage a fuller exchange of information about students. They may, however, demand greater skills in diplomacy than written evaluations or letters home would. In a conference, the teacher must deal with any frustrations and worries of parents as they occur, and not later when the teacher has had lots of time to reflect on them.

values and limits
of conferences

Partly for this reason, conferences run the risk of avoiding the real problems that students may be having in school and avoiding the real concerns of their parents. This risk is increased because conferences often do not last long enough for teachers and parents to establish confidence in one another. Having a conference with every family of an elementary school class, for example, may mean confining each one to only ten or fifteen minutes. Student loads in secondary school often prevent even this much contact, since teachers must often deal with well over one hundred families. The parents, for their part, must go to a half-dozen conferences if all of their child's teachers decide to have them—a challenge for most parents. Probably these facts help explain why parent conferences have been much more popular with teachers of young children than with teachers of adolescents (National Education Association, 1972).

THE NATURE AND USES OF STANDARDIZED TESTS

features of
standardized tests

The limitations of even the best teacher-made evaluations have led to the use of various kinds of *standardized tests* to supplement, but not replace, the information they give. **Standardized tests** have three prominent features: they consist of many well-constructed items or problems; they clearly spell out the procedures for scoring them; and they present information on how large populations of comparable individuals perform on them (Green, 1981). Typically the items are carefully constructed by experts in the subject area and in psychological measurement, and thus they aspire to very high standards of reliability and validity, in the senses described in Chapter 13. Almost every area of behavior evaluated informally by teachers can also be evaluated by such tests—all the way from interests and attitudes to specific abilities and achievements to the general aptitude for school work.

The nature of standardized tests, of course, depends on the purpose of the test. The ones that measure attitudes and interests are often called surveys or **inventories** rather than tests, since they measure typical behaviors and feelings, rather than "best"ones. **Ability tests** try to predict how well students will generally do in school or in some broad skill area. To do so, they draw on skills and knowledge that the students have already acquired, not to assess the past but to predict the future. **Achievement tests** serve the opposite function: they measure how much a student has already learned in a particular area of knowledge or skill. In principle they pertain to the content of the field itself rather than the thinking skills prerequisite to it. Ability and achievement tests are probably the most common standardized tests used in schools, and so we shall examine them in greater detail later in this chapter.

Although in principle standardized tests can guide teachers in planning instruction, in practice they more commonly affect students and teachers in the same way that grades do: as an official report on how well individuals have performed or are likely to perform in the future. In this way standardized tests function differently from teacher-made observations and teacher-made tests, which more often help teachers form and modify instruction as it proceeds and which often are not reported outside the classroom at all.

Like grades, standardized tests help in guiding students into particular classes or instructional programs. Sections of a science course, for example, can be established partly on the basis of standardized test results, with the groups defined in part by how well each has done on the test. Remedial courses can be constructed by the same principle: the students who do very poorly on certain relevant tests may be considered for further special instruction or classes. And as pointed out in the previous chapter, interest and attitude surveys can help students clarify vocational and educational goals—just as informal teacher evaluations can.

Unlike teacher-made grades, standardized tests usually offer information about **norms**—the averages and variabilities of scores across large and supposedly representative samples of students. This fact helps most obviously when a student transfers from one school to another: the teachers at the receiving school can get a better notion of the student's skills and potential by comparing this standardized test's results with the results from their own students. Doing so helps to make up for the ambiguities in the former school's grading and course descriptions: does an *A* in mathematics from the previous school mean the same as an *A* from the new school? Even if it does, what does the previous school do in a course called "mathematics," anyway? Standardized tests can help answer these questions. Or at least they can as long as they correctly reflect the educational goals of teachers in general and are in this sense valid.

inventories

ability tests

achievement tests

tests for reporting

tests for guidance

norms

INTERPRETATION OF TEST SCORES

Administering any standardized test yields a set of scores, typically one for each child or student who takes the test. In order to interpret these numbers—the so-called *raw scores*—they must be converted to forms that allow comparisons with other relevant tests or other students. Test makers use a variety of methods for doing so, some of which are highly statistical. For help in learning more about such techniques, try one of the many books on the topic (for example, Lyman, 1978, or Burns, 1979). The discussion below will consider only relatively simple ways of ordering and interpreting test scores—the ways, as it turns out, that are the most usable in instructional practice. We shall look at two related and basic questions about test interpretation. First, what score is considered typical for the group? And second, how can the variability of individual scores be described most accurately and concisely?

raw scores

Central Tendency: The Typical Score

Central tendency refers to a number that is somehow typical or representative of a group of scores. For any particular group of scores, central tendency is usually defined by one of three measures: the mean, the median, or the mode. Often these three measures have nearly the same value, but they sometimes do differ noticeably from one another.

Table 14–2 Raw Scores for Thirty Students

Arlene	41	Karl	37	Ulman	44
Bob	33	Lois	31	Victoria	45
Carol	34	Martin	29	Wes	46
David	42	Nancy	41	Xyphonie	37
Emily	36	Oscar	42	Zeb	43
Frances	35	Patty	38	Arthur	25
George	39	Quigley	44	Beth	42
Harriet	40	Robert	43	Cory	39
Ike	38	Sam	41	Debbie	42
Joan	43	Tess	36	Esther	39

$$\text{Mean} = \frac{\text{sum of scores}}{\text{number of scores}} = \frac{1140}{30} = 38$$

Median = middle score   = halfway between fifteenth and sixteenth rank
                              = 39.5

Mode   = 42

Range = 46 to 25   = 21

Mean Suppose that a test yielded a set of scores like those listed in Table 14–2. The most common way to describe the typical or central score for such a set is as the arithmetic average, or the **mean**. As most children learn in school, this number equals the sum of all the scores in the group, divided by the number of scores itself. If the scores are distributed fairly evenly around the mean, this figure will usually fall quite close to the middle of the distribution and in this sense can be considered typical or representative of it.

the mean

But a few very extreme scores can influence the value of the mean quite noticeably—so much so, in fact, that it may no longer seem representative of the group. Table 14–3 illustrates this problem. The scores on this test cluster around low values, but the students Frank and Isabelle scored quite a bit higher than the others did. Including their extreme scores would raise the mean to almost 33, higher than any of the scores of the other nine students. Without them, the mean would come only to about 29.5, a value that seems to represent more closely the group as a whole. Yet this lower figure does not really represent the entire group, just the smaller, more closely clustered group of nine.

Median One solution to this dilemma is to describe the central tendency using the *median* rather than the mean. The **median** is whatever score divides the entire distribution of scores into two equal parts, one above it and one below it. Because the median is the middle score, it can be found by arranging the scores in rank order and counting halfway up from the bottom of the distribution (or down from the top). For the eleven scores in Table 14–3, the median would be the sixth score up from the bottom (or down from the top)—in this case 30. For distributions with even numbers of scores, the median can be estimated as halfway between the two most-middle scores in the distribution, since no one of them falls at the actual midpoint. This is the case for the thirty scores in Table 14–2; the median turns out to be 39.5, in between the tenth and eleventh scores.

the median

The median does not vary as much as does the mean, because of a few unusually extreme scores. In Table 14–3, the two extremely high scores cause the median to rise only from 29 to 30—a much smaller influence

Table 14–3 Mean and Median of Eleven Students' Scores

Abe	29	Earl	29	Harry	30
Betty	32	Frank	45	Isabelle	51
Carl	29	Gertrude	30	Jack	28
Darlene	30			Kelvin	29

Mean (all 11 students) = 32.9   Median (all 11 students) = 30
Mean (9 lowest students) = 29.5   Median (9 lowest students) = 29
Mode (all 11 students) = 29   Mode (9 lowest students) = 29

Among other things, summarizing scores requires knowing their central tendency: with these boys, for example, it means deciding on some height typical of the group. (Michael Weisbrot and Family)

than the scores have on the mean. For this reason many test makers consider the median a better indicator than the mean is of the typical or central value in any relatively small group of scores, like those from most classroom tests. Unfortunately, the median often is also more difficult to determine, since the entire distribution first must be rank ordered, and the scores examined individually. But if the teacher has reason to believe that the scores are not distributed fairly evenly around the middle of the group, this work may be worth the effort. Otherwise, the mean will work just as well, and in fact it has certain mathematical advantages if the scores are going to be further manipulated statistically.

Mode   Another way of measuring central tendency is the **mode**, which is simply the most commonly occurring score. In Table 14–3, the mode is 29 because it occurs more often than does any other score (four times); in Table 14–2, the mode is 42 (also occurring four times). The mode has the

the mode

advantage of being relatively easy to determine for small groups of scores—one just has to count how often each score appears. Finding the mode can be cumbersome, though, with very large groups of scores. In addition, the mode is greatly affected by small changes in individual scores. In Tables

14–2 and 14–3, if even one student who scored at the mode happened to have scored one point higher, he or she would have raised the mode by one entire point. It does not seem right that the central tendency—a representative score—should be influenced that much by such a small change.

Variability

A set of scores is not fully summarized without some information about how much they vary from their typical value. One set of test scores may be much more "spread out" than another is, even though they both have the same mean or median, and in many cases this fact may influence the grades or school placements of individual students. How, then can variability be summarized best?

Range   One obvious indicator of variability is the **range** of scores, the difference between the highest and the lowest score. The scores in Table 14–2 have a range of twenty-one points, and those in Table 14–3 have a range of twenty-two. But Table 14–3 shows the limitation of this way of describing variability: by definition, the range is completely influenced by the two most extreme scores. If either or both of these greatly differ from most of the other scores, the range will be much larger than it would otherwise be and in this sense will not represent the variability of the scores in general. For sets of scores without such oddities, however, the range can be a practical measure, that is, a quick and easy one.

the range

Standard Deviation   For various statistical reasons, the most commonly used indicator of variability is the **standard deviation**. This figure takes into account the deviation of each individual score but does so by squaring each deviation rather than finding its absolute value. The squared deviations are averaged, and the square root of the resulting figure indicates the variability. This value is called the standard deviation and is often abbreviated by the Greek letter σ (called **sigma**). Table 14–4 shows how the standard deviation is calculated for a set of seven scores.

the standard deviation

Table 14–4 Standard Deviation for Seven Scores

	Score	Deviation	Square of Deviation		Score	Deviation	Square of Deviation
Archie	55	+5	25	Ernie	65	+15	225
Barry	50	0	0	Farrell	60	+10	100
Cathie	45	−5	25	Gina	40	−10	100
Dolores	35	−15	225			Sum	=700

$$\text{Standard deviation} = \sigma = \sqrt{\frac{(\text{sum of squared deviations})}{(\text{number of scores})}} = \sqrt{\frac{700}{100}} = \sqrt{7} = 2.6$$

For various statistical reasons, the standard deviation is very popular with educators and test makers. Unfortunately, it also requires considerable calculation work if many scores must be accounted for and if their numerical values include fractions or large, multidigit numbers. But teachers **computing the standard deviation** can make a good estimate of the standard deviation by using a much simpler calculation procedure proposed by a number of psychologists (Lathrop, 1961; Sabers & Klausmeier, 1971). The method assumes a reasonably symmetrical distribution of scores, one that does not include overly numerous high values or low values. In essence the shorter method uses the following general formula:

$$\text{Estimate of } \Sigma = \frac{\left(\begin{array}{c}\text{sum of top 1/6}\\ \text{of scores}\end{array}\right) - \left(\begin{array}{c}\text{sum of bottom 1/6}\\ \text{of scores}\end{array}\right)}{(1/2 \text{ the total number of scores})}$$

If this formula were applied to the scores from Table 14–2 at the beginning of this section, it would give the following estimate:

$$\text{Estimate of } \Sigma = \frac{(46+45+44+44+43)-(35+34+33+31+25)}{30 \times 1/2}$$

$$= \frac{222-158}{15} = 4.3$$

Statistical studies of this formula have shown it to give a reasonably accurate estimate for groups having as few as twenty-five scores, as long as the distribution is symmetrical. For most practical classroom evaluations, therefore, this formula is far more usable than is the official definition of the standard deviation described earlier. Teachers must remember, though, that any standard deviations reported by standardized tests probably are based on the more difficult, but more accurate, calculation procedures.

Norms

The information about central tendency and variability are often called the **norms** for the test.

The Standardization Sample   To be most useful, norms must be based on hundreds or even thousands of scores, and they must be collected from students or children who are representative of the ones for whom the **the standardization sample** test is intended. This group—often called the *standardization sample*— may be quite broad. It may consist of all persons of a certain age range, or it may be relatively specific: for example, all Grade 12 males who are eighteen years old and enrolled in a particular course of study. The nature of the reference group will depend on the kinds of comparisons that the test makers expect the test score users to make.

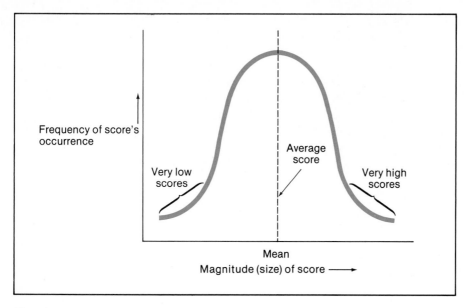

Figure 14–1 The Normal Curve

The Normal Curve   Once the norms for a test are collected, they can help interpret the performance of the individual students or classroom groups who take the test. If John gets 63 on a standardized test, for example, did he do well or not? This question can be answered more easily if we know that several thousand students comparable to him scored an avarage of 52. It can be answered still more easily if we know that the reference group did not vary much around this mean—for example, that 99 percent of them scored between 57 and 47. But to get the latter kind of information, we need more precise ways of defining variability. One of these is described below, using the standard deviation. Some others are described later in this chapter, in the context of standardized achievement and ability tests.

Test makers have found that the scores of many standardized tests distribute themselves very close to a particular pattern called a *normal curve.* Figure 14–1 illustrates this pattern for a hypothetical test. The most common scores on it occur at or around the mean, and the least common ones occur at the extremes of the distribution. If the occurrence of each score is graphed opposite its magnitude or amount, the resulting curve will look like that in the figure, rather like a bell. But the distribution will look like this curve only if very large numbers of test scores are used to construct it. Usually the results from the reference group will approximate a normal curve, but often the results from an individual classroom group will not.

the normal curve

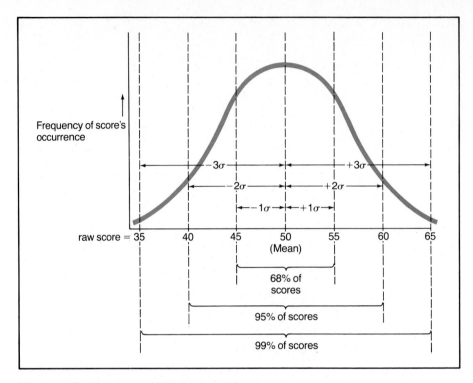

Figure 14–2 Hypothetical Distribution of Scores

When scores are normally distributed, about 68 percent of them fall within one standard deviation of either side of the mean score for the test, at least when very large samples of scores are used. Furthermore, about 95 percent of all scores fall within two standard deviations of either side of the mean, and about 99 percent fall within three standard deviations of either side. Figure 14–2 illustrates these landmarks for an imaginary test whose scores array themselves normally. The scores have a (hypothetical) mean score of 50 and a standard deviation of 5. About 68 percent of all the test takers earned scores between 45 and 55, about 95 percent between 40 and 60, and about 99 percent between 35 and 65.

Z-scores Knowing such landmarks for a distribution helps in estimating how unusual any particular score may be. If Frank scores 57 on the test in Figure 14–2, then we know that his score varies more from the mean than do about two-thirds of the scores of all the individuals who take the test. If Mary scores 61, then we know that her score varies more than about 95 percent of all the scores of the test takers. We can express their raw scores in standard deviation units by using the conversion formula below. Sometimes such a standard score is also called a **z-score**:

$$\text{Standard score} = z = \frac{\text{raw score} - \text{mean}}{\sigma}$$

For Frank and Mary this formula gives the following z-scores:

$$\text{Frank: } z = \frac{57 - 50}{5} = 7/5 = 1.4 \text{ standard deviations}$$

$$\text{Mary: } z = \frac{61 - 50}{5} = 11/5 = 2.2 \text{ standard deviations}$$

calculating z-scores

Scores below the mean yield negative z-scores. If George scores 46, the formula will give this result:

$$\text{George: } z = \frac{46 - 50}{5} = -4/5 = -0.8 \text{ standard deviations}$$

Statisticians have developed ways for estimating fairly precisely how typical or unusual such standard scores may be. These techniques go beyond the scope of this book, but readers interested in learning about them should consult any basic text in statistical measurement (for example, Anastasi, 1976).

STANDARDIZED ACHIEVEMENT TESTS

Uses of Achievement Tests

Standardized achievement tests measure students' success in various specific areas of school learning, all the way from reading readiness to advanced mathematics. By providing norms from large national samples of students, they allow comparisons of local groups with students in general. How well, for example, is a Grade 7 science class doing compared with science classes across the country? A standardized test of science achievement can help answer this question, thanks to the norms that test makers have gathered for it from students in many schools and cities. The performance of the local group helps evaluate the students' learning, and it also evaluates the school curriculum itself: the local class may do badly, for example, because they have been taught the wrong material or because they have been taught badly. But the test results themselves do not identify these possibilities.

Teacher-made tests of achievement resemble standardized tests in that they focus on the results of schooling, but they also differ from them in important ways. Typically, a teacher-made test contains items tailored to the specific objectives of a particular teacher or classroom group, whereas a standardized test must draw on content that the test makers consider common to all teachers and classrooms in that particular field of study. Any one class, then, will probably face questions on the standardized test

teacher-made versus standardized achievement tests

for which it has received little or no instruction. A good teacher-made test will not have this problem and may therefore be considered more equitable by some students and teachers. Indeed, it is more equitable, though only as judged by a local frame of reference; the standardized test usually contains more balanced content from a national perspective.

The quality of items on teacher-made tests probably varies more than does the quality of items on standardized achievement tests. Teachers vary not only in how well they can write items for their own tests but also in how much time they have for the task: their main responsibility, after all, consists of instruction, and evaluation is only part of this job. Because standardized tests are typically constructed by professional test makers, the items on them usually are selected and revised until their reliability is quite high—higher, in fact, than most of those on teacher-made tests. But this advantage may be offset by the fact that standardized tests are used in schools relatively rarely compared with teacher-made tests. Conversely, by using their own tests fairly often, teachers gain more information from them and thereby improve their overall reliability.

Methods of Reporting Scores on Standardized Achievement Tests

Norms for standardized tests can be reported in a number of ways.

Percentile Ranks A **percentile rank** indicates the percentage of students in the standardization sample whose scores were *lower* than a particular raw score. Table 14–5 is an example of norms reported as percentiles. The left-hand column contains the raw scores possible on a hypothetical achievement test in biology. Across from each of these are the percentages of students who scored no higher than that particular raw score: these figures are the percentile scores.

Because percentiles are determined by ranking the students in the original standardization sample, they have nothing to do with the percentage of right answers that a student earns on the test. The seventy-fifth per-

Table 14–5 Raw Scores and Equivalent Percentile Ranks

Raw scores	Percentiles	Raw scores	Percentiles
97	95	62	45
86	85	59	35
78	75	53	25
71	65	42	15
68	55	32	5
65 (mean)	50		

centile means that the student scored higher than did 75 percent of the standardization group; it does *not* mean that he or she got 75 percent of the items correct. For the same reason, the differences among percentile ranks do not necessarily represent equal differences in raw scores or in actual performance. The ninety-fifth and fifty-fifth percentiles, for example, are equally distant in rank from the seventy-fifth percentile, but as the figures in Table 14–5 show, one is much more distant than the other is if measured by raw scores. Typically, the raw scores spread out more at the extremes of a percentile distribution (near the ninety-ninth and the first percentiles) than near its middle.

percentile ranks versus percentages

By the way they are defined, percentiles give only norm-referenced information—comparisons among students. No matter how many or how few items the best student in a group gets right, he or she will still be assigned to the ninety-ninth percentile; and by the same token, the lowest student will be assigned to the first percentile no matter what. Interpreting percentiles therefore depends on knowing the group from which the ranks are constructed: were they made from relatively high scoring individuals or relatively low scoring ones? Knowing the answer helps teachers estimate the absolute level of performance of individual students and thus make more sensible decisions about their promotion and placement.

using percentiles to compare students

The hundred-point scale of percentile ranks has a convenient and familiar relationship to the hundred-point scale of percentages, but it often creates an illusion of precision that it does not really have. What, really, is the difference in performance between a student scoring at the seventy-fifth percentile and one scoring at the seventy-fourth? At best they may differ by only a few points in their raw scores, a difference that is just as likely to occur by chance as to represent any true difference in achievement. Such a difference, furthermore, probably has no educational implications: teachers would not teach a child at the seventy-fifth percentile any differently from one at the seventy-fourth. For practical purposes, therefore, teachers sometimes need a way of reporting achievement test results that has fewer steps in it.

overly precise rankings for instruction

Stanines *Stanines* have this advantage. They divide the distribution of raw scores into only nine steps, numbered simply 1 through 9. Each step is called a **stanine** (a contraction of "standard nine") and refers to a range of scores exactly one-half of a standard deviation wide. The stanines are located by placing the middle of the fifth stanine exactly at the mean of the distribution and assigning its borders one-quarter of a deviation above and below this point. The other stanines are then placed outward from this one. Figure 14–3 illustrates this process, based on the raw scores from Table 14–2. Note that the procedure creates groups of unequal size, with the largest groups occurring at the middle stanines. This happens because stanines essentially "chunk" a normal distribution of scores into intervals with equal ranges.

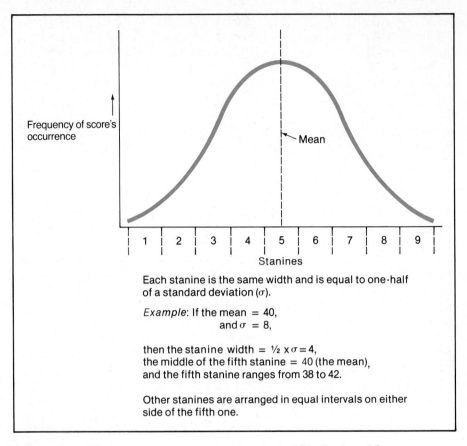

Figure 14–3 Stanine Scores Based on a Hypothetical Distribution of Scores

Grade Equivalents   Standardized achievement tests often report distributions of raw scores as **grade equivalents**. These tell the grade level at which a particular raw score is the average for the group. If a child receives a grade equivalent score of, say, 3, it means that her raw score equals the average raw score of Grade 3 children; if her grade equivalent score equals 7, then it means she scored at about where the average Grade 7 student scores. Typically, such scores also include an estimate of months into the school year. A grade equivalent of 4.2, for example, means that the child performed at the same level as an average Grade 4 student in the second month of the year; a score of 6.8 means that the child performed the same as an average Grade 6 student in the eighth month. The monthly figures, however, do not usually come from testing students during each and every month of the school year, but from estimates of how far the students must have progressed during each month. Usually only the yearly grade equivalent figures come from actual test observations of a standardization sample.

the meaning of grade equivalent scores

A standardized test usually allows comparisons with larger numbers of individuals than is true for most teacher-made tests. (Arthur Grace/Stock, Boston)

As with percentile ranks, grade equivalents provide a convenient and familiar scale for comparing children with one another, in this case a scale tied to the ever-present system of graded instruction in modern schools. Unlike either percentiles or stanines, though, grade equivalents compare an individual child with older and younger students, rather than with peers of his or her own grade level. This practice creates some ambiguity in interpreting grade equivalent scores. If a fourth-grade child scores at the seventh-grade level in math, for example, we are tempted to believe that he can perform math skills in just the same ways as can an average seventh grader. An observation of real children, however, suggests that this conclusion may not always be true.

Take that "fast" fourth grader. He scored at a high grade equivalent level only because he earned the same *total* score as did an average seventh grader, not necessarily because he got correct the very same questions as the older students did. In fact, he may have gotten correct an unusually large number of the easiest questions, whereas the older students may have earned their points more evenly throughout the test. These two patterns of performance do not really indicate that the two students used the

comparing equal scores and equal age groups

same ways of thinking or that the younger one is necessarily ready for more advanced instruction in math.

Types of Standardized Achievement Tests

Because there are standardized tests for almost every possible area of school achievement, we can examine here only a few of the major types. For a more thorough sampling of achievement tests, see Schrader (1980) and for a completely thorough review, see Buros's *Mental Measurements Yearbook* (1972). These sources describe tests in more detail than possible here and give the information necessary to track down copies of the tests themselves. Meanwhile, here is a brief, thumbnail taxonomy of standardized achievement tests.

Reading Tests   *Reading tests* are among the most common achievement tests—perhaps reflecting the importance of this skill to many schoolteachers. Although some of these offer only a single general score, others offer scores on a variety of specific reading skills: vocabulary, comprehension, phonetic decoding, and the like. The second, more diagnostic kind is probably more helpful to teachers. Not only does it identify success and problems with reading in general, but also it gives clues as to their reasons. Note, though, that the scores on a test's diagnostic subscales may lack the reliability of the test as a whole. The difference pertains to the shorter length of the subscales: as a rule, fewer items mean lower reliability than more items do. Ironically, teachers who plan instruction probably need the diagnostic information more than the general assessment, despite its comparative unreliability.

Reading Readiness Tests   *Reading readiness tests* contain elements of both achievement tests and aptitude or ability tests. In principle, they assess the skills of very young children (nursery school or kindergarten age) that are needed to begin instruction in reading. The subscales vary with the test but typically have names like visual discrimination (the ability to see small differences), auditory discrimination (the ability to hear them), following directions, word recognition, and visual-motor coordination (the ability to copy and trace). Each of these subscales refers to a particular ability that young children supposedly need before they can learn to read. These subscales have the same comparatively low reliability of subscales on reading tests and other diagnostic tests. In addition, research suggests that readiness tests do not predict later reading achievement noticeably better than do tests of general intelligence or than do careful ratings by teachers (England & DeNello, 1970; Scott, 1970). But since readiness tests also do not do much worse than general intelligence tests do, the former often are worthwhile for the diagnostic information they provide.

diagnosis of reading-related skills

General Achievement Tests   **General achievement tests**, as their name implies, try to test the whole range of basic skills taught in schools. As a rule, they can do so more easily for the elementary school curriculum than for the high school curriculum. Though teachers of the younger grades may differ in their terminology and emphasis, they tend to agree generally on what elementary-age children should learn in school. Typically the recommended program includes math and reading, followed by a mixture of language arts, social studies, writing, and science. With important exceptions, other major fields of knowledge have failed to establish themselves as part of this core curriculum for younger children. Physical education, for example, and the fine arts are still often considered "frills,"—even though they may be important frills. The relative consensus on the essential curriculum makes general achievement tests comparatively easy to write for the elementary grades.

In high school, however, the curriculum fans out in more diverse directions and thus interferes with constructing valid tests of achievement. This fact has not stopped test makers from trying to construct such tests, but it has presented them with harder problems in deciding on content for their tests. Whereas children in the younger grades may study simply "science," students in high school often choose from any or all of several specialities in this field—typically biology, chemistry, physics, or general science. Even including items from all of these fields does not solve the problem of deciding on the content for the achievement test, since individual students may take different groupings of the specialty subjects. As a result, their achievement scores may not really be comparable.

determining appropriate test content

One solution to this problem is to identify the core skills underlying all the courses offered in high school. In practice such skills have names reminiscent of the school subjects for the elementary curriculum: mathematics, language, social studies, and science, for example—and variations of these terms. Since these skills have no one-to-one correspondence with particular high school courses, the subscales that test them tend to resemble tests of ability rather than achievement: measures of what students *can* learn rather than what they *do* learn.

Criticisms of Standardized Achievement Tests

Despite their careful construction, standardized achievement tests have definite limitations as aids to teaching and instructional guidance.

Low Reliability in Diagnosing Specific Needs   One limitation was mentioned in the preceding section: achievement tests must often touch on relatively few bits of skill or knowledge and so have relatively low reliability in diagnosing deficiencies. If a whole test on, say, mathematics contains about fifty items, then any subscales derived from it must contain only a fraction of this number, and sometimes less than a handful.

subtests less reliable than whole test

If teachers wonder how well their students are doing on, say, long division, the relevant achievement test may have so few items relating to this particular skill that it cannot be used to determine it. To do so properly, teachers may have to construct their own tests of long division. They can, of course, use any diagnostic information from standardized tests as well, but they should not assume that it has the same high reliability that such tests usually have as a whole.

Teaching to the Test   Many teachers also fear that standardized tests will encourage "teaching to the test"—gearing instruction so that students learn the answers to the test that they will eventually take, without necessarily understanding what they are learning. Even if students do learn and understand a test's content, some teachers question whether the content really merits influencing the normal course of instruction. Certain teachers or schools may have special interests or situations, they argue, that should become a part of the normal curriculum only in that particular locale or classroom. A science class in Nevada, for example, may legitimately study the desert in more detail than would a science class in Florida, and a social studies teacher who grew up on an Indian reservation may want to emphasize Indian culture in his teaching more than does a teacher who grew up in a large city. Too much emphasis on standardized achievement tests can discourage these special and desirable biases.

neglect of local or particular priorities

By the same token, standardized tests may promote teaching and learning at the same complexity level of items on the test, to the detriment of the other levels. If the test calls mainly for problem-solving skills (in Gagné's sense), then the teachers and students may work on problem-solving skills—whether or not the students are really ready to learn them. If, as is more common, the test stresses factual knowledge at the expense of complex thinking skills, then the instruction may do the same. Even if teachers do not succumb to such influence, their students may do so nonetheless—especially if they have become relatively "test wise" and anxious to score well.

Less Emphasis on Student Attitudes and Interests   By definition, standardized achievement tests sample the "best" performance of students under conditions of moderate stress. Yet some teachers point out that performance in this sense makes up only part of what education tries to accomplish. In addition, teachers usually wish to influence student attitudes toward and interests in a subject. These, by their nature, can be observed only when the students feel relaxed: only then can they feel free to express themselves sincerely and spontaneously. By creating anxiety about performance, standardized testing reduces the opportunities for students to express their true attitudes and interests, and it may even convey the implicit message that their attitudes and interests are unimportant. Teacher-made achievement tests can have these effects, too, of course. But standardized ones may emphasize them more because they seem especially

anxiety about testing

scientific, accurate, and important—and therefore also especially anxiety provoking.

INTELLIGENCE AND TESTS OF ABILITY

As used by educators and psychologists, the term **intelligence** refers to the ability (or group of abilities) to reason abstractly, learn new material quickly, and integrate old and new knowledge. Though this definition emphasizes verbal and formal thinking, it also encompasses practical skills. Children in Piaget's sensorimotor period, for example, are sometimes said to show sensorimotor intelligence, which means that they learn new material by active manipulation and examination of objects and by using these encounters to build knowledge that is heavily physical and sensory.

Even though older children keep acquiring such knowledge as they grow up, their intelligence takes on an increasingly verbal and symbolic character. This verbal-symbolic ability interests many educators and psychologists because it seems to affect students' educational success in major ways. For this reason a variety of tests have been designed to measure this sort of ability. Some of these ability tests are described later on in this section. On the whole they predict school success fairly well, though they have not been equally successful at diagnosing specific learning needs of individual students or at suggesting remedies for these needs that teachers can use on a daily basis.

The Nature of Intelligence

Several views about the nature of intelligence have emerged during this century. Some, but not all, have developed in conjunction with the ability testing movement.

General Versus Specific Factors
Most test makers have argued that intelligence—or at least performance on intelligence tests—consists of both a general factor or ability and various specific factors. They have disagreed, however, about the relative importance of these factors and about how general (or specific) the factors are.

One early version of this viewpoint postulated the existence of a general ability called g that was common to all tests of ability and another factor called s that was specific to each particular ability test (Spearman, 1927). According to this view, a test of vocabulary and a test of numerical reasoning might both require some of the general g, but each might require specific abilities (the s factors) as well. The general factor would account for why individuals often tend to score at about the same level on several ability tests, and the specific factors would explain why individuals also often vary from one test to another.

Spearman's g and s factors

As more studies of abilities accumulated, other psychologists developed statistical techniques that revealed patterns or relationships among groups of tests. This led many to believe that Spearman's general *g* may not actually be a unified ability but instead consists of several factors, sometimes called *primary mental abilities* by those who studied them (Thurstone, 1938). In the most prominent version of this theory, the primary mental abilities numbered about seven: verbal comprehension, number, spatial visualization, word fluency, perceptual speed, reasoning, and memory. Each of these supposedly contributed to a person's performance on any one ability test, but they did so in varying amounts. In this view, therefore, a person did not have intelligence but rather a moderate number of "intelligences"—more specific than Spearman's *g* but perhaps more general than his *s* factors.

primary mental abilities

A theory strongly emphasizing specific abilities has been developed recently by J. P. Guilford (1977). In his view, sometimes called the *structure of intellect model,* intelligent behavior has three major aspects, each one independent of the others: operations, products, and contents. *Operations* are the mechanisms by which people think; *contents* are what they think about; and *products* are the outcomes of thinking, the results of the other two aspects. Each aspect can take several different forms, and these can combine to make up a great many "kinds" of thinking. Note that one of the operations—divergent production—has formed the basis for much research and many programs about creativity training (see Chapter 7).

Guilford's structure of intellect model

Although some psychologists believe that Guilford's structure of intellect theory carries the idea of specific factors too far, most now agree that some sort of specific-factor theory has much to recommend it. As we shall see below, the notion of several abilities constituting overall intelligence has proved helpful in the diagnosis of learning needs. The notion of one general ability, on the other hand, has been especially helpful in constructing standardized tests that predict school success. The best or most accurate theory must probably integrate both notions (Horn, 1978; Carroll & Horn, 1981).

Conglomeration Versus Compound Theories of Intelligence

Sometimes psychologists and educators describe intelligence as if it were a conglomeration of abilities or skills (Humphreys, 1979): an assortment of talents that do not necessarily resemble one another or relate to one another in any logical way. The conglomeration theory seems to underlie many (but not all) standardized tests of intelligence, especially ones that provide only a single, overall measure of general ability. In essence, such tests sample a variety of thinking skills that seem to illustrate general ability in some way. A person's intelligence is represented by how many items of this sampling he or she can do correctly.

conglomeration of separate abilities

As reasonable as this method of defining intelligence seems, it has a weakness: individuals may achieve the same overall performance score by successfully answering different batches of test items. The same "level" of intelligence may therefore represent somewhat different accomplishments—a fact that critics often point out.

In contrast, compound theories of intelligence assert that the specific skills or factors making up general ability bear a necessary and logical relationship to one another. The cognitive developmental theory of Piaget, discussed in Chapter 2, represents one prominent version of this viewpoint. In Piaget's theory, "more" intelligence does not mean being able to do a greater number of specific, unrelated skills; rather, it means achieving a higher stage of mental development. Achieving a higher stage in turn means organizing or combining previous abilities in logical ways that form new, coherent, and more complex abilities.

compound of related abilities

Although compound theories have a certain logical appeal, the intelligence that they describe has sometimes proved hard to measure reliably. As pointed out in Chapter 2, for example, successes at Piagetian tasks do not always occur at the same age for all children, or even in the same sequence. These facts suggest that Piagetian tasks may not always have the logical, stage-like qualities they are supposed to have. Tests of Piagetian tasks, in addition, do not predict school success as well as traditional, conglomeration-based intelligence tests (Uzgiris & Hunt, 1975). This may mean that schools simply are not rewarding "real" intelligence such as is (possibly) measured by Piagetian tasks, or it may mean that Piagetian tasks, for all their logical qualities, do not constitute "real" intelligence. Or it may mean some of both possibilities. In any event, current evidence does not clearly favor either the conglomeration or the compound views of intelligence.

Fluid Versus Crystallized Intelligence Some psychologists distinguish between fluid intelligence and crystallized intelligence (Horn, 1968; Cattell, 1971; Vernon, 1971). **Fluid intelligence** refers to inborn, general ability, much like Spearman's *g* discussed earlier. It is best illustrated by tests of abstract reasoning that do not require much language—for example, classifying diagrams or figures accurately and intelligently. **Crystallized intelligence** refers to knowledge and skills accumulated by experience; it is best illustrated by tests of vocabulary, reading comprehension, and general information. Any given tests of ability, however, or any given real-life task, may actually use both kinds of intelligence to some extent.

The distinction between fluid and crystallized intelligence helps to explain a curious trend found in ability-testing studies of older people: certain thinking skills decline slowly as a person gets older while others continue to improve virtually until a person's death. The skills that decline, it turns out, tend to be fluid ones; the ones that improve tend to be crystallized ones. The difference occurs, presumably, because fluid skills reflect an individual's current capacity to perform, whereas crystallized skills benefit from a lifetime of practice and overlearning (see Chapter 8) and therefore may not decline easily.

The distinction between fluid and crystallized intelligence also underlies some of the criticisms that ability tests are culturally biased (see Chapter 5). Such bias presumably occurs to the extent that the test measures crystallized, rather than fluid, abilities—vocabulary and reading, for example—which are influenced relatively strongly by life experiences. As shown below, most standardized tests of ability do measure crystallized skills, though usually not exclusively. Tests that confine themselves to measuring only fluid intelligence, however, have not proved entirely successful at their traditional task, predicting school success.

Intelligence and Creativity

Generally, intelligence and creativity seem to have no simple relationship. Two early, classic studies suggested that creative high school students tended to have at least average, and often above-average, intelligence, but that high intelligence by itself was no guarantee of high creativity (Getzels & Jackson, 1962; Wallach & Kogan, 1965). Some students, in other words, were academically bright but not creative. Highly creative students more often reported difficulties getting along with teachers and with the requirements of school life—presumably because they leaned toward divergent thinking and activity (see Chapter 7), which often might not support the educational goals their teachers had set. Academically bright students reported fewer difficulties, whether or not they were also creative.

complex relationship between intelligence and creativity

Guilford's structure of intellect model, discussed above, suggests why creativity and intelligence may only be partly related. Perhaps, as his model implies, creativity is only one part of intelligence—perhaps only the part called *divergent processes,* for example. If so, then an individual could in principle be very intelligent, as judged by Guilford's model, without happening to have strengths in divergent thinking. By the same token, being creative (that is, divergent) would insure at least some intelligence because it would constitute at least part of what the Guilford model means by "intelligence." Likewise, extremely intelligent individuals would usually have at least some divergent thinking skills because by definition such people would not be likely to have gaps in their repertoire of skills.

On the whole, recent research has confirmed these interpretations and predictions about intelligence and creativity (Vernon et al., 1977), but unfortunately it has also confirmed the ambiguity of the relationship. Creativity does seem to be different from intelligence, but only for some people in some circumstances. For many or even most students, the two qualities overlap in essential ways. For them, acquiring more of one quality will provide them with more of the other. Teachers need to remember this fact in evaluating the intellectual and creative potential of their students. More suggestions for aiding creativity—and therefore also intelligence—are discussed in Chapter 7.

Tests of Ability, Intelligence, and Scholastic Aptitude

Although ability tests exist for predicting quite a variety of human abilities, the kind that teachers most frequently encounter measure general **scholastic aptitude**: the ability to succeed in school work. For all practical purposes, scholastic aptitude amounts to what most test makers define as **intelligence**: the ability to reason abstractly, learn new material quickly, and integrate old and new knowledge. Tests that measure these abilities have various names. In addition to scholastic aptitude and intelligence tests, some may be called tests of general ability, or mental maturity, or some other variation of these terms. Although such tests differ in their emphasis on particular elements of intelligence, most require skill with language and other symbolic systems such as mathematics. There are, however, some exceptions, a few of which are noted below.

Some intelligence tests are taken in groups, and others are taken individually. As pointed out in Chapter 13, individual tests tend to be more reliable and valid, but they also require more time and effort to administer. Probably as a result, group tests are more common—at least among educators, who usually must deal with relatively large numbers of students at a time. Group tests tend to have lower reliability and validity— the price paid for greater ease of use. Teachers who must evaluate ability tests scores of students should keep these facts in mind.

individual and group tests compared

Individual Tests   One prominent individual test of general ability is the Stanford-Binet Intelligence Scale (Terman & Merrill, 1974). Like many such tests, it contains a conglomeration of items that emphasize verbal skills, as well as a considerable amount of abstract reasoning. Here are a few items from this test:

Stanford-Binet

> What day comes before Tuesday, Thursday, Friday? [for a typical 8-year-old] (p. 91)
>
> Why is this foolish? 'A man had the flu twice. The first time it killed him, but the second time he got well quickly.' [for a typical 8-year-old] (p. 90)
>
> How are these similar: winter and summer; happy and sad; much and little? [for a typical 14-year-old] (p. 108)
>
> Suppose you are going north, then turn left, then left again, then right, and then right again. In what direction are you going now? [for a typical 14-year-old] (p. 108)*

*L. Terman and M. Merrill, *Stanford-Binet Intelligence Scale: Manual for the Third Revision* (Iowa City, Iowa: The Riverside Publishing Company, 1973). Used by permission.

To take this test, an individual answers a large number of such questions roughly matched to his or her age and ability. It usually requires sixty to ninety minutes to administer the test to each person who takes it—hence its inefficiency for large-scale assessments of entire classrooms or schools. Stanford-Binet results are tabulated as as to yield one particular score, called an *intelligence quotient* or *IQ score,* which is described further below.

Another well-known individual ability test is the Wechsler Intelligence Scale for Children, Revised Form, or WISC-R for short (Wechsler, 1974). The items on the WISC-R generally resembly those on the Stanford-Binet. In addition to giving a single IQ score, however, the WISC-R gives scores for twelve particular subtests, each of which supposedly measures one specific ability. By dividing the overall test performance into subtests, the WISC-R can sometimes help in diagnosing individual abilities—in identifying particular strengths and weaknesses of persons or groups who take **WISC-R** the test. This advantage is reduced somewhat by the fact that the subtests individually are less reliable than the WISC-R taken as a whole. Nevertheless, the diagnostic potential of the WISC-R remains one of its chief attractions. In addition, half of the subtests (those involving picture completion and arrangement, block design, puzzle assembly, coding, and mazes) strive to minimize the use of language, thereby responding to one common criticism of intelligence tests, that they measure language skills too much, rather than true reasoning ability.

Group Tests The number of group tests of ability makes it hard to identify just one or two that are as prominent as the Stanford-Binet and the WISC-R tests are among individual tests. The three described below illustrate the variety possible among group tests:

1. The Otis-Lennon Mental Abilities Tests (1970) are relatively fast to give and score—requiring less than an hour and sometimes as little as thirty minutes. They come in several ability levels, and items consist mainly of reasoning and vocabulary problems presented as multiple-choice items. The items make heavy reading demands on the test taker, which is true of most group ability tests—but not true of the other examples listed below.

2. The Raven's Progressive Matrices Test (1960) contains patterned, but incomplete, figures or diagrams. The test taker completes the figures by choosing from several multiple-choice alternatives, which are also presented as figures rather than as words or descriptions. It therefore responds to the too-much-language criticism of most ability tests, and it is sometimes advocated as a more truly culture-fair test than most. Unfortunately, it also is less accurate and reliable in predicting school success than the best conventional ability tests. This fact, though, may be a reflection more of the schools' inability to be culturally fair than of the test's inadequacies.

3. The Goodenough Draw-a-Man Test (Harris, 1963), as its name implies, asks individuals to draw a pencil picture of a person as well as they

can. The picture is then evaluated by a special scoring system that generally gives a high score to complex drawings—ones with many parts to them. Like the Raven's test, the Draw-a-Man test by definition minimizes reading and the use of language by the test takers; they must, of course, understand the instructions, but they need not understand or read difficult or abstract language, nor produce such language themselves. The test works best with elementary-age children, roughly ages three through ten, rather than with older children or adults. This limitation probably results from the test's asking individuals for a realistic artistic production. Such skill improves regularly during childhood; but as many adults know, drawing ability often stops improving after that time—or even sometimes regresses to earlier, more primitive levels.

Even though the Draw-a-Man test avoids verbal-language bias, it does not escape other types of biases. Minority cultural groups, for example, differ about which parts of the body they emphasize as important and about what a "typical" person looks like. These differences presumably affect the way a child in a minority culture learns to portray a person and therefore also affect his or her score on the Draw-a-Man test. In addition, different styles of drawing evolve gradually over time. At the least, for example, clothing and hair styles change as the years go by; and a scoring system based on earlier styles may not be fair to children growing up at a later time. These possibilities do not discredit the Draw-a-Man test, but they do suggest that, like other ability tests, it has a potential for error.

The Intelligence Quotient   No matter what else they may do, most ability tests provide an overall result often called an *intelligence quotient* or *IQ score*. By definition, individuals with high IQ scores tend to perform well in school or school-like settings, where language and reasoning are heavily in demand, whereas individuals with low IQ scores tend to perform poorly. The score itself makes no comment on whether such differences are inborn or learned, fixed or variable. As a matter of fact, ability scores tend to vary from one testing to the next and over the long run. The variation suggests that both learning and testing conditions may influence IQ scores in significant ways.

IQ scores

Like other standardized measures, intelligence tests provide information about how some large standardization sample has performed on it, and these norms allow teachers to evaluate how well individuals have performed. The norms are often converted statistically from the actual or raw scores to some equivalent standardized form, analogous to the z-scores described earlier in this chapter. These converted scores usually constitute the IQ score actually reported to parents or teachers.

Many intelligence tests have arbitrarily defined the mean score of the standardization sample as 100, and the standard deviation from the mean as some arbitrary number of points, say, fifteen. A person who happens to score exactly at the mean of the standardization sample is therefore assigned an IQ score of 100, whatever his or her raw score on the test may

calculating IQ scores

have been. The IQ scores of other people depend on how many standard deviation units they differ from this arbitrarily defined mean. For example, if the test makers assigned fifteen points for every standard deviation, then the following formula would calculate the standardized IQ on the test:

$$IQ = 100 \text{ points} + (\text{deviation in } \sigma \text{ units} \times 15 \text{ points per } \sigma)$$

Thus if Mary differed from the raw mean by two standard deviations, the formula would give her this IQ:

$$\text{Mary's IQ} = 100 + (2 \ \sigma \times 15 \text{ points per } \sigma)$$
$$= 130 \text{ points}$$

But if George differed from the raw mean by -0.4 standard deviations, it would give this:

$$\text{George's IQ} = 100 + (-0.4 \ \sigma \times 15 \text{ points per } \sigma)$$
$$= 100 - 6 = 94 \text{ points}$$

Uses of Ability Tests

In the past, tests of general ability have helped educators and psychologists decide what sort of educational programs individual students should have. Students scoring low in general scholastic aptitude or intelligence were guided into less academically demanding programs of study, and students scoring high, into more demanding ones. This kind of sorting was, at its best, done in a flexible way, one that took into account other information about the students, such as their grades, other test results, motivation, and personality. General ability tests that provided separate

program guidance scores for particular thinking skills also helped in the diagnosis and division of students. The subscores identified areas of strength and weakness around which teachers could build educational experiences for their students, by either capitalizing on their strengths or building up their weaknesses. Two areas in which such division and diagnosis filled an especially pressing educational need pertained to exceptional children: the very gifted and the mentally retarded. IQ and ability tests eased the difficult and time-consuming process of arranging and conducting special education for these groups.

For the vast majority of ordinary students and schools, however, IQ testing has become a less common experience in the 1980s than it used to

screening and diagnosing special needs be. Many schools have replaced these tests with tests of more specific achievement skills—or have even eliminated standardized testing altogether. General ability and intelligence tests remain an important part of psychological and educational research, but their role in guiding the education careers of students has diminished. We now shall consider the reasons for these changes.

Criticisms of Ability Tests

Some educators have expressed deep concerns about the use of general ability tests in education. Some of their concerns are the same as those for standardized achievement tests, though some are different. As with achievement tests, some educators argue that ability tests may encourage teachers to "teach to the test" rather than to teach the subject itself, that they do not tap complex thinking skills well enough, and that they do not give teachers the specific, criterion-referenced information they need for planning instruction (Gordon & Terrell, 1981; McKenna, 1977; Perrone, 1977).

Imprecision of Scores   In addition to these concerns, some educators point out that the results of ability tests are not really as precise as they first appear. By providing a single number for an IQ score, for example, IQ tests give the impression that they measure intelligence precisely and that intelligence remains fixed for life in the amount indicated by the test. But in fact, IQ scores can vary noticeably from one testing to the next; a five-point difference is common, and even a fifteen-point difference is not uncommon. Such variation is most likely to occur if the time between testings is very great, if the person tested is a young child, or if the conditions of testing vary greatly from one time to the next.

IQ scores imprecise

But even without these factors, small differences in IQ scores are just as likely to come from random fluctuations as from true differences in intelligence. A student with an IQ score of 100 and another with a score of 105 probably have the same true ability for school work, at least for all practical purposes. Teachers should therefore resist the temptation of assigning such students to separate ability groups on the basis of such small differences. Unfortunately, according to testing critics, they do not always do so.

Built-in Biases   Many educators also criticize general ability tests for being prejudiced against particular kinds of children or students. Some minority ethnic groups—American blacks, Chicanos, or native Indians—often score well below the average of the white groups who take the test. Generally, too, children from low-income families score lower than those from more affluent ones. Critics of testing argue that these disadvantages have less to do with innate differences in ability than with differences in life experiences—language and dialect differences, in particular, and unfamiliarity with certain test content that white children take for granted (Cleary et al., 1975). To make the tests fair, they say, there should be special versions of them that take into account ethnic and social class differences. Such tests have in fact been constructed (for example, Raven, 1962), though with only mixed success. In general such *culture-fair tests* have not managed to combine the required fairness to minority groups

prejudice against certain groups

Some intelligence tests try to be more culture fair by including motor and visual tasks as well as verbal ones. (George Bellerose/Stock, Boston)

with high reliability and validity (Reschly, 1981). Reconciling these qualities, in fact, poses a serious problem to test makers.

A variety of other factors have also caused concern among some teachers and educators who must interpret standardized tests, whether of achievement or ability (Cole, 1981). How, for example, does the personality of the test administrator affect the students' performance on the test? Or the administrator's age, or race, or sex? How does a student's anxieties about testing affect his or her performance? Or the student's "test wiseness"— skill with guessing and performing on tests generally? How about the student's motivation to do well? From the standpoint of common sense, all of these factors must surely affect test performance in at least some extreme cases. In fact, research on testing has shown them all to have at least occasional or specific effects (for a review, see Chase, 1978, chap. 13). But this research has also shown that these factors do not influence test results very systematically, as some critics fear. The personality of the test administrator, for example, influences some children but not others

(Galdieri et al., 1971) and may have virtually no effect on tests taken in groups, as usually happens with most school achievement tests.

Lack of Rationale for Test Items   As pointed out earlier in this chapter, the items on many ability or intelligence tests often lack a coherent reason for inclusion on a test other than that they work—that is, predict academic success. Some psychologists and educators argue that predictive ability is reason enough for inclusion, but others object to this basis. In essence, they argue, such "conglomeration tests" lack construct validity (see Chapter 13). Conglomeration tests work only because they have been discovered to work and not because they logically *must* constitute part of general intelligence. They are therefore likely, the critics say, to serve less well wherever the test items are extended to significant new groups of people—to new minorities, for example—who may lack the background experiences assumed by the test items.

lack of inherent validity

Although this criticism remains a constant possibility, thus far it has not been supported strongly by studies of ability tests. The test scores of minority students predict their success in school just about as well as do the scores of everybody else. For minorities with lower-than-average scores, this means lower-than-average school performance. The reasons for their lower performance, however, may have less to do with how the test makers select items than with the various social circumstances that impair success for some minorities. Chapter 5 discusses some of these circumstances— low income, for example, discrimination, and cultural attitudes about language use that may interfere with testing.

Much of the criticism about lack of rationale is based on a concern with knowing the actual, detailed contents and organization of children's thinking, such as Piaget emphasizes in his theory. From this perspective, many ability test items inevitably seem trivial when considered individually. Why, for example, do students really need to know the next number in the series 1, 2, 4, 7, 11, . . . ? Or why should they know the meaning of the word *inadvertent*? The answer is that, on an individual basis, they indeed do not have to know them. Few serious social consequences would result from failing to answer either of these questions. Ability tests, however, base their value not on the importance of test items taken singly but on the importance of large groups of items taken together. Not knowing one arithmetic series or one word may not matter much, but not knowing large numbers of them may. Conversely, success on many test items may also matter in a different way, by signifying exceptional cognitive or academic talent.

Like the question of grading, the issues surrounding standardized testing also involve a question of values: how much should individual children be compared with generalized standards of excellence, assuming that such standards can indeed be defined? Some educators believe that children

In spite of pressures for accountability through testing and evaluation, teachers continue to have a basic obligation to treat each student as a unique person. (Michael Weisbrot and Family)

should be compared, as an aid to instructional and vocational planning. Others believe that they should not, or at least "only very carefully," for the reasons discussed above.

At their best, grades and test scores guide individuals in particular educational or vocational directions, and this guidance benefits both the individual and the community.

As with other human activities, though, grading and standardized testing have their limitations. Teachers and others may forget that grades and standardized tests never achieve complete reliability and validity, and they may thus base their decisions on them inappropriately. The student may wrongly be guided into, or out of, a particular course, or an individual may be hired, or not, on the basis of misunderstood scores or grades. These mistakes can seriously affect anyone, but most especially the economically disadvantaged, who may depend on education for a fair chance in life. But even if such screening decisions could be made perfectly, some educators argue that they *should* not, that instead teachers should focus on bringing students to clearly defined levels of competence and on encouraging them to make wise choices about their lives. Grades and standardized tests do not promote these purposes, some say, because they so often emphasize comparisons among individuals.

A survey of classroom teachers on this question would probably show that they have mixed feelings about it. Their responsibility for instruction teaches them to value the uniqueness of each child or student; yet at some point it usually also requires them to evaluate students and to report these evaluations to the rest of the world in the form of grades and test results. Teachers, then, need grading and testing as part of their work—but they also have reasons not to take these activities too seriously.

Key Points

1. Grading is the assignment of a number or letter to represent the overall quality of a student's performance.

2. Grades can be defined by comparisons either with other students (norm referenced) or with absolute standards (criterion referenced).

3. In addition to the conventional systems of letters and numbers, grading can also be based on systems of pass-fail, credit–no credit, and dual marking.

4. Written evaluations, letters, and conferences provide more detailed evaluations than can single letters or numbers.

5. A standardized test is characterized by large numbers of well-constructed items, clearly defined procedures for scoring and interpreting results, and information about how large populations of individuals perform on the test.

6. Among other things, standardized tests can assess abilities, achieved skills and knowledge, and interests.

7. A standardized test yields raw scores that usually must be converted into other forms for interpretation.

8. Central tendency refers to a typical or representative score, and it is usually measured by either the mean, the median, or the mode.

9. Variability refers to how much a group of scores tends to differ from its central tendency, and it is most commonly measured by the standard deviation.

10. Norms are the information about central tendency and variability for a particular test.

11. Norms must be based on a standardization sample, which is the results from a very large group of individuals who have taken the test.

12. Test scores from very large samples tend to be distributed in a bell-shaped curve called the normal curve.

13. An individual's score can be more meaningfully compared with norms if it is converted to a standardized form called a z-score.

14. Standardized achievement tests usually provide more reliable information about achievement in specific content areas than do teacher-made tests.

15. Standardized achievement tests do not necessarily test content that a particular classroom teacher may consider important.

16. Achievement test scores can be reported in several ways, as percentile ranks, stanines, or grade equivalents.

17. Standardized achievement tests are often used to assess reading ability and reading readiness,

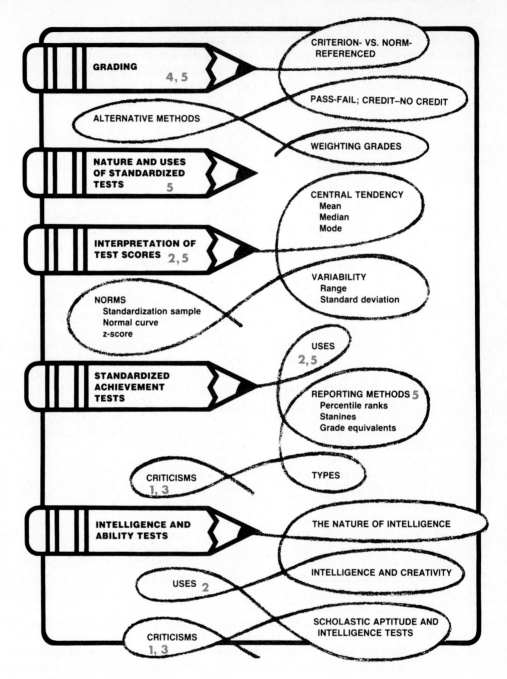

GRADING **4, 5**

CRITERION- VS. NORM-
REFERENCED

PASS-FAIL; CREDIT–NO CREDIT

ALTERNATIVE METHODS

WEIGHTING GRADES

NATURE AND USES
OF STANDARDIZED
TESTS   **5**

CENTRAL TENDENCY
Mean
Median
Mode

INTERPRETATION OF
TEST SCORES **2, 5**

VARIABILITY
Range
Standard deviation

NORMS
Standardization sample
Normal curve
z-score

USES
2, 5

STANDARDIZED
ACHIEVEMENT
TESTS

REPORTING METHODS **5**
Percentile ranks
Stanines
Grade equivalents

CRITICISMS
1, 3

TYPES

INTELLIGENCE AND
ABILITY TESTS

THE NATURE OF INTELLIGENCE

INTELLIGENCE AND CREATIVITY

USES **2**

SCHOLASTIC APTITUDE AND
INTELLIGENCE TESTS

CRITICISMS
1, 3

1 The social context of learning (Chapter 5)

2 Making instruction more effective
    (Chapter 8)

3 Motivation (Part III)

4 The motivation to learn (Chapter 11)

    Making evaluations of learning
5 (Chapter 13)

as well as achievement in a variety of curricular content areas.

18. Standardized achievement tests have been criticized for encouraging teachers to teach to the test and diverting their attention away from their students' attitudes and interests.

19. Ability tests predict performance in some broad skill or area of knowledge.

20. The most commonly used ability tests measure scholastic aptitude or general intelligence—the ability to reason abstractly.

21. Intelligence and tests to measure intelligence are based on various theories: general versus specific factors, conglomeration versus compound abilities, fluid versus crystallized ability, and sequential versus relational ability.

22. All intelligence tests provide at least one standardized score, often called an IQ score; in addition, some tests provide diagnostic scores on specific abilities.

23. Ability tests have been used primarily for guiding students' educational and vocational careers and for research on learning and development.

24. Ability tests have been criticized for lacking precision in their scores, for being biased against certain minority groups, and for lacking a rationale for selecting test items.

Case Study

Assigning Grades and Making Promotions

At the end of the school year, you are faced with deciding on grades and promotions for your class of twenty-five students in ninth-grade mathematics. The information you have for two of the students, John and Gregory, is shown (right). In addition to their scores for classroom tests and term papers, you know the results of two standardized tests given to them during January of that school year. One of these is a group intelligence test, and the other is a test of mathematics achievement. Both John and Gregory have demonstrated competence in the basic skills of ninth-grade mathematics, as judged by the school district's official curriculum guide. Gregory, however, often presents behavior management problems and does not seem consistently motivated to learn.

| | Test (each out of 100 points) | | | Term paper (out of 100 points) | Final grade |
	1	2	3		
John	70	75	90	88	??
Gregory	88	76	90	69	??
Class mean	72	78	81	80	
Class median	73	78	75	82	

Scores on group IQ test (100 = mean; 15 = standard deviation):
John: 105   Gregory: 115   Class average: 105

Scores on *International Test of Mathematical Achievement:*
John: 11.1   Gregory: 11.1   Class average: 9.8
(All scores in grade equivalents.)

Questions for Discussion

1. Taking all the information into account, what grades would you assign to John and Gregory? Explain your decisions and how they relate to the issues regarding evaluation and testing discussed in this and in the previous chapter.

2. Suppose you also had to recommend students from your class for a special accelerated mathematics course next year. Would you recommend either John or Gregory? Both or neither? Again, explain the basis of your decision.

3. What further information would make you feel more sure of your decisions on questions 1 and 2? Be reasonable in your suggestions: remember that actual teachers do not have infinite time to collect observations and give tests but that they can try to manage these activities strategically so as to give as much information as possible.

Suggested Readings

Hawkins, D. *Science and the Ethics of Equality.* New York: Basic Books, 1977.

Strenio, A. J. *The Testing Trap.* New York: Rawson, Wade, 1981.

Both of these books discuss in some detail the ethical issues regarding standardized testing. The first one was written by a philosopher but is quite comprehensible to nonphilosophers; the second one is aimed at teachers and other concerned citizens.

Lien, A. J. *Measurement and Evaluation of Learning.* Dubuque, Ia.: Wm. C. Brown Co., 1980.

Popham, W. J. *Modern Education Measurement.* Englewood Cliffs, N.J.: Prentice-Hall, 1981.

These are two general texts about testing in educational settings. The second one is written by a well-known supporter of behavioral objectives and criterion-referenced testing, and not surprisingly it gives more emphasis to these topics than does the first.

Lyman, H. *Test Scores and What They Mean.* 3rd ed. Englewood Cliffs, N.J.: Prentice-Hall, 1978.

This book gives a relatively simple and short introduction to the nature of standardized tests and the issues regarding their use.

Sattler, Jerome. *Assessment of Children's Intelligence and Special Abilities.* Boston: Allyn and Bacon, 1981.

Vernon, Philip E. *Intelligence: Heredity and Environment.* San Francisco: W. H. Freeman, 1979.

These two books focus on intelligence testing in particular. The first one describes most of the currently used tests in detail and evaluates their effectiveness. The second book discusses the theoretical issues underlying ability testing and the value assumptions it makes.

Shaycroft, M. F. *Handbook of Criterion-referenced Testing.* New York: Garland STPM Press, 1979.

This is a good book to read if you prefer criterion-referenced tests to norm-referenced ones but have not had much experience in constructing them.

Glossary of Terms

ability tests Tests that predict how well students generally will do in school and on some broad skill area.

accommodation The process of changing or modifying existing ideas or schemes to fit new experiences.

achievement tests Tests that measure how much students have learned in a particular area of knowledge or skill.

adaptation The process by which behavior modifies or changes to meet new or emerging conditions in the environment.

adaptive education An approach to education that is individualized and responsive to specific learning needs.

advance organizer A broadly constructed set of statements, either verbally or graphically presented, that puts a particular topic into context.

affective goals Feeling-oriented goals.

analysis The separation of an idea, topic, or learning goal into its elements.

anecdote A brief, verbal description of an incident.

assimilation The process of interpreting or fitting new experiences into existing ideas or schemes.

attention In information-processing theory, the part of learning in which the individual receives perceptions or information.

attitude learning The acquisition of feelings, dispositions, or beliefs about a particular topic, experience, person, or object.

attribution theory The hypothesis that motivation is affected by who or what the individual believes is the source of behavior or outcomes.

authoritarian leadership A dictatorial style of influencing a group; one that allows others little participation in decision making.

authoritative leadership A style of leadership that allows group members some influence, although the leader retains the main influence.

autonomy In Erikson's theory, the independence of action or thought acquired during the second stage of personality development.

babbling An infant's random production of vocal noises; the stage of language acquisition that precedes the production of single words.

basic trust In Erikson's theory, the fundamental confidence in parents and other significant adults acquired by infants in the first stage of personality development.

behavior objective An instructional goal that specifies the behavior to be learned, the minimum level of acceptable performance, and the conditions under which the behavior will be performed.

behaviorism The viewpoint in psychology that focuses only on overt, specific behaviors as legitimate objects of study.

behavior modification A procedure for systematically changing an individual's specific behaviors by applying the principles of behavioral psychology.

belonging needs In Maslow's theory, the motives to be a part of a group which emerge after safety needs have been met but before esteem needs emerge.

bidialecticalism The ability to speak two dialects of one language, though not necessarily equally well.

bilingualism The ability to speak two different languages, though not necessarily equally well.

black English A particular dialect of English spoken by many, but not all, black Americans in many, but not all, situations.

brainstorming The process of listing all the relevant ideas or solutions to a topic or problem without stopping to evaluate them.

central tendency A number that is somehow typical or representative of a group of scores.

chaining A method for conditioning sequences of behaviors using secondary reinforcements to establish intermediate steps.

check list A method for measuring the frequency of occurrence of particular behaviors by noting their occurrence on a prearranged list of behaviors.

chronic condition A condition that persists over long periods of time.

circular reactions In Piaget's theory, the continual repetition of a behavior that often occurs when a child is first learning to use the behavior.

classical conditioning A form of learning in which a behavior that originally followed one stimulus is made to follow another stimulus.

clinical method In Piaget's theory, the method of interviewing children using a guided or semistructured set of questions.

coding The process of classifying and associating new information with old information.

cognition The processes involved in thinking that mediate or guide behavior.

cognitive strategies Procedures for discovering knowledge.

cognitive theory A theory of learning emphasizing inner thinking: acquisition, memory, and relationship of information.

combinatorial thinking A formal operational skill in which relevant factors are systematically combined with other relevant factors.

communication The conveying of information among persons, whether in words or otherwise.

computer-assisted instruction (CAI) Methods of teaching that draw upon computerized storage, retrieval, and presentation of information.

concept An idea or thought referring to a group of objects, perceptions, or experiences.

concrete operational period In Piaget's theory, the stage of cognitive development in which the child can conserve, classify, and mentally reverse logical operations on real objects.

conditioning Learning that occurs through the systematic pairing of stimuli and responses (in classical conditioning) or responses and reinforcements (in operant conditioning).

conservation The belief in invariance despite perceptual changes in an object.

construct validity The extent to which a test actually assesses the quality or skill that it claims to test.

content validity The extent to which a test contains concepts and ideas that relate logically to the skill or quality the test claims to measure.

contiguity learning Two previously unrelated stimuli occurring together in the presence of a response to one of the stimuli.

contingency contracts Agreements to reward students in some specific way if they perform some work or behave in some specified, desirable way.

convergent thinking The ability to produce one relatively well-defined solution to a problem.

creativity The production of new ideas, activities, or objects.

criterion-referenced test A test that is eval-

uated by comparing the results according to some predefined fixed standard.

criterion-related validity The extent to which a test correlates with other, valid tests of a particular quality or skill.

culture The entire pattern of behaviors and beliefs of a group of people.

décallage The lag in time in the appearance of a general stage of thinking when tested by different, but related, tasks.

deep structure The underlying or essential organization of an utterance, to which transformation rules may be applied.

deficiency needs In Maslow's theory, those needs that must be satisfied by sources external to the individual and that become less pressing as they are satisfied.

development The long-run emergence of qualities, abilities, and skills due to the combined effects of spontaneous learning, maturation, and social influences.

diagnosis The measurement or identification of specific qualities, abilities, or skills from among the full range possessed by an individual.

dialect A version of a language that differs from others in its pronunciation, vocabulary, and grammatical features.

discovery learning A method of education that invites students to discover ideas and information on the basis of their own efforts, using learning materials that have been provided for them.

discriminative learning Learning that requires accurately noticing the differences among objects or perceptions.

discriminative stimulus In operant conditioning, the stimulus that signals the availability or nonavailability of reinforcement if operant behavior is emitted.

divergent thinking The ability to produce a wide variety of solutions to a problem, however unusual or unconventional these may be.

double promotion Allowing gifted students to skip a grade.

dual marking Giving one grade for performance and another for effort or improvement.

educational psychology The study of how learning occurs and how teaching may help it occur.

egocentrism The tendency of an individual or child to assume that others view the world in the same way that he or she does or that they hold the same opinions about it.

elaboration The ability to add richness or detail to a response.

enactive learning A mode of learning in which the child acts upon or manipulates objects in order to understand them.

equilibration In Piaget's theory, the balance or harmony achieved between assimilation and accommodation that leads to development through cognitive stages.

equivalent forms A testing method of giving a test twice, each time using a different version of the same general content.

eros In human behavior, the drive toward love.

esteem needs In Maslow's theory, the motives for respect or admiration from others which emerge after the belonging needs are satisfied.

evaluation of learning The process of determining the value of learning through observations or tests and with reference to some sort of standards or criteria.

exceptionality An extreme or unusual quality, ability, or handicap, often requiring special instructional planning and methods.

extinction In operant-conditioning theory, the removal of reinforcement and the consequent disappearance of the operant behavior.

face validity The extent to which a test contains content that appears to relate to the ability, knowledge, or skill that it claims to test.

fixed interval Reinforcement after a fixed amount of time passes.

fixed ratio Reinforcement after a fixed number of responses.

flexibility The ability to approach a problem from a variety of angles, without getting fixed on any one in particular.

fluency The ability to produce, without interruption, numerous responses to a stimulus or problem.

formal discipline The theory that the human mind consists of general abilities that can be trained by learning certain subject matters.

formal operational period In Piaget's theory, the stage following concrete operations, in which the individual can reason abstractly, system-atically, and with only minimal reference to tangible objects.

frame In Skinner's programmed instruction, a small step.

function A psychological process; in language and communication research, the use or purpose of an utterance.

general achievement tests Tests that measure the whole range of basic skills taught in schools.

generalization The application of an idea, behavior, or skill to other, comparable situations or people.

generalized reinforcement or reinforcer A reinforcement or reinforcer leading to many other, more primary reinforcements.

grade A single number or letter assigned to represent the overall quality of a student's performance.

grade equivalent scores On standardized tests, a way of reporting performance as a grade level at which a particular score occurs on the average.

grammar The organization of a language, including its vocabulary and its rules for both relating words into phrases and transforming sentences into other sentences.

growth needs In Maslow's theory, those needs that individuals can satisfy by their own activities, which enhance their sense of individuality and lead to further needs for growth.

habituation The process of becoming accustomed to a stimulus or situation, often leading, as a result, to a decrease or change in some behavior.

halo effect The tendency to respond as though the person being rated were all good or all bad.

hierarchy A fixed order, with each step considered better or more advanced than the ones before it.

holophrase A single word meant to convey an entire thought or message; used by children when they first learn to talk.

humanism A philosophy or viewpoint that places the highest value on individual needs, interests, and dignity.

hypothetical construct A concept or idea that cannot be observed but is proposed or imagined to exist in order to explain certain observations.

hypothetical idea An idea that exists only in the human mind.

iconic learning A mode of learning or thinking that relies on visual representations.

idealism An insensitivity to the practical limits of ideas.

identical elements The theory that transfer occurs only to the extent that elements of the learning situation duplicate those to which the learning is to be applied.

identity The qualities, skills, and behaviors that together define who a person is.

identity crisis In Erikson's theory, the process of facing the question of one's identity.

incidence In special education, the percentage of the population who experience a particular form of exceptionality some time during their lives.

individualized educational plans (IEP) Contracts between students and their teachers specifying the educational goals set for them and the provisions made for reaching those goals; often used for exceptional conditions.

individually prescribed instruction (IPI) A system for coordinating the learning and instruction of entire schools of students and teachers, while at the same time adjusting the content, methods, and pacing to the needs of individual students.

industry Erikson's fourth stage of personality development, in which individuals attempt to learn particular skills through personal concerted efforts.

information-processing theory A cognitive theory of learning in which thinking is modeled after the workings of a high-speed computer.

initiative Erikson's third stage of personality development, in which individuals learn to choose and carry out plans and intentions of their own.

inquiry learning A method of education in which students are encouraged to learn by asking questions, discussing ideas, and searching for their own answers.

insight A relatively sudden perception, understanding, or intuition resulting from the coming together of ideas or experiences.

instinct A natural or innate behavior that is not affected by learning or experience.

instructional management The organization or coordination of all the tasks needed to prepare for and engage in teaching.

integrity In Erikson's theory, one's acceptance of having lived one's life as well as possible in the existing circumstances.

intelligence The ability to reason abstractly, learn new material quickly, and integrate old and new knowledge.

intelligence test A standardized test of the ability to reason logically and understand relationships.

intrinsic motivation An arousal or excitement that originates within the individual and leads to a tendency to act in particular ways.

inventories In education, tests that measure attitudes and interests.

inventories of interests Structured questionnaires that ask one to describe one's interests in a variety of activities, usually vocationally related ones.

IQ score The numerical result of an intelligence test, often expressed in standardized units so that 100 represents an average score.

Keller plan A system for organizing very large courses by using student tutors, self-paced quizzes, and large lectures as rewards for achievement.

LAD (language acquisition device) The name given to the hypothetical processes that must account for the development of language in children.

laissez faire A type of leadership in which the leader takes very little initiative and responds only to direct requests from group members.

language The words and the rules for their use common to a particular community or society.

language styles Unstated rules regarding when and how one should talk.

language universals Features of grammar that exist in all languages and that all children acquire in becoming fully competent in language.

latent learning Any learning or permanent change in behavior that occurs without the learner's conscious intent.

learning Any relatively permanent change in behavior or thinking resulting from a relatively specific experience.

learning disability Achievement that falls below ability, with no obvious cause.

Likert scale A procedure for making a general rating of a person, behavior, or situation by adding together the results of several related, more specific ratings.

locus of control The place or location where individuals believe that the control over their behavior lies.

long-term memory That part of the information-processing model of thinking in which experiences are coded and stored relatively permanently.

MACOS (Man: A Course of Study.) A social studies curriculum for elementary school children covering child-rearing practices, group relationships, and socialization and culture.

mainstreaming The provision of learning and instruction for exceptional children in the least possible restrictive educational environment.

mathamagenic activity Behaviors by learners that lead to real or significant learning.

maturation Long-run changes in behavior and appearance resulting from physical growth or various environmental experiences.

mean The average of a group of test scores; defined as their sum, divided by the number of scores.

measurement The process of quantifying or attaching numbers to observations so as to assist their analysis and comparison.

median A score marking the middle of a group of scores.

mediators Terms or ideas that help in providing links among stimuli and responses or among otherwise unrelated ideas.

mentally retarded Having limited or deficient intellectual ability or intellectual development.

mnemonics Visual or verbal devices or tricks used to help memory.

mode The most commonly occurring score on a test.

modeling Providing a pattern of behavior to imitate.

moral development The long-run emergence of ethical beliefs and ethical conduct, caused by a wide variety of specific experiences.

moral realism In Piaget's theory, a stage of moral development in which the child judges rightness according to the physical consequences of an action rather than by the intentions underlying the action.

moral relativism In Piaget's theory, a stage of moral development in which the child judges rightness according to the intentions underlying a particular action, and not only according to its physical consequences.

morpheme The smallest meaningful unit of language.

motivation The tendency to act in a particular way or engage in particular actions, or the arousal or excitement underlying such a tendency.

motive A particular need or want that leads to motivation.

motor skills learning The learning of active or doing-oriented skills, as opposed to cerebral, thinking-oriented skills.

need for achievement (nAch) The desire to achieve a particular, definable standard of excellence.

negative reinforcement or reinforcer An aversive object removed or event prevented from occurring in consequence of a certain behavior.

negative transfer The application of old learning to new situations in a way that interferes with new, more appropriate learning.

norm-referenced tests Tests in which scores are assigned by comparing individuals with one another or with some standard population of individuals.

norms The scores or numbers summarizing the central tendency and variability of a group of scores.

number In Piagetian theory, a child's ability to establish numerical equivalences, or number correspondences, among sets of objects.

object permanence The belief, acquired in infancy, that objects continue to exist even when not immediately visible or tangible.

observation In education, the collecting of tentative information about students so as to make inferences about their learning needs.

observational learning Significant and relatively permanent changes in behavior caused by seeing another perform the behavior.

open education A method of education that emphasizes self-choice by learners and that offers individualized curricula.

operant The behavior that, when emitted, causes reinforcement to become available and that increases in frequency of occurrence as a result.

operant conditioning The process by which the consequences of certain behaviors influence the chance of those behaviors being repeated in the future. Operant conditioning also can refer to the model itself.

organization In Piaget's theory, the tendency for thinking to become increasingly systematic and logical as it develops.

orienting response In information-processing theory, the initial response of learners to a stimulus that allows them to receive information from the stimulus.

originality The ability to make an unusual or out-of-the-ordinary response.

overlearning The continued practice of a fully learned behavior, even though it produces no further apparent improvement in performance.

partial reinforcement Reinforcement only some of the time.

participation structure The pattern of who gets to participate in activities and discussions, and under what circumstances.

percentile rank The rank of a score on a test indicating the percentage of other scores falling above and below it.

personality All the feelings, abilities, and motives that belong to a person and that altogether define him or her as an individual.

personal originality The ability of an individual to produce an idea or response that is uncommon or new for that particular individual, whether or not it is new for society at large.

phobia A persistent, illogical, abnormal, or intense fear.

phonemes A vocal sound or group of sounds that makes a meaningful difference in the speech of a language.

phrase structure The organization of an utterance into grammatical units.

positive reinforcement or reinforcer A reward given as a consequence of the operant being performed.

positive transfer The correct performance of previously learned behaviors in new situations.

Premack principle The procedure for determining the relative reinforcement value of different objects or events by allowing the learner free choice among them.

preoperational period In Piaget's theory, the stage prior to logical thought, during which the child practices symbolic representations of his or her experiences.

primary reinforcement or reinforcer Primary creature comforts—food, water, and sex—that cause a behavior to occur.

programmed instruction Instruction that has been clearly planned and carefully sequenced so as to ensure maximum success in learning.

projective techniques Tests or other assessment materials that contain very ambiguous stimuli so that test takers have the freedom to attach their own meanings to them.

psychogenic needs Needs or motives that are psychological or mental in origin.

psychology The scientific study of human behavior, thinking, feeling, and motivation.

punishment The administration of an aversive or painful stimulus to an individual following a particular behavior.

range The difference between the highest and the lowest score on a test.

rating A method of measuring a behavior or quality by comparing it according to different amounts of a particular dimension.

recitation A method of education in which the teacher asks questions related to content and students display their knowledge of this content by answering the questions.

reflex connection A stimulus and a response that occur together simply by virtue of how an animal (or person) is physically constructed.

reinforcement Any object or event that causes a particular behavior to increase in frequency of occurrence.

reliability The extent to which a test or observation gives consistent results.

resource teacher A teacher who assists other teachers in planning and carrying out learning activities, especially individualized ones for exceptional children.

response A behavior made in reaction to a stimulus.

response generator The feature of thinking that creates or generates responses.

rules Statements that relate concepts to one another.

running record A method of observation in which all behaviors that occur during a given period of time are written down as they occur.

safety needs In Maslow's theory, the motives to become and remain comfortable and out of danger, which emerge after survival needs but before belonging needs.

schedule of reinforcement In operant conditioning, the pattern or timing by which reinforcements become available.

schemes Ideas or actions that develop from the increasing organization and adaptation of thinking.

scholastic aptitude The ability to succeed in school work.

secondary reinforcement or reinforcer A stimulus that happens to occur with a primary reinforcer and thus acquires reinforcing properties of its own.

self-actualization needs The highest level of motivation in Maslow's theory, in which persons pursue activities that enhance their sense of individuality and their aesthetic and intellectual knowledge.

self-concept One's idea of oneself or one's personality as viewed by oneself.

self-esteem One's evaluation of oneself and one's worth.

self-fulfilling prophecy Any expectation that comes true simply by virtue of being believed.

sensorimotor period In Piaget's theory, the first major stage of cognitive development, in which the child learns primarily by sensing and manipulating objects.

sensory detectors Eyes, ears, nose, mouth, and skin.

sensory synthesis The process of combining sensory experiences or information.

sensory synthesizer The feature of human thinking that combines sensory experiences or information.

serial position effect The tendency for an individual to remember best the beginning and ending material from a list of unrelated terms.

seriation The cognitive skill of sequencing or putting in order a series of objects that differ along some particular dimension.

sex role The pattern of behaviors associated in a society with a particular sex.

shaping The concept of response differentiation; the process of conditioning behaviors that approximate the desired form of a behavior, in which each approximation should be a better approximation than the one before it.

short-term memory In information-processing theory, the cognitive process in which information or perception is held temporarily before being coded and stored permanently.

sigma (σ) A term often used to refer to the standard deviation of a normal distribution.

social class A segment of society defined by particular roles, income levels, and ways of life.

social contract The set of legal and legalistic rules of procedure for setting basic disagreements.

social learning theory A behavioral theory of learning that focuses on the processes of modeling and imitation.

socioeconomic status (SES) The level or place of a person or group in society, defined by particular roles, income levels, and ways of life.

specific learning disability A deficit or difficulty in one relatively precise academic skill that does not generalize to learning or behavior as a whole.

spiral curriculum The doubling back of instruction on itself over time.

split-half reliability A numerical measure of consistency based on how well one half of a test correlates with the other half.

stage A period or level in a sequence of levels that has certain unique properties.

standard deviation A statistical measure for estimating the amount of variability in a normal distribution of scores.

standard English A dialect or version of English commonly used by middle-class speakers in formal situations and often considered the "best" version of the language.

standardized test A test in which the questions and scoring procedures have been carefully prepared so that an individual's performance can be compared meaningfully with that of some larger group or population.

stanine An interval of test scores that is one-half of a standard deviation wide; used sometimes in reporting scores on standardized tests.

stimulus An object or event that causes a learned behavior.

stimulus predifferentiation The ability to detect small or subtle differences in the stimulus that actually requires significantly different responses.

stimulus substitution The process by which one object or event replaces another in eliciting a particular response.

structure The way that objects, events, or ideas are related or organized.

surface structure In a sentence, the actual string of words uttered.

survival needs The lowest level in Maslow's theory, in which the individual seeks to satisfy basic physical needs, such as those for food, water, and sex.

symbol An object, event, or concept that stands for or represents another object, event, or concept.

symbolic learning Learning that requires arbitrary or abstract representations of knowledge.

synthesis The blending or integration of elements or ideas.

table of specifications A table of the relationships among the topics taught in a particular unit and the cognitive activities or skills needed for each of them.

task analysis The process of identifying the specific elements of or steps in a particular activity.

taxonomy A set of categories for classifying objects, events, or ideas.

teacher effectiveness training (TET) A method that draws on humanistic principles to help teachers to establish and maintain better relationships with their students.

teacher-made test A test constructed by a teacher, based on content that the teacher knows the students have covered.

telegraphic speech Speech that omits many prepositions, conjunctions, articles, and other modifiers; used by toddlers as they learn to talk.

test-retest reliability A measure of consistency based on correlating one administration of a test with another one of the same test.

theme-centered discussion A group's discussion of a topic according to several special ground rules.

time sampling A method of observation in which behavior is recorded only at selected intervals of time.

token economy A system of behavior management in which individuals earn tokens for desired behavior which they can later exchange for other rewards.

transfer The generalization or application of learning to new stituations.

transformational grammar A description of a language's organization that establishes rules for converting certain basic sentence forms into other related forms.

usability The ease with which a test can be used under practical circumstances.

validity The extent to which a test or observation measures what it claims to measure.

values Deeply held attitudes toward or beliefs about particular objects, events, or behaviors.

values clarification A method of education using discussion exercises designed to make students' attitudes and beliefs explicit.

variable interval Reinforcement after a variable amount of time passes.

variable ratio Reinforcement after a variable number of responses.

verbal learning The acquisition or modification of concepts or terms that are expressed through language.

vicarious reinforcement The process in which the observer watches the model receive (or fail to receive) reinforcement, without actually receiving it himself or herself.

"withitness" The ability of a teacher to perceive changes in students' behavior even though the teacher's attention may be focused elsewhere.

z-score A score on a standardized test expressed in units of standard deviations.

Bibliography

Adams, C., and R. Laurikietis. *The Gender Trap.* Book 1. London: Quartet Books, 1976.

Airasian, P., and W. Bart. "Validating Prior Instructional Hierarchies." *Journal of Educational Measurement,* 12 (1975), 163–173.

———, G. F. Madaus, and J. J. Padulla. *Minimal Competency Testing.* Englewood Cliffs, N.J.: Educational Technology Pub., 1979.

Allyon, T., and N. H. Azrin. *The Token Economy.* New York: Appleton-Century-Crofts, 1968.

Alschuler, A. *Developing Achievement Motivation in Adolescents.* Englewood Cliffs, N.J.: Prentice-Hall, 1973.

Ames, C., and S. McKelvie. "Evaluations of Student Achievement Behavior Within Cooperative and Competitive Reward Structures." Paper presented at the Annual Meeting of the American Educational Research Association, New York, 1982.

Anastasi, A. *Psychological Testing.* 4th ed. New York: MacMillan, 1976.

Aronso, E., N. Blaney, J. Sikes, G. Stephan, and M. Snapp. *The Jigsaw Classroom.* Beverly Hills, Calif.: Sage Publications, 1978.

Asch, S. "Reformulation of the Problem of Association." *American Psychologist,* 24 (1969), 92–102.

Au, K. H. P., and C. Jordan. "Teaching Reading to Hawaiian Children: Finding a Culturally Appropriate Situation." In *Culture and the Bilingual Classroom.* H. T. Trueba et al. Rowley, Mass.: Newbury House, 1981.

Ausubel, D. *The Psychology of Meaningful Verbal Learning.* New York: Grune and Stratton, 1963.

———. *Educational Psychology: A Cognitive View.* 2nd ed. New York: Holt, Rinehart and Winston, 1978a.

———. "In Defense of Advance Organizers: A Reply to the Critics." *Review of Educational Research,* 48 (1978b), 251–257.

———. "Schemata, Cognitive Structure, and Advance Organizers: A Reply to Anderson, Spiro and Anderson." *American Educational Research Journal,* 17, No. 3 (1980), 400–404.

Axelrod, S. *Behavior Modification for the Classroom Teacher.* New York: McGraw-Hill, 1977.

Ballard, M. "Improving the Social Status of Mainstreamed Retarded Children." *Journal of Educational Psychology,* 69 (1977), 605–611.

Bandura, A. *Principles of Behavior Modification.* New York: Holt, Rinehart and Winston, 1965.

———. *Psychological Modeling: Conflicting Theories.* New York: Aldine-Atherton Press, 1971.

———. *Social Learning Theory.* New York: General Learning Press, 1977.

———, and G. Walters. *Social Learning and Personality Development.* New York: Holt, Rinehart and Winston, 1963.

Baratz, S., and J. Baratz. "Early Childhood Intervention: The Social Science Basis for Institutional Racism." *Harvard Educational Review,* 40 (1970), 28–50.

Bates, E., L. Benigni, I. Bretherton, and V. Volterra. *The Emergence of Symbols.* New York: Academic Press, 1979.

Baumrind, D. "Current Patterns of Parental Authority." *Developmental Psychology Monographs,* 4, No. 1 (1971).

———. "Development of Instrumental Competence Through Socialization." In *Minnesota Symposia on Child Psychology.* Ed. A. Pick. Vol. 7. Minneapolis: Univ. of Minnesota Press, 1973.

Bejar, I. I., and E. O. Blew. "Grade Inflation and the Validity of the Scholastic Aptitude Test." *American Educational Research Journal,* 18, No. 2 (1981), 143–156.

Bellazza, F. S. "Mnemonic Devices: Classification, Characteristics, and Criteria." *Review of Educational Research,* 51, No. 2 (1981), 247–275.

Bennett, N. *Teaching Styles and Pupil Progress.* Cambridge, Mass.: Harvard University Press, 1976.

Berdyne, D. "Arousal and Reinforcement." In *Nebraska Symposium on Motivation.* Ed. D. Levine. Lincoln, Nebr.: University of Nebraska Press, 1967.

Bereiter, C., and S. Engelmann. *Teaching Disadvantaged Chil-*

dren in the Preschool. Englewood Cliffs, N.J.: Prentice-Hall, 1966.

Berelson, B., and G. Steiner. *Human Behavior: Inventory of Scientific Findings.* New York: Harcourt, Brace and World, 1964.

Bergan, J. R. "The Structural Analysis of Behavior: An Alternative to the Learning-Hierarchy Model." *Review of Educational Research,* 50, No. 4 (1980), 625–646.

Berk, L. "How Well Do Classroom Practices Reflect Teacher Goals?" *Young Children,* 32, No. 1 (1976), 64–80.

Bernstein, E. "What Does a Summerhill Old School Tie Look Like?" *Psychology Today,* 2, No. 5 (1968), 37–41.

Berry, J. *Moving Toward Self-Directed Learning.* Alexandria, Va.: Association for Supervision and Curriculum Development, 1979.

Beyer, B. "Conducting Moral Discussions in the Classroom." *Social Education,* 40, No. 4 (1976), 194–202.

Biechlin, H. "Inducing Conservation Through Training." In *Psychology of the 20th Century.* Ed. G. Steiner. Vol. 7. Zurich: Kindler, 1977.

Bingham, W., and E. House. "Counselors' View Women and Work: Accuracy of Information." *Vocational Guidance Quarterly,* 21 (1973), 262–268.

Blank, M. *Teaching Learning in the Preschool.* Columbus, Ohio: Charles Merrill, 1973.

———. *Language of Learning.* New York: Grune and Stratton, 1978.

Blatt, M., and L. Kohlberg. "The Effects of Classroom Moral Discussions on Children's Levels of Moral Judgement." In *Moralization: The Cognitive Developmental Approach.* Ed. L. Kohlberg and E. Turiel. New York: Holt, Rinehart and Winston, 1974.

Block, J., and R. Burns. "Mastery Learning." In *Review of Research in Education.* Ed. L. Shulman. Vol. 4. Itasca, Ill.: F. E. Peacock, 1977.

Bloom, B., M. Engelhart, E. Furst, W. Hill, and D. Krathwohl. *Taxonomy of Educational Objectives: The Cognitive Domain.* New York: Longman's Green, 1956.

Bloom, L. *One Word at a Time.* The Hague: Mouton Pub., 1973.

Bouchard, T., and M. McGue. "Familial Studies of Intelligence: A Review." *Science,* 212, No. 4498 (1981), 1055–1059.

Bower, D. *Child Development and Education: A Piagetian Perspective.* New York: Oxford University Press, 1976, p. 93ff.

Boylan, W. "The Effects on Academic Achievement of Special Education and Regular Classrooms." Ph.D. dissertation, California School of Professional Psychology, San Francisco, 1976.

Brandt, R. *Studying Behavior in Natural Settings.* New York: Holt, Rinehart and Winston, 1972.

Braun, C. "Teacher Expectation: Sociopsychological Effects." *Review of Educational Research,* 46, No. 2 (1976), 185–213.

Brent, S., and E. Katz. "Study of Language Deviations and Cognitive Processes." Report No. 3, Office of Economic Opportunity Job Corps Contract No. 1209, Wayne State University, 1967.

Bronfenbrenner, U. *Two Worlds of Childhood: U.S. and U.S.S.R.* New York: Basic Books, l970.

Brown, R. *A First Language.* Cambridge, Mass.: Harvard University Press, 1973.

———, C. Cazden, and V. Belluyi. "The Child's Grammar from I to III." In *Minnesota Symposium On Child Psychology.* Ed. J. P. Hill. Vol. 2. Minneapolis: University of Minnesota Press, 1969.

Bruner, J. *The Process of Education.* Cambridge, Mass.: Harvard University Press, 1960.

———. "Some Elements of Discovery." In *Learning by Discovery: A Critical Appraisal.* Ed. L. Shulman and E. Keilar. Chicago: Rand McNally Company, 1966a.

———. *Toward a Theory of Instruction.* Cambridge, Mass.: Belknap Press, 1966b.

———. *The Relevance of Education.* New York: W.W. Norton Co., 1971.

———. *Beyond the Information Given: Studies in the Psychology of Knowing.* New York: W.W. Norton, 1973.

———. "Ontogenesis of Speech Acts." *Journal of Child Language,* 2 (1975), 1–19.

———. *On knowing: Essays for the Left-Hand.* Rev. ed. Cambridge, Mass.: Harvard University Press, 1979.

———. "Schooling in a Nasty Climate." *Psychology Today,* 16, No. 1 (January 1982), 57–63.

Burns, E. *The Development, Use, and Abuse of Educational Tests.* Springfield, Ill.: Charles Thomas Publishers, 1979.

Buros, O. K. *Seventh Mental Measurements Yearbook.* Highland Park, N.J.: Gryphon Press, 1972.

Carroll, J. B., and J. L. Horn. "On the Scientific Basis of Ability Testing." *American Psychologist,* 36, No. 10 (1981), 1012–1020.

Case, R. "Gearing the Demands of Instruction to the Developmental Capacities of the Learner." *Review of Educational Research,* 45, No. 1 (1975), 59–87.

———. "A Developmentally Based Theory and Technology of Instruction." *Review of Educational Research,* 48, No. 3 (1978), 439–463.

Cattell, R. B. *Abilities: Their Structure, Growth and Action.* Boston: Houghton Mifflin, 1971.

Cazden, C. "Acquisition of Noun and Verb Inflections." *Child Development,* 39 (1968), 433–438.

———. "The Neglected Situation in Child Language Research and Education." In *Language and Poverty.* Ed. F. Williams. Chicago: Markham Publishers, 1970.

———. *Child Language and Education.* New York: Holt, Rinehart and Winston, 1972.

———, and E. L. Leggett. "Culturally Responsible Education: Recommendations for Achieving *Lau* Remedies." In *Culture and the Bilingual Classroom.* H. T. Trueba et al. Rowley, Mass.: Newbury House, 1981.

Chase, C. I. "Relative Length of Option and Response Set in Multiple-Choice Items." *Educational and Psychological Measurement,* 24 (1964), 861–866.

———. "Often Is Where You Find It." *American Psychologist,* 24, (1969), 1042.

———. *Measurement for Educational Evaluation.* 2nd ed. Reading, Mass.: Addison-Wesley Publishing Company, 1978.

Chomsky, N. "The Case Against B. F. Skinner." *New York Review of Books,* December 30, 1971, 18–24.

———. *Language and Mind.* 2nd ed. New York: Harcourt, Brace, Jovanovich, 1972.

———. *Syntactic Structures.* The Hague: Mouton Pub., 1978a.

———. *Topics in the Theory of Generative Grammar.* The Hague: Mouton Pub.: 1978b.

———. *Language and Learning: The Debate Between Jean Piaget and Noam Chomsky* Cambridge, Mass.: Harvard University Press, 1980.

Cleary, T. A. "Educational Uses of Tests with Disadvantaged Students." *American Psychologist,* 30 (1975), 15–41.

Cogelka, W. *Review of Work-Study Programs for the Mentally Retarded.* Arlington, T.: N.A.R.C. Publications, 1976.

Cohen, D., and V. Stern. *Observing and Recording the Behavior of Young Children.* Rev. ed. New York: Teachers' College Press, 1978.

Cohen, S. "Minimal Brain Dysfunction and Practical Matters such as Teaching Kids to Read." In *Minimal Brain Dysfunction.* Ed. F. de la Cruz et al. New York: Annals of the New York Academy of Science, 1973.

Cohn, R. "Style and Spirit of the Theme-Centered Interactional Method." In *Progress in Group and Family Therapy.* Eds. C. Sagar and H. Kaplan. New York: Brunner/Mazel, 1972.

Colby, A. "Two Approaches to Moral Education." *Harvard Educational Review,* 45, No. 1 (1975), 134–143.

Cole, N. S. "Bias in Testing." *American Psychologist,* 36, No. 10 (1981), 1067–1077.

Coles, R. *Children of Crisis.* Vol. 1–5. Boston: Little, Brown, 1968–1977.

Conger, J. "Freedom and Commitment: Families, Youth, and Social Change." *American Psychologist,* 36, No. 12 (1981), 1475–1484.

Cooley, W., and G. Leinhardt. *The Application of a Model for Investigating Classroom Processes.* Pittsburgh: University of Pittsburgh, Learning Research and Development Center, 1975.

Covington, M. V., R. S. Crutchfield, L. Davies and R. M. Olton. *The Productive Thinking Program: A Course in Learning to Think.* Columbus, Ohio: Charles Merrill, 1974.

———, and R. Beery. *Self-Worth and School Learning.* New York: Holt, Rinehart and Winston, 1976.

Cruickshank, W., and D. Hallahan, eds. *Perceptual and Learning Disabilities in Children.* Vol. 1. Syracuse, N.Y.: Syracuse University Press, 1975.

D'Agostino, P. R., and P. De Remer. "Repetition Effects as a Function of Rehearsal and Encoding Variability." *Journal of Verbal Learning and Verbal Behavior,* 12 (1973), 108–113.

Dasen, P. R., ed. *Piagetian Psychology: Cross-Cultural Contributions.* New York: Gardner Press, 1977.

DeBono, E. *New Think: The Use of Lateral Thinking in the Generation of New Ideas.* New York: Basic Books, 1967.

DeCharms, R. *Enhancing Motivation.* New York: Wiley, 1976.

———, and V. Carpenter. "Measuring Motivation in Culturally Disadvantaged School Children." *Journal of Experimental Education,* 37 (1968), 31–41.

Deci, E. "Intrinsic Motivation, Extrinsic Motivation, and Ineptuity." *Journal of Personality and Social Psychology,* 22 (1972), 113–120.

Dembo, M., and K. Gurney. "The Effects of Cooperative and Individualistic Goal Structure on the Causal Attributions for Performance of Korean and Samoan-American Students." Paper presented at the Annual Meeting of the American Educational Research Association, New York, 1982.

DeVilliers, P. and J. DeVilliers. *Language Acquisition.* Cambridge, Mass.: Harvard University Press, 1978.

———. *Early Language.* Cambridge, Mass.: Harvard University Press, 1979.

Dillard, J. "Bidialectical Education: Black English and Standard English in the United States." In *Case Studies In Bilingual Education.* Ed. B. Spolsky and R. Cooper. Rowley, Mass.: Newbury House, 1977.

Duchastel, P., and P. Merrill. "Effects of Behavioral Objectives on Learning: A Review of Empirical Studies." *Review of Educational Research,* 43, No. 1 (1976), 53–69.

Dunn, L. M., and L. M. Dunn. *Peabody Picture Vocabulary Test—Revised.* Circle Pines, Minn.: American Guidance Service, 1981.

Duska, R. and M. Whelan. *Moral Development: A Guide to Piaget and Kohlberg.* Dublin: Gill and MacMillan, 1977.

Ebel, R. "Criterion-Referenced Measurement: Its Limitations." *School Review,* 79 (1971), 282–288.

———. "Can Teachers Write Good True-False Items?" *Journal of Educational Measurement,* 12 (1975), 31–36.

Elkind, D. "Reading, Logic, and Perception: An Approach to Reading Instruction." In *Childhood and Adolescence: Interpretive Essays on Jean Piaget.* 2nd ed. Ed. David Elkind. New York: Oxford University Press, 1974.

———. *Child Development and Education: A Piagetian Perspective.* New York: Oxford University Press, 1976, p. 93ff.

Elmes, D. G., W. I. Greener, and W. C. Wilkinson. "Free Recall of Items Presented After Massed, and Distributed Practice Items." *American Journal of Psychology,* 85 (1972), 237–240.

Engelmann, S. "How to Construct Effective Language Programs for the Poverty Child." In *Language and Poverty.* Ed. F. Williams. Chicago: Markham Publishers, 1970.

———, J. Osborn, and T. Engelmann. *DISTAR.* Chicago: Science Research Associates, 1978.

England, B., and M. DeNello. "The Relationship of Intellectual, Visual-Motor, Psycholinguistic, and Readiness Skills and Achievement." *Educational and Psychological Measurement,* 30 (1970), 451–456.

Engle, P. L. "Language Medium in Early School Years for Minority Language Groups." *Review of Educational Research,* 45, No. 2 (1975), 283–325.

Ensor, E. G. "Comparison of Dyadic Interactions Between High and Low Self-Concept of Ability Children and Their Teachers." Masters thesis, Bradford University, U.K. Cited in R. B. Burns, *The Self-Concept.* New York: Longman, 1979.

Epstein, N. *Language, Ethnicity, and the Schools.* Washington: George Washington University Institute for Educational Leadership, 1977.

Erikson, E. *Childhood and Society.* 2nd ed. New York: W.W. Norton, 1963.

Erreich, A., V. Valian, and J. Winzemer. "Aspects of a Theory of Language Acquisition." *Journal of Child Language,* 7, No. 1 (1980), 157–179.

Ervin-Tripp, S. "Language Development." In *Review of Child Development Research.* Ed. L. W. Hoffman & M. L. Hoffman. New York: Russell Sage Foundation, 1966.

Fanelli, G. "Locus of control." In *Motivation in Education.* Ed. S. Ball. New York: Academic Press, 1977.

Farnham-Diggory, S. *Specific Learning Disabilities.* Cambridge, Mass.: Harvard University Press, 1978.

Feldhusen, J. F., S. J. Bahlke, and D. J. Treffinger. *The Purdue Creative Thinking Program.* West Lafayette, Ind.: Purdue University, 1975.

———, and D. Treffinger. *Teaching Creative Thinking and Problem Solving.* Dubuque, Ia.: Kendall/Hunt, 1977.

Flavell, J. "Developmental Changes in Memory Processes." *Cognitive Psychology,* 1 (1970), 324–340.

———. *Cognitive Development.* Englewood Cliffs, N.J.: Prentice-Hall, 1977.

———, and H. Wellman. "Metamemory." In *Perspectives on the Development of Memory and Cognition.* Ed. R. Kail and J. Hagen. Hillsdale, N.J.: Lawrence Erlbaum Associates, 1976.

———, J. R. Speer, F. L. Green, D. L. August. "The Development of Comprehension Monitoring and

Knowledge About Communication." *Monographs of the Society for Research on Child Development.* 46, No. 5 (1981), 192.

Fox, M. L. *Pauses in Odawa Speech.* Unpublished paper, 1976.

Fraenkel, J. "The Kohlberg Bandwagon: Some Reservations." *Social Education,* 1976, 216–222.

French, E., and G. Lesser. "Some Characteristics of Achievement Motivation in Women." *Journal of Abnormal Psychology,* 68 (1964), 119–128.

Frisbie, D. "Multiple-Choice versus True-False: A Comparison of Reliabilities and Concurrent Validities." *Journal of Educational Measurement,* 10 (1973), 297–304.

Fundidis, T., I. Kalvin, and R. Garside, eds. *Speech Retarded and Deaf Children: Their Psychological Development.* New York: Academic Press, 1979.

Furst, E. J. "Bloom's Taxonomy of Educational Objectives for the Cognitive Domain: Philosophical and Educational Issues." *Review of Educational Research,* 51, No. 4 (1981), 441–455.

Furth, H., and H. Wachs. *Thinking Goes to School: Piaget's Theory in Practice.* Chapter 1. New York: Oxford University Press, 1975.

Fyan, L. J. *Recent Trends in Achievement Theory and Motivation.* New York: Plenum Press, 1980.

Gage, N. *The Scientific Basis for the Art of Teaching.* New York: Teachers' College Press, 1978.

Gagné, R. *Conditions of Learning.* 3rd ed. New York: Holt, Rinehart and Winston, 1977.

———, and L. Briggs. *Principles of Instructional Design.* 2nd ed. New York: Holt, Rinehart and Winston, 1979.

Galdieri, A. "The Effect of Verbal Approval upon Performance of Middle- and Lower-Class Children on the WISC." *Psychology in the Schools,* 9 (1972), 450–458.

Gallagher, J. *Teaching Gifted Children.* Boston: Allyn and Bacon, 1975.

Gardner, W. *Children with Learning and Behavior Problems: A Behavior Management Approach.* Boston: Allyn and Bacon, 1974.

Garwood, G. "First-Name Stereotypes as a Factor in Self-Concept and School Achievement." *Journal of Educational Psychology,* 68 (1976), 482–487.

Getzels, J. W., and P. W. Jackson. *Creativity and Intelligence.* New York: Wiley, 1962.

Ginsburg, H., and S. Opper. *Piaget's Theory of Intellectual Development.* 2nd ed. Englewood Cliffs, N.J.: Prentice-Hall, 1979.

Glaser, R. *Adaptive Education: Individual Diversity and Learning.* New York: Holt, Rinehart and Winston, 1977.

Glasser, W. *Schools Without Failure.* New York: Harper and Row, 1969.

———. "Disorders in Our Schools: Causes and Remedies." *Phi Delta Kappa,* January 1978.

Goertzel, T., M. Goertzel, and V. Goertzel. *Three Hundred Eminent Personalities.* San Francisco: Jossey-Bass, 1978.

Goldstein, H. *The Social Learning Curriculum.* Columbus, Ohio: Charles Merrill, 1974.

Good, T., and J. Brophy. *Looking in Classrooms.* 2nd ed. New York: Harper and Row, 1978.

Gordon, E. W., and M. D. Ternell. "The Changed Social Context of Testing." *American Psychologist,* 36, No. 10 (1981), 1167–1171.

Gordon, T. *Teacher Effectiveness Training.* New York: Wyden, 1974.

Green, B. "A Primer of Testing." *American Psychologist,* 36, No. 10 (1981), 1001–1012.

Greene, B. F., J. S. Bailey, and F. Barker. "An Analysis and Reduction of Descriptive Behavior on School Buses." *Journal of Applied Behavior Analysis,* 14, No. 2 (1981), 177–192.

Gresham, F. M. "Social Skills Training with Handicapped Children: A Review." *Review of Educational Research,* 51, No. 1 (1981), 139–176.

Grover, S. "An Examination of Kohlberg's Cognitive-Developmental Model of Morality." *Journal of Genetic Psychology,* 136 (1980), 137–143.

Guerin, G., and K. Szatlocky. "Integrative Programs for the Mildly Retarded." *Exceptional Children,* 40 (1974), 173–179.

Guilford, J. *General Psychology.* Princeton, N.J.: Van Nostrand, 1952.

———. *Way Beyond the I.Q.* Great Neck, N.Y.: Creative Synergetic Associates, 1977.

———, and B. Fruchter. *Fundamental Statistics in Psychology and Education.* 6th ed. New York: McGraw-Hill Book Company, 1977.

Guralnick, M. "The Efficacy of Integrating Handicapped Children in Early Education Settings: Research Implications." *Journal of Early Childhood and Special Education,* 1, No. 1 (1981), 57–71.

Hall, C. S., and G. Lindzey. *Theories of Personality.* New York: Wiley, 1970.

Hall, R., and G. Stanley. "Short-Term Verbal Information Processing in Dyslexics." *Child Development,* 44 (1973), 841–844.

Halliwell, J. W., and J. Robitaille. "Relationship Between Theory and Practice in a Dual Report Program." *Journal of Educational Research,* 57, (1963), 137–141.

Hanninen, K. *Teaching the Visually Impaired.* Columbus, Ohio: Charles Merrill, 1975.

Haring, N. "Applications of Behavior Modification Techniques to the Learning Situation." In *Psychoeducational practices.* Vol. 1. Ed. W. M. Cruickshank and D. Hallahan. Syracuse, N.Y.: Syracuse University Press, 1975.

———, and B. Batemen. *Teaching the Learning Disabled Child.* Englewood Cliffs, N.J.: Prentice-Hall, 1977.

Harris, D. B. *Children's Drawings as a Measure of Intellectual Maturity.* New York: Harcourt, Brace, and World, 1963.

Hart, V. "Crippling conditions." In *Children with Exceptional Needs.* Ed. M. S. Lilly. New York: Holt, Rinehart and Winston, 1979.

Hartley, J., and I. Davies. "Pre-instructional Strategies: The Role of Pretests, Behavioral Objectives, Overviews, and Advance Organizers." *Review of Educational Research,* 46, No. 2 (1976), 239–265.

Hartshorne, H., and M. May. *Studies in the Nature of Character.* New York: MacMillan, 1928–1930.

Harzem, P., and T. R. Miles. *Conceptual Issues in Operant Psychology*. New York: Wiley, 1978.

Havighurst, R., P. Bowman, G. Liddle, G. Mathews, and J. Pierce. *Growing Up in River City*. New York: Wiley, 1962.

Henry, R. M. "A Theoretical and Empirical Analysis of 'Reasoning' in the Socialization of Young Children." *Human Development*, 23 (1980), 105–125.

Hersh, R. H., J. P. Miller, and G. D. Fielding. *Models of Moral Education: An Appraisal*. New York: Longman, 1979.

Hewett, F., and P. R. Blake. "Teaching the Emotionally Disturbed." In *Second Handbook of Research on Teaching*. Ed. R. Travers. Chicago: Rand McNally Co., 1973.

Hilgard, E., and G. Bower. *Theories of Learning*. 4th ed. Englewood Cliffs, N.J.: Prentice-Hall, 1975.

Hocevar, D. "Ideational Fluency as a Confounding Factor in the Measurement of Originality." *Journal of Educational Psychology*, 71 (1979), 191–196.

Hoffman, L. "Early Childhood Experiences and Women's Achievement Motivation." *Journal of Social Issues*, 28 (1974), 129–155.

Horn, J. L. "Organization of Abilities and the Development of Intelligence." *Psychological Review*, 75 (1968), 242–259.

———. "The Rise and Fall of Human Abilities." *Journal of Research and Development in Education*, 12, No. 2 (1979), 59–78.

Horner, M. S. "Toward an Understanding of Achievement-Related Conflicts in Women." *Journal of Social Issues*, 28 (1972), 157–175.

Horvath, M. J., C. E. Kass, and W. R. Ferrell. "An Example of the Use of Fuzzy Set Concepts in Modeling Learning Disability." *American Educational Research Journal*, 17, No. 3 (1980), 309–324.

Humphreys, L. G. "The Construct of General Intelligence." *Intelligence*, 3 (1979), 105–120.

Hutt, C. "Exploration and Play in Children." In *Play: Its Role in Development and Education*. Ed. J. Bruner, A. Jully, and K. Sylva. London: Penguin Books, 1976.

Hymes, D. *Foundations of Sociolinguistics*. Philadelphia: University Press, 1974.

Isaacson, R. "Relation Between Achievement, Test Anxiety, and Curriculum Choice." *Journal of Abnormal and Social Psychology*, 68 (1964), 447–452.

Jackson, P. *The Way Teaching Is*. Washington: Association for Supervision and Curriculum Development, 1966.

Jamieson, D., P. Suppes, and S. Wells. "The Effectiveness of Alternative Media." *Review of Educational Research*, 44 (1974), 1–68.

Jay, W. "Sex Stereotypes in Elementary-School Mathematics Textbooks." In *Sex Bias in the Schools*. Ed. Pottker, J. and A. Fishel. London: Associated Universities Press, 1977.

Jaynes, J. "Hello, Teacher: A Review of Fred Keller." *Contemporary Psychology*, 20 (1975), 629–631.

Jencks, C. *Inequality*. New York: Basic Books, 1973.

Jensen, A. C. "How Much Can He Boost IQ and Scholastic Achievements." *Harvard Educational Review*, 39 (1969), 1–121.

John, V. "Cognitive Development in the Bilingual Child." In *Monograph Series In Language And Learning*, 23. Ed. J. Alatis. Washington: Georgetown University Press, 1970.

Johnson, D. "Student-Student Interaction: The Neglected Variable in Education." *Educational Researcher*, 10, No. 1 (1981), 5–10.

———, G. Maruyama, R. Johnson, D. Nelson, and I. Skon. "The Effects of Cooperative, Competitive, and Individualistic Goal Structures on Achievement: A Meta-Analysis." *Psychological Bulletin*, 89 (1981), 47–62.

Jung, C. G. *The Portable Jung*. New York: Viking Press, 1971.

Kamii, C., and L. Derman. "Findings from Administration of Some Piagetian Tasks." In *Measurement and Piaget*. Ed. D. Green, M. Ford, and G. Flamer. New York: McGraw-Hill, 1971.

———, and R. DeVries. *Piaget for Early Education*. Englewood Cliffs, N.J.: Prentice-Hall, 1974.

Kaplan, R., and G. Pascoe. "Humor-

ous Lectures and Humorous Examples: Some Effects on Comprehension and Retention." *Journal of Educational Psychology*, 69 (1977), 61–65.

Karnes, M., and R. Zehrbach. "Educational Intervention at Home." In *The Preschool in Action*. 2nd ed. Ed. M. Day and R. Parker. Boston: Allyn and Bacon, 1977.

Keating, D., ed. *Intellectual Talent: Research and Development*. Baltimore: Johns Hopkins University Press, 1976.

Keele, S. *Attention and Human Performance*. Pacific Palisades, Calif.: Goodyear Publishing Co., 1973.

Keller, F., and J. Sherman. *The Keller Plan Handbook: Essays on a Personalized System of Instruction*. Menlo Park, Calif.: W. A. Benjamin, 1974.

Kephart, N. "Perceptual-Motor Aspects of Learning Disabilities." *Exceptional Children*, 31 (1964), 201.

Kessen, W., ed. *Education in China*. New Haven: Yale University Press, 1975.

Kinsbourne, M. "Hemispheric Specialization and the Growth of Human Understanding." *American Psychologist*, 37, No. 4 (1982), 411–420.

Kirschenbaum, J. "Clarifying Values Clarification: Some Theoretical Issues." In *Moral Education: It Comes with the Territory*. Ed. D. Purpel and K. Ryan. Berkeley, Calif.: McCutchan Publishing Co., 1976.

Kleinfield, J. S. "Intellectual Strengths in Culturally Different Groups: An Eskimo Illustration." *Review of Educational Research*, 43 (1973), 341–359.

Kohl, H. *The Open Classroom*. New York: Vintage Books, 1969.

Kohlberg, L. "The Moral Atmosphere of the School." In *The Unstudied Curriculum*. Ed. H. Overly. Washington: Association for Studies in Curriculum Department, 1970.

———. "A Cognitive-Developmental Approach to Moral Education." *Phi Delta Kappa*, June 1975.

———. "Moral Stages and Moralization: The Cognitive-Developmental Approach." In *Man, Morality, and Society*. Ed. T. Likona. New York: Holt, Rinehart and Winston, 1976.

———, and D. Elfenbein. "The Development of Moral Reasoning and Attitudes Toward Capital Punishment." *American Journal of Orthopsychiatry,* Summer 1975.

———, and E. Turiel. "Moral Development and Moral Education." In *Psychology and Educational Practice.* Ed. G. Lesser. Chicago: Scott, Foresman, 1971.

Kohut, S., and D. Range. *Classroom Discipline: Case Studies and Viewpoints.* Washington: National Education Association, 1979.

Kounin, J. *Discipline and Group Management in the Classroom.* New York: Holt, Rinehart and Winston, 1970.

Krathwohl, D., B. Bloom, and B. Masia. *Taxonomy of Educational Objectives: The Affective Domain.* New York: David McKay, 1964.

———, and D. Payne. "Defining and Assessing Educational Objectives." In *Educational Measurement.* 2nd ed. Ed. R. Thorndike. Washington: American Council on Education, 1969.

Kulik, J., C. C. Kulik, P. A. Cohen. "Effectiveness of Computer-Based College Teaching: A Meta-Analysis of Findings." *Review of Educational Research,* 50, No. 4 (1980), 525–544.

Labov, W. *Language in the Inner City: Studies in Black Vernacular.* Philadelphia: University of Pennsylvania Press, 1972.

———. "The Logic of Nonstandard English." In *Language And Poverty.* Ed. F. Williams. Chicago: Markham, 1980.

Lathrop, R. L. "A Quick but Accurate Approximation of the Standard Deviation of a Distribution." *Journal of Experimental Education,* 29 (1961), 319–321.

LeCompte, M. "The Procrustean Bed: Public Schools, Management Systems, and Minority Students." In *Culture and the Bilingual Classroom.* H. T. Trueba et al. Rowley, Mass.: Newbury House, 1981.

Lepper, M., and D. Greene. "Turning Play into Work: Effects of Adult Surveillance and Extrinsic Rewards on Children's Intrinsic Motivation." *Journal of Personality and Social Psychology,* 34, No. 6 (1976), 1219–1234.

Leslie, G. *The Family in Social Context.* 4th ed. New York: Oxford University Press, 1979.

Lewin, K., R. Lippitt, and R. White. "Patterns of Aggressive Behavior in Experimentally Created Social Climates." *Journal of Social Psychology,* 10 (1939), 271–299.

Lewis, M. *The Culture of Inequality.* Amherst, Mass.: University of Massachusetts, 1978.

Lien, A. *Measurement and Evaluation in Learning.* 4th ed. Dubuque, Iowa: W. C. Brown, 1980.

Lilly, M. S. "Learning and Behavior Problems: Traditional Categorical Overview." In *Children with Exceptional Needs.* Ed. M. S. Lilly. New York: Holt, Rinehart and Winston, 1979.

Lindfors, J. M. *Children's Language and Learning.* Englewood Cliffs, N.J.: Prentice-Hall, 1980.

Lippitt, P., and R. Lippitt. "The Peer Culture as a Learning Environment." *Childhood Education,* 47 (1970), 135–138.

Lockwood, A. "A Critical View of Values Clarification." *Teachers' College Record,* 77a (1975), 35–50.

Loeschke, M. "Mime: A Movement Program for Visually Handicapped." *Journal of Visual Impairment and Blindness,* October 1977.

Lyman, H. *Test Scores and What They Mean.* Englewood Cliffs, N.J.: Prentice-Hall, 1978.

Macarov, David. *Work and Welfare: The Unholy Alliance.* Beverly Hills, Calif.: Sage Publications, 1980.

McClelland, D. *The Achievement Motive.* New York: Appleton-Century-Crofts, 1953.

Maccoby, E., and C. Jacklin. *Psychology of Sex Differences.* Stanford, Calif.: Stanford University Press, 1974.

McCune, S. "What You Can Do About Biased Textbooks." In *Sex Role Stereotypes in the Schools.* Washington: National Education Association, 1977.

McDermott, R. P., and K. Gospondinoff. "Social Contexts for Ethnic Borders and School Failure." In *Nonverbal Behavior: Application and Cultural Implications.* Ed. A. Wolfgang. New York: Academic Press, 1979.

McGuigan, F. J. "Variations of Whole-Part Methods of Learning." *Journal of Experimental Psychology,* 51 (1960) 213–216.

McKeachie, W., and Kulik, J. "Effective College Teaching." In *Review of Research in Education.* Vol. 3. Ed. F. Kerlinger. Washington: American Educational Research Association, 1975.

McKeena, B. "What Is Wrong with Standardized Testing?" *Today's Education,* April 1977.

McReynolds, P. "The Three Faces of Cognitive Motivation." In *Intrinsic Motivation.* Ed. H. I. Day, D. E. Berlyne, and D. E. Hunt. Toronto: Holt, Rinehart and Winston of Canada, 1971.

Maehr, M. L. *Sociocultural Origins of Achievement.* Monterey, Calif.: Brooks/Cole, 1974.

———, and D. A. Kleiber. "The Graying of Achievement Motivation." *American Psychologist,* 36, No. 7 (1981), 787–793.

Mager, R. *Preparing Instructional Objectives.* Belmont, Calif.: Fearon Publishers, 1962.

———, and P. Pipe. *Analyzing Performance Problems.* Belmont, Calif.: Fearon Publishers, 1980.

Mahone, C. "Fear of Failure of Unrealistic Vocational Aspiration." *Journal of Abnormal and Social Psychology,* 60 (1960), 253–261.

Mansfield, R., T. V. Busse, and E. J. Krepelka. "The Effectiveness of Creativity Training." *Review of Educational Research,* 48, No. 4 (1978), 517–536.

———, and T. V. Busse. *The Psychology of Creativity and Discovery: Scientists and Their Work.* New York: Nelson-Hall, 1981.

Marshall, H. H. "Criteria for Open Classrooms." *Young Children,* 28 (1972), 13–19.

———. "Open Classrooms: Has the Term Outlived Its Usefulness?" *Review of Educational Research,* 51, No. 2 (1981), 181–192.

Mehrens, W. A., and I. J. Lehmann. *Standardized Tests in Education.*

New York: Holt, Rinehart and Winston, 1969.

Meisgeier, C. "Review of Critical Issues Underlying Mainstreaming." In *Third Review of Special Education*. Ed. L. Mann and D. Sabatino. New York: Grune and Stratton, 1976.

Mischel, W. "Toward a Cognitive Social Learning Reconceptualization of Personality." *Psychological Review*, 80, No. 4 (1973), 252–283.

———. "The Cognitive Social Learning Approach to Moral and Self-Regulation." In *Man, Morality, and Society*. Ed. T. Likona. New York: Holt, Rinehart and Winston, 1974.

———, and E. Staub. "Effects of Expectations on Working and Waiting for Larger Rewards." *Journal of Personality and Social Psychology*, 2 (1965), 626–633.

Mohatt, G., and F. Erikson. "Cultural Differences in Teaching Styles in an Odawa School: A Sociolinguistic Approach." In *Culture and the Bilingual Classroom*. H. T. Trueba et al. Rowley, Mass.: Newbury House, 1981.

Moran, M. *Assessment of the Exceptional Learner in the Regular Classroom*. Denver: Love Publishers, 1978.

Morse, W. "Helping Teacher/Crisis Teacher Concept." *Focus on Exceptional Children*, 8, No. 4 (1976), 1–11.

Mosher, R., and P. Sullivan. "A Curriculum in Moral Education for Adolescents." In *Moral Education: It Comes with the Territory*. Ed. D. Purpel and K. Ryan. Berkeley, Calif.: McCutchan Publishing Co., 1976.

Mosier, C. "Suggestions for Constructing Multiple-Choice Items." *Educational and Psychological Measurement*, 5 (1945), 261–271.

Murray, H. *Explorations in Personality: A Clinical and Experimental Study of Fifty Men*. New York: Oxford University Press, 1938.

Musgrave, G. R. *The Grading Game: A Public School Fiasco*. New York: Vintage Press, 1970.

Mussen, P., and N. Eisenberg-Berg. *Roots of Caring, Sharing, and Helping: Development of Prosocial Behavior in Children*. San Francisco: W. H. Freeman, 1977.

National Education Association, Research Division. "Reporting Pupil Progress to Parents." N.E.A. Research Memo 1972–10. Washington: N.E.A., 1972.

Neff, H., and J. Pilch. *Teaching Handicapped Children Easily*. Springfield, Ill.: Charles Thomas, Inc., 1978.

Nelson, K. "Structure and Strategy in Learning to Talk." *Monographs of the Society for Research on Child Development*, 38 (1973), No. 149.

Nelson, L., and S. Kagan. "Competition: The Star-Spangled Scramble." *Psychology Today*, 6, No. 1 (1972), 53–56ff.

Newell, A., and H. A. Simon. *Human Problem Solving*. Englewood Cliffs, N.J.: Prentice-Hall, 1972.

Nitko, A. J. "Distinguishing the Many Varieties of Criterion-Referenced Tests." *Review of Educational Research*, 50, No. 3 (1980), 461–485.

Ogbu, J. *The Next Generation: An Ethnography of Education in an Urban Neighborhood*. New York: Academic Press, 1974.

O'Leary, K., and S. O'Leary, eds. *Classroom Management: The Successful Use of Behavior Modification*. 2nd ed. New York: Permagon Press, 1977.

O'Leary, V., and B. Hammock. "Sex-Role Orientation and Achievement Context as Determinants of the Motive to Avoid Success." *Sex Roles*, 1 (1975), 225–234.

Osborn, A. F. *Applied Imagination*. 3rd ed. New York: Scribner's, 1963.

Otis-Lennon Mental Abilities Test. New York: Harcourt, Brace, Jovanovich, 1970.

Palfrey, C. F. "Head Teachers' Expectations and Their Pupils' Self-Concepts." *Educational Researcher*, 15 (1973), 123–127.

Pavlov, I. *Conditioned Reflexes*. London: Oxford University Press, 1927. Also reprinted by Dover Books, New York, 1960.

Pedulla, J. J., P. W. Airasian, and G. F. Madaus. "Do Teacher Ratings and Standardized Test Results of Students Yield the Same Information?" *American Educational Research Journal*, 17, No. 3 (1980), 303–307.

Perrone, V. *The Abuses of Standardized Testing*. Bloomington, Ind.: Phi Delta Kappa Foundation, 1977.

Peters, R. "Why Doesn't Larry Kohlberg Do His Homework?" *Phi Delta Kappa* (June 1975), 678.

Peterson, P. "Direct Instruction Reconsidered." In *Research on Teaching: Concepts, Findings, and Implications*. Ed. P. L. Peterson and H. Walberg. Berkeley, Calif.: McCutchan, 1979.

Pflaum, S. *Language and Reading in Early Childhood Education*. Columbus, Ohio: Charles Merrill, 1974.

Piaget, J. *Plays, Dreams and Imitation in Childhood*. New York: W. W. Norton Company, 1951a.

———. *The Child's Conception of the World*. London: Routledge and Kegan Paul Ltd., 1951b.

———. *The Origins of Intelligence in Children*. New York: International Universities Press, 1952.

———. *Language and Thought of the Child*. Cleveland, Ohio: World Publishing Company, 1955.

———. *The Language and Thought of the Child*. London: Routledge and Kegan Paul, 1976.

———. *The Development of Thought*. Oxford, U.K.: Blackwell Publishers, 1978.

———, and B. Inhelder. *The Child's Conception of Space*. New York: Humanities Press, 1956.

Pietrofesa, J., and N. Schlossberg. "Counselor Bias and the Female Occupational Role." Paper presented at American Education Research Association Annual Conference, 1970.

Piotrkowski, C. *Work and the Family System: A Naturalistic Study of Working-Class and Lower-Middle-Class Families*. New York: Free Press, 1979.

Plowden, Lady B. *Children and Their Primary Schools*. London: Her Majesty's Stationery Office, 1967.

Popham, W. J. *Criterion-Referenced Measurements.* Englewood Cliffs, N.J.: Prentice-Hall, 1978.

———. *Using Instructional Objectives: A Personal Perspective.* Belmont, Calif.: Pitman Learning, 1973.

Posner, M., and S. Keele. "Skill Learning." In *Second Handbook of Research on Teaching.* Ed. R. Travers. Chicago: Rand McNally, 1972.

Postman, N., and C. Weingarten. *Teaching as a Subversive Activity.* New York: Delacorte Press, 1969.

Pottker, J. "Psychological and Occupational Sex Stereotypes in Elementary School Readers." In *Sex Bias in the Schools.* Ed. J. Pottker. London: Associated Universities Press, 1977.

Premack, D. "Reinforcement Theory." In *Nebraska Symposium on Motivation: 1965.* Ed. M. R. Jones. Lincoln, Nebr.: University of Nebraska Press, 1965.

Purkey, W. W. *Inviting School Success.* Belmont, Calif.: Wadsworth, 1978.

Purpel, D., and K. Ryan. "Moral Education in the Classroom." In *Moral Education: It Comes with the Territory.* Ed. D. Purpel and K. Ryan. Berkeley, Calif.: McCutchan Publishing Co., 1976.

Queen, R. "Toward Liberating Toys." In *Perspectives on Non-sexist Early Childhood Education.* Ed. B. Sprung. New York: Teachers' College Press, 1978.

Quick-Word Test. New York: Harcourt, Brace, Jovanovich, 1964.

Rachlin, H. *Introduction to Modern Behaviorism.* San Francisco: W. H. Freeman, 1970.

Ramirez, M. "The Relationship of Acculturation to Cognitive Style Among Mexican-Americans." *Journal of Cross-cultural Psychology,* 5 (1974), 424–433.

———, and A. Castenada. *Cultural Democracy, Bicognitive Development, and Education.* New York: Academic Press, 1974.

———, and D. R. Price-Williams. "Cognitive Styles of Children of Three Ethnic Groups in the United States." *Journal of Cross-cultural Psychology,* 5 (1974), 424–433.

Raths, L., M. Harmin, and S. Simon. *Values and Teaching.* Columbus, Ohio: Charles Merrill, 1966.

Raven, J. *Progressive Matrices.* Form 1962. New York: The Psychological Corporation, 1962.

Reschly, D. J. "Psychological Testing in Educational Classification and Placement." *American Psychologist,* 36, No. 10 (1981), 1094–1102.

Resnick, L. "The Science and Art of Curriculum Design." In *Strategies for Curriculum Development.* Ed. J. Schaffarzick and D. Hampson. Berkeley, Calif.: McCutchan Publishing Co., 1975.

Rest, J. "Developmental Psychology as a Guide to Values Education." *Review of Educational Research,* 44, No. 2 (1974), 241–259.

———. *Development in Judging Moral Issues.* Minneapolis: University of Minnesota Press, 1980.

Reynolds, M. "Some Final Notes." In *Teacher Education: Renegotiating Roles for Mainstreaming.* Ed. M. Reynolds and J. Grosenick. Reston, Va.: Council for Exceptional Children, 1978.

———, and J. Birch. *Teaching Exceptional Children in America's Schools.* Reston, Va.: Council for Exceptional Children, 1977.

Rice, J., C. R. Claninger, T. Reich. "Analysis of Behavioral Traits in the Presence of Cultural Transmission and Assortative Mating: Applications to IQ and SES." *Behavior Genetics,* 10 (1980), 73–92.

Riley, D. "Memory for Form." In *Psychology in the Making.* Ed. L. Postman. New York: Alfred Knopf, 1963.

Roberts, A., and P. Dunston. "Effect of a Conflict Manipulation on Children's Moral Reasoning." *Psychological Reports,* 46, (1980), 1305–1306.

Rogers, C. *Freedom to Learn: A View of What Education Might Become.* Columbus, Ohio: Charles Merrill, 1969.

———, and B. F. Skinner. "Some Issues Concerning the Control of Human Behavior." *Science,* 124 (1956), 1057–1066.

Rosen, H. *The Development of Socio-Moral Knowledge: A Cognitive-Structural Approach.* New York: Columbia University Press, 1980.

Rosenshine, B. *Teacher Behaviors and Student Achievement.* London: National Foundation for Educational Research in England and Wales, 1971.

Rosenthal, R., and L. Jacobson. *Pygmalion in the Classroom.* New York: Holt, Rinehart and Winston, 1968.

Rothkopf, E. "The Concept of Mathemajenic Activities." *Review of Educational Research,* 40 (1970), 325–362.

———. "Experiments on Mathemagenic Behavior and the Technology of Written Instruction." In *Verbal Learning Research and the Technology of Written Instruction.* Ed. E. Z. Rothkopf and P. E. Johnson. New York: Teachers' College Press, 1971.

Ryan, B. A. *PSI: Keller's Personalized System of Instruction: An Appraisal.* Washington, D.C.: American Psychological Association, 1974.

Sabers, D. L., and R. Klausmeier. "Accuracy of Short-Cut Estimates for the Standard Deviation." *Journal of Educational Measurement,* 8 (1971), 335–339.

Sachs, J. "Recognition Memory for Syntactic and Semantic Aspects of Connected Discourse." *Perception and Psychophysics,* 2 (1967), 437–442.

Schrader, W. B., ed. *Measuring Achievement: Progress over a Decade.* San Francisco: Jossey-Bass, 1980.

Scott, R. "Perceptual Skills, General Intellectual Ability, Race, and Later Reading Achievement." *The Reading Teacher,* 23 (1970), 160–169.

Scriven, M. "Problems and Prospects for Individualization." In *Systems of Individualized Education.* Ed. H. Talmage. Berkeley, Calif.: McCutchan Publishing Co., 1975.

Sears, R. R. "Relation of Early Socialization Experience to Self-Concept and Gender Role in Middle Childhood." *Child Development,* 41 (1970), 267–289.

Segalowitz, N. "Communicative Incompetence in Nonfluent Bilinguals." *Canadian Journal of Behavioral Science,* 8 (1976), 122–131.

Selman, R., and L. Kohlberg. *First Things: A Strategy for Teaching Values.* New York: Guidance Associates, 1972.

Sgan, M. R. "Letter Grade Achievement in Pass-Fail Courses." *Journal of Higher Education,* 41 (1970), 638–644.

Shaffer, J. *Humanistic Psychology.* Englewood Cliffs, N.J.: Prentice-Hall, 1978.

Shallcross, D. J. *Teaching Creative Behavior.* Englewood Cliffs, N.J.: Prentice-Hall, 1981.

Shuy, R. W. "Speech Differences and Teaching Strategies: How Different Is Enough?" In *Language and Learning to Read.* Eds. R. E. Hodges and E. Rudorf. Boston: Houghton Mifflin, 1972.

Siegler, R. "Developmental Sequences Within and Between Concepts." *Monographs of the Society for Research on Child Development,* 46, No. 2 (1981), 189.

Silberman, C., ed. *The Open Classroom Reader.* New York: Vintage Books, 1973.

Simon, S. *Beginning Values Clarification: A Guide Book for Use of Values Clarification in the Classroom.* San Diego, Calif.: Pennant Press, 1975.

———, L. Howe, and H. Kirschenbaum. *Values Clarification.* 2nd ed. New York: Hart Publishing Company, 1978.

Simpson, E. "Moral Development Research: A Case Study of Scientific Cultural Bias." *Human Development,* 17 (1974), 81–106.

Skinner, B. F. *Science and Human Behavior.* New York: Appleton-Century-Crofts, 1953.

———. "The Science of Learning and the Art of Teaching." *Harvard Educational Review,* 24 (1954), 86–97.

———. *Verbal Behavior.* New York: Appleton-Century-Crofts, 1957.

———. *Beyond Freedom and Dignity.* New York: Alfred Knopf, 1971.

Slavin, R. "Student Teams and Comparison Among Equals. Effects on Academic Performance and Student Attitudes." *Journal of Educational Psychology,* 70 (1978), 532–538.

Smedslund, J. "Piaget's Psychology in Practice." *British Journal of Educational Psychology,* 47 (1977), 1–6.

Smith, H. "Two Kinds of Teaching." *Journal of Humanistic Psychology,* 15, No. 4 (1975), 3–12.

Snyder, L., E. Bates, and I. Bretherton. "Content and Context in Early Lexical Development." *Journal of Child Language,* 8, No. 3 (1981), 565–582.

Solomon, R. "Punishment." *American Psychologist,* 19 (1964), 239–253.

Somervill, M. A. "Dialect and Reading: Review of Alternative Solutions." *Review of Educational Research,* 95, No. 2 (1975), 247–262.

Spearman, C. *The Abilities of Man: Their Nature and Measurement.* New York: MacMillan, 1927.

Spiro, R. J., and R. C. Anderson. "Much Ado About Next to Nothing: A Rejoinder to Ausubel." *American Educational Research Journal,* 18, No. 3 (1981), 271–272.

Sprung, B., ed. *Perspectives in Nonsexist Early Childhood Education.* New York: Teachers' College Press, 1978.

Stallings, W., and H. R. Smock. "The Pass-Fail Grading Option at a State University: A Five-Semester Evaluation." *Journal of Educational Measurement,* 8 (1971), 153–160.

Stanley, J. "Some Thoughts on Not Having Accelerated." *Intellectually Talented Youth Bulletin,* 3, No. 7 (1977).

———, and K. D. Hopkins. *Educational and Psychological Measurement and Evaluation.* Englewood Cliffs, N.J.: Prentice-Hall, 1972.

Stendler-Lavatelli, C. "Aspects of Piaget's Theory that Have Implications for Teacher Education." In *Educational Implications of Piaget's Theory.* Ed. I. Athey and D. Rubadeau. Waltham, Mass.: Xerox Publishing Company, 1970.

Stewart, J. "Problems and Contradictions in Values Clarification." *Phi Delta Kappa,* June 1975, 684–687.

Stodolsky, S. S., and G. Lesser. "Learning Patterns in the Disadvantaged." *Harvard Educa-*

tional Review, 37 (1967), 546–593.

Stokes, T. F., and D. M. Baer. "An Implicit Technology of Generalization." *Journal of Applied Behavior Analysis,* 10 (1977), 349–367.

Strong, E., and D. Campbell. *Strong-Campbell Interest Blank.* 2nd ed. Stanford, Calif.: Stanford University Press, 1974.

Sutton-Smith, B., and S. Sutton-Smith. *How to Play with Your Children.* Chapter 11. New York: Hawthorn Books, 1974.

Tarpy, R., and R. Mayer. *Foundations of Learning and Memory.* Glenview, Ill.: Scott, Foresman, 1978.

Tennyson, R. D. "Use of Adaptive Information for Advisement in Learning Concepts and Rules Using Computer-Assisted Instruction." *Review of Educational Research,* 18, No. 4 (1981), 425–438.

Terman, L., and M. Merrill. *Stanford-Binet Intelligence Scale.* Rev. Ed. Iowa City, Iowa: Riverside Publishing Company, 1973.

Thorndike, E. *The Psychology of Learning.* New York: Teachers' College Press, 1913.

———. *Fundamentals of Learning.* New York: Teachers' College Press, 1932.

Thurstone, L. L. "Primary Mental Abilities." *Psychometric Monographs,* 1938, 1.

Tolman, E., and C. Honzik. " 'Insight' in Rats." *University of California Publications in Psychology,* 4 (1930), 215–232.

Torrance, P. *Torrance Tests of Creative Thinking.* Personnel Press, 1974.

Tough, J. *Focus on Meaning.* London: Unwin Books Educational, 1974.

———. *Listening to Children Talking.* London: Ward Lock Educational, 1976.

———. *Development of Meaning.* London: Unwin Books Educational, 1977a.

———. *Talking and Learning.* London: Ward Lock Educational, 1977b.

Trachtenberg, D. "Student Tasks in Text Material: What Cognitive Skills Do They Tap?" *Peabody*

Journal of Education, 52 (1974), 54–57.

Trecker, J. "Women in the U.S. History High-School Textbooks." *Social Education,* 35 (1971), 249–261.

Trueba, H. T., G. P. Guthrie, and K. H. P. Au. *Culture and the Bilingual Classroom.* Rowley, Mass.: Newbury House, 1981.

Turnbull, A. *Mainstreaming Handicapped Children: A Guide for Classroom Teachers.* Boston: Allyn and Bacon, 1979.

U.S. Bureau of the Census. *Statistical Abstract of the United States, 1980.* Washington, D.C.: U.S. Government Printing Office, 1981.

U.S. Office of Education. "Assistance to States for Education of Handicapped Children: Procedures for Evaluating Specific Learning Disabilities." *Federal Register,* 42 (1977), 65082–65085.

Uzgiris, I. C., and J. M. Hunt. *Assessment in Infancy.* Urbana, Ill.: University of Illinois Press, 1975.

Vernon, P. E. *Intelligence and Cultural Environment.* London: Methuen, 1971.

———, G. Adamson and D. F. Vernon, *The Psychology and Education of Gifted Children.* London: Methuen, 1977.

Vidler, D. "The Need for Achievement." In *Motivation in Education.* Ed. S. Ball. New York: Academic Press, 1977.

Vygotsky, L. *Thought and Language.* Cambridge, Mass.: M.I.T. Press, 1962.

Walker, J., and T. Shea. *Behavior Modification: A Practical Approach for Education.* 2nd ed. St. Louis: Masby, 1980.

Wallach, M. A., and N. Kogan. *Modes of Thinking in Young Children: A Study of the Creativity-Intelligence Distinction.* New York: Holt, Rinehart and Winston, 1965.

Walters, G., and J. Grusec. *Punish-

ment.* San Francisco: W. H. Freeman Co., 1977.

Waterman, A. "Individualism and Interdependence." *American Psychologist,* 36, No. 7 (1981), 762–773.

Waterson, N., and C. Snow, eds. *The Development of Communication.* New York: Wiley, 1978.

Wechsler, D. *Manual for the Wechsler Intelligence Scale for Children.* New York: Psychological Corporation, 1974.

Weikart, D. "Relationship of Curriculum, Teaching, and Learning in the Preschool Curriculum." In *Preschool Programs for the Disadvantaged.* Ed. J. Stanley. Baltimore: Johns Hopkins Press, 1972.

———. "Effects of Different Curricula in Early Childhood Education." *Educational Evaluation and Policy Analysis,* 3, No. 6 (1981), 25–36.

Weiner, B. "New Conceptions in the Study of Achievement Motivation." In *Progress in Experimental Personality Research.* Vol. 5. Ed. B. A. Maher. New York: Academic Press, 1970, pp. 67–109.

———. *Theories of Motivation: From Mechanism to Cognition.* Chicago: Rand McNally Co., 1972.

Wesman, A. G. "Intelligent Testing." *American Psychologist,* 23 (1968), 267–274.

White, B. *The Origins of Human Competence.* Lexington, Mass.: Lexington Books, 1979.

White, E. M. "Sometimes an A is Really an F." *Chronicle of Higher Education,* 9 (1975), 24.

White. R. T. "The Validation of a Learning Hierarchy." *Review of Educational Research,* 11 (1974), 19–28.

Whitely, J. "Effects of Practice Distribution on Learning a Fine-Motor Task." *Research Quarterly,* 48 (1970), 576–583.

Wilkins, W. E., and M. D. Glock. *Teacher Expectations and Student Achievement: Replication and Extension.* ERIC Documents, No. 080-567, 1973.

Willerman, L. *Psychology of Individual and Group Differences.* San Francisco: W. H. Freeman, 1979.

Witkin, H. "Field-Dependent and Field-Independent Cognitive Styles and Their Educational Implications." *Review of Educational Research,* 47 (1977), 1–64.

———, R. B. Dyk, H. F. Faterson, D. R. Goodenough, and S. A. Karp. *Psychological Differentiation: Studies of Development.* Rev. ed. Potomac, Md.: Erlbaum, 1974.

Wittrock, M. "The Learning by Discovery Hypothesis." In *Learning by Discovery: A Critical Appraisal.* Ed. L. Shulman and E. Keislar. Chicago: Rand McNally, 1966.

Wlodkowski, R. *Motivation in Teaching: A Practical Approach.* Washington, D.C.: National Education Association, 1978.

Wolpe, J. "Behavior Therapy vs. Psychoanalysis: Therapeutic and Social Implications." *American Psychologist,* 36, No. 2 (1981), 159–164.

Wright, J., and S. Wright. "Social Class and Parental Values." *American Sociological Review,* 41 (1976), 527–537.

Yamamoto, K. *Scoring Manual for Minnesota Tests of Creative Thinking and Writing.* Kent, Ohio: Kent State University, 1964.

Yando, R., V. Seitz, and E. Zigler. *Intellectual and Personality Characteristics of Childern: Social-Class and Ethnic Group Differences.* Potomac, Md.: Erlbaum, 1979.

Zigler, E., W. Abelson, and V. Seitz. "Motivational Factors in the Performance of Economically Disadvantaged Children on the Peabody Picture Vocabulary Test." *Child Development,* 44 (1973), 294–303.

Zimring, C. M. "Stress and the Designed Environment." *Journal of Social Issues,* 37, No. 1 (1981), 145–171.

Index